MS-DOS®
Batch File
Programming
3rd Edition

Ronny Richardson

THIRD EDITION
FIRST PRINTING

Library of Congress Cataloging-in-Publication Data

Richardson, Ronny.
    MS-DOS batch file programming / by Ronny Richardson. — 3rd ed.
      p.   cm.
    Includes index.
    ISBN 0-8306-2484-8   ISBN 0-8306-2483-X (pbk.)
    1. Operating systems (Computers) 2. MS-DOS. 3. Electronic data
processing—Batch processing. I. Title.
QA76.76.O63R54 1991 <MRC RR>
005.265—dc20   91-16966
                                    CIP

TAB Books offers software for sale. For information and a catalog, please contact
TAB Software Department, Blue Ridge Summit, PA 17294-0850.

Director of Acquisitions: Ron Powers
Book Editor: Kellie Hagan
Production: Katherine G. Brown
Series Design: Jaclyn J. Boone
                                             WT1

About the author

Ronny Richardson was born in Oak Ridge, Tennessee, and raised in Atlanta, Georgia. He has undergraduate degrees in Electronics and Mathematics, and graduate degrees in Decision Sciences and Business Administration. He is currently a doctoral student in Management at Georgia State University.

Ronny began using computers in 1983. The next year he won an IBM clone at the Atlanta Comdex, which spurred his interest in learning about computers. Later that year he began teaching computer classes at a local computer store. In 1986 he began writing for *Computer Shopper*, and has since then published over 200 articles. He currently writes for *Computer Monthly*, *Atlanta Computer Currents*, and *PC Computing*.

Contents

Acknowledgments   xiii

Introduction   xv

PART 1. BATCH FILE BASICS

Chapter 1. Simple batch files   1

What a batch file is good for *2*

DOS as a programming language *7*

The COPY command *7*

Summary *10*

Chapter 2. Batch file commands   11

"Why in the world did I do that?'' *11*

Communicating with the user *13*

ECHO quirks *16*

Stopping the batch file *20*

Replaceable parameters *22*

SHIFT *25*

SET *29*

ERRORLEVEL *33*

Summary *35*

Chapter 3. Looping and program flow   37

Naming lines of a program *37*

GOTO *38*

IF *39*

EXIST *43*

ErrorLevel   *44*
NOT   *47*
FOR   *48*
Why doesn't my batch file work?   *48*
Summary   *50*

PART 2. PUTTING BATCH FILES TO WORK

Chapter 4. Configuring your computer   53
Starting DOS   *53*
The CONFIG.SYS file   *57*
The AUTOEXEC.BAT file   *66*
Memory-resident software   *71*
Summary   *72*

Chapter 5. Custom configurations   75
Copying over boot files   *75*
Environmental surveying   *77*
Conditionally loading memory-resident software   *83*
Summary   *83*

Chapter 6. Batch file menus   85
Structuring your hard disk   *85*
Introduction to menus   *88*
Displaying the menu   *89*
Making it work   *91*
My menu system   *93*
Summary   *93*

Chapter 7. A document archival system   95
Periodic backups   *96*
Systematically copying critical data files   *99*
Indexing document files   *102*
Summary   *104*

Chapter 8. Anti-viral batch files   105
Write-protect program files   *105*
Hide COMMAND.COM   *106*
Test your critical files   *108*
Summary   *109*

PART 3. SOFTWARE TO TURBOCHARGE YOUR BATCH FILES

Chapter 9. Improving your batch files 111

Check *111*
InKey *118*
Answer *124*
Reboot *125*
The Down and Dirty Dozen Batch Utilities *126*
Get *127*
Menuware Batch File Utilities *128*
SetError *129*
ShowEnvironment *130*
Norton Batch Enhancer *130*
Batchman *137*
Getting your hands on these programs *152*
Shareware *153*
Summary *153*

Chapter 10. Alternatives to the DOS batch language 155

Extended Batch Language Plus *155*
Builder *164*
Bat2Exec *175*
Summary *177*

PART 4. ADVANCED BATCH FILE PROGRAMMING

Chapter 11. Subroutines in batch files 179

Tricking DOS into running subroutines *179*
Copying files to a disk *181*
Distributing files on a hard disk *185*
All-in-one batch files *187*
Summary *190*

Chapter 12. Problem solving with batch files 191

Shelling out to DOS *191*
Changing subdirectories *193*
Running inflexible programs *196*
Custom configurations *199*
Controlling your printer *199*
Finding files *200*

Printing return mailing labels *202*
Remembering batch file names *202*
Accessing the date and time *205*
Running commands occasionally *210*
Using the volume in a batch file *212*
Batch file floppy-disk catalog *216*
Batch files that use less space *218*
Adding to and deleting from your path *221*
Repeating batch files *227*
Controlling a network *229*
Modifying files during installation *232*
Password protection *234*
Summary *236*

Chapter 13. Batch file tricks   237
Dealing with capitalization *237*
Passing complex parameters *242*
Nesting IF statements *248*
Keeping the ErrorLevel *253*
The Case method *261*
Quicker than GOTO END *263*
FOR command tricks *265*
Using reserved names for batch files *268*
The hidden power of CTTY *269*
Running commands inside a batch file *276*
Advanced batch file branching *278*
Tidy cleanups *281*
Selecting a working filename *283*
Saving disk space with environmental variables *284*
Making ErrorLevel easier to use *285*
Summary *286*

Chapter 14. The DOS environment   289
What is it? *289*
The SET command *291*
Using SET variables in batch files *295*
Increasing the size of the environment *297*
Summary *301*

Chapter 15. Modifying DOS   303

A word of warning   *303*
Your AUTOEXEC.BAT and CONFIG.SYS files   *304*
Read only   *305*
Changing DOS   *305*
Changing commands   *308*
Conclusion   *311*

PART 5. REFERENCE

Chapter 16. Quick reference list   313

%0 through %9   *313*
%%j (2.0)   *314*
%variable% (2.0)   *314*
: (2.0)   *314*
^Z   *314*
>NUL   *315*
<   *316*
+   *316*
@ (3.3)   *316*
ANSI.SYS (2.0)   *316*
APPEND (3.3)   *317*
ASSIGN (2.0)   *317*
ATTRIB (3.0)   *317*
AUTOEXEC.BAT   *317*
AUX   *317*
BACKUP (2.0)   *317*
BREAK (2.0)   *319*
BUFFERS (2.0)   *319*
CALL (3.3)   *319*
CHCP   *319*
CHDIR (2.0)   *319*
CHKDSK (1.0)   *319*
CLS (2.0)   *320*
COM   *320*
COMMAND (1.0)   *320*
COMP (1.0)   *321*
COMSPEC (2.0)   *321*
CONFIG.SYS   *321*
COPY (1.0)   *321*
COUNTRY (3.0)   *322*
CTTY (2.0)   *323*

DATE (1.0) *323*
Debug (1.0) *323*
DEL (1.0) *323*
DEVICE (2.0) *323*
DEVICEHIGH (5.0) *324*
Device drivers *324*
DIR (1.0) *324*
DISKCOMP (1.0) *324*
DISKCOPY (1.0) *324*
DO (2.0) *324*
DOS-HIGH (5.0) *325*
DOSKEY (5.0) *325*
DRIVPARM *325*
ECHO (2.0) *325*
EDIT (5.0) *326*
EDLIN (1.0) *326*
EMM386 (5.0) *326*
ERASE (2.0) *327*
ErrorLevel *327*
EXE2BIN (1.1) *328*
EXIST (2.0) *328*
EXIT *328*
External commands *328*
FASTOPEN (3.3) *328*
FC (2.0 MS-DOS only) *329*
FCBS (3.0) *329*
FDISK (2.0) *329*
FILES (2.0) *329*
FIND (2.0) *330*
FOR (2.0) *330*
FORMAT (1.0) *331*
GOTO (2.0) *331*
GRAFTABL (3.0) *331*
GRAPHICS (1.0) *331*
IF *331*
IN (2.0) *333*
INSTALL (4.0) *333*
Internal commands *333*
JOIN (2.0) *333*
KEYB*xx* (3.0) *333*
LABEL (3.0) *334*
LASTDRIVE (3.0) *334*

LINK (1.0) *334*
LOADHIGH (5.0) *334*
LPT *334*
MEM *334*
MIRROR (5.0) *334*
MKDIR (2.0) *334*
MODE (1.0) *335*
MORE (2.0) *335*
NLSFUNC (3.3) *335*
NOT (2.0) *335*
NUL *336*
PATH (2.0) *336*
PAUSE (1.0) *337*
Piping (2.0) *338*
PRINT (2.0) *338*
PRN *338*
PROMPT (2.0) *339*
QBASIC (5.0) *340*
REBUILD (5.0) *340*
RECOVERY (2.0) *340*
REM (1.0) *340*
REN (1.0) *340*
Replaceable parameters *340*
REPLACE (3.2) *340*
RESTORE (2.0) *341*
RMDIR (2.0) *342*
SELECT (3.0) *342*
SET (2.0) *342*
SETVER (5.0) *343*
SHARE *343*
SHELL (2.0) *343*
SHIFT (2.0) *343*
SORT (2.0) *344*
STACKS (3.2) *344*
SUBST (3.1) *344*
SYS (1.0) *345*
TIME (1.0) *345*
TREE (2.0) *345*
TRUENAME (4.0) *345*
TYPE (1.0) *345*
USER *346*
UNDELETE (5.0) *346*

UNFORMAT (5.0) *346*
VER (2.0) *346*
VERIFY (2.0) *346*
VOL (2.0) *346*
XCOPY (3.2) *346*

Chapter 17. Summary table 349

APPENDICES

A. **Editing batch files   363**
B. **DOS redirection   373**
C. **Changes in DOS   377**
D. **Modifying InKey   389**

Index   401

Acknowledgments

Professionally, I want to thank Randy Ross at *PC/Computing*. After the second edition of this book was published, Randy contacted me to write some batch file *Hot Tips!* for the magazine. Several of our conversations were basically Randy asking me if I could make a batch file do this or that. When I succeeded, he would publish that as a Hot Tip. Several of my hints in this edition originally appeared in the pages of *PC/Computing*. Not only that, the thinking Randy encouraged me to do about batch files yielded great dividends while I rewrote this book.

Also, I want to thank Andy Thomas at Microsoft. Andy was my contact for problems with DOS 5.0 while I was a beta tester. In addition, Andy provided some general data to update the information in the reference chapter of this book. His work resulted in my being able to finish the book much earlier than I would have otherwise.

Personally, I want to thank my wife Cicinda, my son Tevin, and my daughter Dawna for their support and patience. Because I have only a limited pool of time available, some of the time I spent writing this book had to come from the time I would have spent with my family. All were very understanding and supportive.

Introduction

Your local bookstore has many books intended to introduce you to your IBM (and clone) personal computers. All of these books spend a lot of time explaining the computer's DOS. Then they usually spend about one chapter explaining the basics of batch file programs. One chapter is enough to convince you that batch files are powerful tools. However, it isn't enough to teach you how to use batch files effectively, much less how to write them.

Who this book is for

This book will help you explore the power of batch files. In writing this book, I'm assuming you have a general understanding of DOS. You don't have to be a computer whiz, but you should know how to boot the computer, format a disk, and how to erase and rename files. If you have a hard disk, you should know how to make, delete, and change directories. In general, you should feel comfortable performing simple tasks from the DOS prompt. If this isn't the case, you should start with a general book first.

How this book is structured

This book introduces one topic at a time. When a topic is introduced, it is explained in detail. Most concepts include an example batch file.

The first time you read this book, you'll get much more from it if you're in front of a computer. As you read about each new concept, you should enter and run the batch file or run the batch file from the program disk. This is also an excellent time to experiment. You'll retain the information much longer if you try to modify it to your own needs. For example, one of the first batch files in this book is A.BAT. It looks like this:

```
DIR A:/P
```

As you read about A.BAT, try to think if you could modify it to list only your .BAK files, or perform some similar task that interests you. This is the best way to learn new material.

Part 1: Batch file basics

Part 1 will teach you the basics of writing batch files. You have a head start writing batch files in DOS that you wouldn't have if you had to learn a programming language; much of what goes into batch files is the straight DOS you already know.

Chapter 1, Simple batch files, teaches you how to create batch files that simply replace DOS commands.

Chapter 2, Batch file commands, introduces simple batch file commands and replaceable parameters. Replaceable parameters are variables that allow you to write batch files that do different things at different times.

Chapter 3, Looping and program flow, explains how to write batch files that respond to their environment by changing the flow of commands.

Part 2: Putting batch files to work

In Part 1 of this book, I describe how to write batch files. In Part 2, it's time to really put batch files to work with several applications you can write using mostly batch files that make using your computer much easier and safer.

Chapter 4, Configuring your computer, covers two user-created files that, to a great extent, determine the configuration of your computer. The first one is the CONFIG.SYS file. It isn't a batch file but is so similar to one I've elected to include it in this book. It's actually an ASCII file that acts very much like a batch file. It contains commands that control both how much memory DOS allocates to certain tasks, and how DOS performs several other tasks. The second is the AUTOEXEC.BAT file. It's a standard batch file with one important difference: DOS automatically runs it each time the computer boots. That makes it a great place to perform those tasks that need to be performed only once, like loading memory-resident software or activating a menu system.

Chapter 5, Custom configurations, shows how to configure the computer's setup differently for different applications.

Chapter 6, Batch file menus, develops a simple menu system using batch files. After finishing this chapter, you'll be able to expand the menu system to cover all the programs you use.

Chapter 7, A document archival system, develops a batch file based system with which you can ensure that you never lose a data file. After finishing this chapter, you'll be able to expand this system to include all the software you currently use.

Chapter 8, Anti-viral batch files, develops a series of batch files and DOS commands that you can use to help protect yourself against computer viruses.

Part 3: Software to turbocharge your batch files

The first two parts of this book deal with basic DOS. You have everything you need for these parts on your DOS disk. As you work through parts 1 and 2, you will often get the feeling that batch files would be much better if only they would _____. (You fill in the blank.) Well, people have had that feeling and some of them did something about it. Part 3 explores the results.

Chapter 9, Improving your batch files, has programs that allow you to overcome some of the weaknesses of batch files.

Chapter 10, Alternatives to the DOS batch language, covers an alternative batch file language and several batch file compilers that turn batch files into programs.

Part 4: Advanced batch file programming

Part 4 shows you how to solve difficult problems using the advanced batch techniques already covered in the book.

Chapter 11, Subroutines in batch files, shows you how to use subroutines in a batch file. The ability to call subroutines was added in DOS 3.3 so this will be of interest mainly to users with an earlier version of DOS.

Chapter 12, Problem solving with batch files, shows how to solve actual, everyday computer problems with batch files. These include controlling the printer, setting the color on the monitor, and prompting for a password. In other words, a bunch of batch file applications too small to get their own chapter. This is my favorite part of the book.

Chapter 13, Batch file tricks, shows some tricks I learned while experimenting to write this book. I could have easily called this chapter "Batch files for power users."

Chapter 14, The DOS environment, explains the DOS environment and how to increase its size. The DOS environment contains information that's stored in the Path, Prompt, and Set variables.

Chapter 15, Modifying DOS, shows several useful patches to the DOS operating system using Debug and The Norton Utilities.

Part 5: Reference

Part 5 is a section for readers who don't understand something specific or who have a quick question.

Chapter 16, Quick reference list, is a quick reference for all the commands covered in this book. After finishing the book, you can consult this chapter for the bare essentials of a batch file command.

Chapter 17, Summary table, is a brief summary table with all the DOS commands that you can use for quick reference.

Appendices

The appendices provide information that will be of interest to only some readers. You might want to skip some or all of them.

Appendix A, Editing batch files, discusses the DOS end-of-file marker, along with the EDLIN and EDIT DOS editors. If your word processor creates ASCII files, then you can probably skip this appendix.

Appendix B, DOS redirection, shows you how to use the DOS piping symbols to route output to different places, and obtain input from locations other than the keyboard.

Appendix C, Changes in DOS, explains how the most recent version of DOS has changed the way certain parts of the computer work.

Appendix D, Modifying InKey, shows you how to modify a simple program for user input that's included with this book.

Hardware and software

Writing a computer book is difficult. You never know what type of hardware and software the reader has. You don't even know what version of the operating system he's using. In writing about batch files, I'm more fortunate than many writers. Most batch files will run on any hardware configuration. And most of the batch files in this book will run on any version of DOS that's 2.0 or higher. I've indicated where this is not true.

For most of the examples in this book, I assume that the files supporting DOS external commands (like FORMAT.COM and BACKUP.COM) are either in the current subdirectory or in the PATH when an example batch file requires one of these programs.

If you're working with floppy disks, you can create a system disk by copying the DOS external files to that disk when you format it. Because DOS limits the number of files in the root directory of a disk to 110, you'll need several storage disks to hold all the example batch files and the required system files.

I personally wrote this book using a Northgate Super Micro 386/20 and an HP Laserjet III. The word processor I used for everything except the batch files and tables was Microsoft Word 5.0. I edited batch files and other ASCII files with the extremely nice editor that's built into DOS 5.0. Finally, I created all the tables using Word for Windows. While too slow for general writing, it has the best table editing engine I've ever seen.

Conventions

There are a few important pieces of information you need to keep in mind when reading this book:

- The numbered function keys on the keyboard are shown as F1 through F12. On most older keyboards there are ten function keys on the left side of the keyboard, labeled from F1 to F10. Newer keyboards have twelve function keys, F1 to F12, along the top of the keyboard.
- Enter stands for the Enter or Return key, which can also be represented on the keyboard as Rtrn or a bent arrow. Most other named keys, like Delete or Tab, are also referred to by their name. The directional keys are simply up, down, right, and left arrow.
- Information you type into the computer and pieces of programs broken out from the regular text is in an alternate typeface. The names of keys you hit, like F6 or Enter, and explanatory text is in regular type.
- The caret symbol, ^, means that you hold down the Control, or Ctrl, key and then tap the following key. So ^Z means hold down the Control key and press the Z key. This type of key combination is also shown as Ctrl−Z.
- Any command inside brackets, [ ], is optional. Brackets are generally used when I'm giving the syntax for a command. In the following, for example:

    DIR [/P]

    The /P switch is optional. It causes the listing to pause each time the screen is full. Pressing any key restarts the listing.
- Most of the commands in this book are shown in uppercase. For the most part, the computer doesn't care. C > DIR, C > dir, and C > DiR are all the same to the computer. About the only time it matters is when you're using the equal sign to compare two things.

Notes

If this book causes you to develop a nice batch hint or raises a batch-related question not currently answered in the book, write to me in care of TAB Books and let me know. While I can't respond to individual letters, your hint or question just might show up in the next edition of this book. The address is:

Ronny Richardson
c/o TAB Books
P.O. Box 40
Blue Ridge Summit, Pennsylvania 17214

I tested all the batch files in this book on a wide variety of DOS versions. TAB Books and I have done everything possible to ensure that the programs and batch files included with this book and on the disk either run under all versions of DOS or are clearly labeled as to which version(s) they require. We have also done our best to make sure that every program and batch file does exactly what we claim it will do. Neither TAB Books or I make any warranty of any type, expressed or implied, regarding the programs, batch files, and documentation included in this book and on the included disk. In addition, we aren't liable for incidental or consequential damages in connection with, or arising from, the performance of these programs and batch files.

Part 1
Batch file basics

1
CHAPTER

Simple batch files

The basic idea of a batch file is really very ingenious. When you want the computer to perform a given task more than once, why not have it store the details of that task? A batch file is DOS's way of doing that. When you tell DOS to execute a batch file, DOS reads and follows that batch file just like an actor reads and follows a script. The concept of the computer following a script is an excellent mental image of a batch file.

In DOS, a batch file must have a .BAT extension. It must have a name that's different from any DOS internal commands. So ERASE.BAT and RENAME. BAT would be invalid names. (This isn't absolute; there's a tricky way around it that I'll discuss later in the book.) A batch file must be an ASCII text file.

The batch file script is a special file containing one or more DOS commands, with each command on a separate line. This is illustrated with the following:

First command
Second command
Third command
Fourth command
Fifth command
and so on . . .

You run a batch file by entering its name at the DOS prompt. You can enter the .BAT extension, but you don't have to. To run a batch file named FRED.BAT, you would enter:

FRED Enter

Some batch files require additional information. You enter this additional information after the batch file name. The batch file name and each separate piece of information must be separated by either a space or a comma. For example:

    FRED Yes,1,*.BAK No

There are four types of commands DOS will accept: internal commands, .EXE program names, .COM program names, and .BAT filenames. Every time DOS receives a command, it first checks to see if that command is an internal command, like ERASE. If so, it executes that command.

Internal commands are commands that are so important that they're built directly into DOS. Internal commands represent a trade-off. If DOS had every possible command built-in, then it would take up so much room that there would be no room left for application programs. If no programs were built into DOS, however, every system disk would require numerous programs to perform every simple task. This would waste a lot of space. The trade-off made by DOS is that the most important commands are built-in. The remaining commands are external programs that require a .EXE or .COM program to run.

The names for internal commands are part of DOS. That's why you can't name your batch files using the same as an internal command. If you do, there's no way to execute your program. If you created a file named COPY.BAT and tried to run it with the command:

    COPY

then DOS would automatically go to the built-in DOS COPY command, and try to COPY nothing to nothing. If you tried to run it using:

    COPY.BAT

then DOS would try to COPY a file named .BAT to nothing and would return an error message. If the command isn't an internal command, DOS next checks the current subdirectory for a .COM file by that name, then an .EXE file, and finally a .BAT file. If DOS finds a program with the correct name, it executes that program. If DOS doesn't find a file with the correct name in the current directory, it searches the PATH for a .COM, .EXE, or .BAT file. If DOS finds a program in the PATH with the correct name, it executes that program. Otherwise, it returns the *Bad command or file name* error message. Figure 1-1 shows the hierarchy of DOS commands.

What a batch file is good for

One use of batch files is to save keystrokes. For example, the command to get a directory from the A drive:

    DIR A:/P

can be shortened if you use the following steps. Without worrying about what

Internal Command	(DOS commands)
.COM	(Program in current subdirectory)
.EXE	(Program in current subdirectory)
.BAT	(Batch File in current subdirectory)
C:\FIRST\.COM	(Program)
C:\FIRST\.EXE	(Program)
C:\FIRST\.BAT	(Batch File)
C:\SECOND\.COM	(Program)
C:\SECOND\.EXE	(Program)
C:\SECOND\.BAT	(Batch File)
C:\THIRD\.COM	(Program)
C:\THIRD\.EXE	(Program)
C:\THIRD\.BAT	(Batch File)

1-1   The hierarchy of DOS commands if PATH = C: \ ;C: \ FIRST;C: \ SECOND;C: \ THIRD.

you're typing, enter the following at the C> DOS prompt:

COPY CON:A.BAT Enter
DIR A:/P F6 Enter

You should see a message *1 File(s) copied*. Now put a disk in drive A and type:

A Enter

If everything goes well, you'll now see a directory of the A drive. You're probably thinking to yourself, "So what? I can simply type DIR A:/P when I want a directory." The advantage of A.BAT is that you can get a directory with two keystrokes instead of nine.

Another use of batch files is to reduce confusion. When I first started using computers, I had a great deal of difficulty remembering the command to check a disk. Instead of trying to force myself to remember CHKDSK (CHecK DiSK), I wrote a batch file called CHECK.BAT, shown in Fig. 1-2. Typing CHECK instead of CHKDSK saves one keystroke, but that isn't the primary purpose of CHECK. BAT. I can remember the word *check* much easier than I can remember the non-word *chkdsk*. Of course, I could have renamed CHKDSK.COM to CHECK. COM and achieved the same thing, but then no one else would have been able to check a disk on my computer. Writing a batch file allowed me to use the name I wanted without interfering with normal operations.

It's time for a simple one-question test. Put away your DOS manual and don't look at the next figure in this book. What's the solution to the following prob-

Batch File Line	Explanation
REM CHECK.BAT	A remark that is not executed. It will still show on the screen since ECHO has not been turned off. This remark gives the name of the batch file, an excellent piece of information to put near the top of a batch file.
CHKDSK	Runs the DOS CHKDSK program. Since the full path to CHKDSK is not specified and the batch file does not change to the DOS subdirectory, the program must be in the PATH for this batch file command to work.

1-2 CHECK.BAT, which runs the DOS CHKDSK program.

lem—We all know how important it is to back up your hard disk. You should be making frequent full backups, say weekly or monthly, and daily incremental backups. Write down the proper syntax of an incremental backup using the DOS program BACKUP.COM.

Most of you probably didn't do well on this test. The point is that you can use the batch file in Fig. 1-3 so you'll never have to remember the syntax. So, in addition to reducing keystrokes, batch files can simplify DOS by giving commands more meaningful names and by storing command syntax in the computer so you can safely forget it.

All the batch files you've seen so far have one thing in common—they each do only one thing. Most of them have two lines, but the first line is only a remark to remind you of the batch file name. It doesn't have to be this way. DOS keeps track of its location in a batch file even while it's doing something else. The batch file in Fig. 1-4 illustrates this.

First, 2THINGS.BAT runs CHKDSK.COM. While CHKDSK is running, DOS maintains its place in 2THINGS.BAT. When CHKDSK finishes, DOS reads the next command in 2THINGS.BAT and runs a directory. Although CHKDSK took only a few seconds to run, it could have been a word-processing program that runs indefinitely. It doesn't matter. DOS remembers and picks up the batch file whenever the program finishes.

Batch File Line	Explanation
REM BACKUP-I.BA	A remark that is not executed. It will still show on the screen since ECHO has not been turned off.
BACKUP C:\ A: /S/M/A//	Runs the DOS BACKUP program. Since the full path to BACKUP is not specified and the batch file does not change to the DOS subdirectory, the program must be in the PATH for this batch file command to work.

1-3 BACKUP-I.BAT, which runs the DOS BACKUP program.

Batch File Line	Explanation
REM 2THINGS.BAT	A remark that is not executed. It will still show on the screen since ECHO has not been turned off.
CHKDSK	Runs the DOS CHKDSK program. Since the full path to CHKDSK is not specified and the batch file does not change to the DOS subdirectory, the program must be in the PATH for this batch file command to work.
DIR	Performs a directory of the current subdirectory. Since this is an internal command, it does not need a path.

1-4   2THINGS.BAT, which runs two programs, one after the other.

In this example, the batch file 2THINGS.BAT has done two important things. First, it saved keystrokes. More importantly, it established a standard script to be followed each time 2THINGS.BAT is run. While not important in this example, it is in the next example. Figure 1-5 shows a batch file for starting the spreadsheet program Lotus 1-2-3. Using GOLOTUS.BAT as a script clearly saves keystrokes, but more importantly, it guarantees that every time you start Lotus you'll have all available memory for spreadsheets and that you can use your mouse. A memory lapse, therefore, won't cause you to skip a step.

A final reason for using batch files is safety. There are some very dangerous DOS commands. Specifying FORMAT instead of FORMAT A: can destroy 100 Meg or more of data. ERASE *.DOC instead of ERASE *.BAK can erase all your documents. Batch files can form a strong line of defense against the indiscriminate use of these powerful commands.

Batch File Line	Explanation
REM GOLOTUS.BAT	A remark that is not executed. It will still show on the screen since ECHO has not been turned off.
POPDROP C	Runs a commercial program called PopDrop. The C switch causes PopDrop to begin a new layer of memory resident programs.
CD\LOTUS	Changes to the Lotus subdirectory. Notice the batch file does not change to the C drive so it would not work properly if run from a floppy drive.
MOUSE	Runs Mouse, a commercial program to add a mouse menu to Lotus.
123	Runs Lotus.
POPDROP D	Runs PopDrop again. The D switch causes it to unload the memory resident Mouse program to reclaim the memory.

1-5   GOLOTUS.BAT, which activates a mouse and then loads Lotus 1-2-3.

Batch File Line	Explanation
ECHO OFF	Turns off echo so the rest of the commands will not show on the screen.
REM FORMAT.BAT	A remark to give the name of the batch file. Since echo is off, it will not show on the screen.
XYZ A:/V	The command to format the disk. Notice that FORMAT.COM must be renamed to XYZ.COM and it must be in your path. Also notice that the batch file will only format the A drive and will not place the system files on the disk.

1-6 FORMAT.BAT, which shows how you can add a safety feature to the potentially dangerous DOS FORMAT command.

You can prevent accidental formatting of a hard disk by first renaming FORMAT.COM to XYZ.COM and then creating FORMAT.BAT, as shown in Fig. 1-6. The ECHO OFF command, which will be explained in detail later, prevents you from seeing the name of the program being used to format the disk. If you saw the name, you might be tempted to enter the following at the C> prompt:

    XYZ

and bypass the batch file. You can reduce accidental file erasures with KILL.BAT, as shown in Fig. 1-7. KILL.BAT uses several commands that I'll explain in detail later. The %1 is replaced with what you enter after KILL, so if you enter:

    KILL *.BAK

then everywhere you have a %1 in KILL.BAT, DOS sees *.BAK. So DOS sees

Batch File Line	Explanation
ECHO OFF	Turns echo off.
REM KILL.BAT	Remark to give the name of the batch file. Since echo is off, it does not show when the batch file runs.
DIR %1/W	Lists all the files in the current subdirectory in wide format.
ECHO Hit Control Break to STOP the erase	The first of two lines telling the user what is going on and how to stop the batch file.
ECHO of these files	The second line of information for the user.
PAUSE	Pauses the batch file until the user presses a key. This gives the user the chance to abort the batch file and not erase the files.
ERASE %1	Erases the batch files specified by the user if Ctrl-Break is not pressed.

1-7 KILL.BAT, which allows you to add a safety feature to the potentially dangerous DOS ERASE command.

DIR *.BAK in place of DIR %1. In summary, DOS batch files have three major functions:

- They can reduce the number of keystrokes needed to execute a command.
- They allow you to store the proper syntax of command sequence in a script file so you do not have to remember this information.
- They can protect you from dangerous DOS commands.

DOS as a programming language

When most computer users think of programming, they think of spending months to learn languages such as Pascal or C. Like programs created with Pascal or C, DOS batch files are programs. Unlike any other programming language, however, DOS commands are already familiar to most of you. Therefore, you already know most of the commands you need to write a batch program. Batch files have only a handful of special commands. The vast majority of batch file commands are the regular DOS commands you use every day. If you know how to use DOS, you know most of what you need to know in order to write effective batch files. The few commands unique to batch files will be covered in the first three chapters of this book.

When you learn to program in most computer languages, you must learn a great deal before you're able to write even the simplest program. This isn't true with batch files. As you've already seen, you can write some very powerful batch files with standard DOS commands and one or two special batch commands.

Although batch files are easy to write, this ease comes at a price: batch files are limited in what they can do. One of your most common thoughts as you study this book will be, "If only . . ." You'll see many situations where you could really automate things if only batch files had specific command. That is the real drawback to batch files. They're easy to learn and easy to write, but they always seem to stop just short of having enough power.

One way to overcome many of the limitations of DOS batch files is with the many batch utilities available in the public domain, as shareware and commercial programs. Many of these are discussed in my book, *MS-DOS Batch File Utilities*, also available from Windcrest.

The COPY command

One of the most basic DOS commands you'll use in batch files is the COPY command. You've probably used this command to copy files in the past. For example:

    COPY A:*.* B:

copies between two DOS logical devices, both of which happen to be files. The COPY command can be used to copy between any DOS logical devices. In addition to files, there are the following kinds of logical devices:

CON

Depending on the usage, this is either the screen or the keyboard. When used as the target, it's the screen. After all, you can't copy to the keyboard! When used as the source, CON is the keyboard.

PRN

The PRN specification refers to your printer.

NUL

This is DOS's version of a black hole. Anything that's copied to NUL is gone. I'll show you later how to send unwanted messages to NUL.

You can copy between files and any of the above DOS logical devices, or between the logical devices. (Not all combinations make sense—for example, copying from NUL or from PRN.) You can view a file called SHOWCON.DOC on the screen, for example, by typing the following:

COPY SHOWCON.DOC CON Enter

This command copies the file to the screen, and results in what you see in Fig. 1-8. You can turn your printer into a simple typewriter with the command:

COPY CON PRN Enter

```
C>COPY SHOWCON.DOC CON
REM SHOWCON.DOC
This is an example of an ASCII file
like the files created by some word-
processors.

C>          1 File(s) copied
```

1-8   What you'll see when you copy a file to the CON device, i.e., the screen.

When you're finished typing, press the F6 key followed by an Enter and what you've typed will be sent to the printer. All the combinations that work with the COPY command, however, don't work with the XCOPY command. Unlike COPY, XCOPY can only copy between files.

You can create simple batch files by copying from the keyboard (CON) to a file. To create a simple batch file called EXAMPLE1.BAT, enter the following command:

COPY CON EXAMPLE1.BAT Enter

What you're telling DOS with this command is *copy from the console to a file called EXAMPLE1.BAT.* Note that the DOS prompt doesn't return when you press Enter. Now enter:

DIR *.* F6 Enter

and you should see the message *1 File(s) copied.* You can use this method to create batch files of any length. In fact, you can use this method to write a file containing a letter or anything for which you'd use a word processor. You could, but you probably wouldn't want to. Once you press Enter, there's no way to go back and edit that line. And once you create a file, there's no way to edit it. If you make a mistake, you must start over! In spite of the fact that editing is limited to the current line, COPY CON is an effective way to create short batch files.

When COPY CON isn't enough

When you need to create a longer batch file, or if you need to edit an existing batch file, COPY CON isn't good enough. You need a word processor. Prior to DOS 5.0, DOS came with a simple line editor called EDLIN. The line editor description means it lets you edit only one line at a time. Most word processors are full-screen editors. They let you edit anywhere on the screen. For this reason, most people don't like EDLIN. But it's free. If you want to try using EDLIN, it's explained in appendix A.

With the release of DOS 5.0, Microsoft scrapped EDLIN and replaced it with Edit. Unlike EDLIN, Edit is a full-screen editor with a very Windows-like appearance. Users of Microsoft's QuickBasic will be immediately familiar with Edit, because it works like QuickBasic. Like EDLIN, its operation is explained in appendix A.

Most full-featured word processors, like Wordstar, can be used to edit batch files. Normally, Wordstar doesn't produce ASCII files. If you copy a Wordstar file to the screen, you'll see that the last letter of most words look funny. To produce ASCII text with Wordstar, you must open your document in what Wordstar calls the nondocument mode. This means that you can't open your batch file at the same time you start Wordstar, using this short-cut:

WS BATCH.BAT

Wordstar lets you specify the filename when you start the program, and thus avoid the opening menu. But this method automatically puts you in document mode and you won't get an ASCII file. Even in nondocument mode, Wordstar won't produce an ASCII file if you use the paragraph reformat command, Ctrl$-$B ($^$B). However, if you follow these few precautions, Wordstar will work well as a batch file editor.

Most other word processors will produce ASCII files. However, ASCII probably won't be the default mode. It might be a separate mode, which will usually have word wrap turned off, or you might need to translate your document into DOS or ASCII format. A simple word processor might work similar to a type-writer with limited editing ability. If in doubt, create a small document. Copy that document to the screen. If you see exactly what you typed, then it's ASCII.

If your chosen word processor doesn't support ASCII or makes working with ASCII files difficult, there are a large number of shareware and even public domain ASCII editors to choose from.

Summary

The major points of this chapter are the following:

- Batch files are a script that you write and DOS follows.
- Batch files save keystrokes.
- Batch files can be used to rename one or more commands to something easier to remember.
- Batch files remember parameters and command order.
- Batch files can be used to reduce problems with dangerous DOS commands.
- Batch files are programs, just like programs written in Pascal or C.
- Batch files can be created with the COPY CON command or any ASCII word processor.

Most of the batch files discussed in this chapter are available on the included disk.

2
CHAPTER

Batch file commands

You've just finished chapter 1. You now know how to create simple batch files using COPY CON on your favorite word processor in ASCII mode. You also know how to create batch files that contain standard DOS commands. Now it's time to add batch commands to batch files.

"Why in the world did I do that?"

One of the worst possible feelings a programmer can have is going back to an old program and not knowing what's going on. BASIC programmers even have a name for the type of code most likely to cause this condition. It's called *spaghetti code* because it twists and turns like cooked spaghetti.

In any programming language, it's important to document your work. That means both written documentation, e.g., a manual, and documentation inside the program. If you look at the source code for any well written program in any language, you'll see lots of documentation. The documentation takes the form of comments. These are lines of text inside the program that have nothing to do with the actual program. They're intended to help you understand the surrounding code, especially when you haven't seen the program for six months.

Internal documentation for a batch file consists of the remark line, or REM. If you start a line with REM followed by a space, you can enter almost anything you want to. The only thing you can't use are the DOS redirection characters. The computer will skip the remark line, so the information on that line are simply comments for anyone who has to go back to modify the code.

Take a look at the sample batch file in Fig. 2-1. This example includes some commands you haven't learned yet, but they're not the important part. The important thing is that %1 takes the place of a filename while the batch file is running. Given that, do you know what the file is doing? Probably not. Now consider the

```
:START
ERASE %1.BAK
COPY %1.DOC B:
COPY C:\WORD\NORMAL\%1.STY B:
ERASE C:\WORD\NORMAL\%1.BAK
COPY \WORD\%1.CMP B:
SHIFT
IF /%1==/ GOTO END
GOTO START
:END
```

2-1   Batch file that has no internal documentation. Can you
tell what it does?

same batch file, properly documented, as shown in Fig. 2-2. Its the same batch
file. None of the working commands are any different. But now you can probably
understand the batch file without my explaining the commands I haven't yet covered.

     This isn't a made-up example. Figure 2-1 is an actual working batch file
that's used every day. The author of the batch file could probably modify it, but it

```
REM YESDOC.BAT
REM Batch file to copy new files to floppy
REM disk. Name top of loop
:START
REM Erase the backup file
ERASE %1.BAK
REM Copy the document file to floppy disk
COPY %1.DOC B:
REM Copy the associated style sheet to
REM floppy disk
COPY C:\WORD\NORMAL\%1.STY B:
REM Erase backup copy of style sheet
ERASE C:\WORD\NORMAL\%1.BAK
REM Copy document dictionary to floppy disk
COPY \WORD\%1.CMP B:
REM Get next name
SHIFT
REM Test for next name existing and go to
REM bottom if does not exist
IF /%1==/ GOTO END
REM Go to top since there is another file
GOTO START
:END
REM Finished copy
```

2-2   The batch file segment from Fig. 2-1, this time with proper documentation.

isn't likely that anyone else could. The point is that batch files aren't so simple that you can skip documentation. No one ever suffered from too much documentation.

All the remark command does, therefore, is allow you to add comments to your batch file. The syntax is REM space, and then your comments. The line length must be 127 characters or less. If ECHO is turned off, the REM line won't be displayed when the batch file is executed.

Communicating with the user

Back in chapter 1, I introduced the concept of a batch file being a script that the computer follows. Well, the computer has a bad habit of reading everything on the script. Take the following, for example:

Billy: Sally, you can't leave me. I need you.
Sally: I'm leaving you.
Sally: Opens door and walks out

While the writer expects Sally to open the door and walk out, he expects her to do it quietly. You also expect the computer to do what you tell it. But while running a tax program, you don't expect to see:

```
Line Input A$
SalesTax = Income * .04 − (State * 2.3)
```

When you use a word processor or spreadsheet, you never see the code running. Why should a batch file be any different?

The process of showing commands on the screen while they're being executed is called echoing. When this echoing is on, you see commands as they execute. When echoing is off, you don't see commands as they execute. With most versions of DOS, every batch file starts with echoing turned on. The echoing can be turned off with the command ECHO OFF.

Because ECHO isn't off when this command is given, you'll see the ECHO OFF command. Many users include the ECHO OFF command as the first command of every batch file. If you need to, you can turn echoing back on with the command ECHO ON. The ECHO command by itself will display the status of ECHO.

The ECHO OFF command turns off just command echoing. It doesn't turn off DOS messages. If you copy a file in a batch file, you'll see the *1 File(s) copied* DOS message. If you use a batch file to start a program, you'll still see that program on the screen. All ECHO OFF affects is the display of batch file commands while that specific batch file is running. Beginning with DOS 3.3, preceding a batch file command with an @ suppresses the display of that command even if ECHO is turned on. A good use for this command is putting @ECHO OFF as the first line of each batch file.

Batch File Line	Explanation
`REM ECHO1.BAT`	Remark giving the name of the batch file.
`ECHO`	Show the status of echo.
`ECHO You should see a message` `    saying ECHO is on`	Tell the user what is happening.
`ECHO OFF`	Turn command-echoing off.
`ECHO`	Show the status of echo.

`ECHO You should not have seen`
`    the ECHO command`
`ECHO However, you should have`
`    seen the ECHO is off message`
`ECHO Unlike the first message,`
`    you should see these`
`ECHO messages only once`
	Tell the user what is happening.

`ECHO ON`	Turn command-echoing on.
`ECHO ECHO is now back ON, and` `    you should see this twice`	Tell the user what is happening.

2-3 ECHO1.BAT, which illustrates the ECHO ON/OFF command.

The ECHO command has another, even more important, function. You can use it to communicate with the user. When the ECHO command is followed with a message, that message is displayed on the screen. When ECHO is on, the message is actually displayed twice. It gets displayed once when the command is executed (echoing) and a second time when the command is carried out. When ECHO is off, the message is displayed only once. The batch file in Fig. 2-3 illustrates this point. Figure 2-4 shows what happens on the screen when ECHO-1.BAT runs.

```
C>echo1

C>REM ECHO1.BAT

C>ECHO
ECHO is on

C>ECHO You should see a message saying ECHO is on
You should see a message saying ECHO is on

C>ECHO OFF
ECHO is off
You should not have seen the ECHO command
However, you should have seen the ECHO is off message
Unlike the first message, you should see these
messages only once

C>ECHO ECHO is not back ON, and you should see this twice
ECHO is not back ON, and you should see this twice
C>
```

2-4 Screen display produced by running the ECHO1.BAT file shown in Fig. 2-3.

For extra effect, make sure the message you echo to the screen is no wider than the screen. You can center the message if you add spaces to the front of the message, as discussed, and you can add emphasis by echoing ASCII characters. These techniques are illustrated by the batch file in Fig. 2-5. Figure 2-6 shows ASCII values that are useful for creating fancy ECHO statements. To create these, hold down the Alt key and enter the number from the keypad. Note that using the numbers at the top of the keyboard won't work.

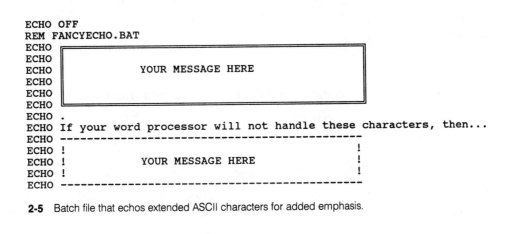

```
ECHO OFF
REM FANCYECHO.BAT
ECHO
ECHO
ECHO                  YOUR MESSAGE HERE
ECHO
ECHO
ECHO
ECHO .
ECHO If your word processor will not handle these characters, then...
ECHO -------------------------------------------------
ECHO !                                               !
ECHO !         YOUR MESSAGE HERE                     !
ECHO !                                               !
ECHO -------------------------------------------------
```

2-5 Batch file that echos extended ASCII characters for added emphasis.

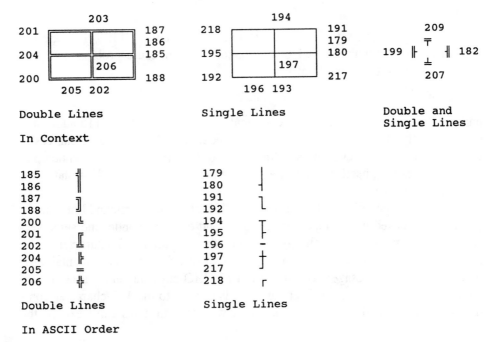

2-6 IBM extended ASCII line drawing characters.

The ECHO command has another little known, and practically useless, function. If you enter ECHO OFF at the DOS prompt, you'll "lose" your prompt. While ECHO is off, the default for all batch files is ECHO OFF and running a batch file won't reset it unless you issue an ECHO ON statement.

ECHO quirks

The ECHO command has had its share of quirks. This section will explain the major ones. Keep in mind that different computer vendors often make minor changes to their version of DOS, so ECHO might exhibit different quirks on your system.

Dots

Prior to version 3.0, you could replace the ECHO statement with a dot. So

. The option you selected is not available

is the same as:

ECHO The option you selected is not available

Because this isn't supported in all versions of DOS, however, it's best to avoid using a dot as a replacement for the ECHO statement.

ECHOs that are too long

Replaceable parameters (%1) and environmental variables (%PATH%) are expanded when used with the ECHO command. This can cause problems. If your batch file has the following line:

ECHO %PATH% 115 additional characters

and you have a long path, then the combination of the ECHO, the 115 additional characters, the dividing spaces, and the expanded %PATH% variable can easily exceed the 127-character command line limit. In fact, the path itself can be up to 122 characters long itself. (Five characters are required for the PATH= statement to install the path.)

On one computer I tested, exceeding the 127-character command line limit in this manner locked up my machine. On a second computer under the same version of DOS, the computer simply truncates the line after 127 characters. The point is that you should use extreme caution when echoing environmental variables inside other messages. When you must ECHO environmental variables, do so on a separate line. Because setting them is subject to the 127-character command line limit, a single ECHO statement with the variables can't exceed the limit.

What you can and can't ECHO

You can't include the symbols <, >, or | in an ECHO statement. These are DOS piping symbols. They're used to move information between sources within DOS. If you include them in an ECHO statement, DOS will try to pipe the data from your ECHO statement, with very unpredictable results.

You can't directly include a percent sign in an ECHO statement. DOS tries to interpret a single percent sign as a variable. If you need a percent sign in your ECHO, include a double percent sign (%%). DOS will display this as a single percent sign.

You can't ECHO any message that begins with a ON space or OFF space because DOS interprets this as an ECHO ON or ECHO OFF command. The solution is to reword the message, to include a space holding printing character (like an exclamation point character) at the beginning of the line, or to include a non-printing character at the front of the message.

Spaces

Older versions of DOS don't display spaces as you would expect them to. You can put any number of spaces between the ECHO command and the message and these older versions of DOS will treat it as a single space. This is illustrated by the batch file in Fig. 2-7. Figure 2-8 shows this batch file running under two versions of DOS. Under one version it works properly, under the other it doesn't.

Batch File Line	Explanation
ECHO OFF	Turn echoing off.
REM SPACE1.BAT	Remark giving name of batch file.
VER	Display the DOS version. This is an internal command.
ECHO ONE SPACE	Echo a message with one space (the minimum) between the ECHO command and the message.
ECHO TWO SPACES	Echo a message with two spaces between the ECHO command and the message. With most versions of DOS, the extra spaces will not appear on the screen.
ECHO THREE SPACES	Echo a message with three spaces between the ECHO command and the message.
ECHO FOUR SPACES	Echo a message with four spaces between the ECHO command and the message.

2-7 SPACE1.BAT, a batch file that uses spaces in the ECHO command.

```
C> SPACE 1
C> ECHO OFF

COMPAQ Personal Computer DOS Version   2.11
ONE SPACE
TWO SPACES
THREE SPACES
FOUR SPACES

C> SPACE1

C> ECHO OFF

COMPAQ Personal Computer DOS Version   3.20
 ONE SPACE
   TWO SPACES
     THREE SPACES
       FOUR SPACES
```

2-8   A screen display of SPACE1.BAT, shown in Fig. 2-7, running on two different computers.

The batch file in Fig. 2-9 shows how to correct this problem by including a leading character. Here I've used an exclamation point, which you can see on the screen. If you want to be fancy, you can include a nonprinting character.

If you're using SideKick or Wordstar, a nonprinting character is a space followed by a ^PH, which is a backspace. Many word processors will allow you to enter special control characters into an ASCII file. The COPY CON method of creating batch files doesn't let you enter a backspace character. It treats a ^H as a command and immediately backspaces the cursor. DOS and some word proces-

Batch File Line	Explanation
ECHO OFF	Turn command-echoing off.
REM SPACE2.BAT	Remark giving the name of the batch file.
VER	Display the DOS version.
ECHO ! ONE SPACE	Echo a message with one space prior to the message. Since the ! is the actual start of the message, this method handles spaces properly, although it is less attractive.
ECHO ! TWO SPACES	Echo a message with two spaces prior to the message.
ECHO ! THREE SPACES	Echo a message with three spaces prior to the message.
ECHO ! FOUR SPACES	Echo a message with four spaces prior to the message.

2-9   SPACE2.BAT, which gives a method for including multiple spaces, using any version of DOS.

sors will let you enter a nonprinting space as an ASCII 255. To enter this, hold down the Alt and Shift keys and type 255 on the number keypad. As stated before, the numbers at the top of the keyboard won't work. Also note that you can use the Alt−Ctrl−255 trick to produce filenames that look like they have a space in them with some, but not all, programs.

As illustrated by the batch file in Fig. 2-10, control characters can be used for other purposes. On a PC, ^G sounds the built-in bell. By echoing a ^G, you can sound the bell to signal a dangerous step or the completion of a long batch file.

The batch file in Fig. 2-11 illustrates another problem with the ECHO command. The ECHO statement in between the two lines is intended to doublespace the two messages. Instead, it displays the status of ECHO, as shown in Fig. 2-12. The solution to this problem is very similar to the above solution. Either echo a single border character like an exclamation point or a nonprinting character like a backspace. This is illustrated by the batch file in Fig. 2-13.

Batch File Line	Explanation
ECHO OFF	Turn echoing off.
REM BELL.BAT	Remark giving the name of the batch file.
ECHO ^G^G^G	Command to ring the bell three times.

2-10 BELL.BAT, which rings the computer's bell.

Batch File Line	Explanation
ECHO OFF	Turn command-echoing off.
REM LINE1.BAT	Remark giving the name of the batch file.
ECHO The next line is intended to be blank	Displaying a message for the user.
ECHO	An attempt to display a blank line. However, it results in an "Echo is off" message instead.
ECHO The above line should be blank	Displaying a message for the user.

2-11 LINE1.BAT, a batch file that incorrectly tries to add a blank line.

```
C>LINE1

C>ECHO OFF
The next line is intended to be blank
ECHO is off
The above line should be blank

C>
```

2-12 A screen display of LINE1.BAT, in Fig. 2-11, running.

Batch File Line	Explanation
`ECHO OFF`	Turn command-echoing off.
`REM LINE2.BAT`	Remark giving the name of the batch file.
`ECHO ! The next line is intended to be blank`	Display a message to the user.
`ECHO !`	Display an (almost) blank line.
`ECHO ! The above line should be blank`	Display a message to the user.

2-13   LINE2.BAT, which forces a blank line and will work with all versions of DOS.

Depending on the version of DOS you use, there are other potential methods to display a blank line. On one of the DOS 2 versions, an ECHO followed by two or more spaces will echo a blank line. Under a DOS 3 version, an ECHO followed directly by a period will echo a blank line. Using these tricks makes it impossible to write a batch file that will work the same under both versions. And when you upgrade DOS, you'll have to modify your batch files.

Because echoing a blank line is such a problem, I wrote SKIPLINE.COM, which is on the enclosed disk. If SKIPLINE.COM is in your path or the current subdirectory, then the SKIPLINE command in a batch file will move the cursor down one line and produce a blank line. It works under all versions of DOS that I've had access to in order to test it. Just enter SKIPLINE on a line by itself.

Other ECHO quirks

One thing I noticed in testing the batch files for this book on different computers running different versions of DOS is that DOS is easily fooled regarding the status of ECHO. It wasn't uncommon for DOS to respond to an ECHO command with *ECHO is off* while echoing every command, or refusing to echo commands when ECHO was on. The problems depended not only on the version of DOS, but also on the brand of computer being used. These ECHO quirks are summarized in Table 2-1.

Stopping the batch file

Normally, DOS executes a batch file without stopping. When the batch file loads a program, DOS stops processing the batch file while the program runs. But as soon as you exit the program, or it automatically terminates, DOS immediately continues processing the batch file on the line following the line that loaded the program.

Normally, this is what you want. But sometimes you want to stop and give the

Table 2-1 ECHO command quirks.

Dots	Version 2.x of DOS let you replace the ECHO command with a dot. So the two batch file lines below are equivalent.
	. Your message here
	ECHO Your message here
Special Characters	< Do not include in an ECHO statement
	> Do not include in an ECHO statement
	| Do not include in an ECHO statement
	% Include a % % in your ECHO statement to ECHO a single %
	ˆH Start your lines with an ECHO ˆH to center messages, ECHO a blank line, or begin a message with ON or OFF
	ˆG ECHO ˆG sounds the PC bell
@	Beginning with DOS 3.3, you can suppress command echoing, even when ECHO is ON by preceding the batch command with a @.
SKIPLINE	With any version of DOS, you can use this command in conjunction with SKIPLINE.COM on the disk to produce a blank line on the screen.

user time to think and react. Take the following three sets of ECHO statements, for example:

You are about to format the hard disk.
Is this what you want?

You are about to erase these files.
Is this what you want?

This program takes six hours.
Do you want to start it now?

The command to stop a batch file is PAUSE. PAUSE stops the batch file until (almost) any key is pressed. Pressing a key, like Shift, that doesn't produce a character on the screen won't restart the batch file. Pressing any other key will restart the batch file.

The user can stop the batch file at any time by holding down the Ctrl key and pressing Break (^Break), or by holding down the Ctrl key and pressing C (^C). DOS will respond by asking if you want to terminate the batch file. Responding Yes will stop the batch file, while a No will allow it to continue. The PAUSE command is illustrated by the batch file in Fig. 2-14.

The PAUSE command isn't very powerful. The keystroke you press to resume processing isn't passed to the batch file, so you can't use this keystroke to make a menu selection. All PAUSE does is stop the batch file until you press (almost) any key.

Batch File Line	Explanation
`REM PAUSEIT.BAT`	Remark giving name of batch file. Since it comes prior to the ECHO OFF command, it shows on the screen when the batch file executes.
`ECHO OFF`	Turns command-echoing off.
`ECHO The next command is a` `    PAUSE. Do NOT press ^Break`	Display a message for the user.
`PAUSE`	Stop the batch file until a key is pressed.
`ECHO Press ^Break this time`	Display a message for the user.
`PAUSE`	Stop the batch file until a key is pressed.

2-14   PAUSEIT.BAT, a batch file that demonstrates the PAUSE command.

Replaceable parameters

DOS batch files would be useful if they did nothing more that what's been covered so far. However, one big limitation of the commands covered so far is that they're "written in stone." If you want to erase a file with a batch file using just these commands, you'll need to physically enter that filename in the batch file code. This is called *hardcoding* or *hardwiring*.

Sometimes you want to hardcode filenames. If you want to copy all your *.WK1 spreadsheet files to a floppy as backup, then hardcoding the COPY *.WK1 A: command is appropriate. Other times, however, you want the flexibility to have the batch file process different files. DOS replaceable parameters offer just such flexibility.

There are two things you need to know in order to use replaceable parameters. First, how to code the replaceable parameters in the batch file. And second, how to give the values for the replaceable parameters to the batch file. The second question is easy. Replaceable parameters are entered after the batch file name and before pressing Enter. For example:

    BATCH Para1 Para2 Para3 Para4

Each parameter is separated by either a space or a comma. How many replaceable parameters does the above line have? The obvious (and wrong) answer is four. DOS counts the name of the batch file as a parameter, so there are five replaceable parameters on this line. Just to make things confusing, DOS names them %0, %1, %2, %3, and %4. Not the %1 through %5 you'd expect. This is illustrated in Fig. 2-15.

DOS uses replaceable parameters as if they don't exist. Everywhere you see a replaceable parameter, DOS sees the value of that parameter. Consider the simple batch file shown in Fig. 2-16. Figure 2-17 shows the results of running this batch file. Notice that, when a batch file executes with ECHO ON, each command in

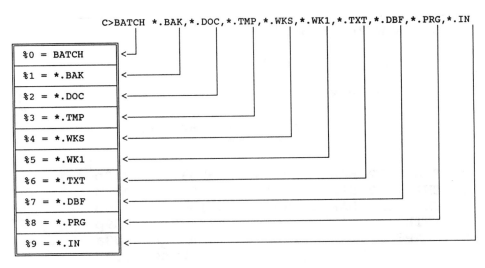

2-15 An illustration of batch file replaceable parameters.

Batch File Line	Explanation
REM SHOWPAR1.BAT	Remark giving the name of the batch file.
DIR %1	Perform a directory on the file mask entered on the command line after the batch file name.
ECHO %1	Echo the first replaceable parameter entered on the command line. If no replaceable parameter was entered, this command will display an "Echo is on" message.
REM %1	A remark to illustrate that DOS replaces every occurrence of the %1 with the replaceable parameter entered on the command line.

2-16 SHOWPAR1.BAT, a batch file that uses replaceable parameters.

the batch file is preceded by the DOS prompt. In other words, DOS treats the commands in the batch file exactly like it would if you entered them from the DOS prompt.

Everywhere there's a %1, DOS sees the value of the first replaceable parameter, which is *.BAK. It's called a replaceable parameter because you can replace it with a new value the next time you use it. DOS is so flexible that the replaceable parameters can be used as commands. This is illustrated in Fig. 2-18. Figure 2-19 shows this batch file running. Note that the %1 is replaced with the DIR command entered from the DOS prompt, after the batch file name.

There are ten replaceable parameters, %0 through %9. %0 always starts off as the name of the batch file, so there are actually nine that you can use. DOS doesn't see %7, for example, it sees the value you enter for it on the command

```
C> SHOWPAR1 *.BAK

C> REM SHOWPAR1.BAT

C> DIR *.BAK

 Volume in drive C is Richardson
 Directory of C\WORD\BOOK

CHAPTER2 BAK     10496    3-15-91    910p
CHAPTER3 BAK      3712    3-15-91    938p
CHAPTER4 BAK     38016    3-19-91    226p
INTRO    BAK      7168    3-15-91    859p
CHAPTER5 BAK     19968    3-19-91    903a
          5 File(s)   2158592 bytes free

C> ECHO *.BAK
*.BAK

C> REM *.BAK
```

2-17 The results of running SHOWPAR1.BAT, shown in Fig. 2-16.

Batch File Line	Explanation
REM SHOWREPL.BAT	Remark giving the name of the batch file.
%1 %2 %3 %4	A batch command line that depends on using the first replaceable parameter as a command.

2-18 SHOWREPL.BAT, which shows using replaceable parameters as commands.

```
C> SHOWREPL DIR *.BAK

C> DIR *.BAK

 Volume in drive C is Richardson
 Directory of C\WORD\BOOK

CHAPTER2 BAK     10496    3-15-91    910p
CHAPTER3 BAK      3712    3-15-91    938p
CHAPTER4 BAK     38016    3-19-91    226p
INTRO    BAK      7168    3-15-91    859p
CHAPTER5 BAK     19968    3-19-91    903a
          5 File(s)   2158592 bytes free
```

2-19 A screen display of the batch file in Fig. 2-18, SHOWREPL.BAT, running.

line. If you don't enter that many values, it sees nothing in place of the replaceable parameter.

There's a bug in some versions of DOS that prevents replaceable parameters from being used from within the AUTOEXEC.BAT file. On some systems it can cause the computer to lock up. That shouldn't be a problem for most users. Because COMMAND.COM automatically runs the AUTOEXEC.BAT file without any parameters, the only parameter that exists is %0 and it's always equal to AUTOEXEC. To avoid problems, don't use replaceable parameters in your AUTOEXEC.BAT file.

SHIFT

I have two computers, and I spend a great deal of my time writing with the Microsoft Word word processor. In addition to the document file, Word can create a *.CMP document dictionary file and a *.STY formatting file. At the end of a

Batch File Line	Explanation
`REM TOA1.BAT`	Remark giving the name of the batch file. Notice that command-echoing is not turned off so all the commands will echo to the screen.
`ERASE %1.BAK`	Erase the backup file for the first filename entered. Notice that the batch file does not check to see if the file exists so a "File not found" error message is possible.
`COPY %1.DOC A:`	Copies the document file for the first filename to the A drive. Notice that the batch file does not check to see if the file exists so a "File not found" error message is possible.
`COPY C:\WORD\%1.CMP A:`	Copies the dictionary file for the first filename to the A drive.
`COPY C:\WORD\NORMAL\%1.STY A:`	Copies the style sheet for the first filename to the A drive.

`ERASE %2.BAK`
`COPY %2.DOC A:`
`COPY C:\WORD\%2.CMP A:`
`COPY C:\WORD\NORMAL\%2.STY A:`
	Repeat the process for the %2 replaceable parameter.

Continues for %3-%8	

`ERASE %9.BAK`
`COPY %9.DOC A:`
`COPY C:\WORD\%9.CMP A:`
`COPY C:\WORD\NORMAL\%9.STY A:`
	Repeat the process for the %9 replaceable parameter.

2-20 TOA1.BAT, which uses multiple parameters to copy files.

working session, I like to copy my work to a floppy disk and use that floppy disk to transfer the modified files to the other computer. This ensures that I have a backup copy of all my files and also that both computers have the latest version of all my files.

My original batch file for doing all this is shown in Fig. 2-20. To use it, first I would generate a directory of all the *.BAK (or backup) files. I would then enter:

TOA *file1 file2 file3*

where the *file* specifications were actual document names without the extension. This batch file would then take care of the actual copying.

There are a couple of problems with this batch file, however. First, it tries to copy nine files even if you don't enter nine filenames. You'll see how to avoid that in the next chapter. Second, it can't copy more than nine names. Third, any changes to the way files are stored must be made nine times, once for each parameter. Finally, the batch file is long and hard to follow.

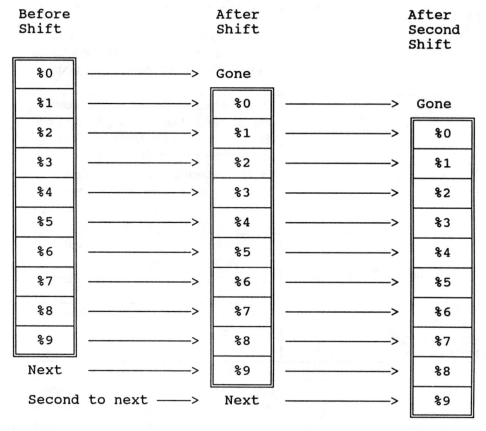

2-21   The action of the SHIFT command.

The SHIFT command can cure all but the first problem. SHIFT discards the %0 parameter, moves the remaining parameters down one value, and brings in a new %9 value if one exists. So, after a SHIFT command, the value in %1 moves into %0, the value in %2 moves into %1, and so on. This is illustrated in Fig. 2-21.

The batch file in Fig. 2-20 can now be replaced with the batch file in Fig. 2-22. The :TOP, :END, and IF lines will be covered in the next chapter. Basically,

Batch File Line	Explanation
REM TOA2.BAT	Remark giving the name of the batch file. Notice that command-echoing is not turned off so all the commands will echo to the screen.
:TOP	A label that can be used by the GOTO command.
ERASE %1.BAK	A command to erase the backup file for the %1 file. Notice it does not check to see if the file exists first.
COPY %1.DOC A:	A command to copy the document file for the %1 file.
COPY C:\WORD\%1.CMP A:	A command to copy the dictionary file for the %1 file.
COPY C:\WORD\NORMAL\%1.STY A:	A command to copy the style sheet file for the %1 file.
SHIFT	Discards the contents of %0, moves the contents of %1 into %0, and moves the contents of %2 into %1. It also adjusts the contents of the remaining replaceable parameters.
IF (%1)==() GOTO END	The next replaceable parameter is blank (one was not entered) so it jumps to a label called END.
GOTO TOP	Jumps back to the top of the file. Since it reached this point, if failed the test just above, so the %1 replaceable parameter is not blank.
:END	A label marking the end of the batch file. Note that the END is just a label name and any other name (including START) would work just as well.

2-22 TOA2.BAT, a much shorter batch file using the SHIFT command, which can replace TOA1.BAT in Fig 2-20.

the program loops through the indented commands as long as there are parameters. This allows the batch file to handle more than nine files and to issue copy commands only when there are files to copy. The number of files isn't unlimited, however, because the command line is limited to 127 characters. The batch file in Fig. 2-23 gives another illustration of the SHIFT command. Figure 2-24 shows the result of running this command.

Note that the command takes more than one line. This is acceptable, as long as the total length is 127 characters or less. DOS won't allow the command line to exceed 127 characters. Also note that there is one parameter (14) that isn't used by the batch file.

The SHIFT command has two major purposes. First, by moving the parameters down into a lower replaceable parameter, a single replaceable parameter can be used for all coding by forcing the program to loop through the code. This makes it much easier to update the code when necessary. Second, it allows the batch file to handle more than nine replaceable parameters. Just keep in mind that the total number of replaceable parameters is constrained by the 127-character command line limitation and the requirement to separate each replaceable parameter with a comma or a space.

Batch File Line	Explanation
`REM REPLACE1.BAT`	Remark giving the name of the batch file.
`ECHO OFF`	Turn command-echoing off.
`ECHO 1=%1 2=%2 3=%3 4=%4 5=%5` `     6=%6 7=%7 8=%8 9=%9`	Display all the replaceable parameters (except %0) that a batch file can display at once.
`SHIFT`	Move all the replaceable parameters down one level.
`ECHO 1=%1 2=%2 3=%3 4=%4 5=%5` `     6=%6 7=%7 8=%8 9=%9`	Display all the replaceable parameters (except %0) that a batch file can display at once.
`SHIFT`	Move all the replaceable parameters down one level.
The batch file repeats this several times.	
`ECHO 1=%1 2=%2 3=%3 4=%4 5=%5` `     6=%6 7=%7 8 9=%9`	Display all the replaceable parameters (except %0) that a batch file can display at once.
`SHIFT`	Move all the replaceable parameters down one level.

2-23 REPLACE1.BAT, a batch file that shows the SHIFT command in another setting.

```
C>REPLACE1 FIRST SECOND THIRD 4TH FIFTH SIXTH SEVENTH EIGHTH NINTH TENTH
11 12 13 14

C>REM REPLACE1.BAT

C>ECHO OFF
1=FIRST 2=SECOND 3=THIRD 4=4TH 5=FIFTH 6=SIXTH 7=SEVENTH 8=EIGHTH 9=NINTH
1=SECOND 2=THIRD 3=4TH 4=FIFTH 5=SIXTH 6=SEVENTH 7=EIGHTH 8=NINTH 9=TENTH
1=THIRD 2=4TH 3=FIFTH 4=SIXTH 5=SEVENTH 6=EIGHTH 7=NINTH 8=TENTH 9=11
1=4TH 2=FIFTH 3=SIXTH 4=SEVENTH 5=EIGHTH 6=NINTH 7=TENTH 8=11 9=12
1=FIFTH 2=SIXTH 3=SEVENTH 4=EIGHTH 5=NINTH 6=TENTH 7=11 8=12 9=13

C>
```

2-24 The screen results of running REPLACE1.BAT, shown in Fig. 2-23.

SET

COMMAND.COM sets aside a portion of memory for storing system-wide variables. This area is called the environment. In addition to storing the value of SET variables, this area stores the PROMPT, PATH, and COMSPEC. The size of the environment is limited. If you exceed the available space, you'll get an *out of environment space* error message. Your DOS manual will explain how to expand the environment if you have DOS 3.1 or later. Variables in this memory are lost when you turn off or reboot the computer.

Although these variables are transient, they can be very useful. As you'll see, these SET variables are useful for communicating between different batch files and storing information for use by more than one batch file.

You can place SET variables into the environment either with a batch file or interactively from the DOS prompt. Other than by placing them in memory and viewing them, you can't access SET variables interactively. The syntax to place a SET variable into the environment, either interactively or in a batch file is:

SET *variable* = *value*

Note that the only space is between SET and the variable name. Don't use spaces around the equal sign. DOS won't report an error but you'll have a space in the variable name and DOS won't be able to properly access it. You'll also have a space in the variable value. SET variables can be used to store any information, commonly filenames and program switches.

The variable you store can be accessed by any batch file and used in commands just like a replaceable parameter. The syntax is *%variable%*, so all you do to use the variable is surround the name with percent signs. Figure 2-25 shows a batch file that uses a SET variable. Figure 2-26 shows interactively setting a SET variable and then running the batch file to access it.

If you enter SET alone, the status of all the SET variables is shown. Figure 2-27 shows what SET does by showing the status of the environment before and after a SET command. Note that some of the information is too wide for the screen and wraps around to the next row.

Batch File Line	Explanation
REM SET1.BAT	Remark giving the name of the batch file.
DIR %TODAY%	Performs a directory on the file mask stored in the environment under then variable name TODAY. This must be set prior to running the batch file.
ECHO %TODAY%	Echoes the contents of the TODAY environmental variable.

2-25   SET1.BAT, a batch file that reads environmental variables.

```
C>SET TODAY=*.BAK

C>SET1

C>REM SET1.BAT

C>DIR *.BAK

 Volume in drive C is Richardson
 Directory of C\WORD\BOOK

CHAPTER2 BAK    10496    3-15-91    910p
CHAPTER3 BAK     3712    3-15-91    938p
CHAPTER4 BAK    38016    3-19-91    226p
INTRO    BAK     7168    3-15-91    859p
CHAPTER5 BAK    19968    3-19-91    903a
         5 File(s)  2158592 bytes free

ECHO *.BAK
*.BAK
C>
```

2-26   A screen display of the SET1.BAT batch file in Fig. 2-25 running.

```
C>SET

COMSPEC=C:\COMMAND.COM
PATH=C:\;C:\BAT;C:\SYSLIB;C:\WORD;C:\NORTON;C:\WINDOWS;C
:\DBASE;C :\RIGHTWRI;C:\BALER
LIB=C:\BALER
BALER=C:\BALER
TEMP=C:\WINDOWS\TEMP
TODAY=*.BAK

C>
```

2-27   The result of using the SET command with no arguments.

You can have batch files communicate with each other by placing values into the environment. Figures 2-28 and 2-29 show two accounting batch files. AC-COUNT1.BAT performs monthly closing. The program CLOSE.EXE sets the ErrorLevel to show whether or not it ran without errors. ACCOUNT1.BAT needs to communicate that information to ACCOUNT2.BAT. It could depend on the ErrorLevel, but that could be reset if you ran another program in between the two batch files. To avoid that problem, ACCOUNT1.BAT places a value into the environment. ACCOUNT2.BAT then checks for that value and won't run without a correct setting. (*Note*: The IF command is explained in the next chapter. The purpose of these batch files is to show how batch files can communicate with each other.)

A logical question is "Why didn't CLOSE.EXE set the information into the environment itself?" Each program is passed a copy of the environment when it starts. When the program terminates, that copy of the environment is erased. So CLOSE.EXE couldn't set the environment directly because those changes would have been lost when CLOSE.EXE terminated. ErrorLevel isn't stored in the environment, so it isn't lost when CLOSE.EXE terminates. The ErrorLevel is explained in more detail later.

SET variables can also be used as a shortcut. Imagine that you're writing a large database program using Quicksilver. You usually work on one program for most of the day, trying to get out all the bugs. You use batch files to start Wordstar in order to edit your program and to run Quicksilver in order to compile the program. If you set the name of the program in the environment as COMPILE, then the batch files in Figs. 2-30 and 2-31 will automate editing and compiling. (Note

Batch File Line	Explanation
ECHO OFF	Turn command-echoing off.
REM ACCOUNT1	A remark line giving the name of the batch file.
CLOSE	A command to run a program called CLOSE.
IF ERRORLEVEL 1 SET ACCOUNT=NO	If CLOSE terminates and sets ERRORLEVEL to 1, then set the environmental variable named ACCOUNT to NO. This is necessary in case another program resets the ERRORLEVEL.
IF ERRORLEVEL 1 GOTO END	If CLOSE terminates and sets ERRORLEVEL to 1, then jump to a label named END.
IF ERRORLEVEL 0 SET ACCOUNT=YES	If CLOSE terminates and sets ERRORLEVEL to 0, then set the environmental variable named ACCOUNT to YES. The if statement is really not needed since the two lines above would cause any value other than zero to skip this line.
:END	A label used by the GOTO command.

2-28 ACCOUNT1.BAT, a batch file that reports an environmental variable that another batch file (ACCOUNT2.BAT) needs.

Batch File Line	Explanation
ECHO OFF	Turn command-echoing off.
REM ACCOUNT2.BAT	Remark giving the name of the batch file.
IF (%ACCOUNT%)==() GOTO ERROR	Skips to a label called ERROR if the environmental variable named ACCOUNT has not been set.
IF %ACCOUNT%==NO GOTO NO	Skips to a label called NO if the ACCOUNT environmental variable has a value of NO.
CLOSE2	If the batch file reaches this line, then the environmental variable ACCOUNT has a value of YES and the batch file runs a program called CLOSE2. Note that YES/NO are the only possible values for ACCOUNT since its value is set by a batch file and not by a user.
GOTO END	After running CLOSE2, the batch file skips to a label called END which is at the end of the batch file.
:ERROR	A label for the GOTO command marking the beginning of the error-handling section of the batch file.
ECHO RUN ACCOUNT1 FIRST	Display a message to the user telling him/her how to correct the problem.
PAUSE	Stop the batch file until the user presses a key to provide time to read the message.
GOTO END	After handling the error, exit the batch file by skipping to a label at the end of the batch file.
:NO	A label marking the beginning of the section to handle the error that occurs if CLOSE does not run successfully.
ECHO WARNING: CLOSE DIR NOT RUN SUCCESSFULLY ECHO FIX THESE ERRORS BEFORE RUNNING ACCOUNT2	Display messages for the user.
PAUSE	Pause the batch file so the user can read the messages.
GOTO END	Skip to a label called END.
:END	A label marking the end of the batch file.

2-29 ACCOUNT2.BAT, which reads the environmental variable reported by the ACCOUNT1.BAT file.

Batch File Line	Explanation
`ECHO OFF`	Turn command-echoing off.
`REM EDIT.BAT`	A remark line giving the name of the batch file.
`WORDSTAR %COMPILE%`	Start Wordstar editing the file stored under the environmental variable named COMPILE.

2-30 EDIT.BAT, a batch file that uses an environmental variable to automate program editing.

Batch File Line	Explanation
`ECHO OFF`	Turn command-echoing off.
`REM COMPILE.BAT`	A remark line giving the name of the batch file.
`DB3C -A %COMPILE%`	Run the Quicksilver compiler and process the file stored under the environmental variable COMPILE.
`DB3L %COMPILE%`	Run the Quicksilver linker on the same file.

2-31 COMPILE.BAT, a batch file that uses an environmental variable to automate the compiling of programs.

that Wordstar must be reconfigured to default to nondocument mode for this to work properly. The Wordstar manual explains how to do this.)

ERRORLEVEL

The DOS environment is a very inhospitable place for programs to store information in order to communicate with each other. Each program is provided with a copy of the environment when it's first loaded. When it reads the environment or writes to it, the program is dealing with its copy of the environment, not the original. When the program terminates, its copy of the environment along with all the changes the program made to it are destroyed.

The DOS ERRORLEVEL command was provided in DOS 2.0 to overcome this problem. The ErrorLevel value isn't stored in the environment, so changes made to it aren't lost when a program terminates. Unlike the environment, there's only one copy of ErrorLevel and every program changes the same one. Error-Level doesn't change unless a program changes it or you reboot, so you can perform multiple tests on it.

ErrorLevel has room for only one byte, so only an ASCII value of 0 to 255 can be stored in it. Using the following statements:

```
IF ERRORLEVEL #
IF NOT ERRORLEVEL #
```

a batch file can test the contents of the ErrorLevel and make decisions based on that content. Unfortunately, the test isn't straightforward. The test IF ERRORLEVEL 5 doesn't test for ERRORLEVEL=5. Rather, it tests for ERRORLEVEL>=5. So

Batch File Line	Explanation
ECHO OFF	Turn command-echoing off.
REM CHECKERR.BAT	A remark giving the name of the batch file.
IF ERRORLEVEL 255 ECHO 255	If the ERRORLEVEL is 255, echo that fact to the screen. Since the ERRORLEVEL test is a greater than or equal test, you must start testing at the highest value of interest and work your way to the lowest.
IF ERRORLEVEL 255 GOTO END	If the ERRORLEVEL is 255, skip to the end of the batch file. Once a match is found, you must exit the batch file because all the lower numbers will also match due to the greater than or equal testing of the ERRORLEVEL test.
IF ERRORLEVEL 254 ECHO 254 IF ERRORLEVEL 254 GOTO END	Test for an ERRORLEVEL of 254.
IF ERRORLEVEL 253 ECHO 253 IF ERRORLEVEL 253 GOTO END	Test for an ERRORLEVEL of 253.
Continues through all the possible ASCII values with two lines per number	
IF ERRORLEVEL 1 ECHO 1 IF ERRORLEVEL 1 GOTO END	Test for an ERRORLEVEL of 1.
IF ERRORLEVEL 0 ECHO 0 IF ERRORLEVEL 0 GOTO END	Test for an ERRORLEVEL of 0. I used the same format for consistency. If the batch file reaches this point, then ERRORLEVEL must equal zero.
:END	Label marking the end of the batch file.

2-32 CHECKERR.BAT, which tests every possible value of the ErrorLevel variable.

any number from 5 to 255 will result in a true on this test. As a result, you must always test from the highest possible ErrorLevel value to the lowest. In addition, you must branch away from the testing after the first match. This is illustrated in Fig. 2-32.

Only a few DOS commands support the ERRORLEVEL command. These are documented along with a list of their codes in your DOS manual. Only a few commercial programs support the ERRORLEVEL command, as well. If a commercial program supports the ERRORLEVEL command, it will be listed in the program documentation. See chapter 3 for more on this feature.

Summary

The major things you should remember to do when you finish reading this chapter are the following:

- Use the REM command to document your batch files.
- Use the ECHO OFF command as the first line to "clean up" batch file execution.
- Use the ECHO *message* command to communicate with the user.
- Use the PAUSE command to suspend a batch file.
- Use replaceable parameters (%0 – %9) to make batch files more flexible.
- Use the SHIFT command if you need to input more than nine variables.
- Use SET variables for communication between batch files.
- Use SET variables to store information to be used more than once.
- Use the DOS ERRORLEVEL command to pass information back to a batch file.

Most of the batch files in this chapter are on the enclosed disk.

3
CHAPTER

Looping and program flow

Looping is nothing more than making a program do the same thing more than once. *Pseudocode* is computer code written in English for later conversion into a programming language. Consider the pseudocode example of a loop, below:

```
Mark the top of a loop
     Do something
     If some test is met, jump out of this loop
Go to top of loop
```

This program goes around in a continual loop until a certain condition forces it to jump out of the loop.

Naming lines of a program

In a batch file, there's no specific marking for the boundary of a loop. Instead, you can give any line a name so the batch file can then jump to that line. To name a line, start with a colon and then type in a name. The name should have the following characteristics:

- It must follow the colon with no spaces between the colon and name.
- There can be nothing after the name.
- The name should have eight characters or less.
- There can be no spaces in the name.
- While not required, it's a good idea to make the name mean something, like :TOP.

GOTO

In a batch file, the command to tell the program to continue processing at a different location is the GOTO command. The syntax is GOTO followed by the name of the line, without the colon. The named line can be above or below the GOTO statement. Control will jump to the named line and won't return to the GOTO line. Figure 3-1 gives a simple example.

The batch file LOOP1.BAT in Fig. 3-1 will continually perform a directory until you use Ctrl−Break to stop it. It won't stop on its own because there's no logic built into it to force it to stop. Note the style used in Fig. 3-1. Everything between the top and bottom of the loop is indented. This is a standard programming practice. It helps you visualize the loop as you look at the code. (Remember the importance of documenting your code in the discussion of the REM command.) DOS doesn't require that the commands be indented. In fact, the indentation slows down the batch file a little. It does, however, make the batch file easier for someone to understand when they look at it.

Now look at a slightly more useful example. The batch file in Fig. 3-2 will copy a list of files to the A drive. When the LOOP2 batch file runs out of files to

Batch File Line	Explanation
`REM LOOP1.BAT`	Remark giving the name of the batch file.
`:TOP`	A name marking a line that the GOTO command can jump to.
`    DIR`	Perform a directory. This is simply an example command so the batch file can perform some task. The command is indented since it is inside a loop. This is a visual clue to help the programmer understand the command flow inside the batch file.
`GOTO TOP`	Command to jump to the line with the name TOP and continue processing. Since there is no IF test to jump out of this loop, this batch file will continue until you press Ctrl-Break to abort it.

3-1   LOOP1.BAT, a simple batch file that uses a batch loop.

Batch File Line	Explanation
`REM LOOP2.BAT`	Remark giving the name of the batch file.
`ECHO OFF`	Turn command-echoing off.
`:TOP`	Label marking a line the GOTO command can jump to.
`    COPY %1 A:`	Copy the file defined by the first replaceable parameter to the A drive.
`    SHIFT`	Replace %0 with %1, %1 with %2, and so on.
`GOTO TOP`	Jump to the line labeled TOP and continue processing.

3-2   LOOP2.BAT, which reads multiple replaceable parameters with a SHIFT command inside a loop.

Batch File Line	Explanation
`REM LOOP3.BAT`	Remark giving the name of the batch file.
`ECHO OFF`	Turn command-echoing off.
`:TOP`	Label marking a line with a name.
`    DIR %1`	Perform a directory using the filename entered as a replaceable parameter.
`    IF %1==STOP GOTO END`	Stop processing if a STOP was entered as a replaceable parameter. The test is case-sensitive so entering stop or Stop will not work.
`    SHIFT`	Copy the file defined by the first replaceable parameter to the A drive.
`GOTO TOP`	Jump to the TOP label and continue processing.
`:END`	Label marking a line with a name.

3-3 LOOP3.BAT, which adds a termination condition with the IF command.

copy, it won't stop. It will try to continue until you use Ctrl–Break to stop it. Clearly, this looping procedure is powerful, but it needs more control. That control is the IF statement. But first, a few notes on loops:

- If the label referenced by the GOTO command doesn't exist, the batch file will stop and give a *Label not found* error message.
- Different versions of DOS handle labels in a slightly difference way. In DOS version 3 and under, only the first eight characters of a label are significant. So the label LABEL12345 is treated as equal to LABEL123, LABEL12399, and LABEL123xxxx. In DOS below version 2, a GOTO LABEL12345 command will only go to the label LABEL123. If you keep your label names to eight characters or less, your batch file will run under any version of DOS.
- The GOTO command has trouble with certain characters in the label name. The usual DOS piping commands (<, >, and ¦) don't work. Other unexpected characters, like square brackets, also don't work. Finally, other characters work only when they aren't the first character of the label. A complete list isn't possible, however, because the symbols depend on the version of DOS being used. You can avoid this problem by using only letters and numbers in your labels.

IF

The IF statement allows a batch file to take one of two paths. The basic syntax of the IF statement is:

IF {*statement is true*} {*do this action*}

If the statement being tested is false, then the batch file will skip to the next line and continue processing. If the statement is true, then the batch file will process the rest of this line. This line can contain a GOTO statement to send processing to another location.

The IF command can be used to test for three types of conditions. It can test the system ErrorLevel; it can compare two strings, including replaceable parameters, to see if they're equal; and it can test to see if a file exists.

The simplest test is to test the replaceable parameter. Unfortunately, DOS isn't very smart in making these comparisons. The batch file in Fig. 3-4 illustrates this point. The intent of this loop is that it should stop when it runs out of replaceable parameters. As Fig. 3-5 shows, that doesn't happen. DOS replaces %1 with the first parameter and then SHIFT brings new parameters into the %1 position until the parameters are exhausted. When this happens, DOS tries to compare nothing to nothing. All this does is confuse DOS, causing it to fail the IF test—which causes the looping to continue.

The solution to this minor dilemma is simple—surround the comparison with a set of symbols so DOS will compare something to something. I always use the ( ) symbols. This is shown in Fig. 3-6. The advantage to surrounding both items to compare with a set of parentheses is that you allow a single test to compare the two strings, while avoiding any problems when one of the strings in the comparison is empty. It even allows testing for an empty string because ( )==( ) is a valid test.

Several IF statements can be combined to handle a complex decision or to overcome the case problem associated with string comparisons. The batch file in Fig. 3-7 makes several tests on the %1 replaceable parameter. In this case, the tests are

Batch File Line	Explanation
REM LOOP4.BAT	Remark line giving the name of the batch file.
ECHO OFF	Turn command-echoing off.
:TOP	Label marking a line with a name.
IF %1== GOTO END	A failed attempt to test for no more replaceable parameters. When the %1 parameter is blank, this test becomes BLANK==BLANK, which confuses DOS enough that it thinks the result is false.
SHIFT	Copy the file defined by the first replaceable parameter to the A drive.
ECHO STILL RUNNING	Display message for the user.
GOTO TOP	Jump to the line labeled TOP and continue processing.
:END	Label marking a line with a name.

3-4 LOOP4.BAT, which becomes confused because DOS expects to see characters on both sides of the == comparison operator.

```
C>LOOP4 1 2 3

C>REM LOOP4.BAT

C>ECHO OFF
STILL RUNNING
STILL RUNNING
STILL RUNNING
Syntax error
STILL RUNNING
Syntax error
STILL RUNNING
Syntax error
STILL RUNNING
Syntax error
STILL RUNNING
^C

Terminate batch job (Y/N)? Y
C>
```

3-5 Running the batch file LOOP4.BAT in Fig. 3-4 produces faulty comparison errors.

Batch File Line	Explanation
REM LOOP5.BAT	Remark line giving the name of the batch file.
ECHO OFF	Turn command-echoing off.
:TOP	Label marking a line with a name.
IF (%1)==() GOTO END	The proper way to test for a blank replaceable parameter. When %1 contains information, this test becomes (INFO)==() and properly evaluates to false. When %1 is blank, this test becomes ()==() and properly evaluates to true.
SHIFT	Copy the file defined by the first replaceable parameter to the A drive.
ECHO STILL RUNNING	Display message for the user.
GOTO TOP	Jump to the line labeled TOP and continue processing.
:END	Label marking a line with a name.

3-6 LOOP5.BAT, which surrounds the comparison operator with parentheses, which allows the batch file to make a null parameter comparison.

meaningless. However, these tests could be used to decide which program to run or which parameters to pass to the program being run. Figure 3-8 shows a simple batch file that will select DOS BACKUP parameters based on the input parameters. If no parameters are entered, it will display the acceptable values.

Batch File Line	Explanation
ECHO OFF	Turn command-echoing off.
REM BIGIF.BAT	Remark giving the name of the batch file.
IF (%1)==() GOTO NONE	Test for a blank %1 and exit the batch file if it is blank. Since the batch file does not use the shift command, this will catch all blank replaceable parameters so the remaining IF tests will not need to be protected against a blank %1.
IF %1==A GOTO ALPHA IF %1==a GOTO ALPHA	Test for %1 containing an A. Since string comparisons are case-sensitive, you must test for upper- and lowercase. This can become difficult when testing for longer words.
IF %1==1 ECHO 1 Entered IF %1==1 GOTO END	Test for %1 containing a 1. If it does, display a message and exit the batch file. Using numbers for replaceable parameters avoids the problem of capitalization.
IF %1==2 ECHO 2 Entered IF %1==2 GOTO END	Test for %1 containing a 2. If it does, display a message and exit the batch file.
GOTO INVALID	If the batch file reaches this point, then the user did not enter one of the three acceptable replaceable parameters (A, 1, or 2) so the batch file jumps to an error-handling section.
:NONE ECHO MUST START WITH VARIABLE AFTER NAME GOTO END	The user failed to enter a replaceable parameter so the batch file displays an error message and exits.
:ALPHA ECHO MUST START WITH A NUMBER GOTO END	The user entered an A, which the batch file does not want, so it displays an error message and exits. Generally, you do not test for each possible invalid entry, rather you first test for the valid entries and then display a generic error message. This approach is appropriate when A was a valid response, but due to changes is no longer valid.

:INVALID
ECHO THE OPTION YOU
    SELECTED IS INVALID.
    CHECK YOUR MANUAL
GOTO END
	A generic error message telling the user he/she entered an invalid response. If only a few responses are valid, the batch file should inform the user what the responses are.

:END	Label marking a line with a name.

3-7 BIGIF.BAT, which uses several tests on a single replaceable parameter.

Batch File Line	Explanation
`ECHO OFF`	Turn command-echoing off.
`REM BACKUP1.BAT`	Remark line giving the name of the batch file.

`IF (%1)==(1)  CD\`
`IF (%1)==(1)  BACKUP C: A: /S`
`IF (%1)==(1)  GOTO END`
	If a one is entered, change to the root directory, perform a full backup, and exit the batch file.

`IF (%1)==(2)  CD\`
`IF (%1)==(2)  BACKUP C: A: /M`
`IF (%1)==(2)  GOTO END`
	If a two is entered, change to the root directory, perform an incremental backup, and exit the batch file.

`IF (%1)==(3)  CD\`
`IF (%1)==(3)  BACKUP C: A: /M /A`
`IF (%1)==(3)  GOTO END`
	If a three is entered, change to the root directory, perform an incremental backup--appending it to any existing backup, and exit the batch file.

`REM If %1 valid, will have`
`    jumped to end by now`
`REM Display error message`
`ECHO YOU ENTERED AN INVALID`
`    PARAMETER`
`ECHO Enter 1 For A Full Backup`
`ECHO Enter 2 For Incremental`
`    Backup`
`ECHO Enter A 3 For An Appended`
`    Incremental Backup`
`GOTO END`
	Deal with a user who either enters no replaceable parameter or enters an invalid one.

`:END`	Label marking a line with a name.

3-8 BACKUP1.BAT, which deals with several different parameters.

EXIST

The IF command is a very powerful command, which can be combined with other commands, like EXIST, for even more power. The EXIST command is used to test to see if a file exists. The syntax is:

IF EXIST *filename action*

Figure 3-9 shows a sample batch file. Note that this command won't have any problem comparing %3 when %3 doesn't exist because the testing problem described applies only to comparing two strings. This example is fairly useless, however. The example in Fig. 3-10 is a more useful version.

Note that the ECHO and DEL lines can't be reversed because the *.OBJ and

Batch File Line	Explanation
ECHO OFF	Turn command-echoing off.
REM IF1.BAT	Remark giving the name of the batch file.
IF EXIST %1 ECHO %1 Exists!!!!!	Test to see if the file named in %1 exists and inform the user if it does.
IF EXIST %2 ECHO %2 Exists!!!!!	Test to see if the file named in %2 exists and inform the user if it does.
IF EXIST %3 ECHO %3 Exists!!!!!	Test to see if the file named in %3 exists and inform the user if it does.

3-9   IF1.BAT, which uses the IF EXIST command.

Batch File Line	Explanation
ECHO OFF	Turn command-echoing off.
REM IF2.BAT	Remark giving the name of the batch file.
IF EXIST *.OBJ ECHO *.OBJ files being erased	Tell the user the batch file is going to erase all the *.OBJ files in the current subdirectory--but only if there are some to erase.
IF EXIST *.OBJ DEL *.OBJ	If the *.OBJ files exist, erase them. Using the IF test avoids the "File not found" error message if there are no *.OBJ files.
IF EXIST *.BAK ECHO *.BAK files being erased	Tell the user the batch file is going to erase the *.BAK files. If there is some change the user might want to abort the erasure, the batch file should have a PAUSE command to give the user a change to press Control-Break.
IF EXIST *.BAK DEL *.BAK	Erase any *.BAK files.
ECHO Finished erasing	Tell the user the batch file is finished.

3-10   IF2.BAT, a more useful batch file using IF EXIST.

*.BAK files wouldn't exist once they were deleted! This type of batch file line is good for cleaning up working and temporary files when you exit a program that automatically creates them.

ErrorLevel

ErrorLevel allows a program to terminate and pass a one-byte code through DOS and back to the calling program. This code can then be accessed from a batch file using the ErrorLevel batch command.

Programs can use ErrorLevel to report back to a batch file if they were successful in their execution. The batch file can then use that information to decide what to do next. Prior to DOS 3.0, BACKUP and RESTORE were the only DOS programs to return an ErrorLevel code. Some after-market products support ErrorLevel. The situation is improving, however, as more DOS commands and programs begin to support ErrorLevel values. The one-byte code assigned to ErrorLevel is retained until you run another program. Even if that program doesn't support ErrorLevel, DOS resets ErrorLevel to zero anytime you run a program. This allows multiple tests on ErrorLevel, as required.

This is illustrated when you use XCOPY to copy files that don't exist. This generates an ErrorLevel code of 1. Figure 3-11 shows a batch file using ErrorLevel and Fig. 3-12 shows it running.

The ErrorLevel test isn't a straightforward test, and you must be very sure of your tests. The ErrorLevel test ERRORLEVEL 7 isn't a test for ErrorLevel equals

Batch File Line	Explanation
`ECHO OFF`	Turn command-echoing off.
`REM IF3.BAT`	Remark giving the name of the batch file.
`XCOPY C:XXXXXXXX.XXX D:`	XCOPY a file named XXXXXXXX.XXX to the D drive. Normally, you would not hardwire the name of the file in the batch file. This was an example to force XCOPY to generate an error.
`IF ERRORLEVEL 1 ECHO FILE NOT FOUND TO COPY, TRY AGAIN`	If ERRORLEVEL is one or greater, display an error message.
`IF ERRORLEVEL 1 GOTO END`	If ERRORLEVEL is one or greater, jump to a line labeled END.
`IF ERRORLEVEL 0 ECHO copy successful`	If the ERRORLEVEL is zero or greater, display a message that the file was copied. Since the line above weeded out all ERRORLEVEL values of one or greater, only a value of zero could reach this line so the IF test is redundant.
`:END`	Label giving the line a name.

3-11 IF3.BAT, which combines the IF and ERRORLEVEL commands.

```
C>IF3

C>ECHO OFF
XXXXXXXX.XXX File not found
        0 File(s) copied
FILE NOT FOUND TO COPY, TRY AGAIN

C>
```

3-12 The result of running IF3.BAT, shown in Fig. 3-11.

seven, but rather for ErrorLevel greater than or equal to seven. Any number greater than or equal to seven will return a true value for this test. So you must test for the highest possible ErrorLevel first, then the next highest, and so on. Not only must you test for the highest values first, you must branch out of the testing as soon as the test is true. The ErrorLevel test is a greater than or equal test, so if it passes at seven, it will pass at six, at five, at four, and so on.

Figure 3-13 shows CHECKERR.BAT, a very long batch file to test for every possible ErrorLevel code and display the single true value. Because most programs that generate ErrorLevel codes generate only a few codes, your batch files won't have to be this long. However, this program does illustrate the technique for identifying the unique ErrorLevel code.

Batch File Line	Explanation
`ECHO OFF`	Turn command-echoing off.
`REM CHECKERR.BAT`	A remark giving the name of the batch file.
`IF ERRORLEVEL 255` `    ECHO 255`	If the ERRORLEVEL is 255, echo that fact to the screen. Since the ERRORLEVEL test is a greater than or equal test, you must start testing at the highest value of interest and work your way to the lowest.
`IF ERRORLEVEL 255` `    GOTO END`	If the ERRORLEVEL is 255, skip to the end of the batch file. Once a match is found, you must exit the batch file because all the lower numbers will also match due to the greater than or equal testing of the ERRORLEVEL test.

`IF ERRORLEVEL 254`
`    ECHO 254`
`IF ERRORLEVEL 254`
`    GOTO END`
	Test for an ERRORLEVEL of 254.

`IF ERRORLEVEL 253`
`    ECHO 253`
`IF ERRORLEVEL 253`
`    GOTO END`
	Test for an ERRORLEVEL of 253.

Continues through all the possible ASCII values with two lines per number	

`IF ERRORLEVEL    1`
`    ECHO 1`
`IF ERRORLEVEL    1`
`    GOTO END`
	Test for an ERRORLEVEL of 1.

`IF ERRORLEVEL    0`
`    ECHO 0`
`IF ERRORLEVEL    0`
`    GOTO END`
	Test for an ERRORLEVEL of 0. I used the same format for consistency. If the batch file reaches this point, then ERRORLEVEL must equal zero.

`:END`	Label marking the end of the batch file.

3-13 CHECKERR.BAT, which tests for all possible values of ErrorLevel.

Batch File Line	Explanation
REM CLIPPER.BAT	Remark giving the name of the batch file.
CLIPPER %1	Use Clipper to compile the file named in the %1 replaceable parameter. Notice there is no testing to make sure a replaceable parameter was entered or that the file exists.
IF NOT ERRORLEVEL 1 PLINK86 %1 LIB	If the ERRORLEVEL is less than one (e.g., zero) then Clipper finds a %1 file and compiles it successfully, so use Plink to link the file.

3-14 CLIPPER.BAT, which calls a linker called Plink only if the compiler, CLIPPER, was successful.

The ErrorLevel command is especially useful with products that support it, like compilers. For example, the batch file in Fig. 3-14 will try to compile a program using Clipper. If the program compiles successfully, the batch file will try to link the program. If the program doesn't compile, the batch file will skip the unnecessary linking. Don't worry about all the extra commands after PLINK86, which is the linking program. They're input parameters for the linker.

NOT

The NOT command is used to reverse a DOS decision. If an IF EXIST statement is true, then the corresponding IF NOT EXIST statement is false. If an IF EXIST statement is false, then the IF NOT EXIST statement is true. Figure 3-15 shows an example of a batch file using the NOT command.

Batch File Line	Explanation
REM SHOWNOT.BAT	Remark giving the name of the batch file.
IF EXIST *.BAK ECHO There are backup files	Check for *.BAK files and tell the user if they exist.
IF NOT EXIST *.BAK ECHO There are no backup files	Check for *.BAT files not existing and tell the user if there are not any. Between this and the prior line, the user will know if any *.BAK files exist.
DEL *.BAK	Delete any *.BAK files. If none exist, DOS will display a "File not found" error message. The batch file could prevent this by using an IF test.
IF EXIST *.BAK ECHO There are backup files IF NOT EXIST *.BAK ECHO There are no backup files	Just for illustration, again check for any *.BAK files and tell the user the results.

3-15 SHOWNOT.BAT, which uses the NOT modifier in an IF test.

FOR

The FOR command causes DOS to loop through a series of files and perform a single action on those files. There are two forms of the command. The first takes a list of files:

    FOR %%h IN (CHAPTER1.BAK CHAPTER2.BAK) DO ERASE %%h

The second form uses DOS wildcards to calculate all applicable files:

    FOR %%j IN (*.BAK) DO DEL %%j

In general, the command is:

    FOR %%variable IN (file set) DO command

The FOR command must be on one line. FOR commands can't be nested, so only one FOR command can be on each line. The %%*variable* must be a single character, for example, %%A through %%Z. In addition, you must use the same case each time you use the single-character variable in the FOR command. Some versions of DOS won't let you use %0 through %9, but it isn't a good programming habit because DOS uses these for other purposes. You can also use the FOR command from the DOS prompt without a batch file. The only change is the %%*variable* must be *%variable*.

The command used in the FOR statement doesn't have to be a direct command as has been used in the above illustrations. The command can also be a logical test. The following, for example:

    FOR %j IN (*.*) DO IF EXIST A:%j DEL %j

will delete files on the C drive only if they exist on the A drive. A few versions of DOS allow the variable name to be more than one character. If yours does, multi-character names will work just like single character names. If your DOS doesn't support multi-character names, you'll see an error message. For general compatibility, you should always use single-character names. The batch file in Fig. 3-16 illustrates using FOR to delete all .BAK files. Figure 3-17 shows a batch file using the FOR command to copy files.

DOS will replace %%1 with %1 when %%1 is displayed on the screen. This is how you enter the command from the DOS prompt without a batch file. When DOS sees *%variable*, it always replaces the variable with its value. The %%*variable* tells DOS to use %1 and not to replace it with a specific value. Table 3-1 gives a summary of the important aspects of the very powerful FOR command.

Why doesn't my batch file work?

By now you should have a good understanding of the basics of writing and using batch files. You should be able to create a batch file that uses standard DOS com-

Batch File Line	Explanation
REM FOR-BAK.BAT	Remark giving the name of the batch file.
DIR *.BAK	Perform a directory of the *.BAK files. If the user might potentially want to abort the erasure, the batch file would need a warning and a PAUSE command to give the user a chance to press Control-Break.
FOR %%h IN (*.BAK) DO DEL %%h	Delete the files one at a time using a FOR loop. Of course, this is just for illustration--normally you would use DEL *.BAK to delete all the files.
DIR *.BAK	Perform a directory of all .BAK files.

3-16 FOR-BAK.BAT, which uses the FOR command to delete all .BAK files.

Batch File Line	Explanation
REM FOR2.BAT	Remark giving the name of the batch file.
FOR %%L IN (*.DOC) DO COPY %%L D:	Copy all the *.DOC files to the D drive one at a time. Of course, COPY *.DOC D: would do the same thing, this is just an illustration of the FOR command.

3-17 FOR2.BAT, which uses a FOR loop to copy files.

mands as well as batch-specific commands. You should also know how to use replaceable parameters and IF tests to control the flow of the batch file. As you begin to use this knowledge in your computing, however, you're going to occasionally have a batch file that doesn't work properly—so you need to know what to do.

If your batch file is in a loop or doesn't appear to be doing anything, hit ^C or ^Break. This should stop the batch file and give you a *Terminate batch job (Y/N)?* prompt. Answer Y for yes and press Enter. This is the only way to stop a batch file. If it doesn't work, you'll have to reboot. Once you get it stopped, you need to locate the problem. You can list the file on screen with the command:

TYPE *file*.BAT

However, you'll need a word processor to make changes so you might as well load it into a word processor to begin with.

The first thing to check is the spelling. It's very easy to make a spelling error, especially when you're copying the file from the console. If all the commands are spelled right, then use the reference section of this book to check your syntax. Finally, make sure your program logic is correct. It's easy to make a logical mistake, especially when you have a lot of IF statements.

Table 3-1   Summary of the FOR command.

The variable must be a single letter for most versions of DOS.
There is no limit on the number of times the variable can be referenced. It can even not be referenced. For example: C: > FOR %%j IN (*.BAK) DO DIR
The list of files must be in parentheses. Each file must be separated by a space or a comma.
The list of files can contain any number of files, except that the command is limited to the DOS command line limit of 127 characters. Normally, you can mix full filenames and filenames with wildcards, however, some versions of DOS have problems when both types are mixed.
Once the FOR command has executed, the %%variable has no further meaning.
If the command at the end of a FOR command is a GOTO command FOR %j in (*.*) DO GOTO END, then the batch file jumps to the GOTO label and does not complete the FOR command.
If the command at the end of a FOR command executes another batch file, the control never returns to the batch file with the FOR command. This can be avoided by using the CALL command that was added in DOS 3.3 or by using the batch file subroutine trick presented in the book.

Summary

The important things to remember about looping and program flow are the following:

- The lines inside a loop should be indented to make it easy to read.
- You can name a line of code with a colon followed by a name.
- The GOTO command can be used to jump to any line to continue processing.
- The IF command can be used to cause the batch file to follow one of two processing paths, depending on whether or not a statement is true.
- You can use multiple IF commands to create complex branching.
- The EXIST command can test for the presence of a file or group of files.

- You can control branching with an ErrorLevel command, depending on whether or not certain external programs were successful.
- The NOT command can reverse any batch file decision.
- The FOR command can construct a loop all on one line.

Most of the batch files in this chapter are on the included floppy disk.

4
CHAPTER

Configuring your computer

This chapter covers two user-created files that, to a great extent, determine the configuration of your computer. They are the basis of how DOS operates on your computer. The first one is the CONFIG.SYS file. The second is the AUTOEXEC .BAT file. This chapter also explains memory-resident software. But to begin with, the following are the three major parts of a computer's disk operating system.

The Basic Input Output System (BIOS) This is made up of two parts: a hardware chip that comes with the computer, and a software portion that's read from the disk. Most computer manufacturers try to make their BIOS chips as close to the IBM BIOS as possible without making an exact copy. The software portion can be licensed from Microsoft Corporation.

The DOS kernel This is the software portion of DOS that provides the interface between your application programs and the hardware.

COMMAND.COM This is the command interpreter. It reads the DOS commands you enter into the computer and takes appropriate action.

Starting DOS

When you first turn on your computer, the BIOS goes through several steps to get the computer ready to use. The first thing it does is a power-on self test (POST). The POST checks the reliability of RAM (some clones skip this step—others let you skip it by pressing the Esc key) and initializes certain chips and disk drives and other standard equipment.

If something fails the POST test, the computer might freeze. The computer might also display a cryptic error message. A failure at this point might be something serious like a bad memory chip or something as simple as the keyboard connector being loose. Newer computers with setup information stored in a CMOS memory chip will fail at this point if the contents of that chip have been lost or don't agree with your current configuration. If your computer fails at this point, there are a couple of things you can try:

- If you've added memory, changed boards, or otherwise changed the configuration of your computer, boot off the setup disk and reconfigure the computer.
- If you haven't changed the configuration, you should still try booting off the setup disk. Your battery could have failed and the computer would have lost all setup information. Generally, if running the setup program will correct the problem, the error message will suggest running the setup program.
- If the problem isn't with the setup, try pushing the F1 key several times. My Compaq at the office always gives me an error message when it boots and pressing F1 always clears it. I haven't been able to identify the reason but it's never caused any other problems.
- Try turning the computer off for thirty seconds or so and then turning it on again. Sometimes, random problems will crop up and turning the computer off for thirty seconds gives all the internal memory a chance to lose its contents.

If all the above fail, you'll need to either get your computer serviced or use the error message number to track down the problem yourself.

After the POST, the boot record is loaded into memory and executed. It doesn't know very much. In fact, all it knows is how to start DOS. This program is called a *bootstrap* program. The bootstrap routine isn't very smart. It doesn't know that it's loading DOS. In fact, it could just as easily load a different operating system. All it does is read the beginning of a disk. If there's a disk in the A drive, it will try to read DOS from that disk. If the A drive is empty, it will try to read DOS from the first hard disk—usually the C drive. If DOS isn't present or if the disk is defective, you'll get a *non-system disk* error message. Following the error, the computer either waits for you to insert a new disk or brings up a limited function version of BASIC (depending on the type of computer).

You might be wondering why the operating system isn't built into the computer. It is, in fact, built into a few Tandy computers. The problem with building the operating system into hardware is that it makes upgrading to a newer operating system expensive and difficult. Over the past few years, there have been so many improvements to DOS that I wouldn't want to still be locked into DOS 2.0 because that was what was built into my machine. Having a built-in DOS would also prohibit you from running an alternative operating system.

On an IBM machine, DOS is made up of three primary programs, IBM BIO.COM, IBMDOS.COM, and COMMAND.COM. IBMBIO.COM and IBM DOS.COM are hidden files. When using non-IBM DOS, these files are usually called SYSBIO.COM, SYSDOS.COM, and COMMAND.COM. You don't see them when you perform a directory. IBMBIO.COM or SYSBIO.COM are a supplement to the internal ROM BIOS routines already in the computer. IBMDOS .COM or SYSDOS.COM handles input-output operations. COMMAND.COM is the command interpreter.

On an IBM system, the bootstrap program loads IBMBIO.COM and IBM DOS.COM. Control is passed to IBMBIO.COM, which initializes all the hardware that's attached to the computer. That's why all the disk drive lights flash and the print head on your dot matrix printer moves to the left. Hardware initialization also moves the part of the operating system from its load position in memory to its final position in low memory, and erases the IBMDOS.COM routines that are no longer needed.

After initializing the hardware, IBMBIO.COM looks for and processes a file called CONFIG.SYS. This is short for CONFIGure the SYStem. If no CONFIG.SYS file is found, IBMBIO.COM continues with the boot process. Like the AUTOEXEC.BAT file, the CONFIG.SYS file must be in the root directory of the boot disk. Unlike the AUTOEXEC.BAT file, however, the CONFIG.SYS file contains unique commands. Most of these commands can't be used outside the CONFIG.SYS file. While these commands are unique, they're very similar to batch commands, which is why I've included them in this book.

After the CONFIG.SYS file is found and processed, control is passed to IBMDOS.COM. This program loads routines that control the information flow to and from the computer and other hardware, like disk drives and printers. After IBMDOS.COM is finished, COMMAND.COM is loaded. When COMMAND .COM first begins operation, the last thing it does is look for a special file called the AUTOEXEC.BAT file. It looks for the AUTOEXEC.BAT file only in the root directory of the boot disk. If it finds the AUTOEXEC.BAT file, it executes it just like any other batch file. This makes the AUTOEXEC.BAT file an excellent place to perform task that are performed only once, like setting the date and time and loading memory-resident software.

Figure 4-1 illustrates the steps that take place when you switch your computer on. Figure 4-2 shows how the computer's RAM is configured with the computer running a program.

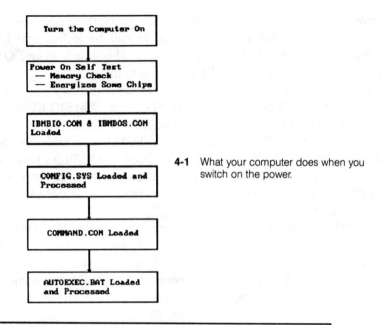

4-1 What your computer does when you switch on the power.

BIOS Area
Device drivers loaded from CONFIG.SYS file
PSP of COMMAND.COM (Program Segment Prefix)
Low memory portion of COMMAND.COM
Master environment block (This is the copy of the environment accessed and modified by batch files.)
Memory resident software (Along with a full copy of the environment for each program.)
Current program's copy of the environment
DOS memory control block (MCB) for the current program
Current program's PSP
Current program's code area
Current program's data area
Free memory

4-2 Configuration of a computer's RAM when it's running a program, including space for memory resident software.

The CONFIG.SYS file

The CONFIG.SYS file is an ASCII file that's very much like a batch file—with commands that control how much memory DOS allocates to certain tasks, and how it performs several other tasks. DOS uses it to control the configuration of the computer. In order to add a mouse or connect to a network, you enter commands into the CONFIG.SYS file. If there isn't a CONFIG.SYS file in the root directory, DOS skips this step and loads COMMAND.COM.

The CONFIG.SYS file is structured just like a batch file, and must be an ASCII file. It must have one command on each line. Unlike a batch file, however, most commands in the CONFIG.SYS file are unique to the CONFIG.SYS file and can't be used elsewhere. There's a reason for this. The CONFIG.SYS file runs before COMMAND.COM loads and configures certain aspects of memory usage. Once COMMAND.COM is loaded, there's no room to change the values set by the CONFIG.SYS file. Because the CONFIG.SYS file isn't a batch file, it can't contain batch file commands.

There are nine commands that can be used in a CONFIG.SYS file under DOS version 3, and most of the commands can be used under earlier versions of DOS. For the most part, they can be in any order. Keep in mind that, while there are nine commands you can use in your CONFIG.SYS file, only three are used a lot. They are BUFFERS=, FILES=, and DEVICE=. Each of the CONFIG.SYS commands is discussed below:

BREAK=on/off

Normally, DOS checks for a Ctrl−Break only during standard input, output, when printing, or when accessing the communications port. This is the default for BREAK OFF. Setting BREAK ON causes DOS to check for a Ctrl−Break whenever a program requests any DOS function. The Off setting is redundant since this is the default setting. I recommend the On setting.

The BREAK command is one of the few CONFIG.SYS commands that you can enter from the keyboard or in a batch file. The syntax is identical to the syntax in a CONFIG.SYS file. Entering BREAK alone (from the keyboard or batch file but not in the CONFIG.SYS file) will display the status of BREAK.

BUFFERS=#

DOS sets up a special place in memory to hold information that's just been read from disk. This area is called a buffer. If the program requests the same information again, DOS can supply it from very fast memory (the buffer) rather than the very slow disk. This is called caching. Up to a point, the larger the buffer, the faster the disk access system works. And the larger the buffer, the more memory it takes and the less you have available for other uses.

In addition to saving time on a disk read, the buffer saves time on a disk write because, before DOS can write a record to a sector, it must first read that sector. So a large buffer saves on both read and write time. The number (#) is between 1 and 99. The default value that DOS uses if there's no BUFFERS command is between 2 and 15, and depends on both the version of DOS you have and your machine's configuration. Each buffer causes DOS to allocate 512 bytes to the buffer. This exactly matches the 512-byte disk sectors that DOS uses. Due to internal overhead, each buffer reduces the amount of memory available to other applications by 528 bytes. So a BUFFERS value of 10 causes DOS to allocate 5280 bytes, or a little over 5K, to the buffer.

A higher buffers statement can dramatically speed up some operations. A program that reads the same information from disk over and over, like a database program, gains a great deal from either a higher level of buffers or a caching program. A program like Lotus, which reads its worksheet into memory and holds the entire set of data in memory, gains little or nothing. In order to load a file into memory, DOS must first load the proper directory. Therefore, systems with a large number of files in a directory or a complex subdirectory structure also gain from a higher buffer setting.

With all the memory-resident programs around, memory is already tight. Making your buffer too large might even slow down a program because it reduces the memory available to the program. Many commercial programs want you to set your buffer to 20. So unless you want to spend a lot of time experimenting to find the best setting or if you have a caching program, just set it to 20 and forget it. In fact, making your BUFFERS setting too high with some versions of DOS can dramatically slow DOS down, as opposed to having no buffers at all.

Much of this, however, has changed with the introduction of DOS 4.0. DOS can now read up to eleven sectors ahead of the sector it's requested to get, and place this additional information into a buffer. The process is called *lookahead*. Earlier versions of DOS were limited to, at most, 99 buffers. That was more than adequate at the time because of the loss of speed at higher buffer setting. DOS 4.0, however, can go up to 999 buffers and can place those buffers in expanded memory using a /X switch.

The DOS BUFFERS command is a very simple cache program. If you install a commercial caching program, like Super PC-Kwik, the installation instructions will probably tell you to set the buffer statement to a very low number—typically one or two. This avoids having two caching programs trying to cache your hard disk. You must have a statement in your CONFIG.SYS file setting BUFFERS to this value. Otherwise, it can default to a value as high as fifteen.

You might be wondering why you would want a separate caching program, because the BUFFERS setting is really a cache. The problem is that BUFFERS is a very simple cache. Before checking the hard disk for data, DOS first checks the buffers. Its search method is very simple; it starts with the first buffer and checks every single buffer sequentially until it either finds the information it's looking for or checks all the buffers. If DOS is always reading new information from the disk but first has to sequentially check all the buffers, the buffers can actually slow down the computer! That's why the DOS manual warns about setting buffers too high.

On the other hand, a good caching program doesn't sequentially check its entire contents. In fact, most caching programs allow you to create multi-mega-byte caches, way too large to check sequentially. Rather, they generate an index as data is being placed in the cache. All they do when DOS requests information is briefly check their index. That tells them right away if the cache has the data DOS is requesting and, if so, where to get it.

COUNTRY =

COUNTRY = # controls how the date and time are displayed. The number (#) represents the country code. Table 4-1 shows all the COUNTRY codes, along with the corresponding default KEYBxx value. The default is USA if no value is entered.

DEVICE =

There are a number of devices attached to your computer. These include disk drives, a hard disk, and printers. Some of these devices are unique and require a *device driver* in order to communicate with your computer. A device driver is a special program provided by the manufacturer to allow a special device to communicate with DOS. A device driver usually ends with the extension .SYS, although .EXE and .COM are also possible extensions. By using device drivers to control special types of equipment, DOS is device independent. You can use almost any type of equipment with DOS as long as a device driver has been written for the equipment.

Device drivers are attached to DOS in the CONFIG.SYS file. For example, the CONFIG.SYS file in Fig. 4-3 is mine from an earlier computer. Note that the path isn't set when DOS reads the CONFIG.SYS file. Therefore, the device driver must be in the root directory (as is mine) or the command must supply the complete path to the driver. If my QUADCLOK.SYS driver were in the C: \ SYSLIB directory, then the line in my CONFIG.SYS file would be:

```
DEVICE = C: \ SYSLIB \ QUADCLOK.SYS
```

When DOS attaches a device driver, that driver becomes a part of DOS. As you can imagine, writing a device driver is complex and difficult. Most memory-resident software would function better if it were written as a device driver. However, the task of writing device drivers as complex as most memory-resident software is too difficult for even big software companies.

Table 4-1 Possible values for the COUNTRY configuration command.

Country	Code	KEYBxx
United States	001	US
Canada (French)	002	CF
Latin America	003	LA
Netherlands	031	NL
Belgium	032	BE
France	033	FR
Spain	034	SP
Italy	039	IT
Switzerland	041	SF, SG
United Kingdom	044	UK
Denmark	045	DK
Sweden	046	SV
Norway	047	NO
Germany	049	GR
Australia (English)	061	-----
Japan	081	-----
Korea	082	-----
People's Republic of China	086	-----
Taiwan	088	-----
Asia (English)	099	-----
Portugal	351	PO
Finland	358	SU
Arabic	785	-----
Hebrew	972	-----

There are a couple of device drivers of particular note because they're included with DOS. They are listed as follows:

ANSI.SYS ANSI.SYS was first included with DOS 2.0 and has been standard since. ANSI.SYS replaces the screen and keyboard handling of DOS with more powerful routines. The details are complex and would require a separate book, but the bare essence of ANSI.SYS is keyboard remapping and screen improvements. ANSI.SYS can function as a poor man's keyboard macro program. The syntax is far more difficult than most memory-resident programs, but ANSI.SYS can remap any key to any other set of keystrokes. For example, in writing this

Batch File Line	Explanation
`SHELL=C:COMMAND.COM` `/P /E:30`	Load COMMAND.COM as the command processor and, in the process, expand the environment.
`FILES=20`	Increase the number of files DOS can open at once.
`DEVICE=QUADCLOK.SYS`	Load the clock driver and set the time in DOS according to the built-in clock. This was used on older PCs that did not have a built-in clock. They relied on an after-market clock built into a memory board.
`BUFFERS=20`	Increase the buffers used for disk caching.
`BREAK=ON`	Turn break on.
`LASTDRIVE=E`	Set the last drive to E. This machine had one hard disk but there were two subdirectories treated like hard disks using the SUBST command.

4-3 My old CONFIG.SYS file.

chapter I've used a keyboard macro program to remap the Ctrl−A (^A) key to AUTOEXEC.BAT. ANSI.SYS can do the same thing. ANSI.SYS can also use special keystrokes to control the screen. The computer magazines are full of hints on how to change your prompt to an imitation of a state flag and other such things using ANSI.SYS screen control commands.

VDISK.SYS VDISK.SYS was first introduced in DOS 3.0. (The source code for it was included with DOS version 2.) It allows you to set aside part of your memory as an electronic floppy disk drive, called a RAM disk. The advantage of a RAM disk drive is speed. They're extremely fast. The disadvantage of a RAM disk is that all the data in them is lost when you turn the computer off or if you lock up the computer, and a RAM disk reduces the memory available to other applications.

DISPLAY.SYS, DRIVER.SYS, and PRINTER.SYS These three new device drivers were added with DOS version 3.3. DRIVER.SYS lets you define an external drive as a logical drive. The primary use for DRIVER.SYS is to define an external 5¼-inch drive as a logical drive on a machine with only 3½-inch drives. The other two drivers, DISPLAY.SYS and PRINTER.SYS, are used for displaying and printing character sets from other countries.

CEMM.SYS CEMM.SYS was first introduced in Compaq DOS, version 3.2. While only available with Compaq DOS, some other versions of DOS include a similar device driver. CEMM.SYS lets you use the memory above 640K as either a RAM disk (like VDISK.SYS) or as expanded memory.

FCB=

This specifies the number of file control blocks (FCBs) that DOS can concurrently open. The format is:

FCBS = m,n

where the m gives the total number of files that can be opened simultaneously by FCBs. The default is 4 and the range of possible values is $1-255$. The n specifies the number of protected file openings—that is, the first n FCBs are protected against being closed if a program tries to open more than m files using FCBs. The default is zero and the range of possible values is $m-255$.

FILES=#

The FILES command controls how many files the entire system can have open at any one time. The default value is 8, which is too few for many applications. The maximum number of files that a process can have open is 20. This twenty includes five predefined files, input, output, error, auxiliary, and printer files. Several major programs, like dBASE, require a FILES value of 20. Some programs offer the ability to shell to other programs, for example, */System* in Lotus, *Run a program* in Wordstar, *Shell* in Basic, or *Escape transfer run* in Microsoft Word. The second application is called a child process. The shelling process can open twenty files, as can the second application, so it's possible, although unlikely, that you could require a FILES specification as high as 40.

If you don't specify a value, the default is 8. Each file above eight requires 48 bytes. The maximum value is 99. As a general rule, set your FILES value to 20. If you ever need more, you'll get an error message like *No free file handles*. If that happens, you need to increase the value of the files statement in your CONFIG.SYS file and reboot. Of course, each file requires only 48 bytes, so setting it too high won't affect your memory too much.

LASTDRIVE=#

This command controls how many disk drives DOS appears to have, and was added with DOS 3.0. The # represents the last drive in the system, which, on a typical XT, would be C. This number only sets an upper limit; DOS still tracks the correct number. Note there isn't a colon after the drive letter. Remember that LASTDRIVE must leave room for any nondisk drives you have. These include RAM disks, any unusual disk or tape drives added as device drivers, any hard disks that have been partitioned into more than one drive, and any "pseudo" drives set up with the SUBST command.

If not specified, LASTDRIVE defaults to the E drive. However, certain software can overwrite the LASTDRIVE setting. Typically, network software will define several drive letters beyond the LASTDRIVE setting as network drives.

For example, on my office computer I have a LASTDRIVE=D setting. Once the Novell network software loads, however, it defines the P, Q, R, S, Y, and Z as network drives.

SHELL=

The DOS command interpreter is called COMMAND.COM. You don't have to use COMMAND.COM in particular; you can use any other one, for example, Command.Plus, 4DOS, or UNIX. You specify another command interpreter with the SHELL command in the CONFIG.SYS file. If, like device drivers, the command interpreter you want to use isn't in the root directory, you must specify the full path. The SHELL command is also used to expand the DOS environment.

Some devices require you to boot from a floppy disk even if you have a hard disk. An example is early Bernoulli boxes. With this type of device, you must keep the boot disk in the A drive because of how DOS works.

DOS takes up a lot of memory. When your computer is short of memory, either because it has less than 640K or you have a lot of memory-resident software, this can be a problem. The lack of memory might prevent some programs from being run or limit the size of others. DOS solves this problem by making part of itself provisionally resident (or transient) in memory. You need this part to enter DOS commands but not to run application programs. If a program needs this space, it can overwrite the transient portion of DOS.

When you exit an application program that's overwritten the transient portion of DOS, DOS is less than complete. If you were to use this version, you wouldn't be able to enter most internal commands. DOS replenishes itself by rereading portions of COMMAND.COM into memory. (*Note*: This is why COMMAND.COM isn't a hidden file like the other two system files.) Usually, DOS reloads itself from the drive it booted from. Using a CONFIG.SYS file with the command:

```
SHELL = C: \ COMMAND.COM
```

on the boot disk, you can force DOS to load and reload itself from the hard disk or anywhere else. Because some viruses infest COMMAND.COM and automatically expect it to be in the root directory, however, many users change this to:

```
SHELL = C: \ DOS \ COMMAND.COM
```

in order to protect the COMMAND.COM file. Of course, this statement requires a copy of COMMAND.COM in the C: \ DOS subdirectory. If you do this, you no longer need COMMAND.COM in the root directory, but many users leave it there to try and fool the virus. This will only fool very simple viruses, however, because the COMSPEC environmental variable always points to the active COMMAND .COM.

If you have hardware that requires you to boot off a floppy disk, you can still cause DOS to reload COMMAND.COM from the hard disk by pointing the COMSPEC variable to the C drive.

The SHELL command doesn't work properly for DOS version 2 because of a bug in DOS. Generally, it works properly the first time, but fails to work after that. If you need to use this command, your best option is to upgrade to a DOS version 3. You can cause DOS to reload COMMAND.COM from other than the boot disk in version 2 DOS by using the following steps:

1. Boot as normal.
2. Copy COMMAND.COM to the disk where you want to reload it. Of course, you only have to perform this step once, while you perform the others each time you boot.
3. Log onto the disk where you want to reload COMMAND.COM, which I will assume is the C drive.
4. Issue the command COMMAND C:.

Replace the C: with the appropriate drive letter if your path specification is different. If you want COMMAND.COM in a subdirectory, you must log onto that subdirectory and issue the command:

    COMMAND C: \ SUBDIRECTORY

This works, but upgrading your DOS version is a less painful method to accomplish the same thing.

The SHELL command can't be used at the DOS prompt. In addition, COMMAND.COM doesn't show up in the environment under SHELL, but under COMSPEC. You can change the location where DOS looks for COMMAND .COM at the DOS prompt with the COMSPEC (or optionally SET COMSPEC) command, like so:

    SET COMSPEC = C: \ COMMAND.COM

or

    COMSPEC = C: \ COMMAND.COM

Like the SHELL command, COMSPEC doesn't work properly for version 2 DOS. In addition to pointing to COMMAND.COM, the SHELL command is used to expand the size of the DOS environment. This is explained later in the book.

STACKS =

Stacks controls the number and size of the stack frames. The command is:

    STACKS = m,s

where m is the number of stack frames. The possible values are 0 or $8-64$, and the default is zero. The *m* value increases memory usage by the size specified by *s*. The *s* value specifies the size of each stack frame. The possible values are 0 or 32 − 512, and the default is zero. The default for stacks is 0,0, which indicates that DOS shouldn't install STACKS support. This is acceptable for most systems. You'll get an error message from DOS if a program requires STACKS support and it isn't installed. A value of 6,512 would tell DOS to install six stack frames of 512 bytes each.

DOS 4.0 adds three new commands to the CONFIG.SYS file. These commands work only with DOS 4.0 and above.

INSTALL=

This command allows you to load some memory-resident software from the CONFIG.SYS file instead of the AUTOEXEC.BAT file. Regardless of the order of the commands in the CONFIG.SYS file, all device drivers are loaded before any TSR software is loaded with the INSTALL command. The memory-resident software currently supported by the INSTALL command are:

- FASTOPEN.EXE
- KEYB.COM
- NLSFUNC.EXE
- SHARE.EXE

The command to load any of these programs in the CONFIG.SYS file is similar to the command below to load SHARE.EXE:

```
INSTALL = C: \ DOS \ SHARE.EXE
```

Because you haven't yet specified a path for CONFIG.SYS, you must specify the full path for the program, including the extension.

REM

This is short for remark and lets you add comments to your CONFIG.SYS file in order to document the logic. This is really no big improvement—I've used REM lines in my CONFIG.SYS file for years. DOS doesn't process any line in the CONFIG.SYS file it doesn't recognize. Therefore, prior to introduction of the REM command, a remark line just resulted in an *Unrecognized command* error message.

SWITCHES=

A SWITCHES = /K line in your CONFIG.SYS file tells DOS to use conventional keyboard functions even if you have an enhanced keyboard installed. You would use this with a program that doesn't understand the enhanced keyboard.

The AUTOEXEC.BAT file

The last step the computer performs when it boots is checking for the AUTO EXEC.BAT file in the root directory. If it finds this file, it runs it automatically—hence the name AUTOmatically EXECuted BATch file. DOS runs this file automatically when you boot or reboot—at least as long as it's in the root directory of the boot disk. Because it runs automatically, AUTOEXEC.BAT is the perfect place to do those things you only do once, like setting the path and loading memory-resident software. With two minor exceptions, the AUTOEXEC.BAT file is just like any other batch file. There are no special AUTOEXEC.BAT commands. The only commands you can use in an AUTOEXEC.BAT file are normal DOS and batch file commands.

Once unusual, but very minor aspect of the AUTOEXEC.BAT is the following: If there's no AUTOEXEC.BAT file, the last thing DOS will do is prompt you for the date and time. If there is an AUTOEXEC.BAT file, DOS will turn control over to it and never prompt for the date and time. Older computers didn't come with a built-in clock. They required a DATE and TIME command in the AUTOEXEC.BAT file so the user could set the clock manually. Later, vendors began selling boards containing a clock. These required running a program in the AUTOEXEC.BAT (some used a device driver in the CONFIG.SYS file) to transfer the date and time from the clock to DOS. Almost all newer computers have a clock built in that automatically communicates with DOS so most users can ignore the clock.

The second unusual aspect of the AUTOEXEC.BAT file involves replaceable parameters. Some versions of DOS don't allow you to specify replaceable parameters in the AUTOEXEC.BAT file, and will lock up if they come across any. This shouldn't be a significant limitation because the AUTOEXEC.BAT file runs automatically, giving you no opportunity to enter a replaceable parameter on the command line.

As I discussed earlier, most system configuration is performed by the CONFIG.SYS file. However, there are several configuration commands that belong in the AUTOEXEC.BAT file. They are as follows:

PATH=

There are four types of commands DOS will accept: internal commands, .EXE program names, .COM program names, and .BAT filenames. Every time DOS receives a command, it first checks to see if that command is an internal command, like ERASE. If so, it executes that command. If the command isn't an internal command, DOS next checks the current subdirectory for a .COM file by that name, then a .EXE file, and finally a .BAT file. If DOS finds a program with the correct name, it executes that program. If DOS doesn't find a file in the current directory, it searches the path for a .COM, .EXE, or .BAT file. If it finds a program in the path with the correct name, it executes that program. Otherwise, DOS returns the *Bad command or filename* error message.

So the path is nothing more than a list of subdirectories for DOS to search when a program isn't in the current subdirectory, and the syntax for the PATH command is:

PATH = C: \ ;*1stsubdirectory;2ndsubdirectory;...;lastsubdirectory*

If your path is:

PATH = C: \ ; \ SYSLIB; \ DATABASE; \ WORDPROCESSOR

then DOS will search only those subdirectories on the default disk. This is normally what you want. However, if you're working on the A drive, then the path is really:

PATH = C: \ ;A: \ SYSLIB;A: \ DATABASE;A: \ WORDPROCESSOR

because A is the default drive. So you're better off to specify the full path, like this:

PATH = C: \ ;C: \ SYSLIB;C: \ DATABASE;C: \ WORDPROCESSOR

A second problem is that the PATH command can contain only the same 127 characters as other DOS commands. Before DOS 3.0, there was simply no way to have a path longer than 127 characters. While DOS 3.0 retained the 127 character command line limit, it introduced the Substitute command. SUBST allows you to substitute a drive letter for a subdirectory, so:

SUBST D: C: \ SYSLIB \ LEVEL1 \ LEVEL2

allows you to use D: anywhere you would have used C: \ SYSLIB \ LEVEL1 \ LEVEL2. Your PATH command can now be:

PATH = C: \ ;D: \

instead of:

PATH = C: \ ;C: \ SYSLIB \ LEVEL1 \ LEVEL2

This makes the PATH command shorter, as well as easier to read. Generally speaking, you won't have set a path before using the SUBST command. Therefore, SUBST.EXE must be in the root directory, you must change to the directory containing the path before you issue the SUBST command, or you must specify the full path to the SUBST program. An example of having SUBST.EXE in the C: \ SYSLIB directory follows:

CD \ SYSLIB
SUBST D: C: \ SYSLIB \ LEVEL1 \ LEVEL2

or

　　　 \ SYSLIB \ SUBST D: C: \ SYSLIB \ LEVEL1 \ LEVEL2

If you enter the PATH command with nothing after it, DOS displays the current path. If you enter the path followed by a semicolon, then DOS resets the path to nothing. This causes DOS to search only the default directory for programs and batch files. If you specify a path incorrectly, DOS will not find the error until it needs to search the path. If you enter an invalid directory in the path, DOS ignores that entry.

　　　The PATH command is really a SET variable. The difference is that you don't have to start the command with a SET, although you could. Like other SET variables, the path is accessible to a batch file with the variable name %PATH%. So a batch file could add the E drive to the path with the command:

　　　PATH = %PATH%;E: \

Like other %variables%, this won't work from the command line, only from a batch file.

PROMPT =

The default DOS prompt is a C>, which tells you that C is the default drive. You can use the PROMPT command to make the DOS prompt display a wide range of information. The PROMPT command is normally just used in the AUTOEXEC .BAT file. When used by itself, PROMPT resets the prompt to C>.

　　　Any printable character string can be included in the PROMPT command. Some characters require special coding. They're shown in Table 4-2. It's important to remember that any PROMPT you develop is stored in the environmental space, along with the PATH and SET variables. A long PROMPT combined with a long PATH and SET variable might require you to expand your environmental space, as explained in chapter 18.

　　　There's an additional drawback to using an expanded prompt. The most common one is PROMPT=pg, which causes DOS to display both the drive and the current subdirectory. However, to display the current subdirectory, DOS must be able to read the disk. That means trouble if you try to switch to an empty floppy disk drive. DOS will try to read the disk to get the information it needs for your prompt. When it fails, you'll get the familiar *Abort, Ignore, or Retry?* error message. Abort won't work. It causes DOS to abort trying to read the disk, but DOS immediately tries to display your prompt, which forces another disk read. You can get out of this loop by putting a disk into the drive. You can also use Ignore (or Fail with some versions of DOS) in order to enter a new drive letter. Fail generally works the first time, but if your system uses the Ignore option you might have to try it several times to get it to work. Figure 4-4 shows this.

Table 4-2 Metacharacters you can use with the PROMPT command.

Command	Action
$$	Display a dollar sign
$t	Display the time
$d	Display the date
$p	Display the current subdirectory
$v	Display the DOS version
$n	Display the current drive
$g	Display a greater than sign
$l	Display a less than sign
$b	Display a vertical bar
$q	Display the equal sign
$h	Display a backspace (thus deleting the prior character)
$e	Include an escape (Useful when ANSI.SYS is loaded)
$_	Include a carriage return and line feed

```
C>REM There is on disk in the B drive
C>B:

Not ready error reading drive B
Abort, Retry, Fail? a

Not ready error reading drive B
Abort, Retrn, Fail? f

Current drive is no longer valid>c:

C>
```

4-4 What happens when you try to switch to the A drive when it doesn't contain a disk.

VERIFY = on/off

From the name, you would expect that VERIFY causes DOS to check data it writes to a disk to make sure it was written properly. You would expect DOS to read back the data as it writes it and compare what it reads back to what it wrote. When they match, it would go on to new data. When they didn't match, it would either retry or signal an error.

This isn't what DOS does, however. When DOS writes information to disk, it also includes a special checksum, called a Cyclical Redundancy Check, or CRC. Writing the same data to disk will always cause DOS to write the same CRC to disk. By including the data and the CRC on the disk, DOS has two versions of the data.

When DOS reads data from disk, it computes the CRC and compares it to the one already read from the disk. If they don't match, DOS knows it's read the data incorrectly. When the two CRCs don't match, DOS tries several more times. If it can't read the data where the CRCs match, it responds with the *Abort, Ignore, or Retry?* error message.

When VERIFY is on, DOS does more than write data to disk. After writing the data, it reads the data and computes a new CRC. If the new CRC matches the CRC stored with the data on the disk, DOS assumes the data was written properly. Note that DOS doesn't compare the data on the disk with the data in memory, which would be the better test. All it does is compare checksums.

So having VERIFY on causes DOS to perform a partial test of the data on the disk after a write operation. This partial test will catch some, but not all, errors. One thing VERIFY on will always do is slow down disk operations. After writing data to disk, DOS must wait for that data area of the disk to rotate back under the head, read in the data, compute a new CRC, and compare it to the existing CRC. All that takes time. So having VERIFY on catches some disk errors, but slows down all disk write operations.

You must decide whether or not to have this tradeoff. My recommendation is to leave VERIFY on (VERIFY=ON). Entering VERIFY alone displays the status of VERIFY.

MODE

The program MODE.COM is used to configure the serial ports on a PC. For example, in order to use my modem at 2400 baud, I have to issue the command:

```
MODE COM1:2400,,,,,
```

Because I always use my modem at 2400 baud, I have this command in my AUTOEXEC.BAT file. Serial printers and plotters typically require a similar command or set of commands. You would also place these in the AUTOEXEC .BAT file. Note that MODE.COM must be in your path statement, and you must have already issued the PATH command or you need to specify the full path to MODE.COM. For example:

```
C:\DOS\MODE COM1:2400,,,,,
```

Memory-resident software

Memory-resident software (also called TSR for terminate and stay resident) is software that stays in memory until you reboot or specifically remove it. There are special problems associated with loading memory-resident software. Generally, the software is only loaded once. Trying to load it a second time when it's already in memory can cause problems. If you load more than one memory-resident software program, there's usually only one loading order that will work.

The problems associated with memory-resident software make the AUTO EXEC.BAT file an excellent way to load it. With the AUTOEXEC.BAT file, you can specify a specific order so you don't have to worry about loading in the wrong order. Because the AUTOEXEC.BAT file automatically loads the programs into memory when the computer is booted, they're always available without you having to remember to load them. My old AUTOEXEC.BAT (AUTO1.BAT on the disk) file is shown in Fig. 4-5.

Batch File Line	Explanation
`PROMPT Ronny Richardson (404) 555-1212$_$p$g`	Change the prompt to show my name and phone number, along with the current subdirectory.
`PATH=C:\;C:\BAT;C:\SYSLIB; C:\WORDSTAR; and so on`	Set the path. Notice that I specified the full path to the subdirectories, including the drive. This is critical if your computer has more than one hard disk or you work with floppy disks a lot.
`subst d: c:\word\money`	Treat this subdirectory as a separate hard disk.
`subst e: c:\word\personal`	Treat this subdirectory as a separate hard disk.
`VERIFY=ON`	Turn verification on.
`DISABLE`	Run a small program to turn the printscreen off.
`mode mono`	Set the display mode using a DOS program.
`popdrop`	Run a commercial memory management program and mark the spot in memory before any TSR programs are loaded.
`CD\KEY`	Change to the SuperKey subdirectory.
`SuperKey`	Load SuperKey.
`popdrop up`	Use Popdrop to place a marker in memory for its memory management functions.
`CD\SIDEKICK`	Change to the SideKick subdirectory.
`SideKick`	Load SideKick.
`MENU`	Run a menu program.

4-5 My old AUTOEXEC.BAT file (AUTO1.BAT).

Summary

Table 4-3 summarizes the CONFIG.SYS commands and Table 4-4 summarizes some common device drivers that come with different versions of DOS. Table 4-5 illustrates some rules of thumb for the CONFIG.SYS file. The major points of this chapter are as follows:

- The three major parts of DOS are the BIOS, the DOS kernel, and COMMAND.COM.
- When you turn on your computer, DOS runs a bootstrap program, which loads the operating system. If PC DOS or MS DOS is the operating system, the CONFIG.SYS and AUTOEXEC.BAT files are processed.
- The CONFIG.SYS file contains special commands to configure the operating system.
- The AUTOEXEC.BAT file is a special batch file containing only normal batch file commands. It's special because DOS automatically runs it when loaded.

Table 4-3 Summary of CONFIG.SYS commands.

Command	Meaning
BREAK=On/OFF	Controls when DOS checks for a Ctrl-Break.
BUFFERS=#	Controls the space allocated for disk caching.
DEVICE=	Expands DOS to handle equipment it does not directly support.
COUNTRY=	Controls how DOS displays the date and time.
DEVICEHIGH	Loads a device driver into high memory.
DOS=HIGH/LOW DOS=UMB/NOUMB	DOS=HIGH loads most of DOS into high memory. The UMB option keeps certain links open, allowing memory resident software to be loaded into free high memory.
FCBs	Specifies the number of file control blocks [FCBs] DOS can concurrently open.
FILES=#	Controls how many files the system can have open at one time.
INSTALL	Installs some system memory resident programs using CONFIG.SYS.
LASTDRIVE=	Controls the maximum number of disk drives DOS can address.
REM	A nonexecuting comment.
SHELL=	Expands the environment and defines an alternate command processor to replace COMMAND.COM.
STACKS	Controls the number of stack frames and their size.
SWITCHES=/K	Tells DOS to use conventional keyboard functions even if an enhanced keyboard is installed.

Table 4-4 Common device drivers with DOS.

Driver	Function
ANSI.SYS	Replaces DOS screen and keyboard handling with more powerful routines.
DISPLAY.SYS	Defines an external drive as a logical drive.
DRIVER.SYS	Used for displaying character sets from other countries.
EMM386.EXE	Converts extended memory into expanded memory and allows for loading memory resident software and device drivers into high memory.
PRINTER.SYS	Used for printing character sets from other countries.
VDISK.SYS	Used to configure part of RAM as an electric disk drive.

Table 4-5 Guidelines for the construction of a CONFIG.SYS file.

Include the CONFIG.SYS file in the root directory of the boot disk.
Include the following commands in your CONFIG.SYS file: BREAK=ON BUFFERS=20 FILES=20 LASTDRIVE=C
The most commonly used CONFIG.SYS commands are: BREAK BUFFERS DEVICE SHELL
The most infrequently used CONFIG.SYS command is FCBS.
To change the country, use the COUNTRY= command. This is not needed in the United States.

Part 2
Putting batch files to work

5
CHAPTER

Custom
configurations

The two files that determine the configuration of your computing environment, as discussed in the previous chapter, are the CONFIG.SYS and AUTOEXEC.BAT files. If you're lucky, you have one of each of these that handles all your programs. However, the nature of programs and their memory demands on your computer are changing so rapidly that one do-it-all environment is not always possible.

For example, the computer at my office usually loads Novell network software. However, with Novell loaded, I then don't have enough memory to run PerFORM or Migrografx Designer. In order to run those programs, I have to do without the network. Because much of the network loads in the CONFIG.SYS file, I can't use memory managers like Mark/Release or PopDrop to unload the network software.

If your computer has extended memory, you might face the same difficulties. Some programs, like Lotus 2.2, need expanded memory, so you need to load an expanded memory simulator like AboveDisc into your CONFIG.SYS file. Other programs, like Lotus 3.1, need extended memory, so you have to skip the expanded memory simulator.

Copying over boot files
One method of booting with different configurations is to maintain multiple copies of your boot files (AUTOEXEC.BAT and CONFIG.SYS) and have a batch file copy the proper ones into place and reboot. That can be done using the BOOT

.COM program, included on the disk that comes with this book. A batch file with three boot options is shown in Fig. 5-1. Note that each set of AUTOEXEC.BAT

Batch File Line	Explanation
`ECHO OFF`	Turn command-echoing off.
`REM AUTOBOOT.BAT`	Remark giving the name of the batch file.
`REM First test for missing` `    parameter and branch`	Documentation remark.
`IF (%1)==() GOTO NOTHING`	Check for missing replaceable parameter and skip to an error routine if needed.

`REM Now test for proper`
`    parameters. If found, copy`
`    files and branch`
	Documentation remark.

`IF %1==001 COPY AUTOEXEC.001`
`    AUTOEXEC.BAT`
`IF %1==001 COPY CONFIG.001`
`    CONFIG.SYS`
`IF %1==001 GOTO BOOT`
	If the user specifies 001, copy those configuration files into place and jump to the rebooting section.

`IF %1==002 COPY AUTOEXEC.002`
`    AUTOEXEC.BAT`
`IF %1==002 COPY CONFIG.002`
`    CONFIG.SYS`
`IF %1==002 GOTO BOOT`
	If the user specifies 002, copy those configuration files into place and jump to the rebooting section.

`IF %1==003 COPY AUTOEXEC.003`
`    AUTOEXEC.BAT`
`IF %1==003 COPY CONFIG.003`
`    CONFIG.SYS`
`IF %1==003 GOTO BOOT`
	If the user specifies 003, copy those configuration files into place and jump to the rebooting section.

`REM Must be wrong parameter.` `    Branch to message`	Documentation remark.
`GOTO WRONG`	Jump to the section to handle the user entering a replaceable parameter that is not acceptable.
`:BOOT`	The section that reboots the computer.
`BOOT`	Run a program to reboot the computer. Of course, that stops the execution of the batch file.
`REM Could also use POPDROP B`	Documentation remark.

`REM Since computer reboots,`
`    rest of this batch file not`
`    executed`
	Documentation remark.

`:NOTHING`	Label to mark the section to handle the user not entering a replaceable parameter.
`ECHO No parameter entered after` `    AUTOBOOT`	Tell the user what is wrong.
`:GOTO MESSAGES`	Skip to help messages.

5-1 AUTOBOOT.BAT, a batch file with three boot options.

5-1 Continued

Batch File Line	Explanation
`:WRONG`	Label to mark the section to handle the user entering an unacceptable replaceable parameter.
`ECHO Wrong parameter entered` `     after AUTOBOOT`	Tell the user what is wrong.
`GOTO MESSAGES`	Skip to the help messages.
`:MESSAGES`	Label to mark the section of help messages.

`ECHO Enter 001 for no memory`
`     resident software`
`ECHO Enter 002 for writing set`
`     of memory resident software`
`ECHO Enter 003 for data base`
`     set of memory resident`
`     software`
	Help messages.

and CONFIG.SYS files could load different memory-resident software and configure the computer in a special way. I use this at the office to load one set of CONFIG.SYS and AUTOEXEC.BAT files when I want to log onto our network, and another set when I don't want to use the network.

Environmental surveying

Another way to solve this problem is to develop several custom sets of CONFIG.SYS and AUTOEXEC.BAT files under different names. This time, rather than having to run a batch file yourself to change the environment, have the batch files you use to start programs figure out if the proper environment is in place. If it is, they can run the application. If not, they need to copy the proper boot files into place, reboot, and then run the application.

CONFIG.001 in Fig. 5-2 and AUTOEXEC.001 in Fig. 5-3 are files that will configure an environment to give a program the maximum amount of memory

Batch File Line	Explanation
`FILES=20`	Set the number of files DOS can have open at once.
`BUFFERS=5`	Set the amount of memory DOS users to buffer the disk.

5-2 CONFIG.001, which configures a system for the maximum amount of available memory.

Batch File Line	Explanation
PROMPT=PG	Set the prompt
PATH=C:\;..;C:\DOS	Set the path.
STARTAPP.BAT	Run a program.

5-3 AUTOEXEC.001, which configures a system for the maximum amount of available memory by not loading memory resident programs.

possible. CONFIG.001 uses low buffers and files and doesn't load any device drivers. AUTOEXEC.001 doesn't load any memory-resident software. CONFIG.002 in Fig. 5-4 and AUTOEXEC.002 in Fig. 5-5 create a more "user friendly" environment, but they require more memory. CONFIG.002 has higher amounts of buffers and files, and loads several device drivers. AUTOEXEC.002 loads two memory-resident programs. As a result, some memory-intensive pro-

Batch File Line	Explanation
FILES=40	Set the number of files DOS can have open at once.
BUFFERS=40	Set the amount of memory DOS uses to buffer the disk.
DEVICE=C:\MOUSE\MOUSE.SYS	Attach the mouse driver.
DEVICE=C:\RAMDISK\RAMDISK.SYS /1000	Set up a 1 Meg RAM disk.
DEVICE=C:\TOOLS\CACHE.SYS /2000	Set up a 2 Meg hard disk cache.
DEVICE=C:\NETWORK\PROGRAM.SYS	Load the network drivers.

5-4 CONFIG.002, which uses more memory than CONFIG.001 in Fig. 5-2 in order to set up a more user-friendly environment.

Batch File Line	Explanation
PROMPT=PG	Set the prompt.
PATH=C:\;..;C:\DOS	Set the path.
CD\SUPERDO	Change subdirectories.
SUPERDO	Load a memory resident program.
CD\SUPERTOO	Change subdirectories.
SUPERTOO	Load a memory resident program.
CD\	Change to the root directory.
STARTAPP.BAT	Run a program.

5-5 AUTOEXEC.002, which, like the CONFIG.SYS file in Fig. 5-4, uses more memory to set up a user-friendly environment.

grams might not run. For this example, the two applications are BIGAPP and TINYAPP. 01.BAT in Fig. 5-6 runs BIGAPP, while 02.BAT in Fig. 5-7 runs TINYAPP.

Batch File Line	Explanation
`@ECHO OFF`	Turn command-echoing off.
`REM 01.BAT`	Remark giving the name of the batch file.
`REM Runs BIGAPP, a Program That`	Documentation line.
`REM Needs a Lot of Memory`	Documentation line.
`IF EXIST FLAG.001 GOTO OK`	If the flag file FLAG.001 exists, the computer was booted with the proper configuration files and the batch file skips to the OK label.
`IF EXIST FLAG.002 GOTO 002`	If the flag file FLAG.002 exists, the computer was booted with the wrong configuration files and the batch file skips to an area that handles this.

`REM At This Point, Flag Does`
`    Not Exist`
`REM Will Assume Files Wrong`
`REM Will Create Flag File, Copy`
`    Over`
`REM Proper Files and Reboot`
	Documentation lines.
	
	If the batch file reaches this point, then neither flag file exists and the batch file will assume the wrong configuration was used.

`TYPE NOFILE > FLAG.002`	Create a zero-length flag file flagging that the computer was booted under CONFIG.002--the wrong one in this case.
`:002`	A label marking the section of the batch file that handles resetting the computer when the wrong configuration is in effect.
`COPY CONFIG.001 CONFIG.SYS`	Replace the current CONFIG.SYS file with the minimum-memory one stored under the name CONFIG.001. There is no need to store the old one since it is stored under the name CONFIG.002.
`COPY AUTOEXEC.001 AUTOEXEC.BAT`	Replace the current AUTOEXEC.BAT file with the minimum-memory one stored under the name AUTOEXEC.001.
`REN FLAG.002 FLAG.001`	Rename the flag file to indicate that the computer was rebooted using the minimum-memory configuration files.
`REM Create Marker File`	Documentation remark.

5-6 01.BAT, which runs BIGAPP.

5-6 Continued

Batch File Line	Explanation
`TYPE NOFILE > START.001`	Create a zero-length file that tells the AUTOEXEC.BAT file that a program is pending to be run.
`BOOT`	Reboot the computer. The balance of this batch file does not present a problem for this segment of code because rebooting causes this batch file to stop execution. Otherwise, you would need a GOTO command to skip over the next section of code.
`:OK`	Label marking the section of code that runs Bigapp if the computer has the proper configuration without rebooting.
`CD\BIGAPP`	Change to the Bigapp subdirectory.
`BIGAPP`	Run the Bigapp application. You might also want to add another line to restart the menu.

You want the batch file for each application to survey the environment and start the application if the environment is the proper one. If not, the batch file should copy the correct set of files over the current CONFIG.SYS and AUTOEXEC.BAT files, reboot the system, and then start the application automatically. This is straightforward except for two problems—figuring out which environment is running and starting the application automatically after booting.

The first problem is easier to handle than the second. You can create a flag file on the hard disk, and maintain its extension where it always matches the current environment. In both 01.BAT and 02.BAT, the batch file changes the environmental files if necessary. If the flag doesn't exist, the batch file assumes the wrong environment is being used. It also has to create the flag file, a zero-length file, by typing an nonexisting file. DOS first creates FLAG.001 and then checks for NOFILE to pipe to it. NOFILE doesn't exist, so nothing ends up in FLAG.001. However, the directory entry already exists. That way, you end up with a zero-length file that serves as a counter without taking up any disk space. Depending on your version of DOS, this line might display an error message on the screen that you can ignore. DOS is simply warning you that NOFILE doesn't exist.

The second problem has a similar solution, but this time the pending flag file is temporary. When DOS reboots, the AUTOEXEC.BAT file checks for all possible pending flag files. If it finds one, it deletes the pending flag file and then runs the associated application. It deletes the pending flag file so it won't run the same application the next time you reboot.

Batch File Line	Explanation
`@ECHO OFF`	Turn command-echoing off.
`REM 2.BAT`	Remark giving the name of the batch file.
`REM Runs TINYAPP, a Program That Does` `REM Not Need a Lot of Memory`	Documentation remarks.
`IF EXIST FLAG.002 GOTO OK`	If flag file FLAG.002 exists, then the computer was booted in the proper configuration so it runs the application.
`IF EXIST FLAG.001 GOTO 001`	If flag file FLAG.001 exists, the computer was booted in the wrong configuration so it jumps to a section to handle this.

`REM At This Point, Flag Does Not Exist`
`REM Will Assume Files Wrong`
`REM Will Create Flag File, Copy Over`
`REM Proper Files and Reboot`
	Documentation remarks.

`TYPE NOFILE > FLAG.001`	If the batch file reaches this point, no flag file exists. It creates one and then continues as though the wrong configuration were in force. 001 is used rather than a .002 so the REN command below will work properly.
`:001`	Label marking the section that handles resetting the configuration files and rebooting.
`COPY CONFIG.002 CONFIG.SYS`	Replace the CONFIG.SYS file with the proper one.
`COPY AUTOEXEC.002 AUTOEXEC.BAT`	Replace the AUTOEXEC.BAT file with the proper one.
`REN FLAG.001 FLAG.002`	Rename the configuration file to flag the appropriate configuration.
`REM Create Marker File`	Documentation remark.
`TYPE NOFILE > START.002`	Create a marker indicating Tinyapp is pending to run.
`BOOT`	Reboot the computer.
`:OK`	Label marking the section that runs Tinyapp if the configuration is correct.
`CD\TINYAPP`	Change to the proper subdirectory.
`TINYAPP`	Run the application.

5-7 02.BAT, which runs TINYAPP.

This is complex, so let's work through an example. Assume that CON-FIG.002 and AUTOEXEC.002 are in effect and you want to run BIGAPP. Because this is the first time you've used the system, FLAG.002 won't exist. Enter 01 at the DOS prompt and the batch file will take over. Its actions are explained in Fig. 5-6. When the computer reboots, it processes the new CON-FIG.SYS file and then the new AUTOEXEC.BAT file. The last line in the AUTOEXEC.BAT file calls STARTAPP.BAT, shown in Fig. 5-8.

As you can see from the batch file listing in Fig. 5-6, 01.BAT reboots the computer only when the wrong configuration files were used with the original boot. Thus, the computer reboots only when the environment is the inappropriate environment, or when it's not sure which environment is in effect. While this example used two environments and two applications, the actual number you can implement is limited only by your needs.

Batch File Line	Explanation
@ECHO OFF	Turn command-echoing off.
IF EXIST START.001 GOTO 001	If the file START.001 exists, it is a flag telling the batch file which program to run, so jump to the appropriate section.
IF EXIST START.002 GOTO 002	If the file START.002 exists, it is a flag telling the batch file which program to run, so jump to the appropriate section.
GOTO END	If neither flag file exists, no application is pending to run, so exit the batch file.
:001	Label marking the section to run the first application.
DEL START.001	Delete the flag file so the batch file will not start the application the next time the computer is rebooted.
1	Run the application by running another batch file. Since the batch file does not use the CALL command, control never returns to this batch file.
:002 DEL START.002 2	Section to handle the second application identically to the way the above section handled the first application.
:END	Label marking the end of the batch file.

5-8 STARTAPP.BAT, which is run from the AUTOEXEC.BAT file and decides if a program is pending to run.

Floppy-disk boot

Having a custom configuration for different applications is a popular enhancement. In addition to the batch file in Fig. 5-1, there's another method to change the configuration—creating a boot floppy for each application. Each boot floppy has its own AUTOEXEC.BAT and CONFIG.SYS file. Note that the AUTOEXEC.BAT file on a boot floppy can load memory-resident software from the hard disk by simply including a C: line in the AUTOEXEC.BAT prior to the commands to load the memory-resident software. Of course, you'll want to use the SHELL command in the CONFIG.SYS file, or the COMSPEC command in the AUTOEXEC.BAT file to have DOS load COMMAND.COM from the hard disk. That way, you don't have to leave the floppy disk in the A drive.

Conditionally loading memory-resident software

Do you find yourself constantly editing your AUTOEXEC.BAT file to change the memory-resident programs (also called TSRs, for terminate and stay resident) you load when the computer boots? There's a better way! Instead of modifying your AUTOEXEC.BAT file, have it ask you if you want to load each TSR program. To do that, do the following:

Modify your AUTOEXEC.BAT file to prompt you before it loads each TSR program. The program you use to do this can be the InKey program included on the disk or any similar program. Have the batch file skip over the commands to load the TSR package unless the user requests the AUTOEXEC.BAT file to load the program.

Figure 5-9 shows a sample AUTOEXEC.BAT file, called AUTOASK.BAT. It prompts you prior to loading each of three TSR packages: Superkey, PrintCache, and Sidekick. You can choose to load any or none of these programs, all without modifying the AUTOEXEC.BAT file. And they're always loaded in the only order that works—Superkey, PrintCache, and then Sidekick—so you don't have to worry about conflicts caused by not loading one or more of them.

Summary

This chapter has presented numerous short hints for booting your computer with different configurations for different applications. Most of the batch files in this chapter are on the included disk.

Batch File Line	Explanation
`@ECHO OFF`	Turn off command-echoing.

`REM AUTOEXEC.BAT File`
`Illustrating`
`REM Conditional TSR Loading`
	Documentation remarks.

`ECHO Do You Want to Load` `Superkey (Y/N)`	Ask the user a question.
`BE ASK "Load TSR ", YN`	Use the Norton Utilities Batch Enhancer to obtain his or her response.
`IF NOT ERRORLEVEL 2 GOTO SKIP1`	If the user answers yes, skip loading Superkey.
`    CD\SUPERKEY`	Change to the Superkey subdirectory.
`    KEY`	Load Superkey.
`    CD\`	Change back to the root directory.
`:SKIP1`	Label marking the end of the Superkey section.

`ECHO Do You Want to Load`
`PrintCache (Y/N)`
`BE ASK "Load TSR ", YN`
`IF NOT ERRORLEVEL 2 GOTO SKIP2`
`    CD\PCACHE`
`    PCACHE`
`    CD\`
`:SKIP2`
	Conditionally load Print Cache if the user answers yes to the prompt.

`ECHO Do You Want to Load`
`Sidekick (Y/N)`
`BE ASK "Load TSR ", YN`
`IF NOT ERRORLEVEL 2 GOTO SKIP3`
`    CD\SIDEKICK`
`    SK`
`    CD\`
`:SKIP3`
	Conditionally load Sidekick if the user answers yes to the prompt.

`REM Rest of AUTOEXEC.BAT File` `Goes Here`	The rest of the AUTOEXEC.BAT would go here.

5-9   AUTOASK.BAT, a version of AUTOEXEC.BAT which will prompt you before loading memory resident programs.

6
CHAPTER

Batch file menus

The purpose of a menu system is to handle much of the overhead involved in performing routine tasks with a hard disk. For the most part, menus are more trouble than they're worth for a floppy-disk system. Before developing a menu system, however, it's important to have a well structured hard disk.

Structuring your hard disk

A floppy disk is like a desk. You can just toss all your papers on a desk and usually find what you need. Similarly, you can copy files on to an available floppy disk and likely find the file later, especially if you label the disk.

A hard disk, on the other hand, is like a filing cabinet. If you just toss in all your papers, it's unlikely that you'll ever find anything. An average user will create or accumulate over one thousand files a year. If they were all in a single directory, simply getting a listing would take a long time. Finding one specific file would be next to impossible. Just as you categorize all the papers in a filing cabinet into files, you should categorize the files on a hard disk into directories and subdirectories.

An additional reason to create these divisions is that DOS places an arbitrary limit on the number of files that can be created in the root directory. When you format a 20 Meg hard disk on an AT using DOS 3.2, it sets aside only enough room in the file allocation table for 512 files. So you can't store more than 512 files on the hard disk without using subdirectories. Other computers and versions of DOS have similar, but not necessarily identical, limits. Because of the way DOS stores subdirectories, this limit doesn't apply to them.

The first division from the root directory is considered a *directory*, and further divisions from there are *subdirectories*. Keep in mind, however, that these two terms are often used interchangeably.

Each subdirectory is stored as a file in the parent directory. Because the subdirectory is a file, it can expand to hold as many files as needed. A subdirectory is a logical subdivision of a disk, much as a folder is a logical division of a filing cabinet. DOS treats each subdirectory much like a separate floppy disk. Each subdirectory has a separate directory listing, and each one can have files with the same name. Subdirectories don't significantly slow down most DOS operations, and they don't take up much room, so there's no real disadvantage to creating as many as you need. Each subdirectory can also grow to fill all the available space on the hard disk, so using subdirectories doesn't make it more difficult to fit files on a hard disk.

While a subdirectory can have as many files as you want, there are technical reasons to limit the number of files in a single subdirectory to a manageable number. DOS tries to hold all the filenames of a subdirectory in memory. This speeds directories and searches. When the number of files is too large to fit into memory, DOS slows down dramatically. You'll notice this problem because DOS will have to read the disk more than once when you perform a DIR. At this point, you should either reduce the number of files in the offending subdirectory or increase the number of buffers specified in the CONFIG.SYS file.

The DOS commands for managing subdirectories are CD (CHDIR), FDISK, FORMAT, MD (MKDIR), and RD (RMDIR). These commands perform the following functions:

CD *path* (or CHDIR *path*)   will change the currently active directory to the one named in the *path*.

FDISK   is used to prepare a new hard disk. If there's any information on the disk, it will be destroyed by the FDISK command.

FORMAT   is used to prepare a new hard (or floppy) disk. FORMAT is run after the FDISK command. If there's any information on the disk, it will be destroyed by FORMAT. Although some utility programs, like the Norton Utilities, can recover much or even all of the data on your hard disk if you accidently format it, nothing can recover the data on a hard disk if it's accidently partitioned with FDISK.

MD *name* (or MKDIR *name*)   will make a subdirectory with the *name* you specify that branches off the currently active directory.

RD *name* (or RMDIR *name*)   will remove the subdirectory *name* if it branches off the current directory and if it doesn't contain any files.

Think of the subdirectories of a disk as a tree. Each disk has only one root (or base) directory. This directory is created automatically when you format the disk. The root directory can contain as many subdirectories as you need, although the technical limit is the number of files DOS allows in the root directory. Each of these subdirectories can have subdirectories, and so on. The limit is that the path statement (C: \ *subdirectory1* \ *subdirectory2* \ etc.) must be less than 63 characters long. When a directory is created, it will be a child (or branch) of the current directory (called the parent). So, if you create a subdirectory while in the root directory, that subdirectory would be a branch off the root directory. If it were created when you're in a subdirectory, it would be a branch of that subdirectory. A drawing of all the subdirectories in a hard disk, therefore, looks a lot like an inverted tree. Figure 6-1 shows a diagram of the subdirectory structure of a typical hard disk.

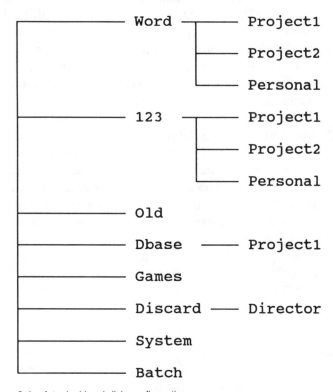

6-1   A typical hard disk configuration.

   Each subdirectory (except the root directory) will automatically contain two files when you create it. These show up as a dot and double dot file when you perform a DIR. These two files have special meanings to DOS and allow for two handy shortcuts. The double dot file stands for the parent subdirectory, so you can move up one subdirectory with the CD.. command. You can continue issuing this command until you reach the root directory. The single dot file represents all the files in the subdirectory, and can be used in place of *.* when copying or erasing files.

To remove a directory, that directory must not have any files except the required dot and double dot files. If you find you can't remove a subdirectory, first check to see if it has any files in it. If so, you need to erase them. When the DIR command doesn't show any files, you most likely have hidden files. These are usually created by a copy protected program, and can usually be removed by the software that created them or with the Norton Utilities program. Remember that, if you erase a file associated with copy protection, you'll most likely render that package permanently unusable.

When you're changing directories, you can move only along a continuous path. For example, in the hard disk diagrammed in Fig. 6-1, you can't move directly from C: \ WORD \ PROJECT1 to C: \ 123 \ PROJECT2. You must first move back to the root directory. However, you can move back to the root directory and on to desired subdirectory with the single command CD \ 123 \ PROJECT2. The CD is the change directory command, and specifying the entire path, from just to the right of the C:, moves you back to the root directory and on to the desired subdirectory. CD \ by itself always returns you to the root directory.

Typically, the first level of subdirectories (or directories) are functional. There is one for system files, one for word processing, one for spreadsheets, and so on. Each of these directories can then have subdirectories. So the word processing directory could have subdirectories for personal letters, course outlines, tests, consulting, and so on. If you teach several courses, the test subdirectory could even be subdivided by course. At some point, however, further division is more trouble than it's worth.

The root directory should have only a few files in it. The operating system requires it to have COMMAND.COM and two hidden system files. If you plan to use an AUTOEXEC.BAT file or a CONFIG.SYS file, they must also be in the root directory.

Introduction to menus

A menu is nothing more than a list of options on the screen. There are several ways to create these, and will be explored later in this chapter. The menu will give numbers for each option. A sample menu is shown in Fig. 6-2. This example menu, along with the hard disk layout in Fig. 6-1, will form the basis for the remaining examples in this chapter. To run any of the programs on the menu, the user can type in the number for the program to run and press Enter.

Entering a 1 at the DOS prompt to run a word processing program when all you have is the menu file does nothing by itself. You must also create a batch file called 1.BAT to perform the action under the first option in the menu. So entering 1 runs 1.BAT. In addition to running the word processor, 1.BAT would typically contain a final command to redisplay the menu. The exact format of that command would depend on the type of menu being used.

PRESS	FOR
1	Run Word Processor
2	Run Spreadsheet
3	Run Database
4	Play Games
5	Format a Disk
6	Backup Hard Disk To Floppies

6-2 A sample menu.

Menu options can do more than just automatically run a program; they can also control how dangerous programs are used. For example, if you try to format a floppy disk without the drive specification (FORMAT A:), you could erase your entire hard disk with some versions of DOS. This can be avoided if you format disks from the menu. The menu option to format a disk runs a batch file, thus preventing the user from entering the format command incorrectly.

Displaying the menu

There are numerous ways to display a menu, and each has its own unique advantages and disadvantages. The easiest way is to use a series of ECHO commands in a batch file. That's how the MENU1.BAT in Fig. 6-3 displays the menu. The problems with this method are that the menu is displayed very slow, it has an unprofessional look, and you must have ANSI.SYS loaded to control the screen color.

A second way is to store the menu in an ASCII file and use the DOS TYPE command to display the file. The batch file to do this is shown in Fig. 6-4, and is

Batch File Line	Explanation
`ECHO OFF`	Turn command-echoing off.
`REM MENU1.BAT`	Remark giving the name of the batch file.

`ECHO =====================================`
`ECHO    PRESS    FOR`
`ECHO`
`ECHO      1    Run Word Processor`
`ECHO      2    Run Spreadsheet`
`ECHO      3    Run Database`
`ECHO      4    Play Games`
`ECHO      5    Format a Disk`
`ECHO      6    Backup Hard Disk To Floppies`
`ECHO =====================================`
	Display the menu on the screen. While you cannot see it, the third row creates a blank line by echoing a backspace.

6-3 MENU1.BAT, a batch file that will create the screen in Fig. 6-2.

Batch File Line	Explanation
`ECHO OFF`	Turn command-echoing off.
`REM MENU2.BAT`	Remark giving the name of the batch file.
`TYPE MENU2.TXT`	Type an ASCII file containing menu text to the screen.

6-4 MENU2.BAT, which uses the TYPE command to display a menu.

an ASCII file containing text similar to that in Fig. 6-3, without the ECHO commands. This method is faster than a series of ECHO statements, but otherwise shares the same problems as the ECHO statements.

A third way to display a menu is by using a high-level programming language. Writing high-level programs is beyond the scope of this book, however, so I haven't covered it. Most high-level programs compile to an executable .EXE file, so all that's required to display the menu is to include the name of the .EXE file in a batch file. In addition, most high-level languages can control the screen color and execute very fast.

Using either of these methods to display a screen is straightforward, but there's a better way. The program disk for this book contains a screen compiler called FastScreen. It will take an ASCII text file and convert it to a small .COM file. When you enter the name of the .COM file, the screen will appear almost instantaneously. To run FastScreen from DOS, simply enter:

    FASTSCRN

at the DOS prompt, with the directory that holds FastScreen active. FastScreen will ask you for the foreground color, the background color, and the name of the ASCII file to turn into a display. The ASCII file must be no more than 79 characters wide, and each line must end with a carriage return. The file must contain no more than 24 lines. FastScreen will read in the ASCII file, process it, and output a small .COM file with the same name. This small .COM file will display the text in the ASCII file to the screen extremely fast. In addition, it will set the foreground and background colors according to your specifications when you compiled the screen. The original ASCII file isn't modified, so you can modify and recompile it if you even need to change the screen. FastScreen makes excellent menus. It also has several other useful functions:

- Several of the programs I use don't properly reset the cursor when they terminate. I end up with a flashing box, or other strange shape, for a cursor. I've compiled an ASCII file that contains a single blank space, called CURSOROK. Running the resulting .COM file will reset the screen colors and sometimes reset the cursor to its proper shape.
- I like my display to have white letters and a blue background. This is initially set by the FastScreen menu that my AUTOEXEC.BAT file displays. However, these colors can be easily reset to white on black by a CLS (clear

screen) command, or by a number of application programs that don't reset screen color when they terminate. I have a FastScreen file called COLOR .COM that was compiled from an ASCII file consisting of a single space. When I issue the COLOR command, the screen is cleared and my colors reset.

- Many times I need to display a message from within a batch file. By compiling it with FastScreen and using a different set of colors, I can generate messages that flash up in unexpected colors. These messages get noticed!

There's one slight problem with using FastScreen. It doesn't work on a few monochrome systems. If your system is monochrome, the only way to see if it will is to try it.

Making it work

After deciding on a method to display the menu on your screen, you need a set of batch files to run the applications on the menu. The batch file in Fig. 6-5 is used to display the menu. Note that a batch file called SHOWMENU.COM actually displays the menu. All SHOWMENU.BAT does is make sure the computer is left in the root directory and then run SHOWMENU.COM to actually display the menu. Also note that SHOWMENU.COM is in the batch subdirectory, which is in the path. The last line of your AUTOEXEC.BAT file should issue the command to display the menu. That way, your menu comes up automatically when you turn on the computer. Figures 6-6 to 6-11 are the batch files that run when you select an option from the menu.

Batch File Line	Explanation
C:	Make sure you are in the C drive. This is necessary only if you have more than one hard disk.
CD\	Make sure the batch file is in the root directory.
SHOWMENU	Run SHOWMENU.COM to display the menu.

6-5 SHOWMENU.BAT, which displays a menu that was created with FASTSCRN.EXE.

Batch File Line	Explanation
C:	Make sure you are in the C drive. This is necessary only if you have more than one hard disk.
CD\WORD	Change to word processing subdirectory.
WORD %1	Start word processor. The %1 allows you to pass parameters to the word processor, e.g., 1 LETTER.TXT.
MENU	Run batch file to display menu.

6-6 1.BAT, which runs the first option of the menu system.

Batch File Line	Explanation
C:	Make sure you are in the C drive. This is necessary only if you have more than one hard disk.
CD\123	Change to word 123 subdirectory.
123	Start 123, which does not allow parameter passing.
MENU	Run batch file to display menu.

6-7   2.BAT, which runs the second option of the menu system.

Batch File Line	Explanation
C:	Make sure you are in the C drive. This is necessary only if you have more than one hard disk.
CD\DBASE	Change to database subdirectory.
DBASE %1 %2	Start dBASE. The %1 and %2 allows you to pass parameters to the database, e.g., 3 DO ACCOUNT.
MENU	Run batch file to display menu.

6-8   3.BAT, which runs the third option of the menu system.

Batch File Line	Explanation
C:	Make sure you are in the C drive. This is necessary only if you have more than one hard disk.
CD\GAME	Change to game subdirectory.
XMAN	Run XMAN game.
MENU	Run batch file to display menu.

6-9   4.BAT, which runs the fourth option of the menu system.

Batch File Line	Explanation
FORMAT A:/V	Format a disk in the A drive. If FORMAT.COM is in the PATH, then you do not need to change directories.
MENU	Run batch file to display menu.

6-10   5.BAT, which runs the fifth option of the menu system.

Batch File Line	Explanation
BACKUP C:\ A:/S	Backup a hard disk to floppies. If BACKUP.COM is in the PATH, then you do not need to change directories.
MENU	Run batch file to display menu.

6-11   6.BAT, which runs the sixth option of the menu system.

This menu system is a simple system with only one menu. One or more of the options could call up other menus, allowing you to develop a system as complex as you require.

My menu system

Back in 1983, the organization I worked for got its first few computers. These computers were shared by over twenty users, most of whom didn't know much about computers. After answering the question "How do I start Lotus?" at least fifty times, I developed a menu system very much like the one I just described for the most frequently used computer. The MIS manager saw it and laughed at it. Several days later, I saw him copying it onto the other computers. The menu had become so popular with the users that he had no choice. I've slightly modified this menu system over the years as programs have been added or deleted, but it's very similar to the system I installed in 1983.

Summary

The major points of this chapter were:

- Before you can develop a menu system, it's important to properly divide your hard disk into sections. Each section, or subdirectory, is devoted to one task.
- The DOS special hard disk commands are CD (change directory), MD (make directory), and RD (remove directory).
- Menus are controlled by batch files. The most important batch files are those that run each menu entry. For example, entry 1 in the menu is controlled by the 1.BAT batch file.
- Menus can be displayed by putting ECHO statements in a batch file, typing an ASCII file to screen, of using either a high-level language or a screen compiler.

Most of the batch files in this chapter are on the disk.

7
CHAPTER

A document archival system

What I'm going to describe in this chapter is a complete system for making sure that you never lose an important file. Because it consists of several major sections, you can adopt only those sections that are critical to your own applications. The major sections to my overall document archival system are as follows:

Periodic backups   Absolutely nothing is more important than periodically backing up your hard disk or important floppy disks. This is the only part of this plan that I recommend to everyone.

Systematically copying critical data files   Many important data files undergo routine revisions. Prior to making a major revision, I copy the file to be revised to a special holding subdirectory.

Maintaining old files   I never erase an old file. Instead, I copy it to a special holding subdirectory. When that subdirectory is full of files, I copy the files to a disk and erase them from the subdirectory. I then store the disk in a safe place. I currently have 78 such disks.

Indexing document files   I use a commercial indexing package to index my word processing documents so I can find them faster.

Each part of my overall document archival system is explained in much more detail, as follows.

Periodic backups

Back when everyone used floppies, the most damage you could do with one "stupid" command was 360K. Like stupid commands, bad disks or defective hardware rarely damaged more than 360K. Large hard disks, however, now give us the ability to damage 70 Megs of stored information or more with one command, or as the result of an errant command or defective hardware. 70 Megs is over 200 floppy disks!

I insure my computer with a company called Safeware. Recently, they sent out a newsletter listing some of the more unusual claims they had paid. This list included the following:

- A California man carried some work home with him. He kept the disks in a box that looked like his cat's litter box. As you might expect, the cat used the disk box to relieve himself and that destroyed all the data on the disks.
- A California boy was hiding behind the family computer during a friendly game of hide-and-seek. When a friend found him, the boy made a heroic dash to avoid being tagged. While dashing, he tripped over the power cord. That sent a shock through the computer that caused the hard disk to crash.
- A Los Angeles motorist collided with a fire hydrant, sending a column of water into the air. That water entered a nearby office building damaging several computers.
- A California man knocked his fish tank over, spilling all the water into his computer.
- A Florida man had his laptop out near the pool. The family dog bumped the table and sent the computer to the bottom of the pool.

As you can see, computers can be damaged by a number of unexpected events. While an insurance policy like the one from Safeware can protect your hardware and even your software programs, it's up to you to protect your data.

Many small businesses maintain all their records on a single microcomputer. All the payroll records, tax information, bid information, and so on. Imagine the impact to that business if those records were lost. I know of one company that had their three computers stolen. Naturally, they didn't have backups. They were so desperate for the data that they ran ads saying that the thieves could keep the computers and they wouldn't press charges if they could just get their data back. They never did, and they ended up going out of business.

I know of a Fortune 500 company that maintains a lot of their legal information on microcomputers. One of the analysts tried to format a floppy with (you guessed it) the FORMAT command at the C prompt. He was lucky. There was a recent backup and he lost only a few hours of work. The manager told me that losing the files on his hard disk would have delayed a billion dollar legal case. He now requires daily backups.

I have about twenty articles in progress, a year's worth of work on my dissertation, a copy of this book, the related batch files, and several other books on my hard disk. Until recently, I make a daily incremental backup and two full weekly backups. One backup is stored at home and the other is stored at my office.

Is this carrying things too far? I don't think so. An incremental backup takes about two minutes and the two full backups take less than half an hour. So I spend about an hour a week on backups. I consider this time to be insurance. It would take an experienced typist over twenty hours to rekey just my dissertation. It would take me thousands of hours to redo the research if I lost the hard disk copy and couldn't locate a printed copy. Even my notes are on the hard disk. Now add in the time to redo all the other files, and you begin to see why I make backups.

As I said, that was my approach until recently. I now have a very fast tape drive that can perform a full backup on both my hard disks in about twenty minutes, which is so fast that I've forgone incremental backups. I now make two full backups daily (one during supper and one after I quit for the night), and I keep the three latest versions of these two backup sets. One set is stored at home and the other is stored at the office.

You should have copies of most of your software on the original distribution disks, so you don't need to back up these files except once after installation. Then put the originals in a safe place so they can't be damaged.

Except during installation, programs don't often change. The software is "tied together" with system files that include batch files, AUTOEXEC.BAT, CONFIG.SYS, and subdirectories. You can safely go a long time between backups of these files. They generally change only when you install new software or remove existing software.

If damaged, these system files can be replaced from an old backup or the original distribution disks. However, things aren't that simple with your data files. You create them and then usually modify them quite often. It's important, therefore, to back up these files frequently.

Your first hard-drive backup should be a full backup. This gives you a good copy of installed software and system files. It also gives you a copy of your data files. When you change a data file, DOS automatically changes a flag it maintains to indicate that a current backup no longer exists. At the end of the day, or week if you want to live dangerously, you can make an incremental backup. The backup software looks through your hard disk for files with the archive flag. The software backs up that file and resets the flag, then looks for the next file.

This process is fairly painless because incremental backups are very quick. As you continue making incremental backups, the disks will begin to pile up. If you're constantly updating a 300K database, then you'll create a new copy of this file on disk every day. Most backup software won't remove earlier versions of this file from the backup disks during an incremental backup. Another problem is that files you've erased from the hard disk still exist on the backup disks. Files that have been renamed will exist on the backup disks under both names. If you have to restore from backup disks, you can end up with a lot of extra files.

You can resolve these minor problems by using the batch file in Figure 7-1. The first line goes to the root directory. The second line is optional. It sorts all the directories in extension order, with the filename as the tie breaker. DIRSORT is one of the programs that come with the Norton Utilities. The third lines uses another Norton Utilities program to find all files (*.*) on the hard disk. DOS piping (>) is used to pipe the output to the file C: \ BAT \ LISTING.TXT, or any

Batch File Line	Explanation
ECHO OFF	Turn command-echoing off.
REM BACKUP-1.BAT	Remark giving the name of the batch file.
CD\	Change to the root directory. Note that the batch file assumes the computer is logged onto the C drive.
DIRSORT EN/S	Run the Norton directory sorting program to sort all the filenames across all subdirectories.
FILEFIND *.* > C:\BAT\LISTING.TXT	Run the Norton file finding program to find all filenames and pipe the results to a file called LISTING.TXT in the \BAT subdirectory.

7-1   BACKUP-1.BAT, which lists all the files on the hard disk using the Norton Utilities program.

other filename you choose. If the file doesn't exist, it will be created automatically. If it does exist, it will be erased. If you don't have Norton Utilities, you can replace this batch file with the simpler batch file in Fig. 7-2. This batch file doesn't sort the directory entries because SORT.COM is very slow on large files.

All this batch file does is create a file containing a list of all the files on the hard disk. By running it before backing up, this file will also be backed up—even by an incremental backup. If you must restore, you can compare the files that exist after the restore to LISTING.TXT. Any files that exist on the hard disk but not in LISTING.TXT were either erased or renamed, so they can be deleted.

This takes time. Depending on the type of system you have, it can take as long as thirty minutes. In addition, all this is cumbersome. At some point you'll have so many disks from incremental backups that it will be time to erase them and make another full backup.

These types of backups will protect you from hardware problems and stupidity, but not from theft, fire, or other types of damage. For that, you need a second backup set, stored off-site. In order to create a second incremental backup, your

Batch File Line	Explanation
ECHO OFF	Turn command-echoing off.
REM BACKUP-2.BAT	Remark giving the name of the batch file.
CD\	Change to the root directory.
CHKDSK/V > C:\BAT\LISTING.TXT	Run CHKDSK in the verbose (/V) mode to list all the files and pipe that listing to a file called LISTING.TXT in the \BAT subdirectory.

7-2 BACKUP-2.BAT, which lists all the files on the hard disk without using the Norton Utilities program.

backup program must give you the option of not resetting the archive flag, and not all of them do.

Many organizations with very critical files maintain their three or so newest incremental backups. These are often called the grandfather, father, and son. The purpose of these multiple backups is that you can recreate changes to important files.

Systematically copying critical data files

If you need multiple backups for only a few files, there's a better way. I have a subdirectory called C:\OLD just for old copies of files. Every time I make a major change to a file, I copy it to this subdirectory with a number extension. So the first version of this chapter is CHAPTER6.001, the second is CHAPTER6.002, and so on. This way, I can always go back to an earlier version if I decide I don't like the changes I've made.

Refer back to Fig. 6-1 for the layout of the example hard disk for this chapter. Figure 7-3 shows a batch file for making these backup copies. Note that it checks to make sure that the target filename doesn't exist before copying.

As these files continue to accumulate, you have a choice. You can erase older versions of the now modified (several times over) files, or you can copy them to floppy disks, as described in the next section. To perform your backup, copy these few files to one or more floppy disks.

One of the things I learned a long time ago is that, just as soon as you erase a file, you end up needing it. As a result, I never completely erase a file unless I can easily recreate it. There are a lot of files on your hard disk that you can easily recreate. For example:

.OBJ files When you run most compilers, they first turn your source code into .OBJ files and then they turn the .OBJ files into .EXE files. If you have the source code, you can easily recreate the .OBJ files by running the compiler again.

.BAK files With most word processors, every time you save a file, the prior version is saved under the same name with a .BAK extension. Because I save all critical

Batch File Line	Explanation
REM BACKUP-3.BAT	Remark giving the name of the batch file. Notice command-echoing is not turned off.
IF \%1==\ GOTO ERROR	If the first replaceable parameter is not entered, jump to an error-handling section.
IF \%2==\ GOTO ERROR	If the second replaceable parameter is not entered, jump to an error-handling section.
IF EXIST C:\OLD\%2 GOTO EXISTS	If the file name entered as the second parameter already exists, jump to an error-handling routine.
COPY %1 C:\OLD\%2/V	Copy the file in the current subdirectory named as the first replaceable parameter to the \OLD subdirectory under the name entered as the second replaceable parameter.
GOTO END	Exit the batch file.
:ERROR	Start of error-handling routine for missing parameters.
ECHO SOURCE OR TARGET FILENAME NOT ENTERED	Tell the user the problem.
ECHO ENTER BACKUP-S SOURCE TARGET	Tell the user how to correct it.
GOTO END	Exit batch file.
:EXISTS	Start of error-handling routine for \OLD already containing a file with the name the user entered as the second replaceable parameter.
ECHO %2 ALREADY EXISTS!	Tell user what happened.
ECHO SELECT ANOTHER FILENAME AND TRY AGAIN!	Tell the user how to correct it.
:END	End of batch file.

7-3   BACKUP-3.BAT, which copies your files to a backup subdirectory.

versions to a special subdirectory (as I explained previously), I routinely erase these files.

.PRN files   These are ASCII files created by printing a spreadsheet file to a document. These can easily be recreated by reprinting the spreadsheet.

.$$$ and .TMP files   These are working files created by some commercial packages. They're usually erased by the package when you exit, but a reboot or disk problem can leave them on your hard disk.

Commercial program files   These are the files that come on your software disks. If you need to recreate these, you can copy them from the original disks.

These are about all the files I erase. For the rest of my files, when I'm finished using them I copy them to a holding subdirectory called C: \ DISCARD, and then I erase the original. Figure 7-4 shows the batch file I use for this. It copies all the files I list on the command line. Prior to copying, it checks to make sure that the file doesn't already exist. After successfully copying the file, it erases the original.

Once I get a lot of files in the C: \ DISCARD subdirectory, I copy them to a floppy disk and then delete them from the hard disk. Each of my floppy disks is numbered, from one to my latest one. Up until very recently, I used 360K floppy disks and had accumulated almost one hundred. After copying the files to a floppy disk, I perform three steps. First I erase the copied files from the hard disk. Next, I create a list of the files on the floppy disk. This list stays on the hard disk for easy retrieval when I want to search for a file. Finally, I index the document files on the hard disk.

Deleting all the files on the hard disk that were copied to the discard floppy disk would be easy if all the files were copied. All it would take is a DEL *.*

Batch File Line	Explanation
ECHO OFF	Turn command-echoing off.
REM DISCARD.BAT	Remark giving name of the batch file.
:TOP	Label marking the top of a loop.
IF \%1==\ GOTO END	Exit the batch file when there are no more replaceable parameters.
IF C:\DISCARD\%1 EXIST GOTO ERROR	If the \DISCARD subdirectory contains a file with the same name as the replaceable parameter, jump to an error-handling routine.
COPY %1 C:\DISCARD\%1/V	Copy the file named as a replaceable parameter to the \DISCARD subdirectory.
IF EXIST C:\DISCARD\%1 DEL %1	Make sure the file was successfully copied and then erase the original file.
SHIFT	Bring the next replaceable parameter into the %1 position.
GOTO TOP	Go back to the top of the loop.
:ERROR	Mark the beginning of the error-handling routine.
ECHO %1 ALREADY EXISTS IN C:\DISCARD SUBDIRECTORY!	Tell the user what the problem is.
ECHO YOU MUST DECIDE WHICH FILE TO KEEP	Tell the user how to correct the problem.
:END	Mark the end of the batch file.

7-4   DISCARD.BAT, a batch file to copy files to a "discard" subdirectory.

command. However, I sometimes have more files than will fit on a single floppy, but not enough to justify using two. The problem is then to delete only those files that were actually copied to the discard floppy disk. Figure 7-5 shows a batch file using the FOR command that does just that.

To create a file on the hard disk containing a listing of all the files on the floppy disk, I change over to the C: \ DISCARD \ SUBDIRECTORY and issue the following command:

```
DIRECTORY A:>99.DIR
```

replacing the 99 with the number of the current floppy disk. By maintaining a directory of all my discard floppy disks on my hard disk, I can rapidly search them for a file.

This might sound like overkill, especially if you rarely go back to a file after you're finished with it. The advantage to this system is that it's dirt cheap. In my area, 360K floppy disks currently cost about $5.00 per box of ten. So I have less than $50.00 invested in storing every one of my old files. The way I figure it, using just one of those files again saves me much more than $50.00. I recently converted to 1.44 Meg floppies, which are a little more expensive for the same amount of storage, so I might have $200 invested. But it's still worth it in my opinion.

Batch File Line	Explanation
`@ECHO OFF`	Turn command-echoing off.
`REM DELOLD.BAT`	Remark giving name of the batch file.
`A:`	Change to the A drive. This batch file deletes all the files in the C:\DISCARD subdirectory. It changes to the A drive as a precaution.
`CD\`	Change to the root directory on the floppy disk.
`FOR %%j IN (*.*) DO DEL` `    C:\DISCARD\%%j`	Delete all the files in the C:\DISCARD subdirectory one at a time using a for-loop.
`C:`	Change back to the C drive.
`CD\DISCARD`	Change to the \DISCARD subdirectory.

7-5 DELOLD.BAT, which deletes all files on the hard disk that exist on the "discard" floppy disk.

Indexing document files

Currently, there are a number of good word processing indexing programs available. These programs take a word processing file or an ASCII file, and create an index of it. These aren't indexes like you find in the back of a book. Rather, they're indexes that allow you to search for every document that contains a specific phrase.

ZyIndex is such a package. It will index most word processing documents, using the format they're stored in. All you have to do is tell ZyIndex the format. I use ZyIndex to index all the text files on my discard floppy disks so I can rapidly locate information on them. A big drawback to ZyIndex, and all other indexing programs, is that it will index only text information. It won't index dBASE database files or Lotus spreadsheet files. To get around that problem, I create a small text file with the same name but a different extension that explains what the attached file does. For example, I create .WKT files to explain worksheet (spreadsheet) files. So HP.WKT explains in ASCII text what the file HP.WK1 does. I use .DBT files to explain the function of .DBF dBASE database files.

ZyIndex lets you assign names to the floppy disks that are up to thirty-characters. These names can't include spaces, so I use an underscore to simulate a space. Because all the floppy disks are numbered, I give them the same name combined with their unique number. Disk number 43 would be named DISCARD_DISK_43.

The batch file in Figure 7-6 runs the indexing program. It knows that the name should include the DISCARD_DISK_ specification, so I don't have to enter that. It also knows a number should be entered, so it checks to make sure that one was.

Batch File Line	Explanation
`ECHO OFF`	Turn command-echoing off.
`REM INDEX.BAT`	Remark giving the name of the batch file.
`CD\ZYINDEX`	Change to the \ZYINDEX subdirectory.
`IF /%1==/ GOTO END`	Skip the processing portion if no replaceable parameter was entered.
`REM INDEX MICROSOFT WORD DOCUMENTS`	Documentation remark.
`IF EXIST A:*.DOC ZYINDEX D:\ZYINDEX\ A:\*.DOC/03 DISCARD_DISK_%1`	If any *.DOC files exist on the A drive, index them with ZyIndex. D:\ZYINDEX is the index file path. A:*.DOC is the data file path. /03 specifies the format and the DISCARD_ DISK_%1 gives the disk name.
`REM INDEX SIDEKICK DOCUMENTS`	Remark

7-6 INDEX.BAT, which allows you to index your floppy disks.

7-6 Continued

Batch File Line	Explanation
`IF EXIST A:*.TXT ZYINDEX D:\ZYINDEX\` `A:\*.TXT/15 DISCARD_DISK_%1`	Index all the SideKick format documents.
The batch file continues on in this fashion for several more types of files.	
`GOTO DONE`	Go to the bottom of the batch file after indexing all the files.
`:END`	Label marking the end of the processing section. Note that :END does not have to mark the physical end of the batch file. The batch file reaches this point only if no replaceable parameter was entered.
`CLS`	Clear the screen.
`ECHO ADD DISK NUMBER`	Display an error message. The batch file repeats this 8 times.
`PAUSE`	Pause so user can read the error messages.
`:DONE`	Label marking the end of the batch file.
`CLS`	Clear the screen.

Summary

This chapter points out how to implement a three-point plan to make sure you never lose a critical file. The first and most important step is to periodically back up your hard disk or floppy disks. Data files can be protected by periodically copying them to a holding subdirectory. If you make changes to the files that you later regret, you can go back and use one of these copies. Finally, you can get the ultimate protection by copying all your files to a storage floppy disk prior to erasing them. Most of the batch files in this chapter are on the enclosed disk.

8
CHAPTER

Anti-viral batch files

I'm not going to get into the controversy about whether viruses are actually a serious problem. Some people believe in them—others claim they're all or mostly marketing hype that's manufactured by the people selling anti-viral software. In either case, it makes sense to protect yourself, and it makes especially good sense to take those protection measures that don't require you to purchase an additional computer program. I'll leave it to others to explain "safe" computing, and I'll show you only how you can use batch files to protect yourself.

If basic safe computing practices aren't enough to make you feel safe, but you don't want to spend the money to purchase an anti-viral software package, then try the following three steps. While they don't offer as much protection as anti-viral software, they use DOS so they're free, and they're all fairly unobtrusive. That is, they rarely get in the way. That's important. If the anti-viral procedures you use generate too many false alarms, you are going to deactivate them. The three DOS-based anti-viral procedures are:

- Write-protect your program files.
- Hide COMMAND.COM.
- Test your critical program files to make sure they have not been altered.

Each of these is discussed in more detail below.

Write-protect program files

DOS comes with a program called ATTRIB that will let you mark files as read-only. While a smart virus can bypass this, it will stop some viruses. Not only that, it will protect you against accidently erasing the program files yourself. The command to mark files as read-only is:

ATTRIB *filename* + r

Attrib accepts wildcards, so you can mark more than one file at a time. You can also use a /s switch to mark all the files along the current path. (This requires DOS 3.3 or later.) You should be able to mark all your program files (*.EXE and *.COM) as read-only without any problems. If you later need to erase a file, you can turn off the read-only setting with the following command:

ATTRIB *filename* − r

Hide COMMAND.COM

More viruses hit COMMAND.COM than any other file, primarily because almost every computer has COMMAND.COM and it runs every time the computer runs. Because COMMAND.COM runs every time the computer boots, infecting it gives a virus the largest opportunity to be running when other disks are available for infection.

Most computers have COMMAND.COM in the root directory, so some viruses won't take the time to look elsewhere. Beginning with DOS 3.0, you can put COMMAND.COM into any subdirectory you like. On my system, I have it in the \ SYSLIB (system library) subdirectory. To move COMMAND.COM to a subdirectory, follow these easy steps:

1. Copy COMMAND.COM to the subdirectory on your hard disk where you store your DOS files.
2. Leave a copy in the root directory as a sacrificial lamb. DOS won't be using that copy, so it doesn't matter if it becomes infected.
3. Add the following line to your CONFIG.SYS file:

    SHELL = C: \ SYSLIB \ COMMAND.COM /P

4. Add the following line to your AUTOEXEC.BAT file:

    SET COMSPEC = C: \ SYSLIB \ COMMAND.COM

5. Replace *C:* \ *SYSLIB* in the above command with the subdirectory you use to store your copy of COMMAND.COM. In step 3, you must specify the .COM after COMMAND and you must specify /P, or DOS won't run your AUTOEXEC.BAT file.

If you need to expand the size of your environment, add a /E:*xxxx* to the line in step 3, with *xxxx* being the new size for your environment. For DOS 3.0 and 3.0, *xxxx* should be a number from 10 to 62, representing the number of 16-byte segments to use for the environment. So 20 gives you a 320-byte environmental space. For DOS 3.2 and beyond, the *xxxx* represents the actual size of the environment. The default and minimum is 160 bytes. The maximum is 32,768. Almost all users can get by with 500 bytes or less for the environment. Figure 8-1 shows my current CONFIG.SYS file. You could rename it to NOTUSED.COM and substitute the line in Fig. 8-2 into the CONFIG.SYS file without any problem. You do have to leave the .COM extension.

Batch File Line	Explanation
`SHELL=C:\SYSLIB\COMMAND.COM /P /E:3000`	Load the version of COMMAND.COM in the \SYSLIB subdirectory and expand the environment to 3K.
`DEVICE=C:\386MAX\386MAX.SYS AUTO`	Load the 386-to-the-Max device driver.
`DEVICE=C:\MOUSE\MOUSE.SYS`	Load the mouse driver.
`FILES=35`	Increase the number of files DOS can have open at once.
`BUFFERS=25`	Increase the DOS buffers.
`BREAK=ON`	Turn break on.
`LASTDRIVE=N`	Set the last drive DOS will use.

8-1 My current CONFIG.SYS file.

Batch File Line	Explanation
`SHELL=C:\SYSLIB\NOTUSED.COM /P /E:3000`	Load the version of COMMAND.COM in the \SYSLIB subdirectory under the name of NOTUSED.COM and expand the environment to 3K.
`DEVICE=C:\386MAX\386MAX.SYS AUTO`	Load the 386-to-the-Max device driver.
`DEVICE=C:\MOUSE\MOUSE.SYS`	Load the mouse driver.
`FILES=35`	Increase the number of files DOS can have open at once.
`BUFFERS=25`	Increase the DOS buffers.
`BREAK=ON`	Turn break on.
`LASTDRIVE=N`	Set the last drive DOS will use.

8-2 NOTUSED.COM, the CONFIG.SYS file in Fig. 8-1 renamed.

This is by no means a fool-proof method. First, your COMSPEC variable points to your real COMMAND.COM, so any virus can check its contents and infect COMMAND.COM no matter where it's located or what it's named. There's also a second, thought less obvious, problem. You have to make sure that your path statement doesn't point to the root directory, or you could end up running the "fake" COMMAND.COM. For example, Microsoft Word lets you shell to the DOS prompt by entering Escape Transfer Run Command. What it does is run a second copy of the command processor. If your root directory is in your PATH and comes before the directory containing the proper version of COM-MAND.COM, Word will run the fake version. No matter how your path is set, Word will run the fake version if it's logged into the root directory when you issue this command.

Test your critical files

You can test COMMAND.COM against a good copy with a batch file. This requires that you have a good copy stored under a different name available for test-

Batch File Line	Explanation
`@ECHO OFF`	Turn command-echoing off.
`REM TESTCOMM.BAT`	Remark giving the name of the batch file.

`REM Simple Anti-Viral Program`
`REM to Test COMMAND.COM`
`REM I Have COMMAND.COM Stored in`
`REM My \SYSLIB Subdirectory Rather`
`REM Than in my Root Directory`
`REM There is an Identical`
`REM Copy in my \MISC Subdirectory`
`REM Under the Name TEST.TXT`
	Documentation remarks.

`FC \SYSLIB\COMMAND.COM` `    \MISC\TEST.TXT`	Run the program File Compare and test COMMAND.COM against a copy stored in a subdirectory under a different name.
`IF ERRORLEVEL 1 GOTO VIRUS`	If the FC program reports an error, jump to an error-handling routine.
`GOTO END`	If the batch file reaches this point, there was no error, so exit the batch file.
`:VIRUS`	Label marking the beginning of the error-handling routine.
`ECHO COMMAND.COM MODIFIED!` `ECHO Find Problem Before Continuing`	Tell the user what has happened.
`PAUSE`	Pause execution of the batch file so the user will have time to read the message.
`:END`	Label marking the end of the batch file.

8-3　TESTCOMM.BAT, which tests your COMMAND.COM against a "good" copy.

ing. The COMP command won't work because it doesn't return a DOS ErrorLevel setting. Most versions of DOS include a program called FC that does return the ErrorLevel of one if the two files are different. The batch file in Fig. 8-3 shows how to perform this test. Notice that here, the good copy can (and should) have a different name. You could add this to your AUTOEXEC.BAT file to test COMMAND.COM every time you boot. You could also run the comparison only occasionally, as explained in the next chapter.

This test isn't restricted to COMMAND.COM, or even program files. You could have the batch file test any or all critical files on your hard disk. That would require a lot of room, however, because you need a second copy of any files you're testing. The test takes about ten seconds on my 386/20, so doing more than one or two tests in the AUTOEXEC.BAT file could significantly slow down booting. For multiple tests, you might want to create a separate batch file that you run once a day or even once every few days.

Summary

The following are points that have been covered in this chapter:

- Making COMMAND.COM and other program files read-only might stop a simple virus.
- Hiding COMMAND.COM in a subdirectory and even changing its name might stop some viruses.
- You can compare COMMAND.COM and other mission-critical programs against known good copies to see if they've been modified.

None of these methods are as good as running a good anti-viral software package, but users with only a low chance of infection will probably find these measures adequate.

Part 3
Software to turbocharge your batch files

9

CHAPTER

Improving your batch files

Communication with a batch file is always in one direction; the batch file "talks" to the user with ECHO statements. The only way you can communicate with a batch file is by using replaceable parameters when you start the batch file. Once it's running, you have no control over it. In addition, a batch file has no way to access the time, disk space, or other useful functions.

Check

A batch file can also execute one or more programs. The programs presented in this chapter takes advantage of that facility in order to allow the user to communicate with the batch file. For example, earlier in this book, you looked at a batch file called KILL.BAT. This batch file (shown in Fig. 9-1) performs a directory of the files to be erased and then pauses while the user decides between pressing Ctrl−Break to stop it or any other key to allow it to continue. A program called Check (CHECK.COM on the disk), allows you to replace this with a question, asking the user what to do and then test on his response.

As useful as this is, Check also does much more. Check uses 16 keywords to communicate with the user. The keywords follow the CHECK command, and are shown in Table 9-1. The best way to learn to use Check is to simply use it. Figure 9-2 shows CHECK1.BAT, a long batch file that uses every keyword of Check. It illustrates the proper syntax, as well as techniques for branching and decision making based on the results of running Check. Figure 9-3 shows CHECK1.BAT running. There are numerous possible usages for this program:

Batch File Line	Explanation
ECHO OFF	Turns echo off.
REM KILL.BAT	Remark to give the name of the batch file. Since echo is off, it does not show when the batch file runs.
DIR %1/W	Lists all the files in the current subdirectory in wide format.
ECHO Hit Control Break to STOP the erase	The first of two lines telling the user what is going on and how to stop the batch file.
ECHO of these files	The second line of information for the user.
PAUSE	Pauses the batch file until the user presses a key. This gives the user the chance to abort the batch file and not erase the files.
ERASE %1	Erases the batch files specified by the user if Ctrl-Break is not pressed.

9-1   KILL.BAT, which allows the user to stop the file deletion process by entering a Ctrl–Break.

Table 9-1   CHECK keywords.

Keyword	Syntax	Function
8087 80287	CHECK 8087 CHECK 80287	Returns a 0 if there is a math coprocessor, a 1 if there is not a math coprocessor.
DAY	CHECK DAY	Returns the day of the month.
DISKSPACE	CHECK DISKSPACE	Returns the amount of free disk space on the default disk drive. Because of the limits of ERRORLEVEL, DISKSPACE cannot simply report the disk space. Instead, it reports the number of full 16K blocks. So 200K is reported as 12. (200/16 = 12.5).
FILEFOUND	CHECK FILEFOUND *file*	Returns a 0 if the file exists and a 1 if it does not exist.
FILESIZE	CHECK FILESIZE *file* (No wildcards)	Returns the size of a file in Ks. The maximum ERRORLEVEL value is 255, so all files 255K or larger return a value of 255.
FILETEXT	CHECK FILETEXT *file text* (No wildcards)	Returns a 0 if the text is found, a 1 if the text is not found or if the program encounters an error, such as the file does not exist. The text must match exactly, including capitalization.
KEYBOARD	CHECK KEYBOARD	Returns a 1 if there are keystrokes in the keyboard buffers, 0 if not.

Table 9-1 Continued

Keyword	Syntax	Function
KEYPRESS	CHECK KEYPRESS	Returns the ASCII value of any key that is pressed. If a key is pressed that produces an extended code (e.g., function key or cursor key) a 0 is returned. Note: lower- and uppercase keys return different values.
MEMORY	CHECK MEMORY	Reports the total memory (not the free memory) in 16K blocks. So 40 corresponds to 640K (40*16). Not all this memory will be available.
MODEL	CHECK MODEL	Returns the computer model number on IBM machines. It might not work on some clones. The codes are: Code Machine 255 PC 254 XT and Portable PC 253 PCjr 252 AT 249 PC Convertible
MONTH	CHECK MONTH	Returns the month, Jan.=1, Feb.=2, and so on.
TIME	CHECK TIME	Returns the current hour in 24-hour format. So 1 PM to 1:59 PM returns a code of 13.
VERSION	CHECK VERSION	Returns the current version of DOS. Only the first number is reported. So 3.3, 3.2, 3.1, and 3.0 all return a 3. This is required since ERRORLEVEL supports only whole numbers. DOS versions prior to 2.0 are not supported.
VIDEOCARD	CHECK VIDEOCARD	Returns a code to indicate the type of video display. The codes are: Code Display Type 0 MDA 1 CGA 2 EGA
VIDEOMODE	CHECK VIDEOMODE	Returns current video mode (1-16).

Batch File Line	Explanation
ECHO OFF	Turn command-echoing off.
REM CHECK1.BAT	Remark giving the name of the batch file.
CHECK 8087 IF ERRORLEVEL 1 ECHO No math coprocessor exists IF ERRORLEVEL 1 GOTO 80287 IF ERRORLEVEL 0 ECHO Math coprocessor exists IF ERRORLEVEL 0 GOTO 80287	Check for 8087 math coprocessor. If found, tell user. Otherwise, look for an 80287 coprocessor.
:80287 CHECK 80287 IF ERRORLEVEL 1 ECHO No math coprocessor exists IF ERRORLEVEL 1 GOTO DAY IF ERRORLEVEL 0 ECHO Math coprocessor exists IF ERRORLEVEL 0 GOTO DAY	Check for 80287 math coprocessor. If found, tell user. Otherwise, skip to next section.
:DAY CHECK DAY IF ERRORLEVEL 31 ECHO 31th of month IF ERRORLEVEL 31 GOTO DISKSPAC IF ERRORLEVEL 30 ECHO 30th of month The batch file continues in a similar fashion for days 29-3 IF ERRORLEVEL 2 ECHO 2th of month IF ERRORLEVEL 2 GOTO DISKSPAC IF ERRORLEVEL 1 ECHO 1th of month IF ERRORLEVEL 1 GOTO DISKSPAC	Run Check to set the ERRORLEVEL equal to the day of the month then perform a series of ERRORLEVEL tests to echo the day. Note that after echoing the day, it jumps to the next test.
:DISKSPAC CHECK DISKSPACE IF ERRORLEVEL 255 ECHO More than 4080K free on hard disk IF ERRORLEVEL 255 GOTO FILEFOUN IF ERRORLEVEL 200 ECHO More than 3200K and less than 4080K free on hard disk IF ERRORLEVEL 200 GOTO FILEFOUN The batch file continues in a similar fashion for 2400K-160K. IF ERRORLEVEL 10 ECHO More than 160K and less than 800K free on hard disk IF ERRORLEVEL 10 GOTO FILEFOUN ECHO Less than 160K free GOTO FILEFOUN	Run Check to set the ERRORLEVEL equal to the amount of free space on the hard disk. Then perform a series of ERROR-LEVEL tests to echo the amount of space on the disk.

9-2 CHECK1.BAT, which uses every CHECK keyword.

9-2 Continued

Batch File Line	Explanation

`:FILEFOUN`
`CHECK FILEFOUND NO-FILE.TXT`
`IF ERRORLEVEL 1 ECHO NO-FILE.TXT missing`
`IF ERRORLEVEL 1 GOTO FILEFOU2`
`IF ERRORLEVEL 0 ECHO NO-FILE.TXT found`
`IF ERRORLEVEL 0 GOTO FILEFOU2`
 	
The batch file repeats this test for the file CHECK1.BAT in order to show what happens when the file exists.
	Run Check to see if NO-FILE.TXT exists and set the ERRORLEVEL accordingly. Then use a series of ERRORLEVEL tests to display the results.

`:FILESIZE`
`CHECK FILESIZE CHECKERR.BAT`
`IF ERRORLEVEL 255 ECHO File was 255K`
`   or larger`
`IF ERRORLEVEL 255 GOTO FILETEXT`
`IF ERRORLEVEL 200 ECHO File was 200-254k`
`IF ERRORLEVEL 200 GOTO FILETEXT`
 	
The batch file continues in a similar fashion for 199K-
 	
`IF ERRORLEVEL 1 ECHO File was 1K`
`IF ERRORLEVEL 1 GOTO FILETEXT`
`IF ERRORLEVEL 0 ECHO File was 0K or did`
`   not exist!`
`IF ERRORLEVEL 0 GOTO FILETEXT`
	Run Check to find the size of a specific file and place it in the ERRORLEVEL. Then use a series of ERRORLEVEL tests to echo that value.

`:FILETEXT`
`CHECK FILETEXT CHECK1.BAT 'CHECK'`
`IF ERRORLEVEL 1 ECHO Text not found in`
`   CHECK1.BAT or error encountered`
`IF ERRORLEVEL 1 GOTO FILETXT2`
`IF ERRORLEVEL 0 ECHO Text found in`
`   CHECK1.BAT`
`IF ERRORLEVEL 0 GOTO FILETXT2`
 	
The batch file performs the same test on a second set of text as an illustration.
	Run Check to see if the text CHECK exists in the file CHECK1.BAT and store the results in the ERRORLEVEL. Then use a series of ERRORLEVEL tests to display the results.

`:KEYBOARD`
`CHECK KEYBOARD`
`IF ERRORLEVEL 1 ECHO Keystroke waiting`
`IF ERRORLEVEL 1 GOTO KEYPRESS`
`IF ERRORLEVEL 0 ECHO Keystroke not waiting`
`IF ERRORLEVEL 0 GOTO KEYPRESS`
	Test for a keystroke waiting and place the results into ERROR-LEVEL. A series of ERRORLEVEL tests displays the results.

9-2 Continued

Batch File Line	Explanation
:KEYPRESS CHECK KEYPRESS IF ERRORLEVEL 122 ECHO z Pressed IF ERRORLEVEL 122 GOTO MEMORY IF ERRORLEVEL 121 ECHO y Pressed IF ERRORLEVEL 121 GOTO MEMORY The batch file continues in a similar fashion for the remaining letters along with all the capital letters.	Run Check to see which key was pressed and place the value in ERRORLEVEL. A series of ERRORLEVEL tests displays the value.
:MEMORY CHECK MEMORY IF ERRORLEVEL 40 ECHO At least 640K RAM available IF ERRORLEVEL 40 GOTO MODEL IF ERRORLEVEL 39 ECHO 624K available IF ERRORLEVEL 39 GOTO MODEL The batch file continues in a similar fashion for 608K-496K IF ERRORLEVEL 30 ECHO 480K available IF ERRORLEVEL 30 GOTO MODEL ECHO Less than 480K available	Run Check to measure the amount of RAM and place the value into ERRORLEVEL. A series of ERRORLEVEL tests displays the value.
:MODEL CHECK MODEL IF ERRORLEVEL 255 ECHO PC IF ERRORLEVEL 255 GOTO MONTH IF ERRORLEVEL 254 ECHO XT or Portable PC IF ERRORLEVEL 254 GOTO MONTH IF ERRORLEVEL 253 ECHO PCjr IF ERRORLEVEL 253 GOTO MONTH IF ERRORLEVEL 252 ECHO AT IF ERRORLEVEL 252 GOTO MONTH IF ERRORLEVEL 250 ECHO Unknown machine IF ERRORLEVEL 250 GOTO MONTH IF ERRORLEVEL 249 ECHO PC Convertible IF ERRORLEVEL 249 GOTO MONTH ECHO Unknown machine	Run Check to find out the type of computer and place the value into ERROR-LEVEL. A series of ERRORLEVEL tests displays that value.
:MONTH CHECK MONTH IF ERRORLEVEL 12 ECHO December IF ERRORLEVEL 12 GOTO TIME IF ERRORLEVEL 11 ECHO November IF ERRORLEVEL 11 GOTO TIME The batch file continues in a similar fashion for October-February. IF ERRORLEVEL 1 ECHO January IF ERRORLEVEL 1 GOTO TIME	Run Check to find the month of the year and place it into the ERROR-LEVEL. A series of ERRORLEVEL tests displays the value.

9-2 Continued

Batch File Line	Explanation
:TIME CHECK TIME IF ERRORLEVEL 23 ECHO After 11PM IF ERRORLEVEL 23 GOTO END IF ERRORLEVEL 22 ECHO 10PM - 11PM IF ERRORLEVEL 22 GOTO END The batch file continues in a similar fashion for 10PM-3AM IF ERRORLEVEL 1 ECHO 1AM - 2AM IF ERRORLEVEL 1 GOTO END IF ERRORLEVEL 0 ECHO Midnight - 1AM IF ERRORLEVEL 0 GOTO END	Run Check to find the time and place it into the ERRORLEVEL. A series of ERRORLEVEL tests displays the value.
:END	Label marking the end of the batch file.

```
C>CHECK1
No math coprocessor exists
28th of month
More than 2400K and less than 3200K free on hard disk
NO-FILE.TXT missing
CHECK1.BAT found
File was 10-19K
Text found in CHECK1.BAT
Text not found in CHECKERR.BAT or error encountered
Keystroke not waiting
OTHER KEY PRESSED
At least 640K RAM available
AT
March
7PM - 8PM
C>
```

9-3 Screen showing the results of running CHECK1.BAT in Fig. 9-2.

- When you start your word processor, erase all the *.BAK files if your B drive is cramped for space.
- The MIS department can distribute a new program that will install itself only if there is enough space for all the files.
- A batch file can decide which version of a program to run depending whether the system has a color or monochrome monitor, or if there is a math coprocessor installed.

Of course, this is just a short list of suggestions. I'm sure you'll have more uses for Check.

InKey

Check is a very powerful program. However, if all you want to do is ask the user a question, it might be too powerful. InKey (INKEY.COM on the disk) is a program that overcomes this problem. InKey was written by Stephen Moore, the TAB Books acquiring editor for this book.

Like Check, InKey can query the user. Unlike Check, that's all InKey can do. A copy of InKey for several different types of keyboard is on the disk. The command to use InKey in your batch file is:

INKEY [*prompt*]

InKey displays the prompt and waits for the user to press any key. InKey sets the ErrorLevel value based on the key the user presses.

The prompt can be up to 80 characters long, and can contain anything except the four DOS redirection operators >, |, <, or > > and the dollar sign ($). The INKEY prompt routine can include almost any character string, including ANSI .SYS cursor positioning and video attribute commands. These provide the opportunity to generate some highly creative menu screens.

For the standard ASCII characters Ctrl−A through lowercase z, InKey returns the normal ASCII value of the key. You need to test the alphabetic characters only for their uppercase forms, ASCII 65 through 90, because InKey converts all lowercase keystrokes to uppercase. This makes testing for menu selections much easier. For the non-ASCII keys (like the function keys), obtain the key's ErrorLevel value from Tables 9-2 through 9-4, depending on your keyboard. If a key you need isn't listed, you can run InKey and then use CHECKERR.BAT (from chapter 2) to test the ErrorLevel value.

An interesting side effect for the standard keys is that Ctrl−C (ASCII 3) is reported just like any other character, without stopping your batch file. Because InKey doesn't flush the keyboard buffer, however, Ctrl−Break brings up the *Terminate batch job (Y/N)?* message. This quirk allows you to give your users the familiar Ctrl−C "escape pod" without bombing the whole routine.

Figure 9-4 shows how 2.BAT from chapter 6 can be modified to load the mouse driver, but only if the user answers Yes to the prompt. Also note the Ctrl−Gs used in the prompt to ring the computer bell so the user won't miss the prompt.

A final note on using InKey. I originally tried to write 2-2.BAT so it would run the commercial memory-resident program manager POPDROP to temporarily load the mouse driver and unload it when I left Lotus. This created a problem, however, because POPDROP sets the ErrorLevel value, which overwrites the value set by InKey. If you need to make multiple tests on the ErrorLevel value set

Table 9-2   Extended keycodes and upshifted ErrorLevel values for 83/84-key keyboards.

Extended Key Code	ERROR-LEVEL	Key	Extended Key Code	ERROR-LEVEL	Key
15	138	Shift-Tab	90	213	Shift-F7
16	139	Alt-Q	91	214	Shift-F8
17	140	Alt-W	92	215	Shift-F9
18	141	Alt-E	93	216	Shift-F10
19	142	Alt-R	94	217	Ctrl-F1
20	143	Alt-T	95	218	Ctrl-F2
21	144	Alt-Y	96	219	Ctrl-F3
22	145	Alt-U	97	220	Ctrl-F4
23	146	Alt-I	98	221	Ctrl-F5
24	147	Alt-O	99	222	Ctrl-F6
25	148	Alt-P	100	223	Ctrl-F7
30	153	Alt-A	101	224	Ctrl-F8
31	154	Alt-S	102	225	Ctrl-F9
32	155	Alt-D	103	226	Ctrl-F10
33	156	Alt-F	104	227	Alt-F1
34	157	Alt-G	105	228	Alt-F2
35	158	Alt-H	106	229	Alt-F3
36	159	Alt-J	107	230	Alt-F4
37	160	Alt-K	108	231	Alt-F5
38	161	Alt-L	109	232	Alt-F6
44	167	Alt-Z	110	233	Alt-F7
45	168	Alt-X	111	234	Alt-F8
46	169	Alt-C	112	235	Alt-F9
47	170	Alt-V	113	236	Alt-F10
48	171	Alt-B	114	237	Ctrl-PrtSc
49	172	Alt-N	115	238	Ctrl-left-arrow
50	173	Alt-M	116	239	Ctrl-right-arrow
59	182	F1	117	240	Ctrl-End
60	183	F2	118	241	Ctrl-PgDn
61	184	F3	119	242	Ctrl-Home
62	185	F4	120	243	Alt-1
63	186	F5	121	244	Alt-2
64	187	F6	122	245	Alt-3
65	188	F7	123	246	Alt-4
66	189	F8	124	247	Alt-5
67	190	F9	125	248	Alt-6
68	191	F10	126	249	Alt-7
84	207	Shift-F1	127	250	Alt-8
85	208	Shift-F2	128	251	Alt-9

Table 9-2   Continued

Extended Key Code	ERROR-LEVEL	Key	Extended Key Code	ERROR-LEVEL	Key
86	209	Shift-F3	129	252	Alt-0
87	210	Shift-F4	130	253	Alt-Hyphen
88	211	Shift-F5	131	254	Alt-=
89	212	Shift-F6	132	255	Ctrl-PgUp

Table 9-3   Extended keycodes and upshifted ErrorLevel values for Tandy keyboards.

Extended Key Code	ERROR-LEVEL	Key	Extended Key Code	ERROR-LEVEL	Key
44	---	Alt-Z	112	184	Alt-F9
45	---	Alt-X	113	185	Alt-F10
46	---	Alt-C	114	186	Ctrl-PrtSc
47	---	Alt-V	115	187	Ctrl-left-arrow
48	---	Alt-B	116	188	Ctrl-right-arrow
49	---	Alt-N	117	189	Ctrl-End
50	---	Alt-M	118	190	Ctrl-PgDn
59	131	F1	119	191	Ctrl-Home
60	132	F2	120	192	Alt-1
61	133	F3	121	193	Alt-2
62	134	F4	122	194	Alt-3
63	135	F5	123	195	Alt-4
64	136	F6	124	196	Alt-5
65	137	F7	125	197	Alt-6
66	138	F8	126	198	Alt-7
67	139	F9	127	199	Alt-8
68	140	F10	128	200	Alt-9
70	142	Alt-PrtSc	129	201	Alt-0
71	143	Home	130	202	Alt-Hyphen
72	144	up-arrow	131	203	Alt-=
73	145	Shift-PgUp	132	204	Ctrl-PgUp
74	146	Shift-Home	133	205	Shift-up-arrow
75	147	left-arrow	134	206	Shift-down-arrow
77	149	right-arrow	135	207	Shift-left-arrow
79	151	Shift-End	136	208	Shift-right-arrow
80	152	down-arrow	140	212	Alt-Backspace
81	153	Shift-PgDn	141	213	Ctrl-Tab
83	155	Shift-Del	142	214	Alt-Tab
84	156	Shift-F1	143	215	Alt-Enter
85	157	Shift-F2	144	216	Ctrl-up-arrow
86	158	Shift-F3	145	217	Alt-up-arrow
87	159	Shift-F4	146	218	Alt-left-arrow
88	160	Shift-F5	147	219	Ctrl-7
89	161	Shift-F6	148	220	Ctrl-8

Table 9-3 Continued

Extended Key Code	ERROR-LEVEL	Key	Extended Key Code	ERROR-LEVEL	Key
90	162	Shift-F7	149	221	Ctrl-4
91	163	Shift-F8	150	222	Ctrl-down-arrow
92	164	Shift-F9	151	223	Alt-down-arrow
93	165	Shift-F10	152	224	F11
94	166	Ctrl-F1	153	225	F12
95	167	Ctrl-F2	154	226	Ctrl-2 (keypad)
96	168	Ctrl-F3	155	227	Shift-0 (keypad)
97	169	Ctrl-F4	156	228	Ctrl-0 (keypad)
98	170	Ctrl-F5	157	229	Ctrl-Del
99	171	Ctrl-F6	158	230	Alt-Del
100	172	Ctrl-F7	159	231	Ctrl-Ins
101	173	Ctrl-F8	160	232	Alt-Ins
102	174	Ctrl-F9	161	233	Shift-. (keypad)
103	175	Ctrl-F10	162	234	Shift-F11
104	176	Alt-F1	163	235	Shift-F12
105	177	Alt-F2	164	236	Ctrl-. (keypad)
106	178	Alt-F3	165	237	Alt-. (keypad)
107	179	Alt-F4	166	238	Alt-Home
108	180	Alt-F5	172	244	Ctrl-F11
109	181	Alt-F6	173	245	Ctrl-F12
110	182	Alt-F7	182	254	Alt-F11
111	183	Alt-F8	183	255	Alt-F12

Table 9-4 Extended keycodes and upshifted ErrorLevel values for enhanced IBM keyboards.

Extended Key Code	ERROR-LEVEL	Key	Extended Key Code	ERROR-LEVEL	Key
44	133	Alt-Z	115	204	Ctrl-left-arrow
45	134	Alt-X	116	205	Ctrl-right-arrow
46	135	Alt-C	117	206	Ctrl-End
47	136	Alt-V	118	207	Ctrl-PgDn
48	137	Alt-B	119	208	Ctrl-Home
49	138	Alt-N	120	209	Alt-1
50	139	Alt-M	121	210	Alt-2
59	148	F1	122	211	Alt-3
60	149	F2	123	212	Alt-4
61	150	F3	124	213	Alt-5
62	151	F4	125	214	Alt-6
63	152	F5	126	215	Alt-7
64	153	F6	127	216	Alt-8
65	154	F7	128	217	Alt-9
66	155	F8	129	218	Alt-0

Table 9-4 Continued

Extended Key Code	ERROR-LEVEL	Key	Extended Key Code	ERROR-LEVEL	Key
67	156	F9	130	219	Alt-Hyphen
68	157	F10	131	220	Alt-=
84	173	Shift-F1	132	221	Ctrl-PgUp
85	174	Shift-F2	133	222	F11
86	175	Shift-F3	134	223	F12
87	176	Shift-F4	135	224	Shift-F11
88	177	Shift-F5	136	225	Shift-F12
89	178	Shift-F6	137	226	Ctrl-F11
90	179	Shift-F7	138	227	Ctrl-F12
91	180	Shift-F8	139	228	Alt-F11
92	181	Shift-F9	140	229	Alt-F12
93	182	Shift-F10	141	230	Ctrl-up-arrow
94	183	Ctrl-F1	142	231	Ctrl-- (keypad)
95	184	Ctrl-F2	143	232	Ctrl-5 (keypad)
96	185	Ctrl-F3	144	233	Ctrl-+ (keypad)
97	186	Ctrl-F4	145	234	Ctrl-down-arrow
98	187	Ctrl-F5	146	235	Ctrl-Ins
99	188	Ctrl-F6	147	236	Ctrl-Del
100	189	Ctrl-F7	148	237	Ctrl-Tab
101	190	Ctrl-F8	149	238	Ctrl-/
102	191	Ctrl-F9	150	239	Ctrl-*
103	192	Ctrl-F10	151	240	Alt-Home
104	193	Alt-F1	152	241	Alt-up-arrow
105	194	Alt-F2	153	242	Alt-PgUp
106	195	Alt-F3	155	243	Alt-left-arrow
107	196	Alt-F4	157	244	Alt-right-arrow
108	197	Alt-F5	159	248	Alt-End
109	198	Alt-F6	160	249	Alt-down-arrow
110	199	Alt-F7	161	250	Alt-PgDn
111	200	Alt-F8	162	251	Alt-Ins
112	201	Alt-F9	163	252	Alt-Del
113	202	Alt-F10	164	253	Alt-/
114	203	Ctrl-PrtSc	165	254	Alt-Tab
166	255	Alt-Enter			

by InKey and you need to run other programs in between these tests, you must store the ErrorLevel value in the environment. Figure 9-5 shows 2-3.BAT, which is 2-2.BAT modified to perform multiple ErrorLevel tests.

InKey is very flexible and can be highly modified. The disk that comes with this book has a version for the regular, enhanced, and older Tandy keyboards. If

Batch File Line	Explanation
ECHO OFF	Turn command-echoing off.
REM 2-2.BAT	Remark giving the name of the batch file.
INKEY-E Do you want to load your mouse driver?	Run InKey with the prompt "Do you want to load your mouse driver?"
CD\123	Change to the Lotus subdirectory.
IF ERRORLEVEL 89 IF NOT ERRORLEVEL 90 123MOUSE	If the user answered yes, run 123Mouse to load the mouse driver.
123	Run Lotus 1-2-3.
MENU	Reload the menu.

9-4 2-2.BAT, a modified version of 2.BAT from chapter 6, which is modified to load a mouse driver.

Batch File Line	Explanation
ECHO OFF	Turn command-echoing off.
REM 2-3.BAT	Remark giving the name of the batch file.
REM Set default value to environment	Remark providing documentation.
SET MOUSE=NO	Set an environmental variable.
INKEY-E Do you want to load your mouse driver?	Run InKey with the prompt "Do you want to load your mouse driver?"
CD\123	Change to the Lotus subdirectory.
REM Change default value only if Y pressed	Remark providing documentation.
IF ERRORLEVEL 89 IF NOT ERRORLEVEL 90 SET MOUSE=YES	If the user pressed yes, store a YES in the MOUSE environmental variable. This is required since PopDrop resets the ERRORLEVEL.
IF %MOUSE%==YES POPDROP U	If the user pressed yes, run PopDrop and set a memory marker so the mouse program can be unloaded.
IF %MOUSE%==YES 123MOUSE	If the user pressed yes, run 123Mouse.
123	Run Lotus.
IF %MOUSE%==YES POPDROP D	If the user pressed yes, unload 123Mouse using PopDrop.
MENU	Reload the menu.

9-5 2-3.BAT, a modified version of 2-2.BAT, which performs multiple ErrorLevel tests.

you have a special application where you need to modify InKey, you'll find complete instructions in appendix B. These instructions are somewhat technical in nature. Most users should be able to ignore appendix B and use just one of the versions of InKey on the disk.

Answer

Answer, from Frank Schweiger, lets you ask a question and then places the response in the environment attached to the variable Answer. You can then set another variable equal to Answer and ask the user another question. Following this procedure, you can obtain as much information from the user as will fit in the environment. Figure 9-6 shows a batch file that does just this.

Batch File Line	Explanation
@ECHO OFF	Turn command-echoing off.
REM This file demonstrates ANSWER.COM	Documentation remark.
SET	Displays the contents of the environment. The batch file does this for illustration purposes.
ANSWER Enter the drive with the file to copy	Run ANSWER.COM with a prompt. Answer takes the user's response and places it into the environment under the name ANSWER.
SET	Displays the contents of the environment.
SET DRIVE=%ANSWER%	Stores the contents of the environmental variable ANSWER in another variable. Since ANSWER.COM uses the same name each time it runs, you must do this if you plan on collecting more than one response. Notice that the batch file used the response without error checking. This is not generally a good idea.
ANSWER Enter the file name to copy	Runs Answer again to get another response.
SET	Displays the contents of the environment.
SET FILE=%ANSWER%	Stores the user's response under an alternative environmental variable.
ANSWER Enter destination	Runs Answer again to get another response.
SET	Displays the contents of the environment.
SET TO=%ANSWER%	Stores the user's response under an alternative environmental variable.
COPY %DRIVE%%FILE% %TO%	Constructs a command using the three user responses. If this were an actual batch file rather than a demonstration, the batch file would need extensive error checking.

9-6   ANSWER1.BAT, which lets you ask a question, and places the answer directly in the environment.

Answer is a very powerful and useful program; however, it does have a couple of problems. The first is that, even if you include spaces after the prompt, the user still has to enter a response justified against the Answer prompt. There seems no way to avoid this. The second problem is that Answer doesn't reset the cursor position when printing the prompt, so the next ECHO or system message gets printed over this line. Of course, you no longer need the prompt but it makes the screen look sloppy. You can avoid this problem by issuing a CLS command immediately after using Answer to obtain information.

A more serious problem is that Answer doesn't work with all versions of DOS. It was written several years ago and the author hasn't updated it. It works with DOS 4.0 and DOS 3.2, but not with Compaq DOS 3.3. Until upgraded, it looks like it'll be hit or miss if it will run on your computer.

Reboot

In this book I discuss several ways to alter the configuration of your environment for different applications. The methods I've discussed are a custom batch file that copies selected files on top of the existing AUTOEXEC.BAT and CONFIG.SYS files and reboots the computer, and a separate boot-floppy disk that's maintained for each application.

Reboot (REBOOT21.EXE on the disk) is a program by Robert L. Miller that automates the batch file described in the first option above. If you enter:

```
REBOOT21 ABC
```

ReBoot will issue the two commands:

```
COPY AUTOEXEC.ABC AUTOEXEC.BAT
COPY CONFIG.ABC CONFIG.SYS
```

and reboot the computer. If you can't remember the specific extension you want to use, you can run Reboot with no command-line arguments. It will present you with a sorted list of AUTOEXEC.* files to select from.

One other note about using Reboot. REBOOT21.EXE must be in your root directory. It won't work from any other subdirectory even if that subdirectory is in your PATH. In addition, all your AUTOEXEC.* and CONFIG.* files must be in the root directory. Using Reboot, you can add a new set of AUTOEXEC.* and CONFIG.* files at any time without having to rewrite anything.

The Down and Dirty Dozen Batch Utilities

The Down and Dirty Dozen Batch Utilities are a collection of 12 utilities that expand the power of DOS batch files. They are listed in Table 9-5. The Down and Dirty Dozen Batch Utilities are shareware, with a very reasonable ten dollar registration fee. A site license is also available. For more information, contact:

G&G COMPUTER SERVICES
39 Cathy Circle
Portsmouth, RI 02871

Table 9-5 The Down and Dirty Dozen Batch Utilities.

Utility	Function
0-9	Waits for a number key from 0 to 9 to be pressed, and then returns the number of that key as the ERRORLEVEL. For example, pressing the 8 key sets ERRORLEVEL to 8. This program greatly simplifies option selection in a batch file if you have ten or fewer options. 0-9 does not display a prompt, so you must take care of that with an ECHO statement first.
BEEP	Makes the speaker beep the same as echoing a Ctrl-G. It cannot control the frequency or duration .
CLW	Clears a part of the screen in a rectangle using the coordinates you specify and sets the foreground and background colors.
DAY	Returns the day of the week as an ERRORLEVEL. It returns a one for Sunday, a two for Monday, and so on.
DR_BOX	Draws a box with single or double lined border at the position you specify. The box is drawn from ASCII characters with an ASCII "shadow." The routine does not reposition the cursor at the bottom of the screen after drawing the box so you must take care of cursor positioning manually or you will end up with a strange looking screen.
FCLS1 FCLS2	Fancy routines to clear the screen.
IS_TODAY	Compares the clock date against a date you specify on the command line. If they match the program returns an ERRORLEVEL of one; otherwise, it returns a zero.
MODE_ON	Returns an ERRORLEVEL code to indicate the system display mode. It incorrectly identified some VGA modes.
PRT_ON	Checks the specified printer port and returns an ERRORLEVEL of one if the printer is off, a zero if it is on.
PRTAT	Locates the cursor at a specified position on the screen and optionally prints the specified text. You would use this to print in the boxes and colored clear areas created by other utilities in this package.
YES_NO	Waits for either the Y or N key to be pressed, and returns an ERRORLEVEL of one for the Y and two for the N. It ignores any other keys. It cannot print an error message if the user presses another key.

Get

Get is an extremely powerful program that you can run from within a batch file to gain additional information for the batch file to act on. What makes Get especially powerful is it not only returns information via DOS ErrorLevel, it also places identical information in an environmental variable called GET. Often, that makes testing much easier. You would access this variable in a batch file using %GET%.

Use Get with the command GET, along with optional parameters to tell it what to do. The parameters it recognizes are listed in Table 9-6. Get was written by Bob Stephan and placed in the public domain. A copy of GET.EXE (the program) and GET.DOC (the documentation) are on the disk.

Table 9-6 GET parameters.

Parameter	Function
7	Checks for a math coprocessor and returns a 1 if one is available and a 0 if no math coprocessor is available. The value is returned to both the GET environmental variable and the ERRORLEVEL.
A	Checks for ANSI.SYS and returns a 1 if it is loaded and a 0 if ANSI.SYS is not loaded. The value is returned to both the GET environmental variable and the ERRORLEVEL.
B	Clears the screen and changes the foreground and background colors. The documentation does not give a list of colors, so you have to experiment to find a setting you like. It stores the color number you use in both the GET environmental variable and the ERRORLEVEL.
C	Causes Get to obtain a single character. Like most utilities of this type, it places the decimal code for the ASCII value in the ERRORLEVEL for standard testing. In addition, it places the capitalized character in the environmental variable GET. Because the value in the environmental variable is always capitalized, it reduces your testing by half. You can add an additional prompt with this command to tell the user which keys to press.
D	Gets the DOS version in use. It stores the major portion only in the GET environmental variable. So 3.0, 3.1 and 3.2 would all have 3 stored in the GET variable. It stores the major portion times ten plus the first decimal place times ten in the ERRORLEVEL. So 3.2 would have 32 (3*10+.2*10) stored in the ERRORLEVEL.
E	Stores the bytes left in the environment in both the ERRORLEVEL and the GET environmental variable. There is an additional optional switch to store the bytes/10 rather than the bytes.
F	Stores the size of a specified file in hex bytes in the GET environmental variable and the kilobytes in the ERRORLEVEL. There is an additional optional switch to store the bytes/10 rather than the bytes.

Table 9-6   Continued

Parameter	Function
K	Stores the kilobytes of free disk space in both the GET environmental variable and the ERRORLEVEL. There is an additional optional switch to store the bytes/10 rather than the bytes.
M	Stores the kilobytes of free memory in both the GET environmental variable and the ERRORLEVEL. There is an additional optional switch to store the bytes/10 rather than the bytes.
N	Just like the C parameter except it accepts only a Y (yes) or N (no). It beeps for any other key.
P	Checks for a printer and returns a 1 if one is available and a 0 if no printer is available. The value is returned to both the GET environmental variable and the ERRORLEVEL.
S	Prompts the user for a character string. It places the actual string in the GET environmental variable without converting it to all capitals. It places the length in the ERRORLEVEL. Like C and N, you can add an optional prompt.
T	A specialized version of the C parameter. Everything except the prompt is identical. Instead of a prompt character string, T takes a file as the prompt. The file must be 4K or smaller without a return or special characters. Get displays this file as a moving prompt at the bottom of the screen. It scrolls through the entire file and then starts over. It repeats this until a key is pressed. It then stores that key in the GET environmental variable and its decimal equivalent in the ERRORLEVEL.
V	Sets the video mode. The documentation does not give a list of modes, so you have to experiment to find a setting you like. It stores the number you use in both the GET environmental variable and the ERRORLEVEL. The documentation warns you not to use this option unless you know what you are doing.
Y	Returns the current subdirectory including the drive in the GET environmental variable. It returns the levels deep in the ERRORLEVEL. There is an optional switch to return the drive rather than the levels deep in the ERRORLEVEL.

Menuware Batch File Utilities

Menuware Batch File Utilities (Menuware for short) is a collection of shareware batch file utilities. There are 12 small utilities in all, listed in Table 9-7. These are shareware programs and you can register the entire package for $10. The author adds a strange extension to the shareware philosophy, called menuware. Under this, the author allows you to register only those programs you want to use. The individual registration fee is one dollar. However, many of the utilities, especially the system variable ones, work together so it seems to me you'd be better off just registering all of them. They are from:

INTERFACES, PEOPLE, AND MAGIC
Post Office Box 4496
Middletown, RI 02840

Table 9-7 Menuware Batch File Utilities.

Utility	Function
Add	Menuware can maintain a single "system variable" in low memory. This variable is not stored in the ERRORLEVEL value but has the same limitation. It must be an integer between -127 and 127. This variable stays in memory until the system is reset. Add increases the value of this variable by a specified amount.
AMIAT	This uses ERRORLEVEL to report if the current subdirectory matches the subdirectory listed after the AMIAT command.
CHTIMER	This reports the time since the STTIMER utility was run. The report is through the DOS ERRORLEVEL although the time is not stored there.
CMP	This compares the system variable to a specified value and reports via the DOS ERRORLEVEL if it is larger, smaller, or equal to the specified value.
CMPDS	This compares disk space to a specified value and reports via the DOS ERRORLEVEL if it is larger, smaller, or equal to the specified value.
DEC	This subtracts one from the system variable.
GDRIVE	This returns the current drive via the DOS ERRORLEVEL. For example, A:=1, B:=2, and so on.
INC	This increases the system variable by one.
STORE	This stores a specified value to the system variable.
STTIMER	This sets/resets the timer to zero.
SUB	This subtracts a specified amount from the system variable.
VALUE	This returns the value of the system variable via the DOS ERRORLEVEL. Since ERRORLEVEL is limited to integers from -127 to 127, the system variable is similarly limited.

SetError

The ErrorLevel feature of DOS is a nice feature; however, in writing this book I found two problems with it. I came across the first problem trying to test error handling routines. It's sometimes very difficult to force a specific ErrorLevel value so you can test what a batch file does when that condition exists. The second problem is that there's no easy way to reset the ErrorLevel to zero. I ran into this problem a lot while writing batch files that do a lot of error checking. I would run them once and force an error to see how they worked. (I originally did things like copying to a disk drive with the drive door open to force an error.) Once I'd run the test, the batch file would stop the next time because I hadn't reset the value.

SetError is a small program I wrote to correct this problem. The syntax is:

```
SETERROR #
```

where # is any integer from 0 to 255. The program sets the ErrorLevel to the number you specify and exits. If you enter anything other than an integer between 0 and 255, the program gives you an error message and exits without setting ErrorLevel. You can add the command:

    SETERROR 0

as one of the first commands (after @ECHO OFF) to any batch file where you use the ErrorLevel value for error trapping. That ensures that the batch file starts with a clean ErrorLevel value.

ShowEnvironment

As you learn more of the things you can accomplish in the DOS environment, you are likely to begin running out of space. ShowEnvironment is a small program I wrote to help you avoid this problem. To run it, enter:

    SHOWENVI

on the command line. The program then shows you how much total environmental space you have and how much of it remains free. That way, you can quickly decide if you need to expand the environment.

Norton Batch Enhancer

Peter Norton includes the Batch Enhancer in his utilities. (With Release 4.0 of the Norton Utilities, there was a standard and advanced version; only the advanced version contained the Batch Enhancer. With Release 5.0, that dual distinction of the utilities has been dropped.) Batch Enhancer began as a couple of small utilities like BEEP.COM. After a couple of rounds, these small utilities were compiled into a single program called BE.EXE. BE (short for Batch Enhancer) contains several different routines you call up with a keyword after the BE. For example, the command BE BEEP would run the Beep program exactly the same way as entering BEEP at the command line with the older version. Figure 9-7 illustrates

Batch File Line	Explanation
`@ECHO OFF`	Turn command-echoing off.
`REM NORTON.BAT`	Remark giving the name of the batch file.
`REM This batch file illustrates`	Documentation remark.
`REM the Norton Batch Enhancer`	Documentation remark.
`CLS`	Clear the screen.

9-7 NORTON.BAT, which illustrates the features of Norton Utilities' BE (Batch Enhancer).

9-7 Continued

Batch File Line	Explanation
BE ASK "Do you want to hear the computer beep (y/n) " ny	Run the Norton Utilities Batch Enhancer to get information from the user. The ny gives the responses it will accept. For the first acceptable response, it sets ERRORLEVEL to 1, and uses 2 for the second. This makes doing the tests easier than looking up ASCII values. It also ignores case.
CLS	Clears the screen.
REM The above line with set ERRORLEVEL to 2 for a y or Y	Documentation remark.
REM and 1 for a n or N	Documentation remark.
IF ERRORLEVEL 2 BE BEEP	Sound the speaker for a y response. No testing is required for an n since it has a lower ERRORLEVEL value.
BE ASK "Do you want to hear a high pitch beep (y/n) " ny DEFAULT=Y TIMEOUT=2	Prompt the user again. This line sets a default if the user presses return or lets the program run out of time. The TIMEOUT=2 says to use the default after two seconds.
CLS	Clear the screen.
REM Notice that this will time out after two seconds	Documentation remark.
REM with a default answer of y	Documentation remark.
IF ERRORLEVEL 2 BE BEEP /F5000 /D18	If the user answered yes, sound the speaker.
REM The tone will sound at 5K Hertz for 1 second	Documentation remark.
REM Notice that duration is specified in 1/18 second intervals	Documentation remark.
CLS	Documentation remark.
REM Now let's draw boxes on the screen	Documentation remark.
BE BOX 0, 0, 5,15,DOUBLE,BOLD,BLUE	Draw a blue, bold, double line on the screen from pixel 0,0 to 5,15.
BE BOX 5,15,10,30,DOUBLE,BOLD,BLUE	Draw a line.

9-7 Continued

Batch File Line	Explanation
BE BOX 10,30,15,45,DOUBLE,BOLD,BLUE	Draw a line.
BE BOX 15,45,20,60,DOUBLE,BOLD,BLUE	Draw a line.
BE ROWCOL 23,0	Position the cursor for the prompt to come next.
BE ASK "Press Any Key To Continue "TIMEOUT=10	Ask the user a question, and either take any answer or continue after ten seconds.
CLS	Clear the screen.
BE BOX 0, 0, 0,10,SINGLE,BOLD,WHITE BE BOX 0,10, 5,25,SINGLE,BOLD,WHITE BE BOX 3,13, 8,28,SINGLE,BOLD,WHITE BE BOX 9,19,14,34,SINGLE,BOLD,WHITE BE BOX 12,22,17,37,SINGLE,BOLD,WHITE BE BOX 15,25,20,40,SINGLE,BOLD,WHITE BE BOX 18,28,23,43,SINGLE,BOLD,WHITE	Draw two boxes on the screen, one line at a time.
BE ROWCOL 23,0	Position the cursor.
BE ASK "Press Any Key To Continue "TIMEOUT=10	Prompt the user.
CLS	Clear the screen.
BE PRINTCHAR -,80	Print one character 80 times.
ECHO Warning: Something is about to happen	Tell the user something is going to happen.
ECHO This is just a test	Message to user.
ECHO If it were a real warning	Message to user.
ECHO instructions would follow	Message to user.
BE PRINTCHAR -,80	Print one character 80 times.
BE ROWCOL 23,0	Position the cursor.
BE ASK "Press Any Key To Continue "TIMEOUT=10	Prompt the user.
CLS	Clear the screen.
BE ROWCOL 0,0,"Cursor is at top left of the screen"	Position the cursor and write to the screen.
BE ROWCOL 10,40,"Cursor is in the middle of the screen"	Position the cursor and write to the screen.
BE ROWCOL 22,79,"X"	Position the cursor and write to the screen.
BE ROWCOL 23,0,"X was printed at bottom right"	Position the cursor and write to the screen.
BE ROWCOL 23,0	Position the cursor.

9-7 Continued

Batch File Line	Explanation
BE ASK "Press Any Key To Set Screen Colors and Exit "TIMEOUT=10	Prompt the user.
CLS	Clear the screen.
BE SA BOLD WHITE ON BLUE	Set the screen colors.

all the features of BE, and the features are listed in Table 9-8. You can use Batch Enhancer to display windows on the screen. NORTON2.BAT in Fig. 9-8 shows a batch file that does windows.

The Norton Utilities Batch Enhancer includes a very nice option called Ask, which lets you get information from the user. Ask has a number of options, listed in Table 9-9. With skillful programming, you can even use Ask to get multiple responses from the user and combine them into a single ErrorLevel value. NOR-

Table 9-8   Norton Utilities Batch Enhancer features.

Features	Function
Ask	Basically an ERRORLEVEL tester you use to get a single byte of information from the user and pass it back in as an ERRORLEVEL. Ask is one of the best ERRORLEVEL testers around. The syntax for the command is BE ASK "*prompt*", *keys*, DEFAULT=*key*, TIMEOUT=#, ADJUST=*n*, *color,* and a typical batch line would be BE ASK "Files will be deleted! Continue (y/n) " ny, DEFAULT=n, TIMEOUT=5. The Ask options are listed in the next table.
Beep	Sounds a tone on the speaker. There are numerous options to control the tone. They include specifying the tone duration, frequency, the number of times the tone is repeated and the delay between repeats. These options let you play a large variations of tones. In fact, prior versions of the Norton Utilities contain a sample batch file that uses the Beep function to play Mary Had a Little Lamb and it does a good job.
Box	Draws a box on the screen. The syntax is BE BOX *top, left, bottom, right, line type, color* where top, left, bottom, and right specify box coordinates. Using the Batch Enhancer ROWCOL function, you can draw a box and then position the cursor to write text inside the box.
Printchar	Repeats a single character a specified number of times. It is a nice way to draw lines in a batch file.
Rowcol	Positions the cursor at a specific row and column on the screen and optionally displays text.
SA	Lets you set the color of the screen and text using English names like Red and Bright. The changes are not permanent unless you have loaded ANSI.SYS in your CONFIG.SYS, otherwise, they are reset by a CLS command.
Window	Much like the Box command except it includes options for zooming in the window and creating a shadow around the window. You specify the location and color just like the Box command.

Batch File Line	Explanation
@ECHO OFF	Turn command-echoing off.
REM NORTON2.BAT	Remark giving the name of the batch file.
REM Window demonstration	Documentation remark.
CLS	Clear the screen.
BE WINDOW 2,2,22,78, BLUE, SHADOW, ZOOM	Draw a window between pixels 2,2 and 22,78. Make it blue with a background shadow and zoom it onto the screen.
BE ROWCOL 12,30, "This is a window"	Position the cursor and write to the screen.
BE ROWCOL 20,4, "press any key"	Position the cursor and write to the screen.
BE ASK " ", TIMEOUT=10	Ask the user a question without a prompt and wait ten seconds for the user to press any key.
CLS	Clear the screen.
BE SA WHITE, RED > NUL	Change the screen colors to white letters on a red background and pipe this command to NUL.
BE WINDOW 8,20,13,60, RED, ZOOM	Draw a red window.
BE ROWCOL 10,25,"A simulated error has occurred", BLINKING WHITE	Position the cursor and write to the screen.
BE ROWCOL 12,25, "Press any key to abort", WHITE	Position the cursor and write to the screen.
BE ASK " ", TIMEOUT=10	Prompt the user.
CLS	Clear the screen.

9-8   NORTON2.BAT, a batch file that shows how the Batch Enhancer can ''do windows.''

Table 9-9   Ask options.

Ask Options	Function
Adjust	Lets you add a specified value to the ERRORLEVEL returned by Ask. By careful coding and decoding, you can use this feature to ask the user multiple questions and pass the answers back to a batch file as one ERRORLEVEL value.
Color	Lets you change the color of the prompt.
Default	The value Ask assigns if the user merely presses Return or the Ask prompt times out.
Keys	This is what really sets Ask apart from other ERRORLEVEL tests. The keys you enter here are the only ones Ask will accept. If the user presses any other key, Ask just beeps and waits for an acceptable keystroke. And no more fooling with ASCII tables to get the ERRORLEVEL values either. Ask sets ERRORLEVEL to one for the first key in the list, two for the second key,

Table 9-9 Continued

Ask Options	Function
	and so on. Ask is case-insensitive, so you do not have to test for Y and y. That effectively cuts your number of tests in half for character responses.
Prompt	The message that Ask displays. Typically, you would want to put a space at the end of the prompt so you do not enter the answer directly next to the prompt.
Timeout	The number of seconds Ask will wait for the user to press any key. If he does not press a key in that period of time, Ask defaults to the value you specify and returns control to the batch file. Note that Timeout uses the clock and is independent of processor speed. You can use the Timeout feature without a prompt to cause a batch file to pause for a given period of time.

TON1.BAT in Fig. 9-9 illustrates this. For more information on Norton Utilities, contact:

Symantec Corporation
100 Wilshire Blvd., 9th floor
Santa Monica, CA 90401
(213) 319-2000

Batch File Line	Explanation
@ECHO OFF	Turn command-echoing off.
REM NORTON1.BAT	Remark giving the name of the batch file.
REM Illustrate the ability of Ask to	Documentation remark.
REM adjust the ERRORLEVEL value to	Documentation remark.
REM return more than one response.	Documentation remark.
CLS	Clear the screen.
BE ASK "Do you want option A, B or C ", abc	Ask the user to select from three options and set ERRORLEVEL according to A=1, B=2, and C=3.
CLS	Clear the screen.
IF ERRORLEVEL 3 GOTO THREE	If ERRORLEVEL is greater than or equal to three, goto THREE. Since Ask had only three alternatives, three will be the maximum value.
IF ERRORLEVEL 2 GOTO TWO	If ERRORLEVEL equals two, jump to TWO. Normally, this would test for greater than or equal to two, but the line above removed all the values of three or larger.

9-9 NORTON1.BAT, which uses Ask to get multiple responses, and then combines them into a single ErrorLevel value.

Batch File Line	Explanation
IF ERRORLEVEL 1 GOTO ONE	If ERRORLEVEL equals one, jump to ONE. Since Ask will require a value, one is the minimum ERRORLEVEL value. The batch file will make it past this point only by using a GOTO command.
:THREE	Label used by a GOTO command.
BE ASK "Do you want option 1 or 2 ",12,ADJUST=10	Ask the user a question and add ten to his or her response.
CLS	Clear the screen.
GOTO NEXT	Continue processing below.
:TWO	Label used by a GOTO command.
BE ASK "Do you want option 1 or 2 ",12,ADJUST=20	Ask the user a question and add twenty to his or her response.
CLS	Clear the screen.
GOTO NEXT	Continue processing below.
:ONE	Label used by a GOTO command.
BE ASK "Do you want option 1 or 2 ",12,ADJUST=30	Ask the user a question and add thirty to his or her response.
CLS	Clear the screen.
GOTO NEXT	Continue processing below.
:NEXT	Label used by GOTO.
IF ERRORLEVEL 32 GOTO A2 IF ERRORLEVEL 31 GOTO A1 IF ERRORLEVEL 22 GOTO B2 IF ERRORLEVEL 21 GOTO B1 IF ERRORLEVEL 12 GOTO C2 IF ERRORLEVEL 11 GOTO C1	A series of ERRORLEVEL tests used to determine which set of responses the user selected above. Notice that the logic allows the batch file to store two responses in the single slot provided by ERRORLEVEL.
:A2 ECHO A2 SELECTED GOTO END	Tell the user what he/she selected and exit the batch file.
:A1 ECHO A1 SELECTED GOTO END	Tell the user what he/she selected and exit the batch file.
:B2 ECHO B2 SELECTED GOTO END	Tell the user what he/she selected and exit the batch file.
:B1 ECHO B1 SELECTED GOTO END	Tell the user what he/she selected and exit the batch file.

9-9 Continued

Batch File Line	Explanation
:C2 ECHO C2 SELECTED GOTO END	Tell the user what he/she selected and exit the batch file.
:C1 ECHO C1 SELECTED GOTO END	Tell the user what he/she selected and exit the batch file.
:END	Label marketing the end of the batch file.

Batchman

Batchman is a collection of useful batch commands that are combined into one program. Having all the commands in one program keeps it small. Otherwise, each command would need one cluster of disk space. To run a command, enter:

BATCHMAN *command*[*options*]

and the commands available in Batchman are the following:

ANSI

ANSI tests to see if ANSI.SYS is loaded. It stores a zero in ErrorLevel if it is, and a one in ErrorLevel if it isn't loaded.

BEEP [*frequency, duration*]

BEEP sounds the bell. You can control the frequency and duration. The frequency is entered in hertz, and the duration is entered in $1/18$ of a second.

BREAK

BREAK tests the status of break. It returns a zero as ErrorLevel if it's off, and a one if it's on.

CANCOPY *file-specification drive*

CANCOPY determines if the drive you specify has enough room for the file specification you enter, and returns the results in an ErrorLevel. That way, if there isn't enough room, the batch file can tell the user to swap disks before it continues.

CAPSLOCK [on/off]

If no option is specified, CAPSLOCK toggles the setting of the CapsLock key. If a specific setting is specified, it sets CapsLock to that value.

CECHO [C] [*color*] *string*

The CECHO command in Batchman is like the ECHO command in DOS, except it lets you avoid a carriage return at the end of the line and you can change the color of the text string. If you specify the optional C, Batchman doesn't move the cursor down to the next line after displaying the string. You can specify a new color using the way you would with CLS (see below). Combining these two options means you can print part of a string in one color and the remaining in another color.

CLS [*colors*]

When used without the optional colors, Batchman clears the screen using the color scheme it finds at the current cursor position. Unlike the DOS CLS command, it properly clears even an EGA screen in 43-line mode or a VGA screen in 43- or 50-line mode.

You can also specify the colors on the command line in order to have Batchman change the default colors. Enter a color, select the number of the foreground and background colors, and compute a single number—(foreground + (background * 16)). It would be much easier if Batchman accepted names like red and blue, but it doesn't.

Some of the available colors are 1=blue, 2=green, 3=light blue, 4=red, 5=purple, 6=orange, 7=white and 8=gray. On my Super-VGA display, Batchman will set the background color correctly, but won't change the foreground color.

COLDBOOT

COLDBOOT performs a cold reboot of the computer.

COLS

COLS returns the number of columns DOS is currently configured for as an ErrorLevel value.

COMPARE *string1* *string2*

COMPARE performs a case-insensitive comparison between the two strings you specify, and returns the results as an ErrorLevel value.

CPU

CPU returns the CPU type as an ErrorLevel, where 1=8086/8088, 2=80186, 3=80286 and 4=80386.

CURSORTYPE [*m,n*]

CURSORTYPE changes the shape of the cursor, where *m* is the beginning scan line and *n* is the ending scan line. Entering CURSORTYPE by itself resets the cursor shape. It returns an ErrorLevel of zero if it's successful, and a zero if it's unsuccessful.

DAY

DAY returns the day of the month as an ErrorLevel value.

DIREXIST [*drive:*] *subdirectory*

DIREXIST checks to see if the specified subdirectory exists, and sets ErrorLevel accordingly.

DISPLAY

DISPLAY returns the type of display as an ErrorLevel value.

DOSVER

DOSVER returns the DOS version in ErrorLevel. However, the format used by DOSVER isn't very useful. It returns an ErrorLevel value of 32 times the major version plus the minor version. Thus, DOS 3.1 returns 32*3+1 or 97.

DRIVEEXIST *drive*

DRIVEEXIST tests to see if the specified drive exists, and sets ErrorLevel accordingly. It checks to see only that the drive exists, not if the drive is ready to receive data.

E43V50

E43V50 sets an EGA display to 43-line mode and a VGA display to 50-line mode. Batchman doesn't have a command to reset either to 24-line mode.

EXPMEN n/r

If you specify an amount of expanded memory (the n), EXPMEN returns an ErrorLevel of zero if you have that much expanded memory, and a one if not. If you specify the r, it reports on the amount of expanded memory. Under DOS 5.0, this option always reports zero memory.

EXTMEN n/r

If you specify an amount of extended memory (the n), EXTMEN returns an ErrorLevel of zero if you have that much extended memory, and a one if not. If you specify the r, it reports on the amount of extended memory. Under DOS 5.0, this option always reports zero memory.

GETKEY [*"string"*]

If you don't specify a string, GETKEY returns the ASCII value of the keystroke as an ErrorLevel. If you specify a string, it returns the first keystroke in the string as a one, the second as a two, and so on. When a string is specified, the testing is case insensitive. According to the documentation, you can specify function keys after the string as F1, F2, and so on. However, this didn't work for me— GETKEY wouldn't recognize the function keys as valid keystrokes.

HOUR

HOUR returns the hour of the day as an ErrorLevel value.

ISVOL [*drive:*] *volume*

ISVOL tests to see if the volume label of a disk matches the one specified on the command line, and sets the ErrorLevel accordingly. The test is case insensitive, but ISVOL can't test for volume labels with spaces in them. DOS can't create these kind of volume labels, but programs like VOLABEL in the Norton Utilities can.

MAINMEN n/r

If you specify an amount of memory (the n), MAINMEN returns an ErrorLevel of zero if you have that much memory, and a one if not. If you specify the r, it reports on the amount of memory.

MINUTE

MINUTE returns the minute as an ErrorLevel value.

MONTH

MONTH returns the month as an ErrorLevel value, where January=1, February=2, and so on.

NUMLOCK [on/off]

If no option is specified, NUMLOCK toggles the setting of the Numlock key. If a specific setting is specified, it sets Numlock to that value.

PRTSC

PRTSC issues a print screen.

PUSHPATH / POPPATH

PUSHPATH stores the current drive and subdirectory in a 408-byte memory area. The POPPATH command returns to that drive and subdirectory. Multiple PUSHPATH commands can be nested, as long as you don't exceed the 408-byte memory space. It returns an ErrorLevel of zero if it's successful, and a zero if it's unsuccessful.

QFORMAT

QFORMAT redoes the formatting of a floppy disk. In the process, it erases all the files and removes any subdirectories. It does this by rewriting to the file allocation table (FAT) and not by overwriting the files themselves, so an unerasing program like the Norton Utilities can still recover the data. QFORMAT returns an ErrorLevel of zero if it's successful, and a zero if it's unsuccessful.

RENDIR *old new*

This command changes the name of the old subdirectory to the new name.

ROWS

ROWS returns the number of rows DOS is currently configured for as an ErrorLevel value.

SCROLLLOCK [on/off]

If no option is specified, SCROLLOCK toggles the setting of the ScrollLock key. If a specific setting is specified, it sets ScrollLock to that value.

SECOND

SECOND returns the second as an ErrorLevel value.

SETCURSOR *line, column*

SETCURSOR locates the cursor at the location specified after the keyword. You can locate the cursor off the screen to hide it. You must be careful with this, however, because a mistake can make the text on the screen invisible. When I tried locating the cursor in column zero by mistake, it locked up my computer.

SETLOOP [*n*] / DECLOOP

The SETLOOP command reserves a small amount of memory and stores the number specified in *n* in that space. Each time you issue the DECLOOP command, it decreases that counter by one. In addition, DECLOOP sets the ErrorLevel value to the counter value, so you can test on ErrorLevel to see if it's time to exit the batch file. Both the area for the counter and ErrorLevel are 1 byte in size, so the counter is limited to 255 or smaller.

SHIFT ALT/CTRL

Returns a one in ErrorLevel if the specified toggle key is pressed, or a zero otherwise.

TYPEMATIC [*repeat rate, initial delay / default*]

TYPEMATIC changes the keyboard typematic built into most AT and above keyboards. You can change the repeat rate and the delay before the keyboard begins repeating, or reset everything to normal.

VIDEOMODE

VIDEOMODE returns the video mode as an ErrorLevel value.

WAITFOR [*mm:*]*ss*

This command pauses the batch file for a specified amount of time (minutes and seconds).

WAITTIL [*hh:mm*[*.ss*]

This command halts execution of the batch file until the specified time (hours, minutes, and seconds).

WARMBOOT

WARMBOOT performs a warm reboot of the computer.

WEEKDAY

This command returns the day of the week as an ErrorLevel, where Sunday = 0, Monday = 1, and so on.

WINDOW *row, column, width, height* [*color, border*]

The WINDOW command draws a box on the screen, using the coordinates specified after the command. It can also set the color, using the same method as the COLOR command, and can specify either a single or double border.

YEAR

YEAR returns the year as an ErrorLevel. Because ErrorLevel is limited to one number, it returns 1980 = 1, 1981-2, and so on. Figure 9-10 shows SHOW-BMAN.BAT, a batch file that illustrates many of the Batchman commands, and

Table 9-10 lists the commands in a quick-reference format. Batchman is clearly one of the most powerful and useful batch file utilities currently available. It suffers from a few bugs, but overall is an excellent package.

Batch File Line	Explanation
`@ECHO OFF`	Turn command-echoing off.
`REM SHOWBMAN.BAT`	Remark giving the name of the batch file.
`REM Illustrate Batchman Program`	Documentation remark.
`BATCHMAN CLS 33`	Clear the screen and reset the color.

`BATCHMAN CECHO C 19 This Batch File`
`BATCHMAN CECHO C 35 Illustrates The`
`BATCHMAN CECHO C 51 PC Magazine Program`
`BATCHMAN CECHO    67 Called Batchman`
	Write a single line to the screen in four different colors.

`BATCHMAN CECHO The Next Message Will`
`BATCHMAN CECHO Show Five Times`
`BATCHMAN CECHO Press Any Key To Start`
`PAUSE > NUL`
	Tell the user what will happen next.

`BATCHMAN SETLOOP 5`
`:LoopTop`
`BATCHMAN CECHO Repeated Message`
`BATCHMAN DECLOOP`
`IF ERRORLEVEL 1 GOTO LOOPTOP`
	Loop through and display the same message five times.

`CLS`
`BATCHMAN CECHO C The Current Subdirectory Is:`
`CD`
`BATCHMAN PUSHPATH`
`CD\`
`BATCHMAN CECHO C Now The Subdirectory Is:`
`CD`
`BATCHMAN POPPATH`
`BATCHMAN CECHO C Location Reset To:`
`CD`
`PAUSE`
	Store the current subdirectory, display that subdirectory, change to another subdirectory, display that subdirectory, then change back to the original subdirectory.

`CLS`
`BATCHMAN ANSI`
`IF ERRORLEVEL 1 ECHO ANSI NOT LOADED`
`IF ERRORLEVEL 1 GOTO SKIPANSI`
`ECHO ANSI LOADED!`
	Determine if ANSI.SYS is loaded and tell the user.

`BATCHMAN BEEP 392,3;523,3;659,3;784,3;`
`            10,3;659,3;784,12`
`PAUSE`
	Play a tune on the speaker.

`CLS`
`ECHO Batch File Will Now Pause For 10-Seconds`
`BATCHMAN WAITFOR 10`
	Pause the batch file for 10 seconds.

`ECHO Cursor Will Now Change`
`BATCHMAN CURSORTYPE 0,15`
`ECHO Notice New Cursor`
`PAUSE`
`ECHO Resetting Cursor`
`BATCHMAN CURSORTYPE`
	Display two different cursor types.

9-10 SHOWBMAN.BAT, which illustrates many of the Batchman commands.

9-10 Continued

Batch File Line	Explanation
BATCHMAN BREAK IF ERRORLEVEL 1 ECHO Break Is On IF ERRORLEVEL 0 IF NOT ERRORLEVEL 1 ECHO Break Off PAUSE	Display the status of break.
CLS BATCHMAN DRIVEEXIST A: IF ERRORLEVEL 1 ECHO A-Drive Exists continues B-I BATCHMAN DRIVEEXIST J: IF ERRORLEVEL 1 ECHO J-Drive Exists	Displays which drives exist.
ECHO BATCHMAN DIREXIST C:\SYSLIB IF ERRORLEVEL 1 ECHO C:\SYSLIB Exists BATCHMAN DIREXIST C:\BAT IF ERRORLEVEL 1 ECHO C:\BAT Exists PAUSE	Check to see if two subdirectories exist and inform the user. The ECHO command is followed by an Alt-255 to display a blank line.
CLS	
BATCHMAN YEAR IF ERRORLEVEL 10 IF NOT ERRORLEVEL 11 ECHO It's 1990 IF ERRORLEVEL 11 IF NOT ERRORLEVEL 12 ECHO It's 1991 IF ERRORLEVEL 12 IF NOT ERRORLEVEL 13 ECHO It's 1992 IF ERRORLEVEL 13 IF NOT ERRORLEVEL 14 ECHO It's 1993 IF ERRORLEVEL 14 IF NOT ERRORLEVEL 15 ECHO It's 1994 IF ERRORLEVEL 15 IF NOT ERRORLEVEL 16 ECHO It's 1995 IF ERRORLEVEL 16 IF NOT ERRORLEVEL 17 ECHO It's 1996 IF ERRORLEVEL 17 IF NOT ERRORLEVEL 18 ECHO It's 1997 IF ERRORLEVEL 18 IF NOT ERRORLEVEL 19 ECHO It's 1998	Display the year.
BATCHMAN MONTH IF ERRORLEVEL 1 IF NOT ERRORLEVEL 2 ECHO It's Jan. IF ERRORLEVEL 2 IF NOT ERRORLEVEL 3 ECHO It's Feb. IF ERRORLEVEL 3 IF NOT ERRORLEVEL 4 ECHO It's Mar. IF ERRORLEVEL 4 IF NOT ERRORLEVEL 5 ECHO It's Apr. IF ERRORLEVEL 5 IF NOT ERRORLEVEL 6 ECHO It Is May IF ERRORLEVEL 6 IF NOT ERRORLEVEL 7 ECHO It's June IF ERRORLEVEL 7 IF NOT ERRORLEVEL 8 ECHO It's July IF ERRORLEVEL 8 IF NOT ERRORLEVEL 9 ECHO It's Aug. IF ERRORLEVEL 9 IF NOT ERRORLEVEL 10 ECHO It's Sep. IF ERRORLEVEL 10 IF NOT ERRORLEVEL 11 ECHO It's Oct. IF ERRORLEVEL 11 IF NOT ERRORLEVEL 12 ECHO It's Nov. IF ERRORLEVEL 12 IF NOT ERRORLEVEL 13 ECHO It's Dec.	Display the month.

BATCHMAN DAY
FOR %%J IN (1 2 3 4 5 6 7 8 9 10)
    DO IF ERRORLEVEL %%J SET DAY=%%J
FOR %%J IN (11 12 13 14 15 16 17)
    DO IF ERRORLEVEL %%J SET DAY=%%J
FOR %%J IN (18 19 20 21 22 23 24)
    DO IF ERRORLEVEL %%J SET DAY=%%J
FOR %%J IN (25 26 27 28 29 30 31)
    DO IF ERRORLEVEL %%J SET DAY=%%J
ECHO Today Is The %DAY%th
	Display the day.

9-10 Continued

Batch File Line	Explanation

BATCHMAN HOUR
FOR %%J IN (1 2 3 4 5 6 7 8 9 10)
    DO IF ERRORLEVEL %%J SET HOUR=%%J
FOR %%J IN (11 12 13 14 15 16 17)
    DO IF ERRORLEVEL %%J SET HOUR=%%J
FOR %%J IN (18 19 20 21 22 23 24)
    DO IF ERRORLEVEL %%J SET HOUR=%%J
ECHO The Hour Is %HOUR%
	Display the hour.

BATCHMAN MINUTE
FOR %%J IN (1 2 3 4 5 6 7 8 9 10)
    DO IF ERRORLEVEL %%J SET MINUTE=%%J
FOR %%J IN (11 12 13 14 15 16 17)
    DO IF ERRORLEVEL %%J SET MINUTE=%%J
FOR %%J IN (18 19 20 21 22 23 24)
    DO IF ERRORLEVEL %%J SET MINUTE=%%J
FOR %%J IN (25 26 27 28 29 30 31)
    DO IF ERRORLEVEL %%J SET MINUTE=%%J
FOR %%J IN (32 33 34 35 36 37 38)
    DO IF ERRORLEVEL %%J SET MINUTE=%%J
FOR %%J IN (39 40 41 42 43 44 45)
    DO IF ERRORLEVEL %%J SET MINUTE=%%J
FOR %%J IN (46 47 48 49 50 51 52)
    DO IF ERRORLEVEL %%J SET MINUTE=%%J
FOR %%J IN (53 54 55 56 57 58 59 60)
    DO IF ERRORLEVEL %%J SET MINUTE=%%J
ECHO The Minute Is %MINUTE%
	Display the minutes.

BATCHMAN SECOND
FOR %%J IN (1 2 3 4 5 6 7 8 9 10)
    DO IF ERRORLEVEL %%J SET SECOND=%%J
FOR %%J IN (11 12 13 14 15 16 17)
    DO IF ERRORLEVEL %%J SET SECOND=%%J
FOR %%J IN (18 19 20 21 22 23 24)
    DO IF ERRORLEVEL %%J SET SECOND=%%J
FOR %%J IN (25 26 27 28 29 30 31)
    DO IF ERRORLEVEL %%J SET SECOND=%%J
FOR %%J IN (32 33 34 35 36 37 38)
    DO IF ERRORLEVEL %%J SET SECOND=%%J
FOR %%J IN (39 40 41 42 43 44 45)
    DO IF ERRORLEVEL %%J SET SECOND=%%J
FOR %%J IN (46 47 48 49 50 51 52)
    DO IF ERRORLEVEL %%J SET SECOND=%%J
FOR %%J IN (53 54 55 56 57 58 59 60)
    DO IF ERRORLEVEL %%J SET SECOND=%%J
ECHO The Second Is %SECOND%
	Display the seconds.

PAUSE SET DAY= SET HOUR= SET MINUTE= SET SECOND=	Reset environmental variables.

BATCHMAN ROWS
FOR %%J IN (1 2 3 4 5 6 7 8 9 10)
    DO IF ERRORLEVEL %%J SET ROWS=%%J
 	
These ERRORLEVEL tests continue for 11-45
 	
FOR %%J IN (46 47 48 49 50 51 52)
    DO IF ERRORLEVEL %%J SET ROWS=%%J
ECHO Your Display Can Show %ROWS% Rows
	Display the number of rows the computer can display given its current configuration.

9-10 Continued

Batch File Line	Explanation

BATCHMAN COLS
FOR %%J IN (1 2 3 4 5 6 7 8 9 10)
    DO IF ERRORLEVEL %%J SET COLS=%%J
 	
These ERRORLEVEL tests continue 11-134
 	
FOR %%J IN (35 36 37 38 39 40 41)
    DO IF ERRORLEVEL 1%%J SET COLS=1%%J
ECHO You Display Can Show %COLS% Columns
	Display the number of columns. Notice that the loop values for the ERRORLEVEL tests above 100 are only used at two digits and the 1 is added as part of % %J.

PAUSE BATCHMAN CLS ECHO Placing Display in Tiny Mode BATCHMAN E43V50 BATCHMAN SETCURSOR 1,1 ECHO Here BATCHMAN SETCURSOR 5,30 ECHO No Here! BATCHMAN SETCURSOR 15,55 ECHO Now Over Here BATCHMAN SETCURSOR 25,1 ECHO Back Over Here BATCHMAN SETCURSOR 36,55 ECHO Now I'm Over Here BATCHMAN SETCURSOR 43,25 ECHO I'm Finished Playing BATCHMAN SETCURSOR 44,25 ECHO Press Any Key To Continue BATCHMAN SETCURSOR 51,1 PAUSE>NUL MODE 80 BATCHMAN CLS	Display messages at various positions on the screen.
SET STRING1=ABCDEF SET STRING2=abcdef ECHO String1 is %STRING1% ECHO String2 is %STRING2% BATCHMAN COMPARE %STRING1% %STRING2% IF ERRORLEVEL 1 ECHO No Match IF ERRORLEVEL 0 IF NOT ERRORLEVEL 1 ECHO Match	Perform a case-insensitive string comparison.
BATCHMAN CANCOPY SHOWBMAN.BAT C:\ IF ERRORLEVEL 1 ECHO No Room For SHOWBMAN.BAT On C:\ IF ERRORLEVEL 0 IF NOT ERRORLEVEL 1 ECHO SHOWBMAN.BAT Will Fit On C:\	Test to see if there is room for SHOWBMAN.BAT in the root directory of the C drive.
ECHO Turning Toggle Switches On BATCHMAN NUMLOCK ON BATCHMAN CAPSLOCK ON BATCHMAN SCROLLOCK ON PAUSE ECHO Turning Them Back Off BATCHMAN NUMLOCK OFF BATCHMAN CAPSLOCK OFF BATCHMAN SCROLLOCK OFF ECHO	Toggle the Numlock, Capslock, and Scrollock keys. Note the ECHO command is followed by an Alt-255 to produce a blank line.
ECHO Your Romdate Is: BATCHMAN ROMDATE PAUSE CLS	Display the ROM date.

9-10 Continued

Batch File Line	Explanation

```ECHO Press Any Letter Key```
 ```ECHO Z Exits This```
 ```:ZTOP```
 ```BATCHMAN GETKEY "ABCDEFGHIJKLMNOPQRSTUVWXYZ"```
 ```IF ERRORLEVEL 1 IF NOT ERRORLEVEL 2 ECHO A Pressed```
 ```IF ERRORLEVEL 2 IF NOT ERRORLEVEL 3 ECHO B Pressed```
 ```IF ERRORLEVEL 3 IF NOT ERRORLEVEL 4 ECHO C Pressed```
 ```IF ERRORLEVEL 4 IF NOT ERRORLEVEL 5 ECHO D Pressed```
 ```IF ERRORLEVEL 5 IF NOT ERRORLEVEL 6 ECHO E Pressed```
 ```IF ERRORLEVEL 6 IF NOT ERRORLEVEL 7 ECHO F Pressed```
 ```IF ERRORLEVEL 7 IF NOT ERRORLEVEL 8 ECHO G Pressed```
 ```IF ERRORLEVEL 8 IF NOT ERRORLEVEL 9 ECHO H Pressed```
 ```IF ERRORLEVEL 9 IF NOT ERRORLEVEL 10 ECHO I Pressed```
 ```IF ERRORLEVEL 10 IF NOT ERRORLEVEL 11 ECHO J Pressed```
 ```IF ERRORLEVEL 11 IF NOT ERRORLEVEL 12 ECHO K Pressed```
 ```IF ERRORLEVEL 12 IF NOT ERRORLEVEL 13 ECHO L Pressed```
 ```IF ERRORLEVEL 13 IF NOT ERRORLEVEL 14 ECHO M Pressed```
 ```IF ERRORLEVEL 14 IF NOT ERRORLEVEL 15 ECHO N Pressed```
 ```IF ERRORLEVEL 15 IF NOT ERRORLEVEL 16 ECHO O Pressed```
 ```IF ERRORLEVEL 16 IF NOT ERRORLEVEL 17 ECHO P Pressed```
 ```IF ERRORLEVEL 17 IF NOT ERRORLEVEL 18 ECHO Q Pressed```
 ```IF ERRORLEVEL 18 IF NOT ERRORLEVEL 19 ECHO R Pressed```
 ```IF ERRORLEVEL 19 IF NOT ERRORLEVEL 20 ECHO S Pressed```
 ```IF ERRORLEVEL 20 IF NOT ERRORLEVEL 21 ECHO T Pressed```
 ```IF ERRORLEVEL 21 IF NOT ERRORLEVEL 22 ECHO U Pressed```
 ```IF ERRORLEVEL 22 IF NOT ERRORLEVEL 23 ECHO V Pressed```
 ```IF ERRORLEVEL 23 IF NOT ERRORLEVEL 24 ECHO W Pressed```
 ```IF ERRORLEVEL 24 IF NOT ERRORLEVEL 25 ECHO X Pressed```
 ```IF ERRORLEVEL 25 IF NOT ERRORLEVEL 26 ECHO Y Pressed```
 ```IF ERRORLEVEL 26 IF NOT ERRORLEVEL 27 ECHO Z Pressed```
 ```IF NOT ERRORLEVEL 26 GOTO ZTOP```
 ```PAUSE```
 ```CLS```
	Continue displaying the letter the user enters until he/she enters a Z.

```ECHO Memory Reports Will Now Appear```
 ```ECHO Press Any Key To Begin```
 ```PAUSE```
 ```BATCHMAN MAINMEM R```
 ```PAUSE```
 ```BATCHMAN EXPMEM R```
 ```PAUSE```
 ```BATCHMAN EXTMEM R```
 ```PAUSE```
 ```CLS```
	Display memory reports.

```BATCHMAN DISPLAY```
 ```FOR %%J IN (1 2 3 4 5 6 7 8 9 10 11)```
 ```   DO IF ERRORLEVEL %%J SET DISPLAY=%%J```
 ```IF ERRORLEVEL 1 IF NOT ERRORLEVEL 2 ECHO MDA```
 ```IF ERRORLEVEL 2 IF NOT ERRORLEVEL 3 ECHO CGA```
 ```IF ERRORLEVEL 4 IF NOT ERRORLEVEL 5 ECHO EGA COLOR```
 ```IF ERRORLEVEL 5 IF NOT ERRORLEVEL 6 ECHO EGA MONO```
 ```IF ERRORLEVEL 6 IF NOT ERRORLEVEL 7 ECHO PGS```
 ```IF ERRORLEVEL 7 IF NOT ERRORLEVEL 8 ECHO VGA MONO```
 ```IF ERRORLEVEL 8 IF NOT ERRORLEVEL 9 ECHO VGA COLOR```
 ```IF ERRORLEVEL 11 IF NOT ERRORLEVEL 12 ECHO MCGA MONO```
 ```IF ERRORLEVEL 12 IF NOT ERRORLEVEL 23 ECHO MCGA COL.```
	Show display mode.

9-10 Continued

Batch File Line	Explanation

`BATCHMAN CPU`
`IF ERRORLEVEL 1 IF NOT ERRORLEVEL 2 ECHO 8086/8088`
`IF ERRORLEVEL 2 IF NOT ERRORLEVEL 3 ECHO 80186`
`IF ERRORLEVEL 3 IF NOT ERRORLEVEL 4 ECHO 80286`
`IF ERRORLEVEL 4 IF NOT ERRORLEVEL 5 ECHO 80386/486`
	Display CPU type.

`BATCHMAN E43V50`
`BATCHMAN WINDOW 1,1,75,10,23,+`
`BATCHMAN WINDOW 2,2,75,30,44,=`
`BATCHMAN WINDOW 25,25,10,10,2,+`
`BATCHMAN WINDOW 26,26,8,8,66,-`
`BATCHMAN WAITFOR 20`
`BATCHMAN CLS`
`MODE 80`
	Draw several windows on the screen.

Table 9-10 Batchman commands.

Keyword	Syntax Usage
ANSI	ANSI Sets ERRORLEVEL to zero if ANSI.SYS is not loaded, and to one if it is loaded.
BEEP	BEEP [*frequency, duration*] Sounds the speaker while letting you control the frequency and duration.
BREAK	BREAK Sets the ERRORLEVEL to indicate if break is on or off.
CANCOPY	CANCOPY *files drive* Measures the space required by the files and the space available on the drive to determine if there is enough space to perform the copy. Returns the results as an ERRORLEVEL value.
CAPSLOCK	CAPSLOCK [on /off] Either toggles the status of Capslock or turns it on or off.
CECHO	CECHO [C] [*color*] *String* Displays text on the screen much like ECHO. Optionally changes the color of the text and optionally writes the string to the display without a carriage return at the end.
CLS	CLS [*color*] Clears the screen and optionally resets the foreground and background colors to those specified by the user.
COLDBOOT	COLDBOOT Performs a cold reboot of the computer.

Table 9-10 Continued

Keyword	Syntax Usage
COLS	COLS Returns the number of columns DOS can display in the current video mode as an ERRORLEVEL value.
COMPARE	COMPARE *string1 string2* Performs a case-insensitive string comparison and places the results in the ERRORLEVEL.
CPU	CPU Returns the type of CPU as an ERRORLEVEL value.
CURSORTYPE	CURSORTYPE [*m,n*] Changes the size of the cursor.
DAY	DAY Returns the day of the month as an ERRORLEVEL value.
DIREXIST	DIREXIST [*drive:*] *subdirectory* Tests to see if the specified subdirectory exists and sets ERROR-LEVEL accordingly.
DISPLAY	DISPLAY Returns the type of display as an ERRORLEVEL value.
DOSVER	DOSVER Returns the DOS version as an ERRORLEVEL value, although in a format that is difficult to use. The ERRORLEVEL value is the major DOS version (1.x, 2.x, and so on) times 32 plus the minor version number.
DRIVEEXIST	DRIVEEXIST *drive* Tests to see if the drive exists and sets ERRORLEVEL accordingly.
E43V50	E43V50 Sets an EGA display to 43-line mode and a VGA display to 50-line mode.
EXPMEM	EXPMEM n/r If an amount of expanded memory is entered, it returns an ERRORLEVEL of one if there is that amount of expanded memory in the system, a zero otherwise. If an r is specified, it reports on the expanded amount of memory.

Table 9-10 Continued

Keyword	Syntax Usage
EXTMEN	EXTMEN n/r If an amount of extended memory is entered, it returns an ERRORLEVEL of one if there is that amount of extended memory in the system, a zero otherwise. If an r is specified, it reports on the amount of extended memory.
GETKEY	GETKEY ["*string*"] Returns the value of the key pressed in ERRORLEVEL. If a string is specified, it returns the first keystroke as an ERRORLEVEL of one, the second as two, and so on. If no string is specified, it returns the ASCII value.
HOUR	HOUR Returns the hour as an ERRORLEVEL.
ISVOL	ISVOL [*drive:*] *volume* Tests to see if the specified volume matches the one on the disk and sets ERRORLEVEL accordingly.
MAINMEM	MAINMEM n/r If an amount of memory is entered, it returns an ERRORLEVEL of one if there is that amount of memory in the system, a zero otherwise. If an r is specified, it reports on the amount of memory.
MINUTE	MINUTE Returns the minute as an ERRORLEVEL value.
MONTH	MONTH Returns the month as an ERRORLEVEL value where January=1, February=2, and so on.
NUMLOCK	NUMLOCK [on/off] Either toggles the numlock status or sets it directly to on or off.
PRTSC	PRTSC Issues a PrintScreen command.
PUSHPATH POPPATH	PUSHPATH POPPATH PUSHPATH stores the current drive and subdirectory into a memory-resident storage area. POPPATH returns to that drive and subdirectory. The total storage area is 408 bytes and sets of these commands can be embedded.

Table 9-10 Continued

Keyword	Syntax Usage
QFORMAT	QFORMAT *drive* Completely erases the files and subdirectories from a floppy disk very quickly. Will not work on a hard disk.
RENDIR	RENDIR *old new* Changes the name of a subdirectory.
ROMDATE	ROMDATE Displays the ROM date.
ROWS	ROWS Returns the number of rows DOS can display in the current video mode as an ERRORLEVEL value.
SCROLLOCK	SCROLLOCK [on/off] Either toggles the status of Scrollock or turns it on or off.
SETCURSOR	SETCURSOR row, column Locates the cursor at a specific position on the screen.
SETLOOP DECLOOP	SETLOOP [*n*] DECLOOP SETLOOP establishes a counter in memory. DECLOOP reduces the value of that counter by one and transfers the counter into ERRORLEVEL so the batch file can test on it.
SHIFT	SHIFT ALT/CTRL Returns a one in ERRORLEVEL if the Alt or Ctrl key is pressed, a zero otherwise.
TYPEMATIC	TYPEMATIC [*repeat rate, initial delay/default*] Changes the keyboard typematic rate or reset it to normal.
VIDEOMODE	VIDEOMODE Returns the video mode as an ERRORLEVEL value.
WAITFOR	WAITFOR [*mm:*]*ss* Pauses the batch file for a specified amount of time.
WAITTIL	WAITTIL *hh:mm*[*.ss*] Halts execution of the batch file until the specified time.

Table 9-10 Continued

Keyword	Syntax Usage
WARMBOOT	WARMBOOT Performs a warm reboot of the computer.
WEEKDAY	WEEKDAY Returns the day of the week as an ERRORLEVEL where Sunday=0, Monday=1, and so on.
WINDOW	WINDOW *row, column, width, height* [*color, border*] Draws a box on the screen using the coordinates specified after the command. Can also set the color using the same method as the COLOR command and can specify either a single or double border.
YEAR	YEAR Returns the year as an ERRORLEVEL. Since the ERRORLEVEL value is limited to one number, it returns 1980=1, 1981=2, and so on.

Getting your hands on these programs

A few of the programs in this chapter, like the Norton Utilities, are commercial programs. Some of them, therefore, aren't included on the disk that comes with this book. Those that aren't included can be purchased from a local computer store or by mail. The programs are generally cheaper by mail. When I'm ordering software by mail, I always check the ads in Computer Monthly, because they generally have the best prices. However, most of the programs in this chapter are shareware.

Shareware

Shareware distribution gives you a chance to try software before buying it. If you try a shareware program and continue using it, you're expected to register. Individual programs differ on details—some request registration while others require it, and some specify a maximum trial period. With registration, you get anything from the simple right to continue using the software to an updated program with a printed manual.

Copyright laws apply to both shareware and commercial software, and the copyright holder retains all rights, with a few specific exceptions. Shareware authors are accomplished programmers, just like commercial authors, and the programs are of comparable quality. (In both cases, there are good programs and bad ones!) The main difference is in the method of distribution. An author of a program specifically grants the right to copy and distribute his software, either to all and sundry or to a specific group. For example, some authors require written permission before a commercial disk vendor copies their shareware.

So shareware is a distribution method, not a type of software. You should find software that suits your needs and pocketbook, whether it's commercial or shareware. The shareware system makes fitting your needs easier, because you can try before you buy. And because the overhead is low, prices are low. Shareware also has the ultimate money-back guarantee—if you don't use the product, you don't pay for it.

You can obtain shareware from various electronic bulletin boards, including CompuServe and PC-Link. Another source is the collection of vendors who specialize in selling shareware by the disk through the mail. With this method, you don't need a modem. Personally, I use Public Brand Software but there are many other good companies.

Summary

The major points of this chapter were as follows:

- Check can be used in batch files to test a number of conditions. Check reports back to the batch file using ErrorLevel. The batch file can use this information to make decisions.
- InKey can be used to query the user. This is useful for menus and also to conditionally load memory-resident software.
- Answer can query the user and accept a multiple-character response. It places the response in the environment.
- REBOOT21.COM will copy the AUTOEXEC.* and CONFIG.* of your choice over the existing AUTOEXEC.BAT and CONFIG.SYS files and reboot the computer. This allows you to store different configurations for different applications.
- The Down and Dirty Dozen Batch Utilities have a number of useful features.
- Get places its results in an environmental variable as well as ErrorLevel. That can make testing easier.
- Menuware Batch File Utilities contain a number of useful features.
- SetError can set the ErrorLevel to any value you like, making batch file debugging easier.
- ShowEnvironment shows you how large your environment is and how much remains free.
- The Norton Utilities has a very powerful query program and a number of other useful features.
- Batchman is one of the most powerful interactive batch utilities available. For many users, it will be the only batch utility you need.

10
CHAPTER

Alternatives to the DOS batch language

Throughout this book, I've stressed using the available DOS commands and a few utility programs to get the most power from your batch files. For most readers, the combination of DOS and utility programs will be enough. A few readers, however, will need more power. Those readers have two choices, alternative languages or a compiler.

An alternative language is a replacement for the DOS batch language. You write standard batch files, but most of the commands are processed by the alternative language. Those commands it doesn't understand are passed on to DOS for processing. I'll discuss one alternative language, Extended Batch Language Plus, in this chapter.

A compiler takes a batch file or batch file-like script and turns it into a stand-alone program. I'll discuss two compilers in this chapter, Builder and Bat2Exec. Builder significantly expands the batch language, while Bat2Exec adds no new commands.

Extended Batch Language Plus

Extended Batch Language Plus (EBL Plus) is a shareware program. It's available from many computer bulletin boards, and for $79.00 from the author, Frank Canova. Write to him in care of Seaware Corporation. The address is P.O. Box 1656, Delray Beach, FL 33444. The phone number is (305) 392-2046. If you order the program from the author, you'll also need to include $3.00 for shipping. Because of the long lead time involved in producing a book, you should write or call to check the price before sending money.

Unlike most shareware programs, EBL Plus doesn't have an ASCII file manual on the disk. If you want documentation, you have to pay the registration fee. You'll need it—the information in this section isn't enough to use EBL Plus without the manual.

Operation

Before a batch file can run an EBL Plus command, it must have a BAT line. This loads the EBL Plus command processor. That requires about 48K, and it remains in memory until the batch file terminates or the batch file specifically unloads it. This EBL Plus command processor is what gives EBL Plus all its power.

With EBL Plus, all your batch files are created just as you create DOS batch files, and a batch file can contain a mixture of DOS and EBL Plus commands. EBL Plus passes only those commands to DOS that it doesn't understand unless you use the SHELL command to force EBL Plus to turn a command over to DOS.

Like DOS, EBL Plus has a number of keywords. They are shown in Table 10-1. EBL Plus adds a number of functions, listed in Table 10-2, to batch files. Figure 10-1 shows a sample batch file called EBL.BAT. It illustrates many of the Extended Batch Language Plus keywords and functions.

EBL Plus is very much a complete batch language. It performs most of the enhancements batch file authors need—all together in one package. It's clearly one of the better batch file enhancements.

Table 10-1   EBL Plus keywords.

Keyword	Operation
*	Identifies an EBL Plus comment.
-	Identifies a name for a GOTO statement.
BEEP	Sounds the speaker.
BEGSTACK	EBL Plus can stuff characters into the keyboard stack for use by applications using the BEGSTACK command.
BEGTYPE	Marks the beginning of lines to be typed to the screen. Typing continues until EBL Plus encounters an END statement.
CALL	Calls a batch file subroutine.
CALL.PURGE	Clears all pending returns.
CLS	Clears the screen just like the DOS command.
COLORCHAR	Changes the color of text.
EXIT	Leaves a batch file and returns to DOS.
GOTO	Jumps to a label, just like the DOS GOTO command.
IF	Similar to the DOS IF statement, its makes decisions based on conditions. Unlike DOS, EBL Plus can make greater than, less than, or case-sensitive comparisons. It can also perform an IF-THEN-ELSE test and the actions taken as the result of passing an IF statement can continue over multiple lines.
INKEY	Reads a single keystroke from the keyboard.

Table 10-1 Continued

Keyword	Operation
INTERPRET	Evaluates an expression and runs EBL Plus command(s) contained in that expression.
LEAVE	Stops EBL Plus and returns control of the batch file to DOS.
LOCATE	Positions the cursor on the screen.
-ON.ERROR-	Marks a special section that is executed if EBL Plus encounters an error.
PARSE	Breaks down an expression into its parts.
READ	Prompts the user for an input and stores that input in a variable or variables. READ can accept values in excess of a single character.
READ.PARSED	Prompts the user for an input, parses that input and stores it in variables.
READSCRN	This reads characters off the screen and can act based on what it reads.
READSCRN.-PARSED	Reads characters off the screen, parses them, and stores them in variables.
REPEAT	Processes an action more than once.
RESUME	Returns control to a program after an error.
RETURN	Causes EBL Plus to exit from a subroutine and resume processing the main batch file.
SHELL	Temporarily exits to DOS to run a single command. EBL Plus remains in memory.
SKIP	Jump forward a specified number of lines.
STACK	Stuffs keystrokes into the keyboard buffers.
STACK.ON/ STACK.OFF	Turns the flow of characters from the stack on and off.
STACK.PURGE	Clears out all the characters in the stack.
STATEOF	Checks to see if a file exists.
TYPE	Displays text on the screen. It works very similar to the DOS ECHO command.
WAIT	Pauses the batch file.

Table 10-2 EBL Plus functions.

Function	Operation
ABS	Returns the absolute value of the number or calculation specified inside the parentheses. Absolute value is a mathematical term. It means that zero or a number above zero is not affected and a number below zero is made positive.
C2H	Converts an ASCII string to hexadecimal.
CENTER	Centers a text string on the screen. It requires two inputs, the string to center and the width in which to center that text. Normally the width will be the screen width of eighty. In a bow to the British, you can also spell the function CENTRE.
CHARIN	Accepts a single keystroke just like INKEY, except the keystroke always comes from the keyboard even if characters have been placed into the buffer.

Table 10-2   Continued

Function	Operation
CHDIR	Just like the DOS CD or CHDIR commands, it changes the current drive and/or subdirectory.
COLOR	Allows the use of colors in menus and text.
COPIES	Returns multiple copies of a string.
CURSOR.ROW CURSOR.COL	Returns the current position of the cursor.
D2H	Converts a decimal (base ten) number into a hexadecimal (base sixteen) number.
DATE	Returns the system date. EBL Plus gives you a great deal of flexibility in how this is displayed.
DELWORD	Removes a portion of a string.
DIR	Returns the specified files.
EDIT	Allows text on the screen to be edited, just like the data entry function of a database.
FIELD	Returns the contents of a field on the screen.
FIND	Locates a phrase in a string.
FLOAT	Returns the value of a calculation with the fractional portion of the number intact.
FRAC	Returns just the fractional part of a number.
GETDIR	Returns the current subdirectory. The real power of this function is you can store it in a variable for later use.
H2C	Converts hexadecimal values to ASCII values.
H2D	Converts hexadecimal values to decimal values.
INT	Returns the integer (non-fraction) part of a number.
INT86	Executes an 8086 software interrupt and is only for very advanced users. Misusing it can cause you to lose data, crash the system, or even destroy disk files.
KEY	Places the named keystroke into the keyboard stack.
KEYPRESSED	Returns a T if a key has been pressed and a F otherwise. Normally, you would use this with functions discussed later to give the user a certain amount of time to respond to a prompt.
LEFT	Returns part of a string of variables. It requires two inputs: the string and the number of characters to return. It returns characters from the left.
LENGTH	Returns the length of a string.
LOCATE x y	Positions the cursor on the screen at a specific location. Generally, you would follow this command with a TYPE command to write information to the screen at that location.
LOWER	Converts all characters in a string to lowercase. Only letters are effected.

Table 10-2 Continued

Function	Operation
MKDIR	Makes a subdirectory.
NOT	Reverses a logical decision just like the DOS NOT function.
PEEK	Like the Basic Peek statement, this returns the value of the byte of memory in hex at the specified location. This is for advanced users only.
PLAY	Plays a note on the speaker.
POKE	Like the Basic Poke statement, this writes the specified value to memory at the specified location. This is for advanced users only.
REBOOT	Reboots the computer just like pressing Ctrl-Alt-Del.
REVERSE	Transposes a string.
RIGHT	The returns the right-most specified number of characters from a character string.
RMDIR	Removes a subdirectory.
SEEK	Finds the position in a file that is being written to.
SELECT	Picks an item from a list on the screen using the cursor control keys.
SPACE	Changes the spacing of a string.
STRIP	Removes extra characters (usually spaces) from both sides of a character string. An optional parameter causes it to strip only extra characters from one side.
SUBWORD	Returns a portion of a string.
TIME	Like DATE, this returns the system time and like DATE, there are a number of parameters to control how it is formatted.
TRACE	A debugging aid that causes additional information to be displayed while the batch file is running.
UPPER	Converts a string to all uppercase.
VERIFY	Checks to be sure that one string is made up of only the characters in another string.
VERSION	Returns the current EBL Plus version.
WHATFUNC	EBL Plus loads its functions separately from the main package because they take up memory all the time. To minimize memory, they are broken down into three partial packages and one full package. That way, if you do not need all the functions you can load only one or two parts. This functions returns a value indicating which functions are loaded.
WINDOW	Draws a window on the screen.
WORD	Returns the specified word.
WORDS	Returns the specified words.

Batch File Line	Explanation
`@ECHO OFF`	Turn command-echoing off.

`REM EBL.BAT`
`REM Sample Extended Batch`
`REM Language Batch File`
	Documentation remarks.

`BAT * Load EBL Into Memory`	BAT loads Extended Batch Language Plus (EBL Plus) into memory. It requires about 48K and automatically unloads when the batch file terminates. The rest of the line is a comment.
`CLS`	Clears the screen.
`ECHO Sound Speaker`	Displays a message.
`BEEP`	An EBL Plus command to sound the speaker.

`BEGSTACK`
`Now is the time for all ;`
`good men to come to the ;`
`aid of their country.`
`Now is the time for all ;`
`good men to come to the ;`
`aid of their country.`
`Now is the time for all ;`
`good men to come to the ;`
`aid of their country.\1A`
`END`
	Everything between the BEGSTACK and END is loaded into the keyboard buffer and supplied to the first program that reads the buffer. The semicolon on the end of some lines causes EBL Plus to ignore the return at the end of those lines. The \1A is hexadecimal for a Ctrl-Z.

`COPY CON NUL`	This copies from the keyboard to NUL, thus using the keystrokes loaded into the buffer above.
`PAUSE`	This pauses the batch file until a key is pressed.
`CLS`	Clears the screen.
`COLORCHAR @ AS COLOR(RED)`	Sets @ as a switch that toggles characters between standard color and red. In addition, EBL Plus prints a space when this character is used to change colors.

`BEGTYPE`
` This line is typed to the screen.`
`@So is this one.@`
` Only the second line was red.`
`@This line is red too.@`
`END`
	Everything between BEGTYPE and END is typed directly to the screen, with the @ acting as a color toggle, as described above.

10-1   EBL.BAT, which illustrates many of the EBL Plus keywords and functions.

10-1 Continued

Batch File Line	Explanation
`COLORCHAR @ AS COLOR(YELLOW)`	Change color toggle to yellow.

`BEGTYPE`
`  This line is plain.`
`@But this line is yellow.@`
`END`
`PAUSE`
	Display more information on the screen.

`GOTO -SKIP`
`ECHO This Lines Will Be Skipped`
`ECHO This Lines Will Be Skipped`
`-SKIP`
	Jump to a label. Works just like a DOS GOTO command except labels are treated differently.

`READ Do You Want To Exit (Y/N) > %A`	Get a character from the user. The READ command is not limited to a single character.
`IF %A=Y EXIT`	If the user enters Y, exit the batch file. Dual testing avoids capitalization problems.
`IF %A=y EXIT`	If the user enters y, exit the batch file. Dual testing avoids capitalization problems.
`CLS`	Clear the screen.
`READ Enter 1 To See Special Screen >%B`	Get more information from the user. Asking for a number avoids capitalization problems.
`IF %B=1 THEN`	While EBL Plus supports standard IF statements, this form is more powerful. THEN tells EBL Plus everything between the BEGIN and END are to be executed only if the IF statement is true.

`BEGIN`
`COLORCHAR @ AS COLOR(BLUE)`
`BEGTYPE`
`@`
`11111111111111111111111111111111111`
`          One Screen`
`11111111111111111111111111111111111`
`@`
`END`
`PAUSE`
`END if`
	This screen is displayed only if the above IF statement is true. Notice the use of the color toggle.

10-1   Continued

Batch File Line	Explanation
CLS	Clear the screen.
REPEAT WITH %I = 1 to 80	Set I=1, and continue until reaching an END. Then, increment I by one and go through the loop again. Continue this until I equals 80.
REPEAT WITH %J = 1 to 20	Set J=1, and continue until reaching an END. Then increment J by one and go through the loop again. Continue this until J equals 20.
LOCATE %I %J	Position the cursor on the screen.
TYPE "O"	Print an O on the screen at the cursor position from above.
END Repeat	Mark the bottom of the J loop.
END Repeat	Mark the bottom of the I loop.
PAUSE	Pause the batch file.
CLS	Clear the screen.
READ Enter Your Name > %1 %2	Request information from the user. Notice the >. Here it marks the end of the prompt and not the normal DOS pipe.
TYPE "Welcome" %1 %2	Type Welcome and then the user's name, as entered above.
TYPE "All Batch Files Are"	Display a message on the screen.

%B=DIR("*.BAT")
REPEAT WHILE %B IS NOT ""
    TYPE %B
    %B=DIR("*.BAT",i)
END REPEAT
	Loop through all the *.BAT files in the current subdirectory and display their name one at a time.

PAUSE	Pause the batch file.
CLS	Clear the screen.
SKIP 10	Skip the next ten lines in the batch file.
TYPE This Is Line 1 TYPE This Is Line 2 Continues Similarly TYPE This Is Line 9 TYPE This Is Line 10	Because of the SKIP 10 command, all of these lines are skipped and not executed.

10-1 Continued

Batch File Line	Explanation
TYPE This Is Line 11	This is the next line after the SKIP 10 line that is executed.
TYPE	Display a blank line on the screen.
TYPE Now I Will Pause TYPE For 10-Seconds	Tell the user what will happen next.
WAIT UNTIL TIME(10)	Pause the batch file for 10 seconds.
TYPE Finished Waiting	Let the user know the wait is over.
PAUSE	Wait for the user to press a key.
TYPE "I'm Thinking of a 2-Digit No."	Tell the user what is happening.
TYPE "Enter Your Guess"	Tell the user to enter a guess.
%1 = 27	Set up the value.
REPEAT WITH %A = 5 DOWN TO 0	Loop through and give the user up to six guesses.
READ %2	Read the users guess.

IF %2 = %1
    BEGIN
        TYPE "Good Guess!!!!!"
        EXIT REPEAT
    END
	Perform these steps if the user guesses the number. The EXIT REPEAT breaks out of the loop early.

IF %A = 0
    BEGIN
        TYPE "The Number Was " %1
        TYPE "This Number Doesn't"
        TYPE "Change When This Is"
        TYPE "Run Again"
        EXIT REPEAT
    END
	IF %A=0, then the user is out of guesses so tell him/her what the number was.

IF %2 > %1 TYPE "Lower:" %A "More Tries"	If the guess was too high, tell the user to guess lower and let him/her how many guesses remain.
IF %2 < %1 TYPE "Higher:" %A "More Tries"	If the guess was too low, tell the user to guess higher and let him/her how many guesses remain.
END REPEAT	End of the repeat loop.

Drawbacks

Extended Batch Language Plus won't run at all under DOS 5.0. As soon as BAT .COM tries to load, the computer locks up. EBL Plus will also not run reliably on an IBM Model 80 running IBM DOS 4.0. In fact, under DOS 4.0, neither the installation program nor the demonstration program will finish running. Both of them terminate in mid-course, but without locking the computer. The sample batch file EBL.BAT in Fig. 10-1 does run successfully under DOS 4.0. Additional drawbacks include:

Portability   An EBL Plus batch file requires EBL to run, so you must purchase a copy of the program for every machine you plan to use EBL Plus on.

Learning difficulty   One of the reasons it's so easy to use DOS batch files is that most of the commands are "regular" DOS commands. You already know how to use them. That isn't true with EBL. It's very much a programming language and, like any other programming languages, it requires study and practice to learn.

DOS compatibility   When using any package that functions as a superset of DOS, you always have to be concerned that it won't be compatible with the next release of DOS. EBL Plus's incompatibility with DOS 5.0 is an excellent example of this. If you depend on EBL Plus batch files and you upgrade to DOS 5.0, none of your batch files will run.

Price   You can write DOS batch files without purchasing any other program. You can purchase the utilities in this book for a small fee. Although EBL is a shareware package, the price is significant.

Conclusion

If you're running DOS 3.3 or earlier and you want to extend your batch files, Extended Batch Language Plus version 1.1 offers a good way to do that. You get most of the utilities you need packaged in a single program. However, if you run DOS 4.0 or later, you'll want to wait until a more compatible version of EBL Plus is released.

Builder

If you're running your batch files through DOS, chances are you're using a number of batch file enhancement programs. If you have Builder, you can discard almost all of those utilities because they're included with this compiler program.

Operation

Builder has two modes of operation, interactive and batch. In the interactive mode, Builder combines the compiler with a simple editor. If you load an exiting batch file, Builder does a good job of converting it into a Builder file with necessary changes made automatically. Some of those changes include:

- Commands to run a program have a RUN command inserted in front of them. So WORDSTAR becomes RUN WORDSTAR. This applies not only to programs, but to commands like CD \ and D:, which are DOS commands and not batch commands.
- A few commands, like FOR, use a slightly different syntax under Builder than they do under DOS. For example, the command

      FOR %%J IN (*.*) DO ECHO %%J

  in DOS becomes

      FOR %%J IN "*.*" DO ECHO %%J

  under Builder. Builder makes all these conversions automatically.

- The @ is stripped off the beginning of commands. Under DOS, @ turns command echoing off for a single line. Commands don't echo in Builder, so it doesn't need this.
- A few label names are converted. For example, Builder objects to END as a label name, but converts it automatically.

When you finish writing your Builder code, press F9 to compile it. You can also press Alt−C to generate the pull-down menu. Strangely, while menus compiled under Builder support a mouse, Builder itself doesn't.

If Builder finds errors while trying to compile a program, it opens a smaller window below the main window. In that window, it gives the line number for each line with an error and a brief error message. Often, the error message is simply *Syntax error*. If there are too many errors to fit on the screen, you can use the menu to switch to that window and scroll around. Once you've corrected all the errors, Builder will compile, link, and write the disk file automatically when you press F9.

While compiled batch files run faster than do regular batch files, the main reason for using Builder are its many enhancements, listed in Table 10-3. Just keep in mind that, because those enhancements have no counterpart under DOS, you can't debug your Builder batch files with DOS. As you can see from the table, Builder offers a wealth of enhancements that will do almost anything any other program listed in this book can do. Figure 10-2 shows a sample Builder program. The included disk has a compiled version of this program that you can run to see Builder perform its tricks. To compile a batch file in batch mode, enter:

    BLD *filename*

on the command line. If the file is a batch file, Builder automatically converts it to a Builder and file then tries to compile it. If it's successful, it creates the program

Table 10-3   Builder's many batch enhancements.

New Commands	Function
'	Adds a comment to the batch file, just like REM in DOS.
BEEP	Sounds the bell.
BOX	Draws a box of the screen. You can set colors at the same time.
CALL	Runs a DOS batch file and then returns control to the Builder compiled batch file. This is the default mode of operation. The command exists only to provide compatibility with DOS batch files which use the CALL command to run another batch file then regain control.
CASE	Allows batch files to be written in case format. You define a test then have a series of CASE statements that define one possible outcome. The statements under a CASE statement are executed only when that CASE is true.
CANCELED	A built-in variable that has a value of one if the last keyboard input ended with the user pressing Escape.
CLOSE	Closes a file and releases the memory associated with that file.
CLOSEALLFILES	Closes all open files and releases all the memory associated with those files.
CLS	Clears the screen, just like in DOS.
CURRENTDRIVE	Places the current drive in a string variable.
DOSERRORLEVEL	Assigns the value of the DOS ERRORLEVEL to a variable for easy storage and easier testing.
DISKFREE	Assigns the amount of free space on a specified drive to a variable.
DISKLABEL	Assigns the volume label to a variable.
DISKREADY	Assigns a value to a variable to indicate if the specified drive is read to use.
DROPDOWN	Creates a drop-down menu for the user to select items from.
ECHO	Works just like the DOS ECHO command. Builder has the more powerful SAY command, so the only purpose of the ECHO command is to maximize compatibility with DOS.
ELSE	Defines those commands to be performed if a statement is false.
EMSAVIL	Assigns the amount of EMS memory that is available to a variable.
EMSINSTALLED	Assigns a one to a variable if EMS is available, a zero otherwise.
EMSMAJOR	Assigns the major (e.g., 3 or 4) EMS version number to a variable.
EMSMINOR	Assigns the minor EMS version number to a variable.
EMSTOTAL	Assigns the total installed EMS memory amount to a variable.
EMSVERSION	Assigns the complete EMS version number to a variable.

Table 10-3 Continued

New Commands	Function
ENVAVAIL	Assigns the amount of free environmental space to a variable.
ENVTOTAL	Assigns the total amount of environmental space to a variable.
EOF	Assigns a zero to a variable if Builder has not yet reached the end of the file it is reading.
EXIT	Stops the batch file and returns control to DOS.
FILE	Configures Builder to begin writing to the specified file.
FILESIZE	Assigns the size of a file to a variable.
FOR	Just like DOS, the FOR command loops through a series of items and performs a single action on each item. Like DOS, FOR commands cannot be nested.
GETKEY	Gets a single keystroke from the user. It works better than programs like Norton's Ask that place their values in ERRORLEVEL because you can test with an equality test rather than the greater than or equal tests DOS uses with ERRORLEVEL.
GETYN	Gets a single keystroke from the user but accepts only a y or n. Like Norton's Ask program, it sets ERRORLEVEL to 0 for an n and 1 for a y.
GOTO	Jumps to another part of the batch file and resumes processing, just like DOS.
GOTOXY	Locates the cursor at a specific location on the screen.
IF	Determines if a command or series of commands is to be executed based on a logical test, just like DOS.
INPUT	Accepts multiple characters from the user and assign them to a variable.
INTEGER	Allocates an integer variable for Builder to use.
LASTKEY	Stores the value from the Getkey command.
LONGINT	Allocates an integer variable for Builder to use. LONGINT integers accept larger numbers than do INTEGER ones.
LIGHTBAR	Chooses an item from a moving lightbar menu.
MAXCOLS	Assigns the current width of the screen to a variable.
MAXROWS	Assigns the current length of the screen to a variable.
MOVE	Copies a file from one location to another (possibly with a new name) and then deletes the original version. This actually copies the file, it does not work like some move commands that simply rewrite the directory information associated with a file without copying it.
ONPATH	Assigns a value to a variable to let you know if the specified file is somewhere in the path.
OPEN	Opens a file so Builder can work with it.
OSMAJOR	Assigns the major DOS version number to a variable.
OSMINOR	Assigns the minor DOS version number to a variable.

Table 10-3 Continued

New Commands	Function
OSVERSION	Assigns the entire DOS version number to a variable.
PARAMCOUNT	A keyword used in an IF test to represent the number of parameters entered on the command line.
PASSWORD	Accepts input from the user and compares it to a password you enter on the command line. If the two are the same, it sets ERRORLEVEL to 0; otherwise it sets ERRORLEVEL to 1.
PAUSE	Like DOS, it causes the batch file to wait until a key is pressed. However, there is no "Strike a key to continue" message.
POPUP	A general menu creation tool.
READLINE	Gets a single line of text from a file and assigns it to a variable.
REBOOT	Performs a warm reboot. This is very useful if you have a batch file modify a CONFIG.SYS or AUTOEXEC.BAT file.
REM	This flags a line as a comment that is ignored by Builder. Builder also uses the apostrophe to mark comments.
RENSUB	Renames a DOS subdirectory.
REPEAT	Repeats a command the indicated number of times.
REWIND	Returns to the top of a file.
ROWCOL	Moves the cursor to a specific location.
RUN	Passes a command out of the compiled batch file to DOS.
SAVEFILE	Saves an open file without closing it.
SAY	Similar to ECHO except you can control the text location and color.
SET	Creates or changes environmental variables.
SHIFT	Just like the DOS SHIFT commands, it moves the contents of %2 into %1, %3 into %2, and so on.
STRING	Allocates space for string variables.
SUB	Marks a section of batch file as a subroutine.
SYSTEM	Passes the contents of a string variable to DOS as a command.
UNSHIFT	The opposite of a DOS SHIFT command. %0 becomes %1, %1 becomes %2, and so on.
USE BIOS/DOS	Selects how the compiled batch file handles text.
WHEREX	Returns the column containing the cursor.
WHEREY	Returns the row containing the cursor.
WHILE	Repeats a command or series of commands until a specific condition takes place.
WRITELINE	Writes a string to a file.

Batch File Line	Explanation

`' REM Builder Example`
`' This Batch File Must Be Compiled To Run`
`' Set Up Variables`
	Documentation remarks. Builder can use either a REM or an apostrophe to indicate a remark.

`STRING   Drive`
`LONGINT FreeSpace`
`INTEGER IsThereEMS`
`LONGINT EMSFree`
`LONGINT EMSThere`
`INTEGER Major`
`INTEGER Minor`
`STRING   All`
`INTEGER E_Available`
`INTEGER E_Total`
`INTEGER F_Size`
`STRING   First`
`STRING   Last`
`STRING   Title`
`INTEGER Rows`
`INTEGER Columns`
`INTEGER Lotus123`
`INTEGER Parameters`
	These statements "declare" variable names and types. Builder requires you to do this prior to using the variables.

`CLS`	Clear the screen.
`' Draw Some Boxes`	Documentation remark.

`DOUBLE BOX   1, 1,80,24 BRIGHT WHITE     ON RED`
`SINGLE BOX   5, 5,20,10 BRIGHT RED       ON BLACK`
`SINGLE BOX 10,10,20,10 BRIGHT RED       ON BLACK`
`SINGLE BOX 10,20,20,10 BRIGHT MAGENTA ON WHITE`
`SINGLE BOX   1,35,15,20 BRIGHT CYAN      ON RED`
	Draw five boxes on the screen.

`SAY @ 10,34 "<BRIGHT WHITE>Press Any Key` `    To Continue"`	Tell the user the batch file has paused until a key is pressed.
`PAUSE`	Pause the batch file. Unlike DOS, this command by itself does not display any message.
`CLS`	Clear the screen.

`DROPDOWN "Select Your Title"`
`    ITEM "          MS          "`
`         Title:="MS. "`
`    ITEM "          MR          "`
`         Title:="MR. "`
`    ITEM "          MRS         "`
`         Title:="MRS. "`
`    ITEM "          DR          "`
`         Title:="Doctor "`
`END`
	Put a drop-down menu on the screen for the user to select a title from. Once the user selects a title, set a variable to the appropriate title.

`CLS`	Clear the screen.

10-2 ZBUILD.BLD, a sample Builder program, which must be compiled with Builder.

10-2 Continued

Batch File Line	Explanation
`SAY "Please Enter Your First Name: ";` `INPUT First`	Request the user's first name and place the response into a variable called FIRST.
`SAY`	Skip a line. Unlike the DOS ECHO command, SAY alone prints a blank line.
`SAY "Please Enter Your Last  Name: ";` `INPUT Last`	Obtain the user's last name and store it in a variable.
`CLS`	Clear the screen.
`SAY "<BRIGHT WHITE>Hello "; Title; First;` `    " "; Last`	Tell the user hello. Notice the use of user-inputted variables and the TITLE variable set using the menu.
`SAY "<BRIGHT WHITE>Sounding Speaker"`	Tell the user what will happen next.
`BEEP`	Sound the speaker.
`Drive:=CURRENTDRIVE`	Store the drive letter to a variable.
`SAY "<BRIGHT RED>The Current Drive Is "; Drive`	Tell the user which drive is the current drive.
`FreeSpace:=DISKFREE Drive`	Store the amount of free space to a variable.
`SAY "<BRIGHT GREEN>The "; Drive; " drive Has` `    "; FreeSpace; "-Bytes of Free Space"`	Tell the user how much space is available.
`IsThereEMS:=EMSINSTALLED`	Perform a logical test to see if EMS memory is installed and store the results in a variable.
`IF NOT IsThereEMS SAY "<BRIGHT MAGENTA>EMS` `    Not Installed"`	If no EMS memory is installed, tell the user.
`IF NOT IsThereEMS GOTO NOEMS`	If no EMS memory is installed, skip the remaining tests.
`EMSFree:=EMSAVAIL`	Store the amount of available EMS memory to a variable.
`SAY "<BRIGHT MAGENTA>There is "; EMSFree;` `    "-Bytes of EMS Available"`	Tell the user how much EMS memory is available.

10-2 Continued

Batch File Line	Explanation
`EMSThere:=EMSTOTAL`	Store the total amount of EMS memory to a variable.
`SAY "<BRIGHT MAGENTA>There is "; EMSThere;` `    "-Bytes of EMS Installed"`	Tell the user.
`Major:=EMSMAJOR`	Store the major EMS version to a variable. If you were running version 4.0, this would store the 4 to the variable. Both this and MINOR are numeric variables while ALL is a string variable.
`Minor:=EMSMINOR`	Store the minor EMS version to a variable. In the above example, this would be a 0.
`All:=EMSVERSION`	Store the EMS version number to a string variable. In the above example, this would be a 4.0.

`SAY "<BRIGHT MAGENTA>The EMS Major Number`
`    is "; Major`
`SAY "<BRIGHT MAGENTA>The EMS Minor Number`
`    is "; Minor`
`SAY "<BRIGHT MAGENTA>The EMS        Number`
`    is "; All`
	Give the EMS information to the user.

`:NOEMS`	Label marking the end of the EMS testing section.
`E_Available:=ENVAVAIL`	Store the amount of free environmental space to a variable.
`E_Total:=ENVTOTAL`	Store the amount of total environmental space to a variable.

`SAY "<BRIGHT GREEN>You Have "; E_Total;`
`    "-Bytes of Environmental Space ";`
`SAY "<BRIGHT GREEN>of That, ";E_Available;`
`    "-Bytes is Free"`
	Give the environmental information to the user.

`F_Size:=FILESIZE "ZBUILD.COM"`	Store the size of ZBUILD.COM in a variable.
`SAY "<BRIGHT BLUE>The Size of ZBUILD.COM is` `    "; F_Size; "-Bytes"`	Tell the user.
`SAY "Only A Y or N Key Will Be Accepted"` `SAY "But Try Other Keys First"`	Tell the user what will happen next.
`GETYN`	Get a Y or N keystroke from the user.

10-2 Continued

Batch File Line	Explanation
`SAY "-Pressed"`	Tell the user what key was pressed. GETYN displays the keystroke itself, so this simply completes the message.
`SAY "Next, Only A Q Will Be Accepted"` `SAY "Note that A Lowercase q Will NOT Work"`	Tell user what will happen next.
`:TOPKEY`	Label marking the top of a loop where the only character that will be accepted is a Q.
`GETKEY`	Get any keystroke from the user.
`IF LASTKEY IS {Q} GOTO DONEKEY`	If that keystroke was a Q, exit the loop.
`BEEP`	The batch file reaches this line only if the user presses an invalid key so the batch file beeps.
`GOTO TOPKEY`	Loops back to the top of the loop.
`:DONEKEY`	Label marking the loop exit point.
`Columns:=MAXCOLS`	Store the maximum number of columns in a variable.
`Rows:=MAXROWS`	Store the maximum number of rows in a variable.
`SAY "You Display Can Show "; Columns;` `SAY " Columns and "; Rows; " Rows"`	Tell the user.
`Lotus123:=ONPATH "LOTUS.EXE"`	Perform a logical test to see if LOTUS.EXE is in the path.
`IF Lotus123 IS 1 SAY "LOTUS.EXE In Path"` `IF Lotus123 IS 0 SAY "LOTUS.EXE Not In Path"`	Tell the user.

`Major:=OSMAJOR`
`Minor:=OSMINOR`
`All:=OSVERSION`
	Store the major, minor, and entire DOS version in variables.

`SAY "Your Major DOS Version Is "; Major;`
`SAY " Your Minor DOS Version Is "; Minor`
`SAY "Your DOS Version Is "; All`
	Tell the user.

`Parameters:=PARAMCOUNT`	Store the number of parameters entered on the command line in a variable.

`SAY "Including The ZBUILD Command, ";`
`SAY "You Entered "; Parameters`
`SAY "Parameters When You Started This Program"`
	Tell the user.

`SAY "<BRIGHT CYAN>Press Any Key To` `    Continue Demonstration"`	Tell the user to press any key to continue the batch file.
`PAUSE`	Pause the batch file until a key is pressed.

Batch File Line	Explanation
`:MENUTOP`	Label marking the top of a menu loop. The loop is required so the user will return to the menu after running a non-exit option.
`CLS`	Clear the screen.
`DROPDOWN "Sample Menu"`	Command to display the menu. Each line below this until the END line that starts with an ITEM keyword will become a menu option.
`    ITEM "         Run Lotus         "`	This line marks the first item in the menu. Notice the spaces around the text, this makes the menu wider.

`        CLS`
`        SAY "I Would Run Lotus Here"`
`        SAY "Then I Would Reload Menu"`
`        SAY "Notice The Mouse Support"`
`        SAY "Press Any Key To Continue"`
`        PAUSE`
`        GOTO MENUTOP`
	All of the command between the above ITEM line and the next ITEM line are executed when this item is selected. Notice the last line goes to the top of the loop to redisplay the menu.

`    ITEM "         Run dBASE         "`
`        CLS`
`        Say "I Would Run dBASE Here"`
`        SAY "Then I Would Reload Menu"`
`        SAY "Notice The Mouse Support"`
`        SAY "Press Any Key To Continue"`
`        PAUSE`
`        GOTO MENUTOP`
	Next menu option.

`    ITEM "         QUIT Menu         "` `        SAY "Exiting Menu"`	Last menu item. Since this is the option to exit the menu, it does not redisplay the menu.
`END`	Keyword marking the end of the menu.
`:MENUTOP2`	Label marking the top of a second menu. A LIGHTBAR menu works just like a DROPDOWN menu, only the display mode is different.

Batch File Line	Explanation
| ```
CLS
LIGHTBAR
   ITEM "Run Lotus  "
       CLS
       SAY "I Would Run Lotus Here"
       SAY "Then I Would Reload Menu"
       SAY "Press Any Key To Continue"
       PAUSE
       GOTO MENUTOP2
   ITEM "Run dBASE  "
       CLS
       Say "I Would Run dBASE Here"
       SAY "Then I Would Reload Menu"
       SAY "Press Any Key To Continue"
       PAUSE
       GOTO MENUTOP2
   ITEM "QUIT Menu"
       SAY "Exiting Menu"
END
``` | A moving lightbar menu. |
| `CLS` | Clear the screen. |
| ```
SAY "Next,I'm Going To Ask You For A Password"
SAY "Remember, The Password Is:"
SAY
SAY "<BLINK><BRIGHT WHITE>Tab Books"
SAY
SAY "Capitalization Is Not Critical"
SAY
SAY "Press Any Key When You Are Ready"
PAUSE
CLS
``` | Tell the user what will happen next. |
| `:NOPASS` | Label marking the top of the section requiring a password. |
| ```
SAY @ 12,30 "<BRIGHT WHITE>Enter Your
    Password: ";
``` | Tell the user to enter a password. |
| `PASSWORD "Tab Books"` | Command to accept the password and tell Builder the password so it can set the ERRORLEVEL accordingly. |
| ```
IF ERRORLEVEL 0 IF NOT ERRORLEVEL 1
    GOTO YESPASS
``` | If ERRORLEVEL is zero, the user entered the proper password, so exit the loop. |
| ```
SAY @ 20,01 "<BLINK><BRIGHT RED>Wrong
    Password! Try Again"
``` | If the batch file reaches this line, an invalid password was entered, so tell the user. |
| `GOTO NOPASS` | Go to the top of the loop. |
| `:YESPASS` | Label marking the exit point of the password loop. |
```

10-2 Continued

Batch File Line	Explanation
| ```
CLS
SAY "This Concludes The Demonstration"
SAY "Thank You For Taking The Time To View It"
SAY
SAY "Ronny Richardson"
SAY "Copyright 1991"
``` | Exit the batch file. |

file automatically. If not, it creates a file containing all the error message, prints a brief error message to the screen, and exits to DOS.

Problems

Builder displays less than clear error messages when it finds an error. And all you get is a line number and this message. The error messages are made even more cryptic because they aren't listed or explained in the manual. Also, as mentioned previously, while compiled Builder menus support a mouse, Builder itself doesn't.

Conclusion

Builder is a fantastic product. It's powerful enough to replace all your batch file utilities and, because the resulting files are compiled, you can distribute them without paying royalties or worrying about other users needing copies of utilities. In fact, SetError and ShowEnvironment in the prior chapter were written with Builder.

Builder costs $149.95 and is well worth it. For more information, contact:

HYPERKINETIX, INC.
666 Baker St., Suite 405
Costa Mesa, CA 92626
(800) 873-9993.

Bat2Exec

PC Magazine introduced their batch file compiler in the August 1990 issue (Volume 9, Number 14) in the Utilities column. The compiler is called Bat2Exec and was written by Douglas Boling. The magazine printed two pages of tiny Basic code with which you could create the program, and an .ASM listing. You can also download the finished program from PC MagNet—complete details are included in most issues of *PC Magazine*.

Bat2Exec is strictly a batch file compiler—it will compile existing DOS batch files, but adds no new features to the language. Thus, you get additional speed and security without the overhead of learning new commands and working with a new environment. You can completely write and debug your batch files using DOS, and then compile them when they're finished.
```

Operation

To compile a batch file, enter:

> BAT2EXEC *filename*

at the DOS prompt. You must include the .BAT extension. When Bat2Exec successfully compiles a batch file, it creates a .COM program that performs the same task. You'll want to keep the batch file in case you ever need to modify it. Because DOS executes .COM programs over batch files, you can store both in the same directory and DOS will always run the compiled program.

Problems

Bat2Exec version 1.0 requires an end-of-file (EOF) marker on the last line of the batch file. This is a holdover from CP/M, a pre-PC operating system. CP/M required an EOF because it stored only the number of clusters in the file, so it didn't know where in the last cluster the file ended. Thus, the EOF marker told it where the file ended. DOS stores the actual length of the file, so an EOF marker is redundant. Most programs don't require an EOF marker and ignore it if it's present. Therefore, most editors don't add one to the end of a file. If your editor doesn't, add a blank line to the bottom of the batch file and enter Alt-2 (you must use the numbers on the keypad) on that line. That should enter a right-pointing arrow—the EOF marker.

Bat2Exec version 1.3 corrects the EOF problem, but introduces a second, and just as annoying, problem. The following line:

> FOR % %J IN (*.DOC) DO ECHO File. . . % %J Found

or any similar line will sometimes work properly, and sometimes display random characters or only part of the line on the screen. Bat2Exec compiled batch files demonstrate a number of problems that further limit their usefulness. The major ones are ErrorLevel and the environment.

Bat2Exec batch files don't respond properly to the ErrorLevel if it's set prior to running the compiled program. It also improperly handles ErrorLevel codes used internally if they're produced by a program that prompts the user for a response and stores that response in ErrorLevel. Finally, it resets the ErrorLevel to zero when it exits or calls an external batch file.

Like any compiled program, batch files compiled with Bat2Exec get a copy of the environment, not the original. Thus, any changes made by a batch file compiled with Bat2Exec are lost when the program terminates. The program gets only enough environmental space to contain the current environment, so trying to add any temporary working variables results in an *Out of environmental space* error message. Not having any extra environmental space also means that existing variables can't be expanded beyond their current length. Occasionally, when a compiled batch file runs out of environmental space, it locks up rather than just aborting with an error message.

Both of these problems are significant limitations for Bat2Exec, but they're not fatal ones. They do mean you'll need to scan your batch files to make sure they're suitable for Bat2Exec. Forget any batch files that prompt the user or depend on the environment. After compiling your batch file, you should test it extensively to make sure it still works properly. Keep in mind, also, that these two errors might mean that other as-yet-undiscovered errors lurk somewhere in the program.

Conclusion

Because Bat2Exec doesn't add any new features to DOS, the best candidates for compiling are those batch files that take a long time to run. The disk includes a copy of FANCYECH.COM, which is FANCYECH.BAT compiled by Bat2Exec.

Summary

Both Extended Batch Language and Builder offer extensive improvements to the batch language. EBL Plus in an interpretative environment and Builder in a compiled environment. Bat2Exec offers no improvements to the batch language, but does allow batch files to run much faster than they do under DOS.

Part 4
Advanced batch file programming

11
CHAPTER

Subroutines in batch files

In programming, a subroutine is a special type of program. When a program calls a subroutine, control is passed to the subroutine. When the subroutine is finished, control is passed back to the calling program. The calling program continues from the point where it passed control to the subroutine. Figure 11-1 illustrates this.

Tricking DOS into running subroutines

Prior to DOS version 3.3, batch files didn't support subroutines. A simple experiment will illustrate this. Figure 11-2 is the main batch file and Fig. 11-3 is the subroutine batch file. Run SUB1.BAT on your system. As you can see, once a batch file passes control to another batch file, control never passes back to the original batch file.

This isn't how a batch file behaves when it passes control to a program. When that program finishes, control is passed back to the calling batch file. This fact can be used to "trick" DOS before version 3.3 into allowing one batch file to call another and gain back control when the subroutine batch file finishes.

Normally, you don't think of COMMAND.COM as a program. Yet it is. Running COMMAND.COM by simply typing COMMAND at the command line runs COMMAND.COM. This loads a second copy of the command processor into memory. The command to exit this second command processor is EXIT, which terminates the second command processor and returns control back to the first (and calling) command processor.

The "trick" involves invoking a second command processor, having that second command processor run the subroutine batch file, and then dropping out of

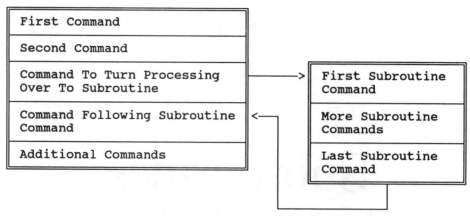

11-1 Illustration of how one program can call another, the second one being the *subroutine*.

Batch File Line	Explanation
REM SUB1.BAT	Remark giving the name of the batch file.
ECHO OFF	Turn command-echoing off.
REM This is the main program REM It will call the subroutine REM on the next line	Documentation remarks.
SUB2	Run SUB2.BAT. Control will not return to this batch file.
ECHO If control returns to SUB1.BAT ECHO you will see this message	Documentation messages.

11-2 SUB1.BAT, a sample batch file that will attempt to call another batch file.

Batch File Line	Explanation
REM SUB2.BAT	Remark giving the name of the batch file.
ECHO This is the last line in SUB2.BAT	Documentation message.

11-3 SUB2.BAT, a sample "subroutine" batch file.

the second command processor to return control to the calling batch file. The syntax to call the second batch file is:

    COMMAND /C *batch file name*

The /C tells COMMAND.COM to run the following command, which, in this case, is a batch file. The last command of the subroutine batch file must be EXIT, which returns control to the original batch file. Figures 11-4 and 11-5 show the batch files from Figures 11-2 and 11-3 modified to take advantage of this technique.

Batch File Line	Explanation
`REM SUB3.BAT`	Remark giving the name of the batch file.
`ECHO OFF`	Turn command-echoing off.

`REM This is the main program`
`REM It will call the subroutine`
`REM on the next line`
	Documentation remarks.

`COMMAND /C SUB4`	Run SUB4.BAT as a subroutine by loading a secondary command processor. This method does not require a later version of DOS where the CALL command is available.

`ECHO If control returns to`
`    SUB3.BAT`
`ECHO you will see this message`
	Documentation messages.

11-4 SUB3.BAT, which is SUB1.BAT from Fig. 11-2, modified to call a subroutine batch file.

Batch File Line	Explanation
`REM SUB4.BAT`	Remark giving the name of the batch file.
`ECHO This is the next TO last` `ECHO line in SUB4.BAT`	Documentation messages.
`EXIT`	Causes control to return to the batch file that invoked this batch file. This line is not needed if the batch file is invoked with the CALL command rather than the COMMAND/C command.

11-5 SUB4.BAT, which is SUB2.BAT from Fig. 11-3, modified to be used as a subroutine.

Note that control did return to SUB3.BAT. Also note that the second command processor was loaded with the normal default of ECHO ON. This trick isn't required in DOS 3.3 or later. DOS 3.3 adds the CALL batch file command, which allows a batch file to call another batch file with the following command:

CALL *batch file*

The batch file being called doesn't even have to end with an EXIT command. That is all well and good, but you might be asking yourself "So what?" I use this technique every day in two sets of batch files, described in the two following sections, and they'll illustrate just how powerful subroutines are.

Copying files to a disk

I keep duplicate copies of all my home files on my computer at the office, and I keep duplicate copies of all my office files on my computer at home. At the end of a work day, I copy all my modified files to a floppy disk and carry them home. At the end of writing in the afternoon, I copy all my modified files to a floppy disk to take to the office. I always know which files have been modified because I do most of my work using Lotus release 3 and Microsoft Word, and both produce .BAK files when a file is modified. So I do a directory of all the .BAK files and enter their name after the TOA command. For example, if a DIR *.BAK showed the files BOOK.BAK, ACCOUNT.BAK, and TOTALS.BAK, I would enter the command:

TOA BOOK ACCOUNT TOTALS

Notice I don't need to enter the file extensions. The above command runs a batch file called TOA.BAT, shown in Fig. 11-6.

Batch File Line	Explanation
@ECHO OFF	Turn command-echoing off.
REM TOA.BAT	Remark giving the name of the batch file.
IF (%1)==() GOTO END	If the first replaceable parameter is empty, exit the batch file.
:START	Label marking the top of a loop.
SET FILE=%1	Store the name of the file to copy in an environmental variable called FILE.
SET DRIVE=A:	Store the target location in an environmental variable called DRIVE.
CALL TO.BAT	Switch to another batch file to handle the actual copying. This allows the use of other batch files to copy to different locations.
IF ERRORLEVEL 1 GOTO END	If a copying error occurred in TO.BAT, exit this batch file. No error-handling tasks are necessary because this is handled in TO.BAT.
SHIFT	Move the replaceable parameters down one level.
IF (%1)==() GOTO END	If there are no more replaceable parameters, exit the batch file.
GOTO START	Continue the loop.
:END	Label marking the (near) end of the batch file.
ECHO FINISHED	Tell the user the batch file is finished.
SET DRIVE= SET FILE=	Reset the environmental variables.

11-6 TOA.BAT, a batch file that controls the process of copying files to the A drive.

TOA.BAT first checks to make sure at least one filename is entered and, if not, it doesn't run. If a filename is entered, it stores it in the environment under the name FILE. It stores the drive to copy the file to (A drive in this case) in the environment under the name DRIVE. I have an almost identical version of this batch file called TOB.BAT that copies to the B drive. Once the environmental variables are set, it calls another batch file called TO.BAT. Because this runs under DOS 4.0, it does not require any tricks to call a subroutine. TO.BAT performs the actual copying and is discussed below. Once control passes back to TOA.BAT, it exits if any error occurred. It doesn't print an error message because TO.BAT takes care of that. It issues a SHIFT command to make the next variable a %1 variable. If there is another value, it loops through again—otherwise, it exits.

TO.BAT in Fig. 11-7 performs the actual copying. It begins by turning the echo off because DOS defaults back on when a batch file is called. It then performs the same couple of steps for .DOC, .CMP, .WK? and .ALL files. You now see why I entered the filenames without the extension—DOS has no way for a batch file to strip off the extension. First, the batch file copies the file if it exists. The >NUL part of the file pipes the *One file(s) copied* message to NUL, so it doesn't show on the screen.

Batch File Line	Explanation
`@ECHO OFF`	Turn command-echoing off.
`REM TO.BAT`	Remark giving the name of the batch file.
`:DOC`	Label marking the beginning of the section to handle copying *.DOC files.
`IF EXIST %FILE%.DOC XCOPY %FILE%.DOC %DRIVE%>NUL`	Copy the files stored in the environmental variable FILE to the location stored in DRIVE. Notice the piping to nul to hide the DOS message.
`IF EXIST %FILE%.DOC IF NOT EXIST %DRIVE%%FILE%.DOC ECHO COPY ERROR`	If the copy was not successful, warn the user.
`IF EXIST %FILE%.DOC IF NOT EXIST %DRIVE%%FILE%.DOC GOTO ERROR`	If the copy was not successful, jump to an error-handling routine.
`IF ERRORLEVEL 1 GOTO ERROR`	If XCOPY reported an error, jump to an error-handling routine.
`IF EXIST %FILE%.DOC FOR %%J IN (%FILE%.DOC) DO ECHO COPIED.....%%J TO %DRIVE%`	If files were copied, tell the user which ones.

The batch file has a number of identical sections for handling other types of files the same way it handles *.DOC files.

11-7 TO.BAT, the program that does the actual copying called for in TOA.BAT in Fig. 11-6.

11-7 Continued

Batch File Line	Explanation
`:ERROR`	Beginning of the error-handling section.

`ECHO WARNING DANGER WILL ROBINSON`
`ECHO XCOPY OF FILE %FILE% WAS NOT`
`ECHO COMPLETED. BATCH FILE TERMINATING`
`ECHO FILES REMAINING TO BE COPIED ARE`
`ECHO LISTED BELOW. A MAXIMUM OF NINE`
`ECHO ARE LISTED`
`ECHO %FILE%, %2, %3, %4, %5, %6, %7,`
`ECHO %8, %9 ^G^G`
	Tell the user about the error. Notice the use of ^Gs to ring the bell.

`GOTO END`	Exit the batch file.
`:END`	Label marking the (near) end of the batch file.
`REM FINISHED COPY`	Documentation remark.

Next, it checks to see if the file was successfully copied. Notice that the following statement uses two IF statements:

```
IF EXIST %FILE%.DOC
IF NOT EXIST %DRIVE% %FILE%.DOC ECHO COPY ERROR ^G
```

This statement is true only if both IF statements are true. It sounds the bell and the next line jumps to an error handling routine. I used this rather than an ErrorLevel test because of two bugs I've discovered in the XCOPY command:

First, under Compaq DOS 3.3, if you have a file called RONNY_FI.DOC (for instance) and you issue the command:

```
XCOPY RONNY_FILE.DOC A:
```

DOS will act like it's copying the file and will even give you a *1 file(s) copied* message, but it won't copy the file! I typically give filenames consisting of the first eight characters of a longer name and I sometimes just type the whole name in on the command line. Doing this works with the COPY command and IBM DOS 4.01 XCOPY, but not the Compaq DOS 3.3 I have at the office.

Second, under IBM DOS 4.0, XCOPY doesn't set the ErrorLevel properly when an error occurs. In fact, it rarely sets the ErrorLevel regardless of whether an error occurs. Testing to make sure the file exists on the source and target drives avoids both these problems. The final line of the batch file echoes a message to the user telling him the file was copied.

TO.BAT loops through and copies each type of file (.DOC, .CMP, .WK? and

.ALL) that exist for each filename. Usually, two files are copied for each name. The .CMP files are special file-specific dictionary files created by Microsoft Word to go along with documents. The .ALL files are Allways formatting files created when you format a worksheet with the worksheet publishing program Allways.

Distributing files on a hard disk

Once I get the disk home (or to the office) with the modified files, I have the problem of distributing the files to the appropriate location. Both of my computers have hard disks that are very similar. I try to use standard names to make determining where the files go easier. For example, all the files for my first book have a 01 in them. Chapter 1 is CHAP0101.DOC, Chapter 2 is CHAP0201.DOC and so on. That was the first edition of this book. When I began this update, those chapters became CHAP011A.DOC, CHAP021A.DOC and so on. My second book has CHAP0102.DOC, CHAP0202.DOC, and so on. My third book has CHAP 0103.DOC, CHAP0203.DOC, and so on. Hopefully, by the time I've written 99 books, Microsoft will have overcome the eight-character limit on filenames.

With these standardized filenames, I use a couple of batch files to automate the process. The first, GET.BAT, copies the files from the floppy into the C: \ A subdirectory. It's shown in Fig. 11-8. Notice the piping in order to answer the prompt about deleting all the files. If I have more than one disk, I just run GET .BAT more than once.

Batch File Line	Explanation
`c:`	Make sure the computer is logged onto the C drive.
`cd\a`	Change to the \A subdirectory.
`xcopy a:`	Copy all the files from the A drive.
`echo y|del a:.`	Delete all the files on the A drive. The ECHO Y| portion of the command pipes the response to the DOS "All files in the directory will be deleted. Are you sure?" prompt so the command runs without user intervention.

11-8 GET.BAT, which copies files from floppy disks to the subdirectory C: \ A.

Once I have all the files copied to the C: \ A subdirectory, I run a batch file called FROMA.BAT, shown in Fig. 11-9. For each file, FROMA.BAT sets the filename in the environmental variable FILE, and the subdirectory to copy it to in the TO environmental variable. It then calls the batch file SUBROUTI.BAT as a subroutine to do the actual processing. Figure 11-10 shows this.

Batch File Line	Explanation
`@ECHO OFF`	Turn command-echoing off.
`CD\A`	Change to the \A subdirectory.

`REM ==============================`
`REM THIS MUST REMAIN THE FIRST`
`    SETTING`
	Documentation remark.

`SET FILE=*.STY` `SET TO=C:\WORD\NORMAL`	Set two environmental variables.
`CALL SUBROUTINE`	Call SUBROUTI.BAT to handle the actual copying based on the values stored in the environmental variables. Two notes: Control returns to FROMA.BAT since it uses the CALL command. Using the longer and more meaningful name for SUBROUTI.BAT does not cause problems for most version of DOS.
`IF ERRORLEVEL 1 GOTO END`	If there was a copying problem, exit the batch file. SUBROUTI.BAT will have alerted the user already.
`REM ==============================`	Documentation remark.

`SET FILE=0?-*.*`
`SET TO=D:\LETTERS`
`CALL SUBROUTINE`
`IF ERRORLEVEL 1 GOTO END`
	A series of commands for handling one type of file.

The above block of four commands are repeated for a large number of files.	
`:END`	A label marking the (near) end of the batch file.
`SET FILE=` `SET TO=`	Reset the contents of the environmental variables to nul.
`ECHO ^G^G`	Ring the bell twice to let the user know this long batch file has finished.

11-9   FROMA.BAT, which copies the files in C:\A to the proper subdirectory.

Batch File Line	Explanation
`echo off`	Turn command-echoing off.
`echo Testing for.....%file%`	Tell the user what is happening. The batch file that calls this batch file sets the value of FILE into the environment.

11-10   SUBROUTINE.BAT, which does the actual copying specified in FROMA.BAT in Fig. 11-9.

11-10 Continued

Batch File Line	Explanation
`if not exist %file% goto end`	If the file whose name is stored under FILE does not exist, exit the batch file.
`xcopy %file% %to% > nul`	Copy the file whose name is stored under FILE to the location stored in the environmental variable TO. The calling batch file sets the value of TO.
`if errorlevel 1 echo ^G^G`	If XCOPY reports an error, ring the bell.

`if errorlevel 1 echo`
`***WARNING*** Problem`
`copying %file%`
	If XCOPY reports an error, inform the user.

`if errorlevel 1 goto end`	If XCOPY reports an error, exit the batch file.
`for %%j in (%file%) do echo` `Moved..........%%j to %to%`	If the batch file reaches this point, the copy was successful, so tell the user what has happened.
`del %file%`	Delete the file that was copied. Thus, the batch file performs a move rather than a straight copy.
`:end`	Label marking the (near) end of the batch file.
`exit`	This is required if the batch file is called using the COMMAND/C trick for a version of DOS prior to 3.3.

All-in-one batch files

Each batch file you write takes up a minimum of one cluster of disk space. Depending on several factors, that can be up to 8K and will most likely be at least 2K. If you're running very short of hard disk space, that can seem like a large price to pay for a relatively small subroutine. You can avoid this by bundling all the subroutines within the main batch file. BIGSUB.BAT in Fig. 11-11 illustrates the technique.

While bundling subroutines within the main batch file is possible, I strongly recommend that you don't do it. As you can see by quickly scanning Fig. 11-11, it's a complicated process. You have to design your IF tests to skip the subroutines the first time the batch file is called and to skip the main portion of the batch file when it's called as a subroutine. The result is one very complex batch file. It would have taken me about five or ten minutes to put together a simple multi-batch file system to do what BIGSUB.BAT does. The extra complexity of bundling all the files together resulted in my having to spend over an hour getting BIGSUB.BAT debugged and running properly. It will be just as difficult if I have

Batch File Line	Explanation
`@ECHO OFF`	Turn command-echoing off.

`REM BIGSUBBAT`
`REM Sample Batch File That`
`REM Calls Itself When It`
`REM Needs To Run A Subroutine`
	Documentation remarks.

`IF NOT (%1)==(SUBROUTINE)` `    GOTO TOP`	If BIGSUB.BAT is not called as a subroutine, jump to the main part of the batch file. Notice there is no error checking that prevents the user from entering SUBROUTINE as a replaceable parameter.

`IF (%1)==(SUBROUTINE)`
`    IF (%2)==(1) GOTO 1`
`IF (%1)==(SUBROUTINE)`
`    IF %2)==(2) GOTO 2`
`IF (%1)==(SUBROUTINE)`
`    IF (%2)==(3) GOTO 3`
`IF (%1)==(SUBROUTINE)`
`    IF (2)==(4) GOTO 4`
	If BIGSUB.BAT was called as a subroutine, decide which subroutine to run and jump to that subroutine.

`GOTO ERROR`	If the batch file reaches this point, it was called as a subroutine but the second replaceable parameter was not a number 1-4. As currently written, that is an error so jump to a section to handle that.
`:1`	Label marking the beginning of the first subroutine.
`ECHO Run Word Processing Here`	If this were a working batch file, the commands to run the word processor would be here.
`SETERROR 0`	This is required because when the batch file exits the subroutine and returns to the main routine, it will have more ERRORLEVEL tests. Since the smallest ERRORLEVEL test it will make is for one, this will make sure it fails the remaining test. That is necessary to keep from running another subroutine.
`GOTO END`	Exit the subroutine.

`:2`
`ECHO Run Database Here`
`SETERROR 0`
`GOTO END`
	Second subroutine.

11-11   BIGSUB.BAT, which bundles many subroutines into one file.

11-11 Continued

Batch File Line	Explanation
:3 ECHO Run Spreadsheet Here SETERROR 0 GOTO END	Third subroutine.
:4 ECHO Run Games Here SETERROR 0 GOTO END	Fourth subroutine.
:TOP	Label marking the top of the actual batch file.

BE ASK "Run Word Processing (1)
    Database (2) Spreadsheet (3)
    Games (4) Quit (5) ", 12345
	Run the Norton Utilities Batch Enhancer and ask the user to make a selection.

IF ERRORLEVEL 5 GOTO END	If the user selected option five, jump to the end of the batch file to exit.
IF ERRORLEVEL 4 CALL BIGSUB SUBROUTINE 4	If the user selected option four, call the batch file and run subroutine four.
IF ERRORLEVEL 3 CALL BIGSUB SUBROUTINE 3	If the user selected option three, call the batch file and run subroutine three. If the user had selected option four, the batch file would make this test as soon as it exited the subroutine. That is why the ERRORLEVEL has to be reset when exiting the subroutine.
IF ERRORLEVEL 2 CALL BIGSUB SUBROUTINE 2	If the user selected option two, call the batch file and run subroutine two.
IF ERRORLEVEL 1 CALL BIGSUB SUBROUTINE 1	If the user selected option one, call the batch file and run subroutine one.
GOTO TOP	The batch file reaches this point after running the option the user selects. (It can not reach this point due to an invalid selection because the Batch Enhancer will not allow an invalid selection.) Since this batch file is functioning as a quasi-menu, it loops through again for the user to make another selection.
:ERROR ECHO AN ERROR HAS OCCURRED GOTO END	Error-handling section.
:END	Label marking the end of the batch file.

to go back and add additional options to BIGSUB.BAT. In general, the increased complexity is simply not worth the extra time it takes to get the batch file running properly.

Summary

Subroutines are special programs that a batch file calls to perform a special task. As such, subroutines can make batch file programming much easier.

12
CHAPTER

Problem solving with batch files

This chapter has two purposes. First, I want you to see how you can use fairly simple batch files to solve everyday problems with a computer. Second, by presenting you with batch files that are used for unusual purposes, I hope to start you thinking about how you can solve your own unique problems with a batch file.

Shelling out to DOS

Many programs allow you to temporarily exit to DOS (for example, /S in Lotus) but users often forget they have a program running and try to start another program (or even reload the program they shelled out of). Sometimes it will start but run very slow due to low memory, and other times it will fail to load at all.

To avoid this problem, you need a way to remind users that they have another program in memory. This is very easy if you start your programs with a batch file or with a menu program that allows you to issue multiple DOS commands. Just change the prompt from the regular pg to something like *Type EXIT to return to Lotus$_$p$g* just before the application starts, and change it back to pg just after the application terminates. With ECHO OFF, the user will never see this until they shell out to DOS. Then the prompt is a constant reminder that a program is loaded in memory. Notice that the prompt contains both the name of the program and instructions on how to return to that program. To do this, you need a custom prompt for each application. Figure 12-1 shows an example of a batch file using this technique to start Lotus.

The technique in Fig. 12-1 doesn't prevent the user from trying to run a second program while shelled to DOS, however, it just displays an explanatory

Batch File Line	Explanation
`@ECHO OFF`	Turn command-echoing off.
`REM LOTUS.BAT`	Remark giving the name of the batch file.
`C:`	Make sure the computer is logged onto the C drive.
`CD\123`	Change to the Lotus subdirectory.
`PROMPT=Type EXIT to return to` `  Lotus$_$p$g`	Change the prompt so if a user shells out of Lotus (using the /System command), he/she will know that Lotus is still loaded into memory and will have a visual reminder of how to return to Lotus.
`123`	Start Lotus.
`PROMPT=$p$g`	Reset the prompt once the user exits Lotus.

12-1   LOTUS.BAT, which generates a custom prompt to remind users to reenter Lotus when they're finished with DOS.

prompt to tell the user that one program is already in memory. If you start all your applications with batch files and you're willing to occasionally surprise your users, there's a way to prevent them from loading a second program while shelled to DOS. This method relies on the fact that the EXIT command will unload a second copy of COMMAND.COM (which programs load in order to shell to DOS) but has absolutely no impact on the first copy of COMMAND.COM. By including EXIT near the top of each batch file, as shown in Fig. 12-2, you prevent the program from being loaded under a second copy of COMMAND.COM. If the batch file is run under the first copy of COMMAND.COM, the EXIT command is ignored. If it's run under a second copy of COMMAND.COM, however, the EXIT command unloads the second copy of COMMAND.COM and, in doing so, causes DOS not to execute the remaining portion of the batch file. Not only that, it immediately returns to the original program.

This technique can surprise a new or even an experienced user. Imagine the surprise if a user shells from Microsoft Word using the Escape Library Run command and then runs LOTUS.BAT expecting to load Lotus. Instead, LOTUS.BAT gives the EXIT command and returns the user to Microsoft Word. While this technique works fine with batch files, it won't work with all menu programs. Some menu programs run under a second copy of COMMAND.COM, and the EXIT command can unload them or cause other problems. Only experimentation will tell you if this technique will work with your menu program.

You can use either of the methods or both of them in combination. Of course, they work only when users start their programs with batch files or menu programs that allow you to issue multiple DOS commands for each selection.

Batch File Line	Explanation
@ECHO OFF	Turn command-echoing off.
REM LOTUS1.BAT	Remark giving the name of the batch file.
EXIT	If the user is running this batch file for the first time, this command has no effect. If the user runs this batch file to try and restart Lotus after shelling out of Lotus, it returns him or her to Lotus and causes the remainder of the batch file not to execute. If he/she uses this batch file to start Lotus while shelled out of another program (Escape Library Run in Microsoft Word for example) then this batch file returns him/her to that application and causes the remainder of the batch file not to execute.
C:	Make sure the computer is logged onto the C drive.
CD\123	Change to the Lotus subdirectory.
PROMPT=Type EXIT to return to Lotus$_$p$g	Change the prompt so if a user shells out of Lotus (using the /System command), he/she will know that Lotus is still loaded into memory and will have a visual reminder of how to return to Lotus.
123	Start Lotus.
PROMPT=pg	Reset the prompt once the user exits Lotus.

12-2 LOTUS1.BAT, a modified version of LOTUS.BAT in Fig. 12-1, which won't allow you to load a second copy of COMMAND.COM (and thus another copy of the Lotus program).

Changing subdirectories

Many users have a very complex directory structure that's nested several levels deep. They often need to leave one subdirectory to check something in another subdirectory and later switch back, and are looking for a way to automate this.

There are actually a couple of different ways to attack this problem. The best way is probably using a quick directory changing program like the NCD program in the Norton Utilities, or the shareware QC (Quick Change) program from Steven Flores. You can find QC on many bulletin board services, like Compu-Serve or PC-Link. You can also get it from many local users groups. If you want to order it directly, send $20 to:

STEVEN FLORES
11711 East 27th St.
Tulsa, OK 74129

and be sure to tell Steven where you heard about his program. If you need or want
to tackle the problem with batch files, you have a couple of alternatives. If you're
always switching between just a couple of subdirectories, you can write a custom
batch file to change to each subdirectory. For example, you could write a batch
file called 0-9.BAT with the single command:

CD \ D \ LOTUSFIG \ 0-9

to change to that subdirectory. I use this method to change back to my home directory on the network at the office, because entering CD \ D \ USERS \ RICH-
ARDS is a bit much.

Of course, this can become a complex solution if you have a lot of subdirectories to change between. You can write a batch file to partially solve this problem.
This batch file marks the current directory as home and builds a second batch file
to always return you to the home directory. The next time you run this batch file, it
creates a new home directory and a new batch file to change there. It does, however, always use the same name.

The batch file, RETURN.BAT, is shown in Fig. 12-3. It copies a file called
RETURN to the batch file named RETURNTO.BAT. RETURN contains the single following line:

CD ^z

Batch File Line	**Explanation**
`@ECHO OFF`	Turn command-echoing off.
`REM RETURN.BAT`	Remark giving the name of the batch file.
`COPY C:\BAT\RETURN C:\BAT\RETURNTO.BAT`	Copy the file RETURN to the file RETURNTO.BAT. RETURN contains the line CD\ and nothing more.
`CD >> C:\BAT\RETURNTO.BAT`	Pipe the current subdirectory to RETURNTO.BAT. If the current subdirectory were \BAT, the last two lines would result in RETURNTO.BAT containing the line CD\BAT.

12-3 RETURN.BAT, which constructs a batch file returns you to a specific subdirectory.

where ^z is an end-of-file marker. Because there's no Return in the file, when the next line of RETURN.BAT pipes in the subdirectory, it gets added to the same line as the CD. The result is a line similar to this:

CD C: \ D \ LOTUSFIG \ 0-9

Because the batch file must be in a subdirectory that's in the path to work, RETURN.BAT is configured to always use the C: \ BAT subdirectory. For that reason, every time you run RETURN.BAT, it overwrites RETURNTO.BAT with a new version. You can expand RETURN.BAT to handle multiple subdirectories by using a replaceable parameter on the command line and creating RETURN1 .BAT, RETURN2.BAT, and so on. I'll leave this up to you.

If you don't want to create a custom batch file, you can use the batch file RETURN2.BAT in Fig. 12-4. There's no way to pipe the current subdirectory

Batch File Line	Explanation
CD %HOME%	Changes to the subdirectory stored in the environmental variable HOME.

12-4 RETURN2.BAT, which returns you to a subdirectory stored in the environment.

into the environment, so this batch file requires you to manually issue the command:

SET HOME = C: \ D \ LOTUSFIG \ 0-9

to tell RETURN2.BAT which subdirectory is home. The only real drawback to RETURN2.BAT is that you have to manually type the home subdirectory into the environment. You can avoid that, as shown in RETURN3.BAT in Fig. 12-5. Using RETURN3.BAT to change to a subdirectory originally (which you have to do anyway) records that subdirectory into the environment automatically. When you use RETURN3.BAT without a subdirectory, it changes back to the last subdirectory you changed to, using RETURN3.BAT with a subdirectory name. Like RETURN1.BAT, you can modify RETURN3.BAT to record multiple home subdirectories in the environment.

Batch File Line	Explanation
@ECHO OFF	Turn command-echoing off.
REM RETURN3.BAT	Remark giving the name of the batch file.
IF (%1)==() GOTO GOHOME	If the user did not enter a subdirectory on the command line, then jump to a section that changes to the subdirectory currently stored in an environmental variable.

12-5 RETURN3.BAT, which records your home directory into the environment when you originally change to it, allowing you to automatically change to it later.

12-5   Continued

Batch File Line	Explanation
`CD\%1`	Change to the subdirectory entered on the command line.
`SET HOME=%1`	Store the subdirectory entered on the command line in the environmental variable HOME so the batch file can use it again later.
`GOTO END`	Exit the batch file.
`:GOHOME`	Label marking the beginning of the section to change subdirectories.
`CD %HOME%`	Change to the subdirectory the batch file stored earlier in the environmental variable HOME.
`:END`	Label marking the end of the batch file.

Running inflexible programs

At my office, we have one computer that we use for all our communications. One of the things we do is log onto a remote database. This database supplies us with custom communications software. Because of the unique features of this database, we must use their software. One limitation of this software is that it stores the account number, password, and other information in a file called MENU.INF. We have two people who use this database, and they both have different account number, passwords, and so on. This communications software can't handle multiple users. The vendor suggested keeping two versions in two different subdirectories. We use batch files as a better solution.

The first user ran the configuration program to create MENU.INF with his information. We then copied MENU.INF to a file called RONNY.INF. The second user ran the configuration program and we once again copied MENU.INF to a file—this time DAVID.INF.

The problem with the database software is that it requires one special file for each user. We created several versions of that special file under different names. The batch file in Fig. 12-6 copies the appropriate one to MENU.INF.

This same technique can be used with any program that stores the defaults values in a special file. For example, Microsoft Word stores the document you're working on, your place, and several optional settings in a file called MW.INI. Figure 12-7 shows a batch file that Ronny and David could both use to maintain their own versions of MW.INI. There's only one major difference between the batch files in Figs. 12-6 and 12-7. Because Microsoft Word allows you to change the defaults while running the program, each user's defaults are copied back to the holding file when that user exits Word. The /L is required to force Word to use some of the defaults from the MW.INI file.

Batch File Line	Explanation
ECHO OFF	Turn command-echoing off.
REM STARTDATA.BAT	Remark giving the name of the batch file.
IF (%1)==() GOTO NOTHING	If the user did not enter a replaceable parameter, jump to an error-handling section.
IF %1==DAVID GOTO OK IF %1==David GOTO OK IF %1==david GOTO OK IF %1==RONNY GOTO OK IF %1==Ronny GOTO OK IF %1==ronny GOTO OK GOTO ERROR	David and Ronny are the only acceptable inputs to the batch file. These lines test for the more common capitalizations and assume that anything that does not match them is an error.
:NOTHING	Beginning of section to handle the error of the user not entering his or her name.
ECHO Enter your name after the STARTDAT command	Tell the user what happened.
GOTO END	Exit the batch file.
:ERROR	Beginning of section to handle an invalid name.
ECHO Invalid user name. Try ECHO again or see system manager.	Tell the user what happened.
GOTO END	Exit the batch file.
:OK	Section marking the beginning of the section of the batch file that handles running the application.
COPY %1.INF MENU.INF	Two different files exist with setup information, DAVID.INF and RONNY.INF. This line copies the right one for the current user to the name MENU.INF, which the program requires to run.
MENU /1200/5551212	This line starts the program. It tells the program the computer has a 1200-baud modem and the phone number to call is 555-1212.
:END	Label marking the end of the batch file.

12-6 STARTDATA.BAT, which activates different setups for an application program.

Batch File Line	Explanation
ECHO OFF	Turn command-echoing off.
REM STARTWORD.BAT	Remark giving the name of the batch file.
IF (%1)==() GOTO NOTHING IF %1==DAVID GOTO OK IF %1==David GOTO OK IF %1==david GOTO OK IF %1==RONNY GOTO OK IF %1==Ronny GOTO OK IF %1==ronny GOTO OK GOTO ERROR	David and Ronny are the only acceptable inputs to the batch file. These lines test for the more common capitalizations and assume that anything that does not match them is an error.
:NOTHING	Beginning of section to handle the error of the user not entering his or her name.
ECHO Enter your name after the STARTWOR command	Tell the user what happened.
GOTO END	Exit the batch file.
:ERROR	Beginning of section to handle an invalid name.
ECHO Invalid user name. ECHO Try again or see system manager.	Tell the user what happened.
GOTO END	Exit the batch file.
:OK	Beginning of the section to run Microsoft Word.
CD\WORD	Change to the Word subdirectory.
COPY %1.INI MW.INI	Two different files exist with setup information, DAVID.INI and RONNY. INI. This line copies the right one for the current user to the name MENU.INF, which the program requires to run.
WORD/L %2	This line starts Microsoft Word. The /L is required to force Word to use some of the information in MW.INI. The %2 allows the user to enter a file on the command line to edit.
COPY MW.INI %1.INI	Since the user could make changes to the defaults while in Word (these are stored in MW.INI), the contents of MW.INI could be different now than when the application started. This copies the new defaults to the storage file under the user's name.
:END	Label marking the end of the batch file.

12-7   STARTWORD.BAT, a word processing version of STARTDATA.BAT, the batch file in Fig. 12-6.

Several readers of an earlier version of this book have told me that they use this same method with Ventura Publishing by using multiple copies of its VP.INI file. However, rather than using this trick for multiple users, they report using it to store multiple configurations of Ventura for a single user.

Custom configurations

The two files that determine the configuration of your computing environment are the CONFIG.SYS and AUTOEXEC.BAT file. If you're lucky, you have one of each of these that handles all your programs. However, the nature of programs and their memory demands on your computer are changing so rapidly that one do-it-all environment isn't always possible.

For example, the computer at my office usually loads Novell network software. However, with Novell loaded, I don't have enough memory to run Per-FORM or Migrografx Designer. In order to run those programs, I have to run without the network. Because much of the network loads in the CONFIG.SYS file, memory managers like Mark/Release or PopDrop can't unload the network software.

If your computer has extended memory, you might face the same difficulties. Some programs, like Lotus 2.2, want expanded memory, so you need to load an expanded memory simulator like AboveDisc in your CONFIG.SYS file. Other programs, like Lotus 3.0, want extended memory, so you have to skip the expanded memory simulator.

This same method can be used to load custom computer setups. All you do is save multiple copies of the AUTOEXEC.BAT and CONFIG.SYS files. These are copied by a batch file, which then forces the computer to reboot. That can be done using the BOOT.COM program included on the disk for this book. A batch file with three boot options is shown in Fig. 5-1. Note that each set of AUTOEXEC .BAT and CONFIG.SYS files can load different memory-resident software and configure the computer in a special way. I use this at the office to load one set of CONFIG.SYS and AUTOEXEC.BAT files when I want to log onto our network and another set when I don't want to use the network.

Another way to solve this problem is to develop several custom sets of CON-FIG.SYS and AUTOEXEC.BAT files under different names. When you need to change the environment, you copy the appropriate files to the names CON-FIG.SYS and AUTOEXEC.BAT and then reboot. Refer to chapter 5, *Environmental surveying*, for more information on this.

Controlling your printer

Changing your dot-matrix printer between compressed and regular print or between type styles can be a real problem. First you have to remember the proper syntax, then you have to start up Basic. Then you run a Basic program. All this can be done with batch files. Figure 12-8 shows the basic outline of such a batch file. This batch file configures an Epson printer for compressed print. If you need to include an Escape, enter Shift−Alt−155. The 155 must be entered from the number pad. Depending on which word processor you use, you'll see a cent sign, ^[, or ^O on the screen. The >LPT1 is used to pipe the setup string to the printer. You can change this to another port if your printer is connected differently. This doesn't work reliably under DOS 2.x. It will usually work the first time but after that give you a *File creation error*. This is a bug in DOS. It's been corrected in DOS 3.0 and later.

Batch File Line	Explanation
ECHO OFF	Turn command-echoing off.
REM COMPRESS.BAT	Remark giving the name of the batch file.
ECHO ^[> LPT1	Echo the appropriate character(s) to the printer to turn on compressed printing. This will vary for different printers.

12-8   COMPRESS.BAT, a batch file that reconfigures an Epson printer to produce compressed print.

Finding files

You can use the batch file in Fig. 12-9 to find a file on your hard disk. The CHKDSK/V command causes the CHKDSK program to also list all the files. The FIND command then finds the specific file. You must enter the filename in upper-case. You don't have to enter the entire filename—just enough to make it unique. You can't use wildcards with this batch file. Note that this batch file takes a *long* time to run. Many commercial and shareware disk utility sets, like the Norton or Mace Utilities, include a program to perform this same file finding function. These programs are usually very fast and generally more flexible than DOS. For example, the Norton Utilities current file finding program will let you simultaneously look for filenames and text in the files, and instantly jump to the subdirectory containing the file you're looking for.

While it's not as flexible as some of the commercial programs, if you have DOS 3.3 or later you can at least write a fast file searching program. DOS 3.0 introduced a program called Attrib (short for Attribute) to change the archive and read-only status of files. The original version worked only in the current subdirectory. With DOS 3.3, it was upgraded to work across subdirectories using a /S switch. Because running Attrib without any switches to change the status of the archive and read-only bits causes it to list all the files it finds and because the /S switch causes it to search subdirectories, these combined cause it to find files. Figure 12-10 shows the resulting batch file and explains how it operates.

Batch File Line	Explanation
ECHO OFF	Turn command-echoing off.
REM FILEFIND.BAT	Remark giving the name of the batch file.
IF (%1)==() GOTO ERROR	Jump to an error-handling section if the user fails to enter a filename.
CHKDSK/V | FIND "%1"	List all the files using the CHKDSK program with the /V (verbose) switch. Use FIND to find matches to the replaceable parameter.
GOTO END	Exit the batch file.
:ERROR	Label marking the error-handling section.
ECHO Must enter filename to match	Tell the user what went wrong.
GOTO END	Exit the batch file.
:END	Label marking the end of the batch file.

12-9   FILEFIND.BAT, which uses CHKDSK and FIND to allow you to locate files on a hard disk.

Batch File Line	Explanation
@ECHO OFF	Turn command-echoing off.
REM FASTFIND.BAT	Remark giving the name of the batch file.
IF (%1)==() GOTO NOFILE	Jump to an error-handling section if the user does not enter a filename on the command line.
GOTO FILE	Jump to a section to handle finding the file.
:NOFILE	Label marking the beginning of the section to handle the user not entering a filename.
ECHO No File Entered On Command Line ECHO Syntax is C>FASTFIND file ECHO Where file is the File You ECHO Wish to Find	Explain the problem to the user.
GOTO END	Exit the batch file.
:FILE	Label marking the beginning of the section that handles finding the file.

12-10   FASTFIND.BAT, which uses Attrib to create a very fast file-searching program (only for DOS 3.3 and later).

12-10 Continued

Batch File Line	Explanation
`ATTRIB \%1 /S	MORE`	Use the DOS ATTRIB program to list all the files matching the replaceable parameter and pipe to MORE to handle the display. Note that the backslash before the %1 forces ATTRIB to begin its search in the root directory and the /S forces it to search all the subdirectories. NOTES: This method requires DOS 3.3 as the /S option was not available earlier. Unlike the method used in FILEFIND.-BAT of piping CHKDSK/V through a FIND filter, this method works with wildcards. It is also much faster.
`:END`	Label marking the end of the batch file.

Printing return mailing labels

You can use a batch file to create your own return address labels. The standard 1×3.5-inch labels have room for five lines of text. They also require a sixth blank line to skip over the blank area between labels. Create a text file called LABEL.TXT with six lines. The last line must be blank. Figure 12-11 shows the batch file that actually creates the labels. It will run continually, so you need to press Ctrl−Break to stop it.

Batch File Line	Explanation
`REM LABEL.BAT`	Remark giving the name of the batch file.
`:TOP`	Label marking the top of the loop.
`COPY LABEL.TXT LPT1:`	Copy an ASCII file to the printer. For this example, the file contains an address label.
`GOTO TOP`	Jump back to the top of the loop and continue processing. This loop will continue until you press Ctrl-break.

12-11 LABEL.BAT, a batch file that sends mailing label information to a printer.

Remembering batch file names

One problem with having a lot of batch files is that it's difficult to remember which batch file does what. One way around this is with a menu, as discussed in

chapter 6. Another way is by writing your own help file. The batch file HELP
.BAT shown in Fig. 12-12 will display a friendly reminder of the purpose of your
batch files. As the batch file in Fig. 12-13 shows, you can use IF statements to
make this help batch file somewhat context sensitive. You could also write custom
help screens using a screen compiler.

Batch File Line	Explanation
ECHO OFF	Turn command-echoing off.
REM HELP.BAT	Remark giving the name of the batch file.
CLS	Clear the screen.
ECHO DISCARD.BAT Will move all unwanted files ECHO to a directory for holding ECHO SYNTAX: DISCARD FILE1 FILE2 ECHO MAINTAIN.BAT Will erase temporary files, ECHO sort files, and run your ECHO file defragmentation program ECHO SYNTAX: MAINTAIN ECHO WARNING: Takes two hours to run ECHO PRINT.BAT Print ASCII files automatically ECHO SYNTAX: PRINT FILE1 FILE2 FILE3 ECHO WARNING: Make sure printer is on ECHO or computer will lock up	Print help information on the screen.

12-12   HELP.BAT, which displays a help menu of other batch files.

Batch File Line	Explanation
ECHO OFF	Turn command-echoing off.
REM HELP1.BAT	Remark giving the name of the batch file.
CLS	Clear the screen.

12-13   HELP1.BAT, which adds limited context sensitivity to a batch-based help facility.

12-13 Continued

Batch File Line	Explanation
`IF (%1)==() GOTO NOTHING`	Jump to NOTHING section if no replaceable parameter was entered.
`IF NOT %1==UTILITY GOTO NOUTIL`	If %1 is not UTILITY, skip to the NOUTIL section.

`ECHO    DISCARD.BAT  Will move all unwanted files`
`ECHO                 to a directory for holding`
`ECHO                 SYNTAX: DISCARD FILE1 FILE2...`
`ECHO MAINTAIN.BAT  Will erase temporary files, sort`
`ECHO                 files, and run your`
`ECHO                 file defragmentation program`
`ECHO                 SYNTAX: MAINTAIN`
`ECHO                 WARNING: Takes two hours to run`
`GOTO END`
	Display the help messages and exit the batch file.

`:NOUTIL`	Label marking the beginning of the NOUTIL section.
`IF NOT %1==PRINTING GOTO NOPRINT`	Skip to the next section if the printing help was not selected.

`ECHO    PRINT.BAT  Will print ASCII`
`ECHO               files automatically`
`ECHO               SYNTAX: PRINT FILE1 FILE2 FILE3`
`ECHO               WARNING: Make sure printer is on`
`ECHO               or computer will lock up`
`GOTO END`
	Display the printing help messages and exit the batch file.

`:NOPRINT`	Label marking the beginning of the NOPRINT section.
`IF NOT %1==BACKUP GOTO NOBACK`	If backup was not selected, skip to the next section.

12-13 Continued

Batch File Line	Explanation
ECHO BACKUP.BAT Will backup all (or some) ECHO subdirectories on your hard disk ECHO SYNTAX: BACKUP ECHO for entire hard disk ECHO SYNTAX: BACKUP directory ECHO for one subdirectory GOTO END	Display the backup help messages and exit the batch file.
:NOBACK	Label for NOBACK section.
IF NOT %1==MISC GOTO WRONG	If misc was not selected, skip to next section.
ECHO GAME.BAT Will bring up the game menu ECHO SYNTAX: GAME GOTO END	Display help message and exit batch file.
:WRONG	Section for invalid replaceable parameter.
ECHO INVALID SYNTAX GOTO NOTHING	Display help message and skip to nothing section for additional help.
:NOTHING ECHO SYNTAX IS HELP1 CATEGORY ECHO ENTER CATEGORY IN ALL UPPER CASE ECHO Valid categories are: ECHO Utilities, Backup, Printing, Misc	Display general help information.
:END	Label marking end.

Accessing the date and time

One limitation of DOS is that a batch file can't directly access the date and time while running. This makes it tricky to run a batch file at a certain date or time. If DOS had access to the date, you could automatically run a backup batch file every Friday when you started the computer. The following set of batch files shows how to construct a system to do this automatically. The methodology can be expanded to run any program or set of programs on specific dates. First, add these two lines as the last two lines in your AUTOEXEC.BAT file:

```
ECHO | MORE | DATE > STOREDATE.BAT
STOREDATE
```

The first line creates a batch file called STOREDATA.BAT with the output of the DATE prompt. ECHO | MORE is used to supply the Return that's needed so you don't have to answer the DATE question. STOREDATA.BAT will contain the following two lines:

```
Current date is Mon 10-14-1991
Enter new date (mm-dd-yyyy):
```

The last line of the AUTOEXEC.BAT file runs STOREDAT.BAT, which runs a batch file you create called CURRENT.BAT and passes five parameters. Those five parameters are:

%0 Current
%1 date
%2 is
%3 Mon (This will change each time the batch file is run.)
%4 10-14-1991 (This will change each time the batch file is run.)

Finally, Fig. 12-14 shows CURRENT.BAT configured to automatically back up

Batch File Line	Explanation
`ECHO OFF`	Turn command-echoing off.
`REM CURRENT.BAT`	Remark giving the name of the batch file.
`IF (%1)==() GOTO END`	Exit the batch file if the first replaceable parameter was not entered.
`IF (%2)==() GOTO END`	Exit the batch file if the second replaceable parameter was not entered.
`IF (%3)==() GOTO END`	Exit the batch file if the third replaceable parameter was not entered.
`IF (%4)==() GOTO END`	Exit the batch file if the fourth replaceable parameter was not entered.
`REM JUMP TO TESTING SECTION`	Documentation remark.
`GOTO TESTS`	Jump down to the section of the batch file that tests the parameters.

`:BACKUP`
`BACKUP C:\ A: /S`
`GOTO ENDBACK`
	Perform a full backup and exit this section of the batch file.

`:PARTBACK`
`BACKUP C:\ A: /S/M`
`:GOTO ENDPART`
	Perform an incremental backup and exit this section of the batch file.

12-14 CURRENT.BAT, which is configured to do backups on Wednesdays and Fridays.

12-14   Continued

Batch File Line	Explanation
REM OTHER OPERATIONS HERE REM JUMP TO THEM USING TESTS	This batch file is a simple illustration. You could have many more sections to perform different operations on different days.
:TESTS	The section of the batch file that decides what to do each day.
IF %3==Fri GOTO BACKUP	If it is Friday, perform a full backup. A trick in the book sends the day of the week to this batch file.
:ENDBACK	The full backup jumps back to this label so the batch file can test to see if it needs to perform any other operations today.
IF %3==Wed GOTO PARTBACK	If it is Wednesday, the batch file performs an incremental backup.
:ENDPART	The incremental backup returns to this point.
REM OTHER TESTS HERE	This batch file is for illustration and only performs two tests on the day of the week. You might also want to optimize the hard disk on certain days or perform other tasks.
:END	A label marking the end of the batch file.

the hard disk every Friday and automatically perform an incremental backup every Wednesday. Additional commands can be added to conditionally run other programs. You can make the day and date available to other batch files by adding these lines to include the date and time in the environment:

```
SET DAY = %3
SET DATE = %4
```

One drawback to this method is that CURRENT.BAT is run every time you boot your computer. This isn't a problem if you never have to reboot; however, if computer problems sometimes cause you to have to reboot, then this can be a significant problem. The reason for running a batch file only occasionally is that you don't want to have to fool with it all the time. As written, however, CURRENT .BAT will run a backup every time the computer is rebooted on Friday.

You can eliminate the problem you'll have if you reboot by having the batch file create a dummy file after a successful backup. If the dummy file exists, it won't make a second backup on Friday. Of course, the batch file would need to delete the dummy file after Friday. CURRENT1.BAT in Fig. 12-15 does just this.

Batch File Line	Explanation
ECHO OFF	Turn command-echoing off.
REM CURRENT1.BAT	Remark giving the name of the batch file.

IF (%1)==() GOTO END
IF (%2)==() GOTO END
IF (%3)==() GOTO END
IF (%4)==() GOTO END
	Exit if the batch file does not receive the appropriate replaceable parameter. A trick discussed in the book sends DOS information from the TIME command to this batch file.

REM Notice that in the GOTO REM statement below I use the REM %3 variable as the basis of REM the goto. This assumes that REM the batch file is never run REM from the command line. REM I could avoid this by REM testing on each day REM value of %3 separately	Documentation remarks.
GOTO %3	The day of the week comes into the batch file as the third replaceable parameter. This line uses that to jump to a section to handle the specific day.
:Sun	The section to handle the Sunday commands.
REM Sunday commands go here	What ever commands you wanted to perform every Sunday would go here. If they took a long time, you would need a flag file like FLAGWED to make sure they were not repeated if you rebooted on Sunday.
IF EXIST FLAGFRI DEL FLAGFRI IF EXIST FLAGWED DEL FLAGWED	If any of the flag files exist, delete them.
GOTO End	Exit the batch file to avoid processing the other days.
:Mon REM Monday commands IF EXIST FLAGFRI DEL FLAGFRI IF EXIST FLAGWED DEL FLAGWED GOTO End	Perform the tasks for Monday.
:Tue REM Tuesday commands IF EXIST FLAGFRI DEL FLAGFRI IF EXIST FLAGWED DEL FLAGWED GOTO End	Perform the tasks for Tuesday.

12-15   CURRENT1.BAT, a modified version of CURRENT.BAT in Fig. 12-14 that will perform a task only the first time a computer is booted on the assigned day.

12-15   Continued

Batch File Line	Explanation
`:Wed`	Perform the tasks for Wednesday.
`REM Wednesday commands`	Documentation remark.
`IF NOT EXIST FLAGWED BACKUP C:\` `   A: /S`	If the file FLAGWED does not exist, perform a full backup. Once this backup is completed, the batch file will create FLAGWED to signal that the Wednesday backup has been completed. That way, if the computer is rebooted on Wednesday, it is not backed up twice on the same day. Tomorrow, or the next day the computer is used, FLAGWED is deleted since the backup would no longer be current.
`REM Create flag file`	Documentation remark.
`TYPE Nofile > FLAGWED`	This command creates a zero-length flag file that does not take up any disk space. Note that the NOFILE <u>must NOT exist</u>. This is explained in more detail in the book.
`IF EXIST FLAGFRI DEL FLAGFRI`	Since it is not Friday, the batch file deletes the Friday flag.
`GOTO End`	Exit the batch file.

`:Thu`
`REM Thursday commands`
`IF EXIST FLAGFRI DEL FLAGFRI`
`IF EXIST FLAGWED DEL FLAGWED`
`GOTO End`
	Perform the tasks for Thursday.

`:Fri`
`REM Friday commands`
`IF NOT EXIST FLAGFRI BACKUP`
`   C:\ A: /S/M`
`TYPE Nofile > FLAGFRI`
`IF EXIST FLAGWED DEL FLAGWED`
`GOTO End`
	Perform the Friday tasks, including an incremental backup and creating a flag file as discussed above.

`:Sat`
`REM Saturday commands`
`IF EXIST FLAGFRI DEL FLAGFRI`
`IF EXIST FLAGWED DEL FLAGWED`
`GOTO End`
	Perform the tasks for Saturday

`:End`	Label marking the end of the batch file.

Running commands occasionally

One significant problem with the previous approach is that you miss your backup altogether if you don't use the computer on Friday. Another approach is to occasionally back up the computer.

Normally, you think of batch files as being either the AUTOEXEC.BAT file, which is run every time you turn your computer on, or a stand-alone batch file that's run only when you enter its name. However, there are some things you want your computer to do only occasionally, like make a backup.

OCCASIONAL.BAT in Fig. 12-16 illustrates this concept. To run this from your AUTOEXEC.BAT file, you'll need a CALL OCCASIONAL.BAT statement if you use DOS 3.3 or later, or a COMMAND/C OCCASIONAL.BAT if you run an earlier version of DOS. Using the second method also requires the last line of OCCASIONAL.BAT to contain the EXIT command.

Batch File Line	Explanation
`@ECHO OFF`	Turn command-echoing off.
`FOR %%J IN (00 01 02 03 04 05 06 07 08 09) DO IF EXIST COUNT.%%J GOTO %%J`	This batch file uses a zero-length counter file called COUNT.00, COUNT.01 and so on, to keep track of the last time it ran. This FOR loop figures out which version of the counter exits and jumps to the appropriate place in the batch file.
`GOTO NOFILE`	If all the tests above fail, then the counter file does not exist. This command causes the batch file to jump to a section to handle that.
`:00`	This section handles the situation where COUNT.00 exists--so none of the other versions exists.
`REM All Work Done Here`	Documentation remark.
`BACKUP C:\ A:`	The command performs a full backup.
`REN COUNT.00 COUNT.01`	Increments the counter by one by changing the name of the counter file.
`GOTO END`	Exits the batch file.
`:01`	This section handles the situation where COUNT.01 exists.
`REN COUNT.01 COUNT.02`	Increments the counter by one. Since the batch file performs a backup only when the counter is named COUNT.00, there is nothing else to do in this section.
`GOTO END`	Exits the batch file.

12-16   OCCASIONAL.BAT, which backs up the hard disk once every ten times the computer is rebooted.

12-16 Continued

Batch File Line	Explanation

`:02`
`REN COUNT.02 COUNT.03`
`GOTO END`
	This section handles the situation where the counter is named COUNT.02.

`:03`
`REN COUNT.03 COUNT.04`
`GOTO END`
	This section handles the situation where the counter is named COUNT.03.

`:04`
`REN COUNT.04 COUNT.05`
`GOTO END`
	This section handles the situation where the counter is named COUNT.04.

`:05`
`REN COUNT.05 COUNT.06`
`GOTO END`
	This section handles the situation where the counter is named COUNT.05.

`:06`
`REN COUNT.06 COUNT.07`
`GOTO END`
	This section handles the situation where the counter is named COUNT.06.

`:07`
`REN COUNT.07 COUNT.08`
`GOTO END`
	This section handles the situation where the counter is named COUNT.07.

`:08`
`REN COUNT.08 COUNT.09`
`GOTO END`
	This section handles the situation where the counter is named COUNT.08.

`:09`
`REN COUNT.09 COUNT.00`
`GOTO END`
	This section handles the situation where the counter is named COUNT.09.

`:NOFILE`	Label marking the beginning of the section that handles a missing counter file.
`REM Restore Counter File` `REM Then Restart Process`	Documentation remark.
`TYPE NOFILE > COUNT.00`	Create the zero-length counter file.
`GOTO 00`	Jump to the section of the batch file that performs the backup.
`:END`	Label marking the end of the batch file.

This batch file maintains a counter in the form of a file. When the batch file first starts, it creates COUNT.00. The next time it runs, it renames this file COUNT.01, the next time it renames it COUNT.02, and so on. When it encounters COUNT.09, it renames it COUNT.00 and performs the task it's suppose to perform occasionally, the backup in this example. That gives this batch file a period of ten.

The batch file counts reboots, not days. If you're working with problem software that frequently locks up, therefore, it could end up running backups several times a day. If you leave your computer on for days at a time, ten reboots could end up being several weeks.

OCCASIONAL.BAT has two interesting tricks in it. The first trick is the counter test on line 2. The batch file needs to perform ten IF EXIST COUNT.00 GOTO 00 tests. Because these tests will be exactly the same except for the digit used, all ten tests are combined into a single FOR command. The second trick is the 0-length file.

You can also use occasional batch files for other kinds of applications. For example, my disk testing program has two levels of testing. The first is the quick mode that takes only a few minutes to run. The complete mode spots more errors, but takes much longer to run. The batch file that runs the program normally runs it in quick mode; however, it occasionally runs it in complete mode. You can have as many different occasional batch files as you need. The only trick is to remember to use a different name for each counter.

Using the volume in a batch file

As you recall, the basic trick in using the DATE and TIME was to pipe the output of these commands to a file and then run the resulting file. That places the rest of the line into replaceable parameters the batch file can access. The exact trick works with the volume label.

The batch file GETVOL.BAT in Fig. 12-17 gets the volume label and pipes it

Batch File Line	Explanation
@ECHO OFF	Turn command-echoing off.
REM GETVOL.BAT	Remark giving the name of the batch file.
VOL > STOREVOL.BAT	Pipe the volume into a filenamed STOREVOL.BAT.
STOREVOL	Run STOREVAL.BAT for additional processing.

12-17   GETVOL.BAT, which gets the volume label and pipes it to a file.

to the file STOREVOL.BAT. Notice that the |MORE specification is missing. The VOL command doesn't expect an input, so you don't need to echo a Return. The file STOREVOL.BAT in Fig. 12-18 shows the typical contents of this file. The second line was added in DOS 4.0, so you might not see this line in your own files. Its presence doesn't affect this procedure.

The batch file VOLUME.BAT actually places the volume label into the environment. Figure 12-19 shows this file. The steps in the process are:

Batch File Line	Explanation
`Volume in drive C is Richardson`	Note that this batch file is created by another batch file issuing a VOL command and piping the results to STOREVOL.BAT. When this batch file is run, it runs VOLUME.BAT and passes the following parameters: %1 in %2 drive %3 C %4 is %5 Richardson and thus VOLUME.BAT has access to the volume label. As explained in the text, %5 cannot contain all the volume.
`Volume Serial Number is 2F47-0FE7`	This line contains the serial number of the disk for later versions of DOS, but there is no way to access this information in this batch file since, the first time VOLUME.BAT runs, it never returns control to this batch file.

12-18 STOREVOL.BAT, which contains the volume label along with the rest of the message that DOS displays for the VOL command.

Batch File Line	Explanation
`@ECHO OFF`	Turn command-echoing off.
`REM VOLUME.BAT` `REM Stores Volume in Environment`	Documentation remarks.
`SET VOLUME=%5`	STOREVOL.BAT passes VOLUME-.BAT the volume label as %5. Since some after-market utilities allow you to have a volume label with spaces, %5 might not contain the entire volume label. VOLUME1.BAT handles that.

12-19 VOLUME.BAT, which actually places the volume label into the environment.

1. Run GETVOL.BAT (Fig. 12-17). This file first pipes the volume label into the file STOREVOL.BAT, and then runs STOREVOL.BAT. Because the CALL command isn't used, control never returns to GETVOL.BAT.

2. STOREVOL.BAT (Fig. 12-18) runs and enters the single command VOLUME to run VOLUME.BAT. The word *in* is passed as %1, *drive* is passed as %2, *C* is passed as %3, *is* is passed as %4, and the volume label is passed as %5. The CALL command isn't used, so control never returns to STOREVOL.BAT.

3. VOLUME.BAT (Fig. 12-19) runs and places the contents of the volume label into an environmental variable.

So far, the process has been fairly simple; however, there's a major complication you have to consider. Many utilities allow you to enter a volume label with a space in it. In fact, your volume label could be *a b c d e f*, which has five spaces in it. Using the process above, only the *a* part of the volume label would be placed into the environment. Although GETVOL.BAT and STOREVOL.BAT can remain the same, VOLUME.BAT must be modified to handle volume labels with spaces.

Figure 12-20 shows VOLUME.BAT with the necessary modifications, now called VOLUME1.BAT. A couple of comments are in order:

- The most difficult volume label you can have is six individual characters separated by a single space each. This fills up the entire eleven spaces allocated for the volume label. When this happens, the replaceable parameters out to %9 are one short of the necessary six parameters. The single SHIFT command changes this.
- The %SPACE% variable contains a single space, so the batch file requires a space after the equal sign and before the Return.
- The lack of spaces on the last line is critical. If you include spaces, DOS incorporates those spaces into the environmental variable as well. While this line looks confusing, DOS handles it properly.

Figure 12-21 shows running GETVOL.BAT with a volume label that has spaces and VOLUME1.BAT in the place of VOLUME.BAT. As you can see, it handles even this complex volume label properly.

Of course, once you get the volume label into the environment, you need something to do with it. The typical thing is to test to see if it matches some predefined value. You could do this with a standard IF test. It's important to remember that many aftermarket utilities allow volume labels with lowercase letters, so you can't make any assumptions about the capitalization.

Batch File Line	Explanation
`@ECHO OFF`	Turn command-echoing off.
`REM VOLUME1.BAT`	Remark giving the name of the batch file. This is an alternative version of VOLUME.BAT for handling a volume label with spaces.
`REM Stores Volume in Environment`	Documentation remark.
`SET SPACE=`	Store a space in the environmental variable SPACE. This is used to replace the space with transferring the volume label to the environment.
`SHIFT`	Move the environmental variables down one level. A volume label has up to 11 characters. With file spaces, a volume label like A B C D E F requires five replaceable parameter to store the entire label. Since STOREVOL.BAT passes the volume label beginning at %5, there is the potential to lose the last character without the SHIFT.
`SET VOLUME=%4%SPACE%%5%SPACE%%6` `%SPACE%%7%SPACE%%8%SPACE%%9`	Store the volume label as an environmental variable. Notice the use of %SPACE% as spaces. With actual spaces, like %4 %5, DOS treats the space as a divider and does not store the space in the environment.

12-20 VOLUME1.BAT, a modified version of VOLUME.BAT in Fig. 12-19 that will properly handle spaces in the volume label.

```
C>vol

 Volume in drive C is a b c d e f
 Volume Serial Number is 2F47-0FE7

C>getvol

C>
C>Volume in drive C is a b c d e f

C>set
COMSPEC-C:\COMMAND.COM
PROMPT=$P$G
PATH=C:\;\C:\WORD;C:\LOTUS;C:\BAT;C:\DBASE;C:\WINDOWS
SPACE=
VOLUME=a b c d e f

C>
```

12-21   The results of running GETVOL.BAT in Fig. 12-17 with VOLUME1.BAT in Fig. 12-20.

Batch file floppy-disk catalog

Batch files can catalog disks and work fairly well if you have only a few disks. If you have more than a few, however, you're probably better off buying one of the many shareware disk cataloging programs that are available, because the batch file method is fairly slow and lacks important error checking. So use at your own risk!

Figure 12-22 shows the batch file that creates the catalog. Notice that it lacks any error-checking at all. I've left this for the user to add. The batch file should determine that it's logged into the proper drive and subdirectory before running.

Batch File Line	Explanation
`@ECHO OFF`	Turn command-echoing off.
`REM CATALOG.BAT`	Remark giving the name of the batch file.

`REM Program for entering files on a`
`    diskette`
`REM into a catalog called`
`    CATALOG.TXT.`
`REM Assumes you are using the`
`    A drive`
`REM for the floppies and the C drive`
`REM for the catalog.`
	Documentation remarks.

`IF (%1)==() GOTO NONAME`	Jump to an error-handling section if the user did not enter a replaceable parameter.

`ECHO Insert disk to catalog into`
`    A drive`
`ECHO and press any key when ready`
	Tell the user to insert the floppy disk to catalog.

12-22   CATALOG.BAT, a batch file that creates a catalog of files on a floppy disk.

12-22 Continued

Batch File Line	Explanation
PAUSE>NUL	Wait for the user to press a key. Also, pipe the DOS message from the PAUSE command to NUL so the user will not see it.
FOR %%j in (A:*.*) DO ECHO %%j %1 >> C:CATALOG.TXT	Echo the name of each file on the A drive and the text entered as the first replaceable parameter and pipe it into a file called CATALOG.TXT.
GOTO END	Exit the batch file.
:NONAME	Label marking the start of a section to handle the error when the user fails to enter a replaceable parameter.
ECHO You must enter CATALOG Name ECHO Where Name describes the disk	Explain the problem to the user.
GOTO END	Exit the batch file.
:END	Label marking the end of the batch file.

As written, the batch file makes sure the user enters a name and then uses the FOR command to cycle through all the files on the A drive. As it echoes each filename, it adds two tab characters (^I) to make formatting with a word processor easier. Notice that this would be a good application for grabbing the volume label and including it in the ECHO command.

You could also pad with spaces, but the line of names would be jagged because not all filenames are the same length. An alternative would be to echo the name first, followed by spaces and the filename. This would avoid the jagged column problem.

Figure 12-23 shows another batch file for removing entries. It also lacks much error checking, but it's impossible to add enough error checking with batch commands. The basic problem is using the FIND command to select lines to delete. If you start the batch file with the replaceable parameter OFFICE, it will not only delete the lines with the added label OFFICE, it will also delete the file OFFICE.TAX and any other line containing the line OFFICE. For this reason, this cataloging method must be used with a great deal of care and frequent back-ups.

Batch File Line	Explanation
`@ECHO OFF`	Turn command-echoing off.
`REM REMOVE.BAT`	Remark giving the name of the batch file.
`REM Removes entries from floppy` `    catalog`	Documentation remark.
`IF (%1)==() GOTO NoName`	If the user did not enter a filename to delete from the catalog on the command line, jump to an error-handling section.

`ECHO All floppy catalog entries`
`ECHO containing %1 will be`
`ECHO deleted. If this is not`
`ECHO OK, press Ctrl-Break`
`ECHO Otherwise, press any other`
`ECHO key`
	Tell the user what is happening.

`PAUSE>NUL`	Pause execution of the batch file so the user has the opportunity to abort the batch file by pressing Ctrl-Break.
`TYPE CATALOG.TXT	FIND/V "%1"` ` > JUNK.TMP`	Type the catalog to the screen. Pipe that output to Find and have it delete all lines with an entry matching the user's input. Pipe that output to a filenamed JUNK.-TMP to create the new catalog.
`DEL CATALOG.TXT`	Delete the old catalog.
`REN JUNK.TMP CATALOG.TXT`	Rename the new catalog to the proper name.

12-23   REMOVE.BAT, which will remove entries from the catalog.

Batch files that use less space

MS-DOS allocates disk space to files in blocks called clusters. Clusters range in size from 1K to 8K. The DOS directory entry that's maintained for every file contains the actual size of the file. This is the size you see when you do a DIR. This isn't the actual size.

On my hard disk, every file gets allocated space in 4,096-byte clusters. The 0-length files discussed above are an exception. If a file has one character in it, it's allocated 4,096 bytes. If it has 4,097 bytes, it's allocated two clusters, or 8,192 bytes. Some versions of DOS allocate space in clusters up to 8,192 bytes. This large space requirement for small files is especially hard on batch files because they're typically small files.

I keep most of my batch files in a subdirectory called C: \ BAT, and I used the Norton Utilities program FILESIZE to get the true size of the files. The batch files have only 5,203 bytes of information in them, yet they require 43,012 bytes of disk space. That means that 88% of the space allocated to these files is wasted.

The directory with all the batch files I'm writing for this book is even worse. With only 19,172 bytes of information, the files require 182,272 bytes!

There are no complete solutions to this dilemma, but there are two partial solutions. The first is to upgrade to a newer version of DOS. Typically, newer releases have reduced the cluster size. This isn't always true and often the cluster size is a function of the hard disk size. So check first.

Upgrading DOS versions has a temporary drawback. You must back up your hard disk, reformat it, and restore the data before the change is effective. All this takes time. There is the additional payback in that the space reduction applies to all files—not just batch files. Because file size behaves much like a random variable, on average files waste one half of their final cluster allocation. If cluster size is reduced from 8K to 4K, then the space wasted by an average file will be reduced from 4K to 2K, a savings of 2K per file. Some time ago, when I upgraded my full 20-Meg hard disk from DOS 2.1 to DOS 3.2, I freed up almost 4 Megs of space as a result of reducing the cluster size from 8K to 4K.

The second solution is to combine multiple small batch files into one larger batch file. For example, if you have a menu with eight options and each option requires a batch file, you could combine all these into one batch file called MENU.BAT. You would pass it the menu option you wanted as the first replaceable parameter. Figure 12-24 shows BIGMENU.BAT. This batch file runs all six of the menu options developed in another chapter.

This solution has two primary drawbacks. The resulting batch file runs slower than six individual batch files, and this long complex batch file is more difficult to write, debug, and maintain than six shorter batch files.

Batch File Line	Explanation
`ECHO OFF`	Turn command-echoing off.
`REM BIGMENU.BAT`	Remark that gives the name of the batch file.

`REM THIS BATCH FILE REPLACES`
`   1.BAT, 2.BAT, 3.BAT, 4.BAT,`
`   5.BAT, AND 6.BAT`
	Documentation remark.

`IF (%1)==() GOTO NOCODE`	If the user fails to enter a replaceable parameter, jump to an error-handling section.

`IF %1==1 GOTO ONE`
`IF %1==2 GOTO TWO`
`IF %1==3 GOTO THREE`
`IF %1==4 GOTO FOUR`
`IF %1==5 GOTO FIVE`
`IF %1==6 GOTO SIX`
	If the user enters one of these values, he/she has made a proper selection and the batch file jumps to the appropriate section to handle it.

12-24 BIGMENU.BAT, which consolidates six different batch files to save space.

12-24 Continued

Batch File Line	Explanation
GOTO NOTRIGHT	The user entered an invalid replaceable parameter and the batch file jumps to an error-handling section.
:ONE	Label marking the top of the section of the batch file that handles the first option.
C:	Make sure the computer is logged onto the C drive.
CD\WORD	Change to the Microsoft Word subdirectory.
WORD %2	Run Word using a replaceable parameter if the user specified one.
GOTO MENU	Jump to the section of the batch file that redisplays the menu.
:TWO C: CD\123 123 GOTO MENU	The section of the batch file that handles the second option.
:THREE C: CD\DBASE DBASE %2 %3 GOTO MENU	The section of the batch file that handles the third option.
:FOUR C: CD\GAME XMAN GOTO MENU	The section of the batch file that handles the fourth option.
:FIVE FORMAT A:/V GOTO MENU	The section of the batch file that handles the fifth option.
:SIX BACKUP C:\ A: /S GOTO MENU	The section of the batch file that handles the sixth option.
:NOCODE	Label marking the section that handles the error when the user fails to enter a menu selection code.
CLS	Clear the screen.
ECHO ENTER BIGMENU FOLLOWED BY A MENU CODE TO RUN A PROGRAM	Tell the user what happened.
ECHO FOR EXAMPLE BIGMENU 1 ECHO TO RUN WORD PROCESSOR	Give the user an example.
PAUSE	Wait for the user to read the message.

12-24 Continued

Batch File Line	Explanation
GOTO MENU	Redisplay the menu.
:NOTRIGHT	Label marking the section of the batch file that handles the user entering an invalid code.
ECHO YOU ENTERED AN INCORRECT CODE ECHO ONLY THE CODES 1-6 ARE ALLOWED ECHO ENTER BIGMENU FOLLOWED BY A MENU CODE TO RUN A PROGRAM ECHO FOR EXAMPLE BIGMENU 1 ECHO TO RUN WORD PROCESSOR PAUSE GOTO MENU	Tell the user what happened and how to correct the problem.
:MENU	Label marking the section of the batch file that displays the menu.
REM ENTER COMMANDS HERE TO DISPLAY MENU REM FOLLOWING COMMAND ASSUMES A PROGRAM CALLED MENU.COM OR MENU.EXE EXISTS	Documentation remarks.
MENU	Display the menu.

Adding to and deleting from your path

Most people simply include every subdirectory they need DOS to search through in the path and forget it. There are occasions, however, when you might want to have two separate paths. For example, if you're testing a new program and you don't want DOS to search anywhere other than the current subdirectory; if you have added a subdirectory for a special program and you want it in the path for only a short period of time; or if you have so many subdirectories to search that you want to have a separate path for each task. The plan of attack is the same for each of these problems. The steps are as follows:

1. Store the current path to a variable in the environment.
2. Replace the path with a new path or modify the existing path.
3. Restore the old path from the environment.

Figure 12-25 shows PATH1.BAT, which will replace the current path with one specified on the command line. Figure 12-26 shows PATH2.BAT, which returns the path to the value stored in the environment. Figure 12-27 shows PATH3.BAT, which will append a new value onto the existing path. Again, PATH2.BAT can be used to return to the old path. PATH4.BAT in Fig. 12-28 allows you to easily switch between three paths.

Batch File Line	Explanation
ECHO OFF	Turn command-echoing off.
REM PATH1.BAT	Remark giving the name of the batch file.
IF (%1)==() GOTO NOPATH	If the user did not enter a replaceable parameter, jump to an error-handling routine.
SET OLDPATH=%PATH%	Set an environmental variable called OLDPATH equal to the current path. This allows for restoring the original path later.
SET PATH=%1	Set the current path to the value entered as a replaceable parameter. Since a semicolon on the command line is treated as a parameter divider, this is limited to setting the path equal to a single subdirectory.
GOTO END	Exit the batch file.
:NOPATH	Label marking the beginning of a section to handle the error of the user not entering a path on the command line.
ECHO NO PATH SPECIFIED	Tell the user what happened.
:END	Label marking the end of the batch file.

12-25   PATH1.BAT, a batch file that dynamically changes the path.

Batch File Line	Explanation
ECHO OFF	Turn command-echoing off.
REM PATH2.BAT	Remark giving the name of the batch file.
SET PATH=%OLDPATH%	Restores the path to the original value after being change by PATH1.BAT.

12-26   PATH2.BAT, a batch file that restores the path to the value stored in PATH1.BAT, shown in Fig. 12-25.

Batch File Line	Explanation
ECHO OFF	Turn command-echoing off.
REM PATH3.BAT	Remark giving the name of the batch file.
IF (%1)==() GOTO NOPATH	Jump to an error-handling routine if the user did not enter a subdirectory on the command line.
SET OLDPATH=%PATH%	Store the old path in an environmental variable.

12-27   PATH3.BAT, which appends a subdirectory onto the current path.

12-27 Continued

Batch File Line	Explanation
`SET PATH=%PATH%;%1`	Add the subdirectory entered on the command line to the path.
`GOTO END`	Exit the batch file.
`:NOPATH`	The beginning of an error-handling routine.
`ECHO NO PATH SPECIFIED`	Tell the user what happened.
`:END`	Label marking the end of the batch file.

Batch File Line	Explanation
`ECHO OFF`	Turn command-echoing off.
`REM PATH4.BAT`	Remark giving the name of the batch file.
`IF (%1)==() GOTO NOPATH`	If the user did not enter a number on the command line, jump to an error-handling routine.
`IF %1==1 PATH=C:\WORD` `IF %1==1 GOTO END`	If the user entered a one on the command line, set the path accordingly and exit the batch file.
`IF %1==2 PATH=C:\LOTUS` `IF %1==2 GOTO END`	If the user entered a two on the command line, set the path accordingly and exit the batch file.
`IF %1==3 PATH=C:\DBASE` `IF %1==3 TOTO END`	If the user entered a three on the command line, set the path accordingly and exit the batch file.
`GOTO ERROR`	If the batch file reaches this point, the user entered an invalid selection so jump to an error-handling section.
`:ERROR`	Label marking the beginning of the section to handle invalid entries.
`ECHO ONLY 1, 2, OR 3 ARE` `    VALID PATH SELECTIONS`	Tell the user what happened.
`GOTO END`	Exit the batch file.
`:NOPATH`	Label marking the beginning of the section to handle no input on the command line.
`ECHO NO PATH SELECTED`	Tell the user what happened.
`:END`	Label marking the end of the batch file.

12-28 PATH4.BAT, which allows for easy switching among three different paths.

A batch file can also remove subdirectories, although the process is a little tricky. A batch file has access to the %PATH% environmental variable, but has no way to strip it into its component parts. However, the different subdirectories in a path are separated by semicolons, which DOS treats as legal dividers for replaceable parameters. If you could issue the command:

BATCH %PATH%

and have DOS treat %PATH% as the environmental variable, then the first subdirectory in the path would be %1, the second would be %2, and so on. Unfortunately, you can't use environmental variables on the command line in this fashion. Luckily, batch files can, so if one batch file invokes another with this exact same command, the subdirectory components are passed as separate replaceable parameters—just as you would expect.

This method takes one more piece of information in order for it to work. The batch file doing the work needs to know how much of the path to keep. EDIT PATH.BAT in Fig. 12-29 is the first of two batch files. It expects you to enter the number of subdirectories to keep on the command line. The batch files keep this many subdirectories from the front of the path and discard the rest. EDIT PATH.BAT limits you to keeping the first eight; however, with the addition of a

Batch File Line	Explanation
`@ECHO OFF`	Turn command-echoing off.
`REM EDITPATH.BAT`	Remark giving the name of the batch file.
`REM Keep first n elements` `   of PATH`	Documentation remark.
`IF (%1)==() GOTO ERROR`	If the user does not enter a replaceable parameter, jump to an error-handling section.

`IF %1==1 GOTO OK`
`IF %1==2 GOTO OK`
`IF %1==3 GOTO OK`
`IF %1==4 GOTO OK`
`IF %1==5 GOTO OK`
`IF %1==6 GOTO OK`
`IF %1==7 GOTO OK`
`IF %1==8 GOTO OK`
`GOTO ERROR`
	This illustrates one way to make sure the user only enters the digits 1-8 as the first replaceable parameter.

`:ERROR`
`ECHO Number of elements to`
`   retain not specified`
`ECHO or specified`
`   incorrectly`
`GOTO END`
	Deal with the problem of the user entering an invalid replaceable parameter or not entering one at all.

`:OK`	Section that edits the PATH if the user runs the batch file appropriately.

12-29 EDITPATH.BAT, a batch file that can remove extra subdirectories from your path.

12-29 Continued

Batch File Line	Explanation
EDIT1 %1 %PATH%	Calls EDIT1.BAT and passes the PATH as a series of replaceable parameters. Since EDIT1.BAT is run without the CALL command, control does not pass back to EDITPATH.BAT.
:END	Label marking the end of the batch file.

SHIFT command, you could keep as many as you like. It would also be a simple modification to delete subdirectories from the front of the path rather than from the rear. You might also want to modify the batch files to delete a single subdirectory. EDIT1.BAT in Fig. 12-30 actually performs the editing. Because EDIT PATH.BAT performs all the error checking, EDIT1.BAT has none.

Batch File Line	Explanation
@ECHO OFF	Turn command-echoing off.
REM EDIT1.BAT	Remark giving the name of the batch file.
REM Reconstruct first n elements of REM PATH. N assumed to be less REM than or equal to eight.	Documentation remarks.
PATH=%2	Set the PATH to the second replaceable parameter. The first replaceable parameter stores the number of subdirectories to keep.
IF %1==1 GOTO END	If just keeping the first subdirectory, exit the batch file.
PATH=%PATH%;%3	Add the second subdirectory onto the existing PATH--which currently contains only the first subdirectory.
IF %1==2 GOTO END	If just keeping two subdirectories, exit the batch file.
The batch file continues in a similar fashion through %8	
IF %1==7 GOTO END	If adding seven subdirectories, exit the batch file. If this test fails, the batch file assumes an eight was entered without testing for an invalid response.

12-30 EDIT1.BAT, which actually performs the work of changing your path and must be called by EDITPATH.BAT, shown in Fig. 12-29.

12-30 Continued

Batch File Line	Explanation
`PATH=%PATH%;%9`	Add the final subdirectory to the PATH.
`ECHO Path now set to %PATH%`	Tell the user what has happened.
`:END`	A label marking the end of the batch file.

While all these forward and backward deleting methods are quite useful, they're very inflexible if you want to delete a single subdirectory in the middle of your PATH. On the other hand, EDITPATH2.BAT in Fig. 12-31 is very flexible. It calls EDIT2.BAT in Fig. 12-32, which prompts you whether you want to keep each subdirectory, one at a time. Using this method, you can easily delete one subdirectory in the middle of your PATH. EDIT2.BAT uses the Norton Utilities Ask program to set the ErrorLevel, but you could easily use the InKey program that comes with this book.

Batch File Line	Explanation
`@REM EDITPAT2.BAT`	Remark giving the name of the batch file.
`@REM Selectively Delete` `  Subdirectories`	Documentation remark.
`@EDIT2 %PATH%`	Run another batch file while passing the PATH as a series of replaceable parameters. A couple of notes are important: Since the batch file runs EDIT2.BAT without the CALL command, control never returns to EDITPAT2.BAT. The semicolons in the current PATH statement are treated as replaceable parameter dividers by DOS. That causes each subdirectory to become a separate replaceable parameter but it also strips the semicolons out of the PATH so EDIT2.BAT has to add them back.

12-31 EDITPAT2.BAT, which allows you to remove subdirectories from your path and is much more powerful than EDITPATH.BAT, shown in Fig. 12-29.

Batch File Line	Explanation
`@ECHO OFF`	Turn command-echoing off.
`REM EDIT2.BAT`	Remark giving the name of the batch file.
`REM Selectively Delete Path` `  Subdirectories`	Documentation remark.

12-32 EDIT2.BAT, a batch file that lets you decide whether or not to keep each subdirectory in your path.

12-32 Continued

Batch File Line	Explanation
`PATH=;`	Reset the PATH to nul.
`:TOP`	Label marking the top of a loop.
`  IF (%1)==() GOTO END`	If the first replaceable parameter is empty, exit the batch file.
`C:\SYSLIB\SKIPLINE`	Skip a line on the screen. (SKIPLINE.-COM is included on the disk that comes with this book.)
`C:\NORTON\BE ASK "Keep %1 in` `    PATH (Y/N)  " NY`	Ask the user about keeping a subdirectory in the PATH. (This batch file is called by another batch file that passes the current PATH as a series of replaceable parameters.

`IF ERRORLEVEL 2 IF NOT`
`   (%PATH%)==() PATH=%PATH%;%1`
`IF ERRORLEVEL 2 IF`
`   (%PATH%)==() PATH=%1`
	If the user wants to keep this subdirectory in the PATH, add it to the end. The additional IF statements handle the special case of adding the first subdirectory to the PATH--when you do not want to add a semicolon before the subdirectory.

`  SHIFT`	Move all the replaceable parameters down one level.
`  GOTO TOP`	Continue the loop.
`:END`	Label marking the (near) end of the batch file.
`ECHO PATH now set to %PATH%`	Message telling the user the current PATH.

Notice that every program that EDIT2.BAT calls has the full path specified. That's because the first thing EDIT2.BAT does is reset the path to nul. As a result, there's no path when it starts running, so it can find programs only in the current subdirectory. This method of specifying the full path to a program won't work prior to DOS 3.0. Users with earlier versions of DOS will need a different approach. An alternative is to leave the path in place, and construct a second environmental variable that contains the new path. If this environmental variable was NEW, then the last line of EDIT2.BAT would be PATH = %NEW%. You could also begin by changing to the subdirectory containing the batch files, so the path isn't needed.

Repeating batch files

I used to use a computer with two hard disks. The computer didn't recognize the D drive when it booted. When I rebooted, however, it did recognize the D drive. I spent several hours troubleshooting, but was unable to resolve the problem. Because the computer always recognized the D drive after rebooting once, or occasionally twice, I decided that finding the problem just wasn't worth any more of my time. I created a zero-length file in the root directory of the D drive called TEST, and formatted it as hidden and read-only so no one would accidently erase it. I then added these three lines at the top of the AUTOEXEC.BAT file.

```
IF EXIST D:\TEST GOTO SKIP
BOOT
:SKIP
```

If DOS doesn't recognize the D drive, then D:\TEST won't exist and the AUTOEXEC.BAT file will run BOOT.COM, which reboots the computer. It will do this over and over until DOS recognizes the D drive. Of course, this kind of a problem can be indicative of additional problems and really should be fixed. Because I decided not to fix it, I did take the extra precaution to make very frequent backups.

This hint might not work under all versions of DOS. Some versions will fail to read the D drive and give you a *Not ready reading drive D, Abort, Ignore, or Fail?* error message. You then might have to respond to this error message several times, eliminating any time savings over simply rebooting the machine. Only experimentation can tell.

Like the problem accessing the D drive above, when I purchased a new computer I faced a problem of occasional lockups. Right after I received my new Northgate 386/20, I was transferring files from old 360K disks to 1.44 Meg disks. About every fifth disk, the computer would lock up completely, forcing me to reset the computer. Technical support was sure it wasn't the computer, but was rather a memory-resident program.

I wanted to test, so I wrote the batch file in Fig. 12-33. This batch file copies all the files in a subdirectory to the floppy disk, then deletes those files and begins

Batch File Line	Explanation
`@ECHO OFF`	Turn command-echoing off.
`REM MUL-COPY.BAT`	Remark giving the name of the batch file.
`ERASE COUNTER`	Erase the counter file.
`:TOP`	Label marking the top of the loop.
`ECHO Y| DEL B:*.*`	Delete all the files on the B drive. The ECHO Y| keeps the user from having to answer yes to the DOS prompt.
`COPY C:\TESTFILE\*.* B: /V`	Copy all the files in a subdirectory to the B drive.

12-33 MUL-COPY.BAT, which copies files repeatedly until the user issues a Ctrl – Break.

12-33 Continued

Batch File Line	Explanation
ECHO 1 >> COUNTER	Echo a 1 to the file. Using the double pipe appends the one to the existing file. That way, there is a single 1 in the file for each loop.
GOTO TOP	Command to restart the loop.

again. It also echoes a 1 to a file for each loop, so I'll know how many times it successfully completed the Copy command. I rebooted off a clean AUTOEXEC .BAT and CONFIG.SYS files with only the commands necessary for the system to run. (In this case, the only command absolutely necessary was a line loading SHARE.EXE in the CONFIG.SYS file.) With this clean system, I let MUL-COPY.BAT run all night several times. It did that successfully, so I was sure nothing was wrong with the Northgate computer. I then began adding back commands to the CONFIG.SYS and AUTOEXEC.BAT files one at a time and letting MUL-COPY.BAT run all night. When it finally locked up, I knew I had found the problem memory-resident program.

Controlling a network

Consider a network administrator I know. The network he manages has 50 users and over 25 software applications. He typically doesn't buy 50 versions of each package; rather, he buys the network version with permission to run 10 copies at once. Except for Lotus and Microsoft Word, 10 copies of most packages is enough so users never have to wait too long for the software he wants to run. This administrator has no problems with the network programs. However, he has no way to control the non-network programs. For example, their art program runs only as a stand-alone program but, because it's on the network, everyone can load and run it at once. How can he make sure that no more than 10 copies are running at any one time?

This is a very good application for a batch file, and the approach is very simple. Simply maintain a counter that starts off with the number of authorized copies of the program you have. The batch file decreases the counter anytime someone begins to run a program and increases the counter when they exit. With a properly maintained counter, the batch file uses the counter to decide if a user can run the requested program.

Figure 12-34 shows just such a batch file. Because batch files can't perform mathematics, I've used a series of IF statements to properly increment the counter when the program is started and stopped. Notice the CALL statement, which calls the batch file to start the program. You could omit the second batch file and start the application from within this batch file.

Batch File Line	Explanation
`@ECHO OFF`	Turn command-echoing off.

`REM Use this batch file to control`
`REM starting of non-network versions`
`REM of software on a network. It`
`REM prevents users from running more`
`REM copies than are available.`
`REM Assumes the environmental variable`
`REM COUNTWP is set to the maximum`
`REM authorized copies at the beginning`
`REM of the day and that five is the`
`REM maximum.`
	Documentation remarks.

`IF %COUNTWP%==0 GOTO SORRY`
`IF %COUNTWP%==1 GOTO START1`
`IF %COUNTWP%==2 GOTO START2`
`IF %COUNTWP%==3 GOTO START3`
`IF %COUNTWP%==4 GOTO START4`
`IF %COUNTWP%==5 GOTO START5`
`GOTO STARTERR`
	The host computer maintains an environmental variable called COUNTWP that stores the number of copies that remains available to run. This routes the batch file to the appropriate section depending on the value of the counters.

`:START1`
`SET COUNTWP=0`
`CALL WP`
`GOTO END`
	When the value of the counter is one, reset it to zero and run the application.

`:START2`
`SET COUNTWP=1`
`CALL WP`
`GOTO END`
	Section for starting the application when the counter equals two.

`:START3`
`SET COUNTWP=2`
`CALL WP`
`GOTO END`
	Section for starting the application when the counter equals three.

`:START4`
`SET COUNTWP=3`
`CALL WP`
`GOTO END`
	Section for starting the application when the counter equals four.

`:START5`
`SET COUNTWP=4`
`CALL WP`
`GOTO END`
	Section for starting the application when the counter equals five.

`:SORRY`	Label marking the beginning of the section that tells the user no copies are available to run.

12-34 NETWORK.BAT, which will restrict the number of users of software application to five.

12-34 Continued

Batch File Line	Explanation
ECHO Sorry, but not more versions ECHO of this software are available ECHO at this time. Please try later.	Tell the user what has happened. It might be a good idea to add a PAUSE after this so the user will have time to read the messages.
REM You should log this to count how REM often in happens. This is REM discussed elsewhere in the book.	Documentation remarks.
GOTO EXIT	Exit the batch file.
:END	Label marking the end of the section of the batch file that starts the application. The remaining portion of the batch file handles exiting the application.
IF %COUNTWP%==0 GOTO END0 IF %COUNTWP%==1 GOTO END1 IF %COUNTWP%==2 GOTO END2 IF %COUNTWP%==3 GOTO END3 IF %COUNTWP%==4 GOTO END4 GOTO ENDERROR	The counter needs to be reset when a user exits the application, so that copy is available for someone else to run. These IF statements directs the batch file to the appropriate section to handle that.
:END0	Label marking the beginning of the section for when the counter equals zero.
SET COUNTWP=1	Increase the counter by one.
GOTO EXIT	Exit the batch file.
:END1 SET COUNTWP=2 GOTO EXIT	Section for handling when the counter equals one.
:END2 SET COUNTWP=3 GOTO EXIT	Section for handling when the counter equals two.
:END3 SET COUNTWP=4 GOTO EXIT	Section for handling when the counter equals three.
:END4 SET COUNTWP=5 GOTO EXIT	Section for handling when the counter equals four.

12-34 Continued

Batch File Line	Explanation

`:STARTERR`
`ECHO WP can not start properly`
`ECHO Please call system administrator`
`GOTO EXIT`
	Section for handling an error when trying to start the application. The likely error is the counter variable somehow being deleted or set to an invalid value.

`:ENDERROR`
`ECHO WP has detected an error while`
`ECHO stopping. Please contact`
`ECHO system administrator at once.`
`GOTO EXIT`
	Section for handling an error when trying to exit the application.

`:EXIT`	Label marking the exit point for the batch file.

Of course, this batch file won't prevent a user from entering WP directly and avoiding this check. Also, you'll need a separate batch file and environmental variable for each application you want to track this way. With a lot of programs, you're going to need a fairly large environment.

You can avoid the need for a larger environment by using 0-length files as the counter, as discussed above. However, this adds two other problems. First, when the network has to be rebooted because of a lockup, the startup files must delete all the counter files or application programs will be assigned as being in use when they're not. Second, the user might need write privileges to the area where the counter is maintained in order for the batch file to rename the counter file. That could give the user the ability to accidently or purposefully damage network-related files.

Modifying files during installation

It's not unusual for an installation program to want to modify the CONFIG.SYS or AUTOEXEC.BAT file during installation. You can "sort of" do this with batch files, but you're limited to adding text above or below the existing AUTOEXEC .BAT and both locations have problems. If you choose to add the commands at the top, you can't change the path, and no path will be in effect so you can't access DOS programs. If you choose to add the commands at the bottom, it's possible that they'll never be run. If the last line in the existing AUTOEXEC.BAT file runs a menu program, that menu program might never turn control back over to the batch file, so your commands will never be executed.

The basic approach is to rename the AUTOEXEC.BAT file to something else and use the Copy command to combine a file containing the new text with the renamed AUTOEXEC.BAT file. Figure 12-35 shows some text to add to the

Batch File Line	Explanation
@ECHO OFF	Turn command-echoing off.
REM ADD.BAT	Remark giving the name of the batch file.
REM Appends commands to an AUTOEXEC.BAT file	Documentation remark.
REM Would have commands here to run a new program	Documentation remark.
PATH=C:\NEWPROGRAM;\%PATH%	Adds C:\NEWPROGRAM as the first entry in the current path.

12-35 ADD.BAT, a batch file that list the commands to add to the top or bottom of an existing AUTOEXEC.BAT file.

AUTOEXEC.BAT file, and Fig. 12-36 shows the batch file to perform the modification. Notice that I've left out error checking. The batch files need to have error checking in order to make sure that the subdirectory and drive are proper and that an AUTOEXEC.BAT file exists. You should add these. To add the text to

Batch File Line	Explanation
@ECHO OFF	Turn command-echoing off.
REM DOADD.BAT	Remark giving the name of the batch file.
CLS	Clear the screen.
ECHO ---UPDATING AUTOEXEC.BAT---	Tell the user what the batch file is doing.
REN AUTOEXEC.BAT *.OLD	Save a copy of the existing batch file under a new name. For complete protection, the batch file should check to make sure this name does not exist first. DOS will not let you rename a file to an existing name so, if it already exists, this command does not execute and the next command operates improperly.
COPY AUTOEXEC.OLD+ADD.BAT AUTOEXEC.BAT	Copy the old AUTOEXEC.BAT file and the lines to add to the name AUTOEXEC.BAT. This effectively adds commands to the end of the AUTOEXEC.-BAT file.

12-36 DOADD.BAT, which adds the commands specified in ADD.BAT, shown in Fig. 12-35, to an existing AUTOEXEC.BAT file.

the top rather than the bottom, you should reverse the order of the Copy command.

If you want to add the text to the end, you could also use the appending pipe symbols > >. However, this will cause a problem if the last line of the AUTOEXEC.BAT file doesn't contain a Return because the pipe adds a Return only after the line, not before—and that could cause two commands to be on the same line.

Password protection

One way to keep casual users from accessing your hard disk is to add password protection. Password protections range from simple programs that require you to enter a password to complex systems that encrypt the file allocation table (FAT) and won't access the hard disk at all until the proper password is entered. If all you need is light protection, then you can put together a batch file password system that's very effective.

Keep in mind that this system won't keep a user from booting off a floppy disk and then accessing your hard disk. In addition, because you can't encrypt the batch file, anyone with access to the hard disk can look at the batch file and figure out your password. With that caveat in mind, let's construct the password system.

The password batch file is shown in Fig. 12-37. It uses InKey to get the first character of the password. If that character is correct, it uses InKey to get the second character. If the first character is incorrect, it increments a counter and asks again. It repeats this process for the second and third character. Any time an incorrect character is entered, the program begins prompting for the password from the beginning. Once the counter reaches three—which is after you've entered three incorrect passwords—the batch file will enter an endless loop and appear to lock up.

With any batch file, you have the problem of the user pressing Ctrl−Break to stop the batch file. PASSWORD.BAT avoids this problem almost completely by using the CTTY NUL command at the top. This turns off the console so the computer won't accept most inputs from the keyboard, and won't write output to the screen. It's interesting to note that the batch file will still accept the Ctrl−Break, but won't accept the *y* in response to the *Terminate batch job (y/n)* message—effectively locking the computer. Notice that, after the correct response is entered, the batch file restores the screen and keyboard with the CTTY CON command.

Because the keyboard and screen don't respond to the batch file under the CTTY NUL command, the batch file forces them to work by piping output to the screen with the > CON piping command and grabbing input from the keyboard with the < CON piping command.

Batch File Line	Explanation
`ECHO OFF`	Turn command-echoing off.
`REM PASSWORD.BAT`	Remark giving the name of the batch file.
`IF (%1)==() GOTO NOPASS`	If the user did not enter a password on the command line, jump to an error-handling routine.
`IF (%PASSWORD%)==() GOTO NOTSET`	If the environmental variable PASSWORD is blank, jump to an error-handling routine.
`IF NOT %1==%PASSWORD% GOTO NO`	If the user's password does not match the one stored in the environmental variable, jump to an error-handling routine.
`PROGRAM` `GOTO END`	If the user's password matches the environmental variable, run the program then exit the batch file.

`:NOPASS`
`ECHO You must enter a password.`
`ECHO See manual for syntax.`
`GOTO END`
	If the user did not enter a password, explain the problem and exit the batch file.

`:NOTSET`
`ECHO Password not set.`
`ECHO Call system operator.`
`GOTO END`
	If the password has not been set, explain the problem to the user then exit the batch file.

`:NO`	Label marking the beginning of the section for handling an incorrect password.
`ECHO INCORRECT PASSWORD` `ECHO LOCKING SYSTEM`	Explain the problem.
`PAUSE>NUL`	Simulate a locked computer by pausing execution and piping the DOS message to NUL. Pressing any key will restart the batch file and allow the user to continue using the computer. The computer could be completely locked up with a CTTY NUL command followed by a PAUSE command. Using this method, the user would have to reboot the computer to use it again.
`GOTO END`	Exit the batch file if the user presses a key to restart the batch file.
`:END`	Label marking the end of the batch file.

12-37 PASSWORD.BAT, which requires the user to enter the correct password (RON in this example) in three tries or less.

Notice the trick that the batch file uses for testing for the appropriate ErrorLevel. DOS treats the ErrorLevel test unusually. When ERRORLEVEL=1, the IF ERRORLEVEL 0 test is also true because it's really a greater than or equal to test. For any ErrorLevel value of n, you can simulate an equality test with the line IF ERRORLEVEL n IF NOT ERRORLEVEL $n+1$. It will pass only the first part of the test when ERRORLEVEL $> = n$, and will pass only the second part when ERRORLEVEL $< n+1$, thus only ERRORLEVEL$=n$ passes the test. This means that you don't need to test for every possible ErrorLevel value because only one character is valid at each stage of the password.

If you add the password to the top of your AUTOEXEC.BAT file, anyone booting the computer from the hard disk will have to enter a password. It should be at the very top of the AUTOEXEC.BAT file so the user won't have time to enter Ctrl−Break before the password part of the AUTOEXEC.BAT file takes over. You should also create a stand-alone batch file with a name like LOCK.BAT so you can lock your computer but leave it running when you have to leave it.

Summary

This chapter has presented numerous short hints for using batch files to solve specific problems. Most of the batch files in this chapter are on the disk.

13
CHAPTER

Batch file tricks

You've seen how to write batch files. You've also seen how to use batch files to solve a bunch of ordinary problems. Now let's look at batch files that can do things you don't expect. In other words, let's look at batch files from a power-user's point of view. (If you don't feel like a power user yet, you can come back to this chapter later, or even skip it altogether.)

Dealing with capitalization

Managing capitalization in batch files is a real pain. Consider the batch file CAPITAL1.BAT in Fig. 13-1. CAPITAL1.BAT is designed to run one of three programs (DAILY.EXE, MONTHLY.EXE, or ANNUAL.EXE) depending on the replaceable parameter you enter. The code that just handles the most likely capitalizations takes up nine lines, where three would work if capitalization weren't a problem.

Even this elaborate scheme won't respond properly to replaceable parameters like DAIly. There are a number of ways of dealing with the capitalization problem quickly without a lot of extra code. Each method has unique advantages.

The first way to avoid the capitalization problem is to use the replaceable parameter as a label for the GOTO command because labels are case-insensitive. Keep in mind that DOS always replaces the replaceable parameters with their value. Take a look at CAPITAL2.BAT in Fig. 13-2. If you run this batch file with the command line:

CAPITAL2 daily

DOS replaces the GOTO %1 line with GOTO daily, and the batch file runs properly. Using the GOTO %1 method, however, is only a partial solution. If the user starts the batch file with an invalid parameter, yearly, for example, the batch file

Batch File Line	Explanation
`@ECHO OFF`	Turn command-echoing off.
`REM CAPITAL1.BAT`	Remark giving the name of the batch file.
`IF (%1)==()          GOTO NOTHING`	Jump to an error-handling section if the user did not enter a replaceable parameter.

`IF (%1)==(DAILY)    GOTO ONE`
`IF (%1)==(daily)    GOTO ONE`
`IF (%1)==(Daily)    GOTO ONE`
	Jump to the section to handle daily closings if either of these three common capitalizations of the replaceable parameter was entered.

`IF (%1)==(MONTHLY) GOTO TWO`
`IF (%1)==(monthly) GOTO TWO`
`IF (%1)==(Monthly) GOTO TWO`
	Jump to the monthly section if that is appropriate.

`IF (%1)==(ANNUAL)   GOTO THREE`
`IF (%1)==(annual)   GOTO THREE`
`IF (%1)==(Annual)   GOTO THREE`
	Jump to the annual section if that is appropriate.

`:NOTHING`
`ECHO This Batch File Requires`
`ECHO A Parameter. The Valid`
`ECHO Ways To Start It Are:`
`ECHO CAPITAL1 daily`
`ECHO CAPITAL1 monthly`
`ECHO CAPITAL1 annual`
`GOTO END`
	Section that tells the user the batch file was run improperly and tells the user how to run it properly.

`:ONE`
`DAILY`
`GOTO END`
	Daily section.

`:TWO`
`MONTHLY`
`GOTO END`
	Monthly section.

`:THREE`
`ANNUAL`
`GOTO END`
	Annual section.

`:END`	Label marking the end of the batch file.

13-1 CAPITAL1.BAT, which tries to handle the most likely types of capitalization.

Batch File Line	Explanation
`@ECHO OFF`	Turn command-echoing off.
`REM CAPITAL2.BAT`	Remark giving the name of the batch file.
`IF (%1)==() GOTO NOTHING`	If the user did not enter a replaceable parameter, jump to an error-handling section.

13-2 CAPITAL2.BAT, which uses a GOTO command to avoid the capitalization problem.

13-2 Continued

Batch File Line	Explanation
`GOTO %1`	Jump to the label that corresponds to the first replaceable parameter. If the user uses a replaceable parameter that does not have a corresponding label, the batch file will abort on this line with a "missing label" error message.

`:NOTHING`
`ECHO This Batch File Requires`
`ECHO A Parameter. The Valid`
`ECHO Ways To Start It Are:`
`ECHO CAPITAL2 daily`
`ECHO CAPITAL2 monthly`
`ECHO CAPITAL2 annual`
`GOTO END`
	Section that tells the user the batch file was run improperly and tells the user how to run it properly.

`:ONE`
`DAILY`
`GOTO END`
	Daily section.

`:TWO`
`MONTHLY`
`GOTO END`
	Monthly section.

`:THREE`
`ANNUAL`
`GOTO END`
	Annual section.

`:END`	Label marking the end of the batch file.

will abort on the GOTO yearly line with a *Label not found* error message. Therefore, you should use this method only when you're sure the user will be able to recover from this error message without any help from the batch file.

Environmental variables

A second method is to store the selected option in the environment as an environmental variable. Figure 13-3 illustrates this method. First, each possible environmental variable is deleted, and then the line SET %1=YES creates a single

Batch File Line	Explanation
`@ECHO OFF`	Turn command-echoing off.
`REM CAPITAL3.BAT`	Remark giving the name of the batch file.

`SET DAILY=`
`SET MONTHLY=`
`SET ANNUAL=`
	Reset the environmental variables used in this batch file.

13-3 CAPITAL3.BAT, which creates an environmental variable to avoid the problems in CAPITAL2.BAT, shown in Fig. 13-2.

13-3 Continued

Batch File Line	Explanation
SET %1=YES	Store YES to the environmental variable corresponding to the first replaceable parameter.
IF %DAILY%==YES GOTO DAILY IF %MONTHLY%==YES GOTO MONTHLY IF %ANNUAL%==YES GOTO ANNUAL	Test on the three environmental variables to decide which section to jump to.
GOTO ERROR	If the batch file reaches this point, the user entered an invalid replaceable parameter so jump to an error-handling section.
:ERROR ECHO This Batch File Requires ECHO A Parameter. The Valid ECHO Ways To Start It Are: ECHO CAPITAL3 daily ECHO CAPITAL3 monthly ECHO CAPITAL3 annual GOTO END	Section that tells the user the batch file was run improperly and tells the user how to run it properly.
:ONE DAILY GOTO END	Daily section.
:TWO MONTHLY GOTO END	Monthly section.
:THREE ANNUAL GOTO END	Annual section.
:END	Label marking the end of the batch file.

environmental variable with the name of the replaceable parameter and a value of YES.

This method works well for most replaceable parameters and avoids the missing label problem associated with the GOTO %1 method, but has a minor problem of its own. If the replaceable parameter the user enters can be a number, the batch file will end up making unexpected tests. Suppose you want to use CAPITAL3.BAT to run Lotus 1-2-3, so the user could be expected to use 123 as a replaceable parameter. The SET %1=YES line would work properly. In order to run Lotus, you would need a test line of IF %123%==YES. However, DOS would translate the %1 as the first replaceable parameter.

The path

The path is the only environmental variable DOS converts to uppercase. You can convert a replaceable parameter to uppercase by performing the following steps:

1. Store the current path under another variable name.

2. Set the path equal to the replaceable parameter. Note that you must use PATH= and not SET PATH=, because some versions of DOS won't convert the path to uppercase with the SET PATH= method.
3. Store the replaceable parameter now stored under the path to another variable name.
4. Restore the proper path using the holding variable created in step 1.
5. Clear out the holding variable created in step 1.

CAPITAL4.BAT in Fig. 13-4 illustrates this. This method handles all possible inputs without problem, but requires the most environmental space because DOS must store two versions of the path and the first replaceable parameter in memory at once.

Neither of these three methods is perfect. Each has its own drawbacks. You have to decide which one is best suited to each situation and use it accordingly.

Batch File Line	Explanation
`@ECHO OFF`	Turn command-echoing off.
`SET OLDPATH=%PATH%`	Store the current PATH under the name of OLDPATH.
`PATH=%1`	Set the PATH equal to the first replaceable parameter. Since DOS converts the PATH to uppercase, this will convert the first replaceable parameter to uppercase. Note that SET PATH=%1 will not work because not all versions of DOS convert the PATH to uppercase using this method.
`SET VARIABLE=%PATH%`	Store the uppercase replaceable parameter under another variable name.
`PATH=%OLDPATH%`	Restore the PATH.
`SET OLDPATH=`	Reset the temporary variable to empty.

`IF (%VARIABLE%)==(DAILY)`
`   GOTO DAILY`
`IF (%VARIABLE%)==(MONTHLY)`
`   GOTO MONTHLY`
`IF (%VARIABLE%)==(ANNUAL)`
`   GOTO ANNUAL`
	Jump to the appropriate section depending on the replaceable parameter the user enters.

`GOTO ERROR`	If the batch file reaches this point, the user entered an invalid replaceable parameter so jump to an error-handling section.

13-4 CAPITAL4.BAT, which uses the PATH command to convert the replaceable parameter in order to avoid the problems with environmental variables, but also requires a large environment.

13-4 Continued

Batch File Line	Explanation

`:ERROR`
`ECHO This Batch File Requires`
`ECHO A Parameter. The Valid`
`ECHO Ways To Start It Are:`
`ECHO CAPITAL4 daily`
`ECHO CAPITAL4 monthly`
`ECHO CAPITAL4 annual`
`GOTO END`
	Section that tells the user the batch file was run improperly and tells the user how to run it properly.

`:ONE`
`DAILY`
`GOTO END`
	Daily section.

`:TWO`
`MONTHLY`
`GOTO END`
	Monthly section.

`:THREE`
`ANNUAL`
`GOTO END`
	Annual section.

`:END`	Label marking the end of the batch file.

Passing complex parameters

Some programs like the Norton Text Search (TS.EXE) can accept a parameter with a space in it as part of an input. For example,

TS *.BAT "ECHO OFF"

would search through all the batch files in the current directory for the line ECHO OFF. Forget the quotes and it will ignore the OFF and just search for ECHO. Batch files don't have any trouble with quotes. If you were running this program with the batch file TEXTFIND.BAT in Fig. 13-5 and entered:

TEXTFIND *.BAT "ECHO OFF"

Batch File Line	Explanation
`@ECHO OFF`	Turn command-echoing off.
`REM TEXTFIND.BAT`	Remark giving the name of the batch file.
`TS %1 %2 %3 %4 %5`	Run the Norton Utilities Text Search program. This program was discontinued after Release 4.5. Beginning with the Norton Utilities Release 5, text searching was integrated into the File Find program. This line has a problem, as discussed in the text.

13-5 TEXTFIND.BAT, which runs the Norton Text Search program.

then the replaceable parameters would be:

%1   *.BAT
%2   "ECHO
%3   OFF"

If you're like me, however, you often forget the quote marks. I set out to have the batch file add the quotes for me, but it proved to be tougher than I'd expected. My first attempt was TEXTFND2.BAT in Fig. 13-6. It worked sometimes. The problem was my selection of four replaceable parameters inside the quotes. If there

Batch File Line	Explanation
`@ECHO OFF`	Turn command-echoing off.
`REM TEXTFND2.BAT`	Remark giving the name of the batch file.
`TS %1 "%2 %3 %4 %5"`	Run the Norton Utilities Text Search program. This line has a problem, as discussed in the text.

13-6   TEXTFIND2.BAT, which is a failed attempt to modify the Norton Text Search program.

were less than four, DOS still used the spaces between the replaceable parameters and spaces matter to a text search program. If there were more than four words, then not all the text was used. My next attempt was to use more replaceable parameters inside the quotes and to remove the spaces. That resulted in TEXT FND3.BAT, as shown in Fig. 13-7. This didn't add any extra spaces before the

Batch File Line	Explanation
`@ECHO OFF`	Turn command-echoing off.
`REM TEXTFND3.BAT`	Remark giving the name of the batch file.
`TS %1 "%2%3%4%5%6%7%8%9"`	Run the Norton Utilities Text Search program. This line has a problem, as discussed in the text.

13-7   TEXTFIND3.BAT, which is another failed attempt to modify the Norton Text Search program.

final quote if I didn't use all the replaceable parameters, but it also failed to add any spaces at all. For example, if I entered:

TEXTFND3 *.BAT REM ECHO IS OFF

then the batch file issued the command:

TEXTFND3 *.BAT "REMECHOISOFF"

which clearly didn't work. Those experiments made it clear that the batch file was going to have to intelligently construct the command.

At this point, I had two choices: the brute force method or the finesse method. I actually decided to try both. TEXTFND4.BAT in Fig. 13-8 represents

Batch File Line	Explanation
`@ECHO OFF`	Turn command-echoing off.
`REM TEXTFND4.BAT`	Remark giving the name of the batch file.
`REM BRUTE-FORCE WAY`	Documentation remark.
`IF (%1)==() GOTO ERROR1`	If no replaceable parameters were entered, jump to an error-handling section.
`IF (%2)==() GOTO ERROR2`	The program requires a minimum of two parameters so, if the second was not entered, jump to an error-handling section.
`IF (%3)==() TS %1 %2` `IF (%3)==() GOTO END`	If no third parameter was entered, run the program with parameters and exit the batch file.
`IF (%4)==() TS %1 "%2 %3"` `IF (%4)==() GOTO END`	If no fourth parameter was entered, run the program with three parameters and exit the batch file.
`IF (%5)==() TS %1 "%2 %3 %4"` `IF (%5)==() GOTO END`	If no fifth parameter was entered, run the program with four parameters and exit the batch file.
`IF (%6)==() TS %1 "%2 %3 %4 %5"` `IF (%6)==() GOTO END`	If no sixth parameter was entered, run the program with five parameters and exit the batch file.

`IF (%7)==() TS %1 "%2 %3 %4 %5`
`%6"`
`IF (%7)==() GOTO END`
	If no seventh parameter was entered, run the program with six parameters and exit the batch file.

`IF (%8)==() TS %1 "%2 %3 %4 %5`
`%6 %7"`
`IF (%8)==() GOTO END`
	If no eighth parameter was entered, run the program with seven parameters and exit the batch file.

`IF (%9)==() TS %1 "%2 %3 %4 %5`
`%6 %7 %8"`
`IF (%9)==() GOTO END`
	If no ninth parameter was entered, run the program with eight parameters and exit the batch file.

`TS %1 "%2 %3 %4 %5 %6 %7 %8 %9"` `GOTO END`	If the batch file reaches this point, then at least nine replaceable parameters were entered, so use all nine. Note that any replaceable parameters after %9 are lost. After running the program, exit the batch file.
`:ERROR1`	Label marking the beginning of the error-handling section for no replaceable parameters.

13-8 TEXTFIND4.BAT, which is a "brute force" method to add quotes into the Norton Text Search program.

13-8 Continued

Batch File Line	Explanation
ECHO No Files to Search Specified	Tell the user what happened.
GOTO END	Exit the batch file.
:ERROR2	Label marking the beginning of the error-handling section for only one replaceable parameter.
ECHO No Text to Search For Specified	Tell the user what happened.
GOTO END	Exit the batch file.
:END	Label marking the end of the batch file.

the brute force method. This batch file simply searches for the first blank replaceable parameter, so it knows how many words were entered to search for. It then constructs a custom command line for that specific number of words. It only has one main drawback, it can't handle more than eight words to search for. If you enter more than that, it ignores all the words after the eighth. You could extend this to nine by adding a SHIFT command so the files to search on became the %0 parameter rather than the %1.

The finesse method proved to be more difficult and ended up taking most of the afternoon to debug. TEXTFND5.BAT in Fig. 13-9 is the result. It works by

Batch File Line	Explanation
@ECHO OFF	Turn command-echoing off.
REM TEXTFND5.BAT	Remark giving the name of the batch file.
REM Allows multiple word searches	Documentation remark.
IF (%1)==() GOTO NOFILE	If the user did not enter files to search, jump to an error-handling routine.
SET FILE=%1	Store the files to search in the environment.
SHIFT	Move all the replaceable parameters down one level.
IF (%1)==() GOTO NOTEXT	If the user did not enter any text to search for, jump to an error-handling routine.
SET TEXT="%1	Store the beginning quote and the text in the environment.
SHIFT	Move the replaceable parameters down one level.

13-9 TEXTFIND5.BAT, which is a "finesse" method for adding quotes into the Norton Text Search program.

13-9 Continued

Batch File Line	Explanation
`IF (%1)==() GOTO STOP`	If only one word was entered to search for, jump to the section named STOP to continue processing.
`:TOP`	Label marking the top of a loop.
`SET TEXT=%TEXT% %1`	Add a space and the next word to the environmental variable storing the text to search for. You must add the space since DOS strips out the spaces when it separates multiple words into individual replaceable parameters.
`SHIFT`	Move the replaceable parameters down one level.
`IF (%1)==() GOTO STOP`	Once the replaceable parameter are exhausted, jump to the next portion of the batch file to continue processing.
`GOTO TOP`	Continue the loop.
`:STOP`	Label marking the next section of the batch file.
`SET TEXT=%TEXT%"`	Add the closing quote to the environmental variable storing the text.
`GOTO START`	Jump to the section of the batch file that handles the actual searching.
`:NOFILE`	Label marking the error-handling section for when the user does not enter files to search.
`ECHO No files to search entered`	Tell the user what happened.
`GOTO END`	Exit the batch file.
`:NOTEXT`	Label marking the error-handling section for when the user does not enter text to search for.
`ECHO No text to search for entered`	Tell the user what happened.
`GOTO END`	Exit the batch file.
`:START`	Label marking the section of the batch file that performs the actual searching.

13-9 Continued

Batch File Line	Explanation
TS %FILE% %TEXT%	Run the Norton Utilities Text Search program and pass it the two values stored in the environment.
:END	Label marking the end of the batch file.

looping through all the replaceable parameters and constructing a custom environmental variable containing the phrase to search on.

Both the brute force TEXTFND4.BAT in Fig. 13-8 and the finesse TEXT-FND5.BAT in Fig. 13-9 share a common problem, they require the user not to enter the proper quotes. The batch files themselves will work properly but then the command passed to DOS will look something like:

TS *.BAT ""REM ECHO IS OFF""

The basic technique presented by this series of batch files in the technique in TEXTFND5.BAT, to cycle through all the replaceable parameters and build a custom environmental variable based on their content. In this example, I have used the contents of each replaceable parameter as found. That is not necessary. The batch file can use those contents to make decisions about constructing an environmental variable without using their contents exactly. TRANSFORM.BAT in Fig. 13-10 shows a nonsense example of this. I leave it to the reader to develop practical applications for this technique.

Batch File Line	Explanation
@ECHO OFF	Turn command-echoing off.
REM TRANSFORM.BAT	Remark giving the name of the batch file.
REM RESET ENVIRONMENTAL VARIABLE TO NUL	Documentation remark.
SET TEST=	Reset the environmental variable.
IF (%1)==() SET TEST=BLANK IF (%1)==() GOTO END	If the first replaceable parameter is empty, set the environmental variable TEST to a value of BLANK and exit.
SET TEST=INVALID	Set the environmental variable to a value of INVALID. Any of the valid setting below will reset this to another value.
REM Of course, one of the tests REM below overwrites this REM setting	Documentation remarks.

13-10 TRANSFORM.BAT, which constructs a custom environmental variable based on replaceable parameter values without using them exactly.

13-10 Continued

Batch File Line	Explanation
IF %1==1 SET TEST=ONE IF %1==2 SET TEST=TWO IF %1==3 SET TEST=THREE IF %1==4 SET TEST=FOUR IF %1==5 SET TEST=FIVE	If the first replaceable parameter has a value of 1-5, reset the environmental variable TEST to that value.
:END	Label marking the end of the batch file.

Nesting IF statements

It's possible to place more than one IF statement on a line. The format is:

IF *condition1* IF *condition2* . . . *do this*

For example:

IF %1 = = BAK IF %2 = = OLD IF %3 = = TXT DEL *.%1

Generally, this isn't worth the confusing code that results. One place it's useful is when you have to make a lot of tests. Batch files make these tests very slow and the fewer tests the better. Back in chapter 3, I introduced a batch file called CHECKERR.BAT for displaying the current value in ErrorLevel. It required 510 lines of IF statements while it tested each possible value of ErrorLevel twice. One test was to display its value and a second test was to jump out of the testing when it passed because all smaller tests would pass as well.

By nesting two IF statements on one line, this batch file can be reduced to half the length. While it doesn't reduce the number of IF tests, the new arrangement runs faster and doesn't require any GOTO statements. CHECKER2.BAT is shown in Fig. 13-11.

Under certain conditions, nesting IF statements can save a lot of testing. For example, the batch file fragment NEST1.BAT in Fig. 13-12 requires four lines to make sure that a Y or N was entered as the first replaceable parameter. (In this example, NEST1.BAT does nothing useful with %1 after testing it. That's

Batch File Line	Explanation
ECHO OFF	Turn command-echoing off.
REM CHECKER2.BAT	Remark giving the name of the batch file.
IF ERRORLEVEL 255 ECHO 255	If ERRORLEVEL equals 255, it echoes that fact. Since 255 is the maximum possible value, only one test is required.

13-11 CHECKER2.BAT, which combines IF and IF NOT statements on one line, allowing an individual ErrorLevel value to be tested by each line.

13-11 Continued

Batch File Line	Explanation
IF ERRORLEVEL 254 IF NOT ERRORLEVEL 255 ECHO 254	This multiple IF test overcomes the limitation of the greater than or equal ERRORLEVEL test. All values greater than or equal to 254 pass the first test. Without the NOT, all values 255 or greater pass the second test and the NOT reverses it so only values less than 255 pass the test. The result is a test only 254 passes.
IF ERRORLEVEL 253 IF NOT ERRORLEVEL 254 ECHO 253	All values greater than or equal to 253 pass the first test. Without the NOT, all values 254 or greater pass the second test and the NOT reverses it so only values less than 254 pass the test. The result is a test only 253 passes.
IF ERRORLEVEL 252 IF NOT ERRORLEVEL 253 ECHO 252	Test for an ERRORLEVEL value of 252.

The batch file continues in a similar fashion for ERRORLEVEL values of 251-4

Batch File Line	Explanation
IF ERRORLEVEL 3 IF NOT ERRORLEVEL 4 ECHO 3	Test for an ERRORLEVEL value of 3.
IF ERRORLEVEL 2 IF NOT ERRORLEVEL 3 ECHO 2	Test for an ERRORLEVEL value of 2.
IF ERRORLEVEL 1 IF NOT ERRORLEVEL 2 ECHO 1	Test for an ERRORLEVEL value of 1.
IF ERRORLEVEL 0 IF NOT ERRORLEVEL 1 ECHO 0	Test for an ERRORLEVEL value of 0.

Batch File Line	Explanation
ECHO OFF	Turn command-echoing off.
REM NEST1.BAT	Remark giving the name of the batch file.
IF (%1)==() GOTO NONE	If no replaceable parameter was entered, go to a special section.
IF %1==Y GOTO OK IF %1==y GOTO OK IF %1==N GOTO OK IF %1==n GOTO OK	If the user entered an upper- or lowercase n or y, jump to a section for an appropriate input.
GOTO ERROR	A non-acceptable input was used, so jump to a special error-handling section.
:OK ECHO CORRECT VALUE ENTERED GOTO END	A correct command was entered, so normally there would be commands here to execute.

13-12 NEST1.BAT, which uses four IFs to test for a Y or N answer.

13-12 Continued

Batch File Line	Explanation
:NONE ECHO NO VALUE ENTERED GOTO END	No replaceable parameter was entered, so tell the user that and exit the batch file.
:ERROR ECHO INVALID VALUE ENTERED GOTO END	An invalid replaceable parameter was entered, so tell the user that and exit the batch file.
:END	Label marking the end of the batch file.

because it's an example. In practice, after testing %1, the batch file accomplish something useful.) These four tests can be reduced to one in NEST2.BAT, shown in Fig. 13-13.

Be sure to use nested IF statements with care, because they can be difficult to write and debug later.

Batch File Line	Explanation
ECHO OFF	Turn command-echoing off.
REM NEST2.BAT	Remark giving the name of the batch file.
IF (%1)==() GOTO NONE	If no replaceable parameter was entered, jump to a special section to handle that error.

IF NOT %1==Y IF NOT %1==y
   IF NOT %1==N IF NOT %1==n
   GOTO ERROR
	If none of the four acceptable responses were entered, jump to an error-handling section.

GOTO OK	An acceptable response was entered, so go to the appropriate section.
:OK ECHO CORRECT VALUE ENTERED GOTO END	A correct command was entered, so normally there would be commands here to execute.
:NONE ECHO NO VALUE ENTERED GOTO END	No replaceable parameter was entered, so tell the user that and exit the batch file.
:ERROR ECHO INVALID VALUE ENTERED GOTO END	An invalid replaceable parameter was entered, so tell the user that and exit the batch file.
:END	Label marking the end of the batch file.

13-13 NEST2.BAT, which simplifies string comparisons by using multiple IF statements on one line.

Even shorter ErrorLevel tests

CHECKER2.BAT in Fig. 13-11 shows how to use combined IF tests to shorten DOS ErrorLevel testing. You can make these tests even shorter, however, with the FOR command. As you recall, the FOR command lets you perform the same test over and over for different values, which is exactly what you do with a typical ErrorLevel test.

CHECKER3.BAT in Fig. 13-14 shows just such a batch file. I have only ten tests on most lines but you could stuff as many as you wanted on each line, up to the 127-character limit DOS places on command lines. Notice that the tests are in descending order. This is consistent with ErrorLevel because it's always a greater than or equal test.

Batch File Line	Explanation
`@ECHO OFF`	Turn command-echoing off.
`REM CHECKER3.BAT`	Remark giving the name of the batch file.
`REM Checking ERRORLEVEL Values` `   Using FOR`	Documentation remark.

`FOR %%j IN (255 254 253 252 251 250)`
`   DO IF ERRORLEVEL %%j ECHO`
`ERRORLEVEL is %%j`
	The line loops through six possible ERRORLEVEL values and echoes the ERRORLEVEL value for every passing test. Since the ERRORLEVEL test is a greater than or equal to test, once a value passes the test, it will pass all the remaining tests.

`FOR %%j IN (249 248 247 246 245 244`
`   243 242 241 240) DO IF ERRORLEVEL`
`%%j ECHO ERRORLEVEL is %%j`
	More ERRORLEVEL tests.

The batch file continues in a similar fashion for ERRORLEVEL values of 20-239	

`FOR %%j IN (19 18 17 16 15 14 13 12 11`
`   10) DO IF ERRORLEVEL %%j ECHO`
`ERRORLEVEL is %%j`
	More ERRORLEVEL tests.

`FOR %%j IN (9 8 7 6 5 4 3 2 1 0) DO IF`
`   ERRORLEVEL %%j ECHO ERRORLEVEL`
`is %%j`
	More ERRORLEVEL tests.

13-14   CHECKER3.BAT, which uses the FOR command to shorten the IF tests in CHECKER2.BAT, shown in Fig. 13-11.

While this batch file is interesting because it's so brief, it's also not very practical. It just echoes the ErrorLevel—it doesn't perform anything useful. An even greater limitation is that it doesn't stop when it finds a match. As a result, all the tests for lower ErrorLevel tests are passed as well.

CHECKER4.BAT in Fig. 13-15 avoids all the problems of CHECKER3.BAT branching as soon as the batch file finds an ErrorLevel match. Notice that this batch file uses the replaceable parameter % %j as the name of the label to branch to. This is completely legal. You can use it as the entire label, as I have, or as a small portion of the label, e.g., JUMP%%j in order to jump to the label JUMP003.

Batch File Line	Explanation
`@ECHO OFF`	Turn command-echoing off.
`REM CHECKER4.BAT`	Remark giving the name of the batch file.

`REM Test and use the results`
`REM Get an ERRORLEVEL value`
`    using the Norton Utilities`
	Documentation remarks.

`BE ASK "Enter an ERRORLEVEL` `    Value  1-9   " 123456789`	Prompt the user to make a selection using Ask. The "Enter an ERRORLEVEL Value 1-9" is the prompt and "123456789" are values for Ask to accept.
`FOR %%j IN (9 8 7 6 5 4 3 2 1)` `    DO IF ERRORLEVEL %%j GOTO %%j`	This FOR loop jumps to the label corresponding to the appropriate ERROR-LEVEL value. Because the ERROR-LEVEL test is a greater than or equal to test, the ERRORLEVEL values must be tested in reverse order. Otherwise, if the batch file always tested for one first, it would always pass that test.

`:1`
`ECHO 1 SELECTED`
`GOTO END`
	Section to tell the user that one was selected.

`:2`
`ECHO 2 SELECTED`
`GOTO END`
	Section to tell the user that two was selected.

`:3`
`ECHO 3 SELECTED`
`GOTO END`
	Section to tell the user that three was selected.

`:4`
`ECHO 4 SELECTED`
`GOTO END`
	Section to tell the user that four was selected.

13-15 CHECKER4.BAT, which improves the branching structure in CHECKER3.BAT, shown in Fig. 13-14.

13-15 Continued

Batch File Line	Explanation
:5 ECHO 5 SELECTED GOTO END	Section to tell the user that five was selected.
:6 ECHO 6 SELECTED GOTO END	Section to tell the user that six was selected.
:7 ECHO 7 SELECTED GOTO END	Section to tell the user that seven was selected.
:8 ECHO 8 SELECTED GOTO END	Section to tell the user that eight was selected.
:9 ECHO 9 SELECTED GOTO END	Section to tell the user that nine was selected.
:END	Label marking the end of the batch file.

Keeping the ErrorLevel

Every time DOS runs a program, it resets ErrorLevel to zero. As a result, batch files that need to run more than one program based on the ErrorLevel have to be complex. For example, consider an accounting batch file that prompts whether it's a daily, weekly, or monthly closing. For a daily closing, it runs DAILY.COM. For a weekly closing, it runs DAILY.COM followed by WEEKLY.COM. For a monthly closing, it runs DAILY.COM, WEEKLY.COM, and then MONTHLY.COM. This batch file has to jump to a separate section to handle daily, weekly, and monthly closing because running DAILY.COM resets the ErrorLevel. As a result, DAILY.COM is run in three different places, and WEEKLY.COM is run in two different places. Not only is that complex, it makes updating the batch file more difficult. CLOSE.BAT in Fig. 13-16 illustrates this. You could avoid this problem if you could store the ErrorLevel.

Batch File Line	Explanation
@ECHO OFF	Turn command-echoing off.
REM CLOSE.BAT	Remark giving the name of the batch file.
C:	Make sure the computer is logged onto the C drive.
CD\CLOSING	Change to the proper subdirectory.

13-16 CLOSE.BAT, a batch file that has to run DAILY.COM three times and WEEKLY.COM twice.

13-16 Continued

Batch File Line	Explanation
BE ASK "D)aily, W)eekly or M)onthly Closing? " DWM	Use the Norton Utilities Batch Enhancer (BE) to ask the user which closing to perform. Note that BE will assign an ERRORLEVEL of one for a D, a two for a W and, a three for a M.
IF ERRORLEVEL 3 GOTO 3	If the user selected a monthly closing, jump to the appropriate section.
IF ERRORLEVEL 2 GOTO 2	If the user selected a weekly closing, jump to the appropriate section.
IF ERRORLEVEL 1 GOTO 1	If the user selected a daily closing, jump to the appropriate section.
GOTO ERROR	The batch file should never reach this point. If it does, a major error has occurred and it jumps to an error-handling section.
:1 DAILY /First_National_Bank /Branch_3 /Teller_4 GOTO END	Section that handles a daily closing.
:2 DAILY /First_National_Bank /Branch_3 /Teller_4 WEEKLY /First_National_Bank /Branch_3 /Manager_CLR GOTO END	Section that handles a weekly closing. Notice that it performs a daily closing first. It could not perform a daily closing, and then test on ERRORLEVEL to see if it should do a weekly closing, because running DAILY.COM would reset ERRORLEVEL to zero.
:3 DAILY /First_National_Bank /Branch_3 /Teller_4 WEEKLY /First_National_Bank /Branch_3 /Manager_CLR MONTHLY /First_National_Bank /Branch_3 /VP_JCK GOTO END	Perform a monthly closing. Note that it performs both a daily and weekly closing first. As above, it could not perform daily closing first, then test ERRORLEVEL to see if it needed to perform the other closings, because running DAILY.COM would reset ERRORLEVEL to zero.
:ERROR ECHO An Internal Error Has Happened! ECHO Contact B. Smith In Accounting. ECHO His Number Is 555-1234.Call Now! GOTO END	If an error occurs, tell the user about it.
:END	Label marking the end of the batch file.

Storing the ErrorLevel is simple if you're obtaining it through a program like the Batch Enhancer (BE) in the Norton Utilities program. With BE, the batch file would have a line like the following:

BE ASK "D)aily, W)eekly, or M)onthly closing " DWM

and BE would set the ErrorLevel to one for D, two for W, and three for M. There are only a few possible ErrorLevel values, so storing the ErrorLevel in the environment is easy. KEEP.BAT in Fig. 13-17 shows a batch file that will store the

Batch File Line	Explanation
`@ECHO OFF`	Turn command-echoing off.
`REM KEEP.BAT`	Remark giving the name of the batch file.

`FOR %%J IN (0 1 2 3 4 5 6 7 8 9 10)`
`    DO IF ERRORLEVEL %%J SET ERROR=%%J`
	This is the same as the following series of IF tests:
	
	`IF ERRORLEVEL 0 SET ERROR=0`
	`IF ERRORLEVEL 1 SET ERROR=1`
	
	`and so on`
	
	`IF ERRORLEVEL 10 SET ERROR=10`
	
	It will continue to pass these tests and update the value of ERROR until it reaches the current ERRORLEVEL value. After that, it will begin failing the tests and ERROR will no longer be changed. Note that as written the batch file will work only for ERRORLEVEL values of ten or smaller. For higher values, see SAVE-BIG.BAT.

`ECHO ERRORLEVEL is %ERROR%`	Tell the user the value of ERROR.

13-17 KEEP.BAT, which will store the ErrorLevel in the environment, as long as it's a value of ten or less.

ErrorLevel in the environment under the name of ERROR, as long as the ErrorLevel is ten or less. The environmental variable ERROR has two advantages over an ErrorLevel value:

- Equality tests work.
- DOS doesn't reset ERROR when you run a program.

As a result, CLOSE.BAT in Fig. 13-16 needs far fewer lines. This is shown by CLOSE2.BAT in Fig. 13-18. This method will also work for storing the exit codes for most programs because they tend to be small numbers.

Batch File Line	Explanation
`@ECHO OFF`	Turn command-echoing off.
`REM CLOSE2.BAT`	Remark giving the name of the batch file.
`C:`	Make sure the computer is logged onto the C drive.
`CD\CLOSING`	Change to the closing subdirectory.
`BE ASK "D)aily, W)eekly or` `   M)onthly Closing?   " DWM`	Ask the user which closing to perform.
`CALL KEEP.BAT`	Call KEEP.BAT to convert the ERROR-LEVEL to an environmental variable called ERROR.

`IF NOT %ERROR%==3 IF NOT`
`   %ERROR%==2 IF NOT %ERROR%==1`
`   GOTO ERROR`
	If the ERRORLEVEL is anything other than a 1, 2, or 3 then jump to an error-handling routine. This should not happen.

`DAILY /First_National_Bank` `   /Branch_3 /Teller_4`	Perform a daily closing. Since all three closing require a daily closing, this does not require an IF test.

`IF NOT %ERROR%==1 WEEKLY`
`   /First_National_Bank`
`   /Branch_3 /Manager_CLR`
	Both the weekly and monthly closing require a weekly closing so run the program unless this is a daily closing. Since the test is on an environmental variable rather than ERRORLEVEL, WEEKLY.COM will not reset its value. In addition, this is no longer a greater than or equal test.

`IF %ERROR%==3 MONTHLY`
`   /First_National_Bank`
`   /Branch_3 /VP_JCK`
	If this is a monthly closing, run MONTHLY.COM.

`GOTO END`	Exit the batch file.

`:ERROR`
`ECHO An Internal Error Has`
`Happened!`
`ECHO Contact B. Smith In`
`Accounting.`
`ECHO His Number Is 555-`
`1234.Call Now!`
`GOTO END`
	If an error occurs, tell the user about it.

`:END`	Label marking the end of the batch file.

13-18   CLOSE2.BAT, which runs both DAILY.COM and WEEKLY.COM once.

However, many batch file prompting programs will accept any ASCII character, and set ErrorLevel equal to the ASCII value of the character. This method will work, but it'll result in the long, slow batch file SAVE-BIG.BAT, shown in Fig. 13-19.

Batch File Line	Explanation
@ECHO OFF	Turn command-echoing off.
REM SAVE-BIG.BAT	Remark giving the name of the batch file.
SET ERROR=0	Set the environmental variable ERROR to zero.
FOR %%J IN (1 2 3 4 5 6 7 8 9 10) DO IF ERRORLEVEL %%J SET ERROR=%%J	Test for the first ten possible values. Since ERROR is already set to zero, the batch file does not have to test for zero. Until the batch file reaches the actual ERRORLEVEL value, it passes this test and the value of ERROR is updated. After reaching the value of ERRORLEVEL, it begins failing this test so the value of ERROR is not changed.
FOR %%J IN (11 12 13 14 15 16 17 18 19 20) DO IF ERRORLEVEL %%J SET ERROR=%%J	Test for the next ten possible values.
The batch file continues in a similar fashion for 21-240	
FOR %%J IN (241 242 243 244 245 246 247 248 249 250) DO IF ERRORLEVEL %%J SET ERROR=%%J	Test for ERRORLEVEL values of 241-250.
FOR %%J IN (251 252 253 254 255) DO IF ERRORLEVEL %%J SET ERROR=%%J	Test for ERRORLEVEL values of 251-255.
ECHO ERRORLEVEL is %ERROR%	Tell the user the value of ERRORLEVEL.

13-19 SAVE-BIG.BAT, which will save any ErrorLevel value to the environment, although the program is long, slow, and complex.

Clearly, this method is too long to use. An easier way is to test each of the three digits individually, First, find out if the left digit is a 0, 1, or 2. This takes only one FOR loop. DIGIT-1.BAT in Fig. 13-20 does this. Next, find out if the middle digit is 0−9. That takes only one FOR loop, as well. DIGIT-2.BAT in Fig. 13-21 does this. DIGIT-2.BAT requires that DIGIT-1.BAT run first, but

Batch File Line	Explanation
@ECHO OFF	Turn command-echoing off.
REM DIGIT-1.BAT	Remark giving the name of the batch file.
FOR %%J IN (0 1 2) DO IF ERRORLEVEL %%J00 SET ERROR=%%J	This line breaks down ERRORLEVEL into three categories, 0-99, 100-199 and 200-255. It also stores the first digit in the environment under the name ERROR.
ECHO Left Digit Was %ERROR%	Tells the user the results of running the batch file.

13-20   DIGIT-1.BAT, a batch file that will find the left digit of an ErrorLevel.

Batch File Line	Explanation
@ECHO OFF	Turns command-echoing off.
REM DIGIT-2.BAT	Remark giving the name of the batch file.
FOR %%J IN (0 1 2 3 4 5 6 7 8 9) DO IF ERRORLEVEL %ERROR%%%J0 SET ERROR=%ERROR%%%J	This line loops through the ten possible digits to find the middle digit of ERRORLEVEL. Although this batch file requires that DIGIT-1.BAT runs first, there is no error-checking to enforce that. When ERROR has a value of 1, this line becomes: FOR %%J IN (0 1 2 3 4 5 6 7 8 9) DO IF ERRORLEVEL 1%%J0 SET ERROR=1%%J
ECHO Left Two Digits Are %ERROR%	Tells the user the result of running the batch file.

13-21   DIGIT-2.BAT, a batch file to find the middle digit of an ErrorLevel.

there's no error checking to enforce that. Notice that the variable ERROR is being built as you go, from left to right. Testing for the right digit works the same way. DIGIT-3.BAT in Fig. 13-22 will find the right digit. Notice that it calls the two prior batch files to find their digits, because it requires that information to run properly.

Batch File Line	Explanation
@ECHO OFF	Turn command-echoing off.
REM DIGIT-3.BAT	Remark giving the name of the batch file.
SET ERROR=	Reset the environmental variable.
CALL DIGIT-1 CALL DIGIT-2	Run the two batch files that must run first. (That is why DIGIT-2.BAT does not run DIGIT-1.BAT and lacks error-checking.) There is no reason to separate the three main lines into separate batch files. I did it here only for illustration purposes.
FOR %%J IN (0 1 2 3 4 5 6 7 8 9) DO IF ERRORLEVEL %ERROR%%%J SET ERROR=%ERROR%%%J	Tests for the right-hand digit in ERROR-LEVEL and adds it to the environmental variable.
ECHO ERRORLEVEL is %ERROR%	Tells the user the results of running the batch file.

13-22 DIGIT-3.BAT, which will find the right digit of an ErrorLevel.

This method works properly for ErrorLevel values of 0 to 199, but there's a problem for ErrorLevel value over 200. There are no restrictions in the batch file, so, when the first digit is a two, it ends up testing for values of 256−299. The maximum ErrorLevel value is 255, and DOS doesn't handle tests above 255 properly. As a result the batch file needs some complex branching. If the first digit is a two, it must branch to a separate test to make sure the test on the second digit doesn't exceed five. If the second digit is a five, it must branch again to make sure the test on the final digit doesn't exceed a five. That way, the batch file never tests for an ErrorLevel greater than 255. The resulting batch file is SAVE- ERR.BAT, in Fig. 13-23.

Batch File Line	Explanation
@ECHO OFF	Turn command-echoing off.
SET ERROR=	Reset the environmental variable to nul.

13-23 SAVE-ERR.BAT, which will store the ErrorLevel in the environment for all possible values.

13-23 Continued

Batch File Line	Explanation
REM SAVE-ERRORLEVEL.BAT	Remark giving the name of the batch file.
FOR %%J IN (0 1 2) DO IF ERRORLEVEL %%J00 SET ERROR=%%J	Find out if a) ERRORLEVEL>200 b) ERRORLEVEL>100 c) ERRORLEVEL>0
IF %ERROR%==2 GOTO 2	Jump to a special section if the ERRORLEVEL is 200 or larger. This is required because the maximum ERRORLEVEL is 255 and DOS does not handle ERRORLEVEL tests for numbers over 255 in a manner that will work with this batch file. When testing ERRORLEVEL 260 (for example) DOS subtracts increments of 256 until the number is less than 256, or 4 in this example.
FOR %%J IN (0 1 2 3 4 5 6 7 8 9) DO IF ERRORLEVEL %ERROR%%%J0 SET ERROR=%ERROR%%%J	As complex as this looks, DOS understands it. If the value of ERROR was 1 coming into this test and the FOR loop is on 6, the test line reads: IF ERRORLEVEL 160 SET ERROR=16 This test sets the value of the tens digit.
FOR %%J IN (0 1 2 3 4 5 6 7 8 9) DO IF ERRORLEVEL %ERROR%%%J SET ERROR=%ERROR%%%J	This test sets the value of the ones digit.
GOTO END	Jump to the end of the batch file.
:2	This marks the beginning of the section that handles ERRORLEVEL greater than or equal to 200.
FOR %%J IN (0 1 2 3 4 5) DO IF ERRORLEVEL %ERROR%%%J0 SET ERROR=%ERROR%%%J	Test for the tens digit. Since the maximum ERRORLEVEL value is 255, the test does not need to exceed 5.
IF %ERROR%==25 GOTO 25	If the ERRORLEVEL is 250 or larger, jump to a special section because the batch file needs to test only to five.
FOR %%J IN (0 1 2 3 4 5 6 7 8 9) DO IF ERRORLEVEL %ERROR%%%J SET ERROR=%ERROR%%%J	Test for the ones digit.
GOTO END	Exit the batch file.

13-23 Continued

Batch File Line	Explanation
:25	Label marking the section of the batch file to testing ERRORLEVEL values greater than or equal to 250.

FOR %%J IN (0 1 2 3 4 5) DO
   IF ERRORLEVEL %ERROR%%%J
   SET ERROR=%ERROR%%%J
	Test for the ones digit.

:END	Label marking the end of the batch file.

The Case method

Performing multiple tests on a variable in a batch file requires a series of complex IF statements. Many other languages use a much simpler case construct. With a case construct, you signal the start of a case test then just list all the cases and what to do if the situation matches that case. Figure 13-24 illustrates this. The

```
Signal The Start Of The Test
      CASE1 =
             Instructions For Case 1
      CASE2 =
             Instructions For Case 2
      CASE3 =
             Instructions For Case 3
      CASE4 =
             Instructions For Case 4
      CASE5 =
             Instructions For Case 5
      CASE OTHERWISE =
             Instructions For Otherwise
Signal The End Of The Test
```

13-24 The typical structure of a case construct.

batch language does not have a case construct; however, it is possible to simulate one using the FOR statement, as shown in Fig. 13-25.

Notice that the ErrorLevel tests in CASE.BAT are performed in ascending order rather than the typical descending order. There is a reason for this. Because the ErrorLevel test is a greater than or equal test, this test passes until the test exceeds the ErrorLevel. Because the variable is reset each time, this results in the proper value. For example, assume the ErrorLevel is three. The following happens:

Batch File Line	Explanation
`@ECHO OFF`	Turn command-echoing off.
`REM CASE.BAT`	Remark giving the name of the batch file.

`REM Simulates a case structure`
`REM in a batch file`
`REM Gets input using Norton`
`    Utility`
`REM program, Inkey from the book`
`REM would work just as well`
	Documentation remarks.

`:TOP`	Label marking the top of the batch file.
`CLS`	Clear the screen.

`ECHO NUMBER      OPTION`
`ECHO ======      ======`
`ECHO    1        Lotus`
`ECHO    2        dBASE`
`ECHO    3        Microsoft Word`
`ECHO    4        Games`
	Display the menu.

`SKIPLINE`	Use the Skipline program included on the disk to display one blank line.
`BE ASK "Press option number" 1234`	Use the Norton Utilities Batch Enhancer to request a number from the user.

`REM I am adding the logic to`
`    handle non-valid`
`REM responses even though the`
`    Norton Utilities`
`REM Ask program takes care of`
`REM that automatically`
	Documentation remarks.

`SET NO=CASE0`	Set the environmental variable NO equal to zero.
`FOR %%j IN (1 2 3 4) DO IF` `    ERRORLEVEL %%j SET NO=CASE%%j`	Use a FOR loop to set the value of NO equal to the ERRORLEVEL plus a string. Since ERRORLEVEL is a greater than test, NO will be set to four for all values of ERRORLEVEL greater than or equal to four.
`GOTO %NO%`	Jump to the label corresponding to the value of NO. The five possible values are CASE0, CASE1, CASE2, CASE3 and CASE4.

13-25   CASE.BAT, which illustrates a more readable case construct in a batch file.

13-25 Continued

Batch File Line	Explanation

`:CASE0`
`CLS`
`ECHO Invalid selection`
`PAUSE`
`GOTO TOP`
	Section for handling an invalid response.

`:CASE1`
`REM Commands to run Lotus`
`GOTO TOP`
	Section for handling a response of 1.

The batch file repeats CASE1 for a response of 2, 3 and 4.	

1. It tests for an ErrorLevel of 1. Because 3 is greater than or equal to 1, the test passes and it sets NO equal to CASE1.

2. It tests for an ErrorLevel of 2. Because 3 is greater than or equal to 2, the test passes and it sets NO equal to CASE2. This removes the NO=CASE1 setting.

3. It tests for an ErrorLevel of 3. Because 3 is greater than or equal to 3, the test passes and it sets NO equal to CASE3. This removes the NO=CASE2 setting.

4. It tests for an ErrorLevel of 4. Because 3 isn't greater than or equal to 4, the test fails and the value of NO isn't reset. This doesn't remove the NO=CASE3 setting.

Thus, this batch file exits with the value for the environmental variable set properly for the ErrorLevel statement.

Quicker than GOTO END

In many of the examples in this book, the batch file jumps to the end of the batch file with a GOTO END statement. Generally, the batch file has to test for several conditions. After successfully performing the task for a condition, the batch file jumps to the end of the file to avoid repeating the task for another condition.

Each time a batch file searches for a label, it searches the entire file from top to bottom. Exiting a batch file by going to the end forces the longest and slowest possible search, because the batch file must be searched from top to bottom. A much faster way to exit a batch file is to run a second dummy batch file. Control never returns to the first batch file, so this is the same as an exit. Using GOTOEND.BAT in Fig. 13-26, enter:

    GOTOEND A

Batch File Line	Explanation
ECHO OFF	Turn command-echoing off.
REM GOTOEND.BAT	Remark giving the name of the batch file.
IF (%1)==(A) GOTO END	Test to see if an A was entered.
IF (%1)==(B) GOTO END	Test to see if an B was entered.
IF (%1)==(C) GOTO END	Test to see if an C was entered.
The batch file continues in a similar fashion for D-X	
IF (%1)==(Y) GOTO END	Test to see if an Y was entered.
IF (%1)==(Z) GOTO END	Test to see if an Z was entered.
IF (%1)==(a) GOTO END	Test to see if an a was entered.
IF (%1)==(b) GOTO END	Test to see if an b was entered.
IF (%1)==(c) GOTO END	Test to see if an c was entered.
The batch file continues in a similar fashion for d-x	
IF (%1)==(y) GOTO END	Test to see if an y was entered.
IF (%1)==(z) GOTO END	Test to see if an z was entered.
ECHO If you reached this point ECHO then a letter was not entered ECHO as a replaceable parameter	Tell the user what has happened.
:END	Label marking the end of the batch file.
ECHO FINISHED!	Tell the user what has happened.

13-26 GOTOEND.BAT, which demonstrates the GOTO END statement, a foolproof way to slow down batch file execution.

And note how long it takes to run. Now, using SKIPEND.BAT in Fig. 13-27 and DUMMY.BAT in Fig. 13-28, enter:

    SKIPEND A

and note how much faster the batch file performs essentially the same task.

Batch File Line	Explanation
ECHO OFF	Turn command-echoing off.
REM SKIPEND.BAT	Remark giving the name of the batch file.

13-27 SKIPEND.BAT, which, by calling the batch file DUMMY.BAT, ends its own execution very quickly.

13-27 Continued

Batch File Line	Explanation
IF (%1)==(A) DUMMY	If the user entered an A on the command line, run a program called DUMMY. Two notes are important: 1. DUMMY does not exist. Running a nonexistent program is a fast way to exit a batch file. 2. Rather than testing for an empty replaceable parameter first, this batch file adds the parentheses to every test so a blank replaceable parameter never represents a problem.
IF (%1)==(B) DUMMY	Test for B.
The batch file continues in a similar fashion for C-Y.	
IF (%1)==(Z) DUMMY	Test for Z.
IF (%1)==(a) DUMMY	Test for a.
IF (%1)==(b) DUMMY	Test for b.
The batch file continues in a similar fashion for c-y.	
IF (%1)==(z) DUMMY	Test for z.

Batch File Line	Explanation
ECHO OFF	Turn command-echoing off.
REM DUMMY.BAT	Remark giving the name of the batch file.
ECHO FINISHED!	Echo a message to the user.

13-28 DUMMY.BAT, which is the file called by SKIPEND.BAT, shown in Fig. 13-27, in order to stop its execution.

FOR command tricks

The following are several ways you can use the FOR command to make your batch file programming easier:

Nested FOR statements

One of the things I said about the FOR statement is that you can't nest them. It is possible to do this, however, using the same trick I used to add subroutines to batch files. Consider NESTFOR1.BAT in Fig. 13-29. When it runs you get an error message.

Batch File Line	Explanation
ECHO OFF	Turn command-echoing off.
REM NESTFOR1.BAT	Remark giving the name of the batch file.
FOR %%a IN (NESTFOR?.BAT) DO FOR %%b IN (NEST?.BAT) DO ECHO %%a %%b	Attempting to run one FOR loop inside another one (called nesting) results in a DOS error message.

13-29   NESTFOR1.BAT, which attempts to nest FOR statements and results in an error message.

By calling a second COMMAND.COM, however, as shown in NESTFOR 2.BAT in Fig. 13-30, you can construct a nested FOR statement. When the second COMMAND.COM is called, ECHO reverts to On.

Batch File Line	Explanation
ECHO OFF	Turn command-echoing off.
REM NESTFOR1.BAT	Remark giving the name of the batch file.
FOR %%a IN (NESTFOR?.BAT) DO COMMAND/C FOR %%b IN (NEST?.BAT) DO ECHO %%a %%b	By calling a second command processor, you can fool DOS into nesting two FOR loops.

13-30   NESTFOR2.BAT, which shows how you can trick DOS into executing a nested FOR command by loading a secondary command processor.

Using FOR to add wildcard support

Most DOS commands, like DEL and COPY, support wildcards. You can, for example, enter

    COPY *.* A:

rather than having to enter one copy command for each file you want to copy. However, a few DOS commands, like TYPE, don't support wildcards. If you want to TYPE three files to the screen, you must enter three commands

    TYPE FILE1 | MORE
    TYPE FILE2 | MORE
    TYPE FILE3 | MORE

This process is long and cumbersome. You can automate it with the FOR command. The FOR equivalent to the above would be

    FOR %j IN (FILE?) DO TYPE %j | MORE

Having FOR do commands

Every so often, the computer magazine "hint columns" will have a tip from some-one who's just discovered that the things you put in the list of variables for a FOR command can be commands themselves. Figure 13-31 shows just such a batch file. 3COMMANDS.BAT will first issue a DIR command, then a CHKDSK command, and finally a CD \ command. The authors of these hints are excited because the batch file runs faster this way. DOS processes batch files one line at a time, and this allows you to put more commands on a single line.

Batch File Line	Explanation
`@ECHO OFF`	Turn command-echoing off.
`REM 3COMMANDS.BAT`	Remark giving the name of the batch file.
`FOR %%j IN (DIR CHKDSK CD\) DO %%j`	Run three commands with one line using the FOR command. This is not recommended.

13-31 3COMMANDS.BAT, which uses the FOR command to put multiple commands on the same line.

But don't be fooled. While the batch files *are* a little faster, this method has a couple of drawbacks that greatly outweigh the slight dose of speed. The biggest drawback is human readability. You and I could probably look at a batch file with the lines:

```
DIR
CHKDSK
CD \
```

and tell exactly what it's suppose to do. However, the function of a batch file with the line:

```
FOR % %j IN (DIR CHKDSK CD \) DO % %j
```

isn't nearly as clear. In the end, you'll waste more time writing and debugging such complex code than you'll save by stacking more commands on a single line.

This method has another drawback. You can't use this trick with any com-mand that requires more than one word. For example, you might want to run CHKDSK and then ring the bell using Norton's batch enhancer, which requires the command BE BEEP. With two lines, you would enter the commands:

```
CHKDSK
BE BEEP
```

Using the FOR command, you would enter the command:

```
FOR % %j IN (CHKDSK BE BEEP) DO % %j
```

but because of the space, DOS would actually try to run:

```
CHKDSK
BE
BEEP
```

The final drawback is the switches. Generally, you would run CHKDSK/F rather than CHKDSK; however, under some versions of DOS the / is treated as a divider in FOR, so the command CHKDSK/F in a FOR statement becomes two commands: CHKDSK and F. (The / is a divider, so it's dropped, just like a space.) So while you can stack multiple commands in a FOR statement, there are some very good reasons not to.

Using reserved names for batch files

You might recall an earlier discussion where I pointed out that you can't normally run a batch file if you give it the same name as a DOS internal command, like ERASE. Figure 13-32 shows just such a batch file, ERASE.BAT. If you try to run it with an ERASE command, DOS aborts with an error message like *Required*

Batch File Line	Explanation
`@echo off`	Turn command-echoing off.
`REM ERASE.BAT`	Remark giving the name of the batch file.
`ECHO Worked!`	Echo a message to the user.

13-32 ERASE.BAT, which you can't run because ERASE is an internal DOS command.

parameter missing. While the error message is different for different DOS versions, the effect is the same. When you enter a command, the first thing DOS checks is to see if it's an internal command. If it is, DOS doesn't check any further; rather, it executes the appropriate internal command.

Beginning with DOS 3.0, DOS allows you to add a path before a command. For example, if you wanted to run a program called INFO.EXE on the A drive and the A drive wasn't in your path, you could specify a full path to INFO.EXE with the following command:

```
A:INFO
```

It turns out that DOS is smart enough to know that, if you specify a path, you're not running an internal command. As a result, it doesn't check its list of internal commands before searching for the program. Thus, the command:

```
C:ERASE
```

will run ERASE.BAT. My first reaction to learning this was "So what!" While it worked, I didn't see any practical application for it. Then it hit me. Earlier, I had suggested renaming FORMAT.COM to XYZ.COM and writing FORMAT.BAT to handle formatting. This approach lets you make sure that no one formats your hard disk; however, it has a flaw. If someone gets a directory of the subdirectory you have XYZ.COM in, they're going to see a program they've never heard of . . . and what better way to find out what it does than to run it. Of course, running XYZ (really FORMAT) with no parameters is a sure way to format a hard disk. Now rename FORMAT.COM to RENAME.COM and no one will be able to find out what it does by entering RENAME in order to run the program, because DOS will execute its internal command. Your batch file can run it by specifying the full path to RENAME.COM, and thus you have even more protection against someone accidently running FORMAT.COM. Next to erasing FORMAT.COM altogether, this is the best protection you can get.

The hidden power of CTTY

CTTY is a very powerful command that allows you to hide batch file operation, create a log of computer use, and create better messages.

Hiding everything a batch file does

Between commands like @ECHO OFF and COPY *.* A: > NUL, you can hide much of what goes on in your batch files; however, some DOS error messages still get through. When the batch file NOT-DEL.BAT in Fig. 13-33 tries to delete a file that doesn't exist, the DOS error message is displayed in spite of the > NUL and @ECHO OFF commands.

Batch File Line	Explanation
`@ECHO OFF`	Turn command-echoing off.
`REM NOT-DEL.BAT`	Remark giving the name of the batch file.
`REM FILE C:\QQQ DOES NOT EXIST`	Documentation remark.
`DEL C:\QQQ > NUL`	Delete a nonexistent file and try to pipe messages to NUL.

13-33 NOT-DEL.BAT, which will try to delete a nonexistent file and produce an error message.

There are several other DOS error messages, like the *File not found* one, that you can't turn off with the ECHO command or pipe to the NUL device. However, you can still get rid of them. DOS has an internal command called CTTY. When you first start the computer, DOS recognizes your keyboard as the default input device and your screen as the standard display device. Normally, you use the CTTY command to change to an alternative input/output device—for example, a data collection device connected to COM1. However, CTTY has two features that make it useful here. First, you can use any legal device name as console, including NUL. With NUL as the alternative console, DOS has no way of receiving input or displaying output. That's where the second advantage of CTTY comes in—programs continue to run while a CTTY NUL command is in effect.

Figure 13-34 shows a batch file that takes advantage of CTTY. Nothing, including DOS error messages, shows on the screen between the CTTY NUL command and the CTTY CON command. In fact, the console (keyboard) is almost completely inactive. Ctrl−Break will stop the batch file, but any other keystrokes simply remain in the keyboard buffer waiting for control to return to the console. As a result, you can't regain control by issuing a CTTY CON command from the keyboard. To regain control, you must reboot.

Batch File Line	Explanation
`@ECHO OFF`	Turn command-echoing off.
`REM NOT-DEL1.BAT`	Remark giving the name of the batch file.
`REM FILE C:\QQQ DOES NOT EXIST`	Documentation remark.
`CTTY NUL`	Turn the console off.
`DEL C:\QQQ`	Delete a nonexistent file as a demonstration. Since the console is turned off, no message will show up on the screen.
`CTTY CON`	Turn the console back on. The batch file must do this because turning the console off with CTTY NUL also turns off the keyboard so the user cannot turn the console on once the batch file terminates.

13-34 NOT-DEL1.BAT, which uses the CTTY command to keep error messages from showing on the screen.

Logging computer usage

You can create a log that records every time a computer is rebooted with the CTTY command. While a log doesn't require the CTTY command to operate, you greatly reduce the chance that the log will be spotted and neutralized by using the CTTY command to hide the logging activity. Figure 13-35 shows the code that creates the log. The important points are as follows:

- ECHO | MORE is used to supply the Return needed so you don't have to answer the DATE and TIME questions.
- The >> piping symbol is used to add the new text to the bottom of the log, rather than overwriting it.
- You should probably change the name of the log file to something less meaningful, like ABC.QVL. You can also specify a full path to the file so it doesn't have to be in the root directory.

Batch File Line	Explanation
@ECHO OFF	Turn command-echoing off.
REM LOGBOOT.BAT	Remark giving the name of the batch file.
REM Normally, this would be part of AUTOEXEC.BAT file	Documentation remark.
CTTY NUL	Turn the console off so nothing shows up on the screen.
ECHO | MORE | TIME >> BOOTLOG.TXT	Pipe the time to a log file. Piping through MORE keeps you from having to press Return and the > > causes the information to be appended to the end of the file.
ECHO | MORE | DATE >> BOOTLOG.TXT	Pipe the date to a log file.
CTTY CON	Return control to the screen/keyboard.

13-35 LOGBOOT.BAT, which creates a log of every time the computer is booted without the user knowing it.

The log doesn't show how long the computer was used, so it would be difficult to use it for client billing or even to determine the utilization of certain computers. You could, however, combine it with a batch file menu system and have the batch files that run the specific applications record additional information. Figure 13-36 shows just such a batch file. Keep in mind that these batch files will run without the CTTY commands, but it will be easier for the user to see what's going on.

Batch File Line	Explanation
@ECHO OFF	Turn command-echoing off.
REM 1-LOG.BAT	Remark giving the name of the batch file.
CTTY NUL	Turn the console off by turning on the alternative console of NUL. This way, nothing except what is explicitly piped to the console is shown.
ECHO Starting Lotus >> C:\LOG\LOTUSLOG.TXT	Pipe a message to the log file indicating the batch file is starting Lotus. Since the batch file uses a > > to pipe, the message is appended to the bottom of the file.
ECHO | MORE | TIME >> C:\LOG\LOTUSLOG.TXT	Pipe the time to the log file. The piping through MORE adds the return the TIME command needs to continue after displaying the time.
ECHO | MORE | DATE >> C:\LOG\LOTUSLOG.TXT	Pipes the date to the log file.
CTTY CON	Turns the console back on.

13-36 1-LOG.BAT, a batch file for tracking Lotus usage.

13-36   Continued

Batch File Line	Explanation
C:	Make sure the computer is logged onto the C drive. This is a very good idea when the computer has more than one hard disk or the user sometimes uses the floppy drives.
CD\123	Change to the Lotus subdirectory.
123	Start Lotus.
CTTY NUL	Turn the console off.
ECHO Finishing Lotus >> C:\LOG\LOTUSLOG.TXT	Pipe the closing message to the log file.
ECHO | MORE | TIME >> C:\LOG\LOTUSLOG.TXT	Pipe the finishing time to the log file.
ECHO | MORE | DATE >> C:\LOG\LOTUSLOG.TXT	Pipe the finishing date to the log file.
CTTY CON	Turn the console back on.
MENU	Reload the menu.

Better messages

I routinely use programs that stubbornly refuse to allow their messages to be turned off with ECHO OFF command, or rerouted with >NUL. That's acceptable for an experienced user who would understand what was going on, but would only add more confusion for a new user. I could add explanations using ECHO statements, but they tend to get lost inside the multiple messages from the programs I use. The File Attribute program in the Norton Utilities is one of the main offenders.

When you issue a CTTY NUL command, all output is directed to the Nul device, including all DOS error messages and messages from programs like File Attribute. However, the output from the ECHO command is also routed to Nul. Luckily, DOS piping still works, so an ECHO statement can be piped to the screen using >CON, where Con is short for console.

PREPARE.BAT in Fig. 13-37 illustrates this. I perform a backup every few days with Fastback. In between, I like to make twice-daily incremental backups. An incremental backup is one where only the few files that have changed are backed up. I also rotate my backups and store the most recent one off-site. Unfortunately, Fastback makes it difficult to make an incremental backup if you don't have the original backup handy, so I use the DOS backup program. Because it's much slower than Fastback, I want to back up only important files. That's where Prepare comes in. It goes through my hard disk and makes sure the archive bit is set Off for all the working files I don't want to back up. That makes my backup much faster. Notice that I use a CTTY NUL to stop all the File Attribute mes-

Batch File Line	Explanation
`@ECHO OFF`	Turn command-echoing off.
`CD\`	Change to the root directory.
`COLOR`	Run a small .COM program that clears the screen and resets the colors to white on blue.
`CTTY NUL`	Turn the console off.

`ECHO Please Wait > Con`
`ECHO Clearing Archive Attributes>Con`
`ECHO *.BAK files > Con`
	Pipe messages to the console to inform the user what is happening.

`FILEATTR *.BAK /S /A-`	Use the Norton Utilities Fileattr program to reset the archive bit on all .BAK files on the hard disk so they will not be backed up in an incremental backup. If you are using DOS 3.3 or later, you could also use the DOS ATTRIB command for this.
`ECHO *.TMP files > Con`	Tell the user which files are next.
`FILEATTR *.TMP /S /A-`	Clear archive bit on .TMP files.
`ECHO JUNK*.* files > Con`	Tell the user which files are next.
`FILEATTR JUNK*.* /S /A-`	Clear archive bit on JUNK*.* files.
`ECHO FRECOVER.* > Con`	Tell the user which files are next.
`FILEATTR C:\FRECOVER.* /A-`	Clear archive bit on FRECOVER.* files.
`ECHO Selected PC-Link Files > Con`	Tell the user which files are next.
`FILEATTR C:\PCLINK\DB01.PCL /A-` `FILEATTR C:\PCLINK\DMCSR.CFG /A-`	Clear archive bit on selected PC-Link files. The program updates these each time it runs, but the updates are so minor they would not prevent PC-Link from running with an older version.
`ECHO MW.INI > Con`	Tell the user which files are next.
`FILEATTR C:\WORD\MW.INI /A-`	Update the Microsoft Word initialization file. Each time you run Word, it stores the name of the last document you edited here. Word will run with an older version or no MW.INI file at all.

13-37 PREPARE.BAT, which gets a hard disk ready for an incremental backup.

13-37 Continued

Batch File Line	Explanation
ECHO Headroom files > Con	Tell the user which files are next.
FILEATTR C:\HEADROOM\SWAP*.* /A- FILEATTR C:\HEADROOM\HRSWAP.SWP /A-	Clear archive bit on selected Headroom files.
ECHO Selected Fastback Files > Con	Tell the user which files are next.
FILEATTR C:\FB-OFFIC*.* /A- FILEATTR C:\FB-HOME*.* /A- FILEATTR C:\FASTBACK*.* /A-	Clear archive bit on selected Fastback file. You need Fastback to restore, so backing up Fastback files is redundant.
ECHO TREEINFO.NCD > Con	Tell the user which files are next.
FILEATTR C:\TREEINFO.NCD /A-	This is a Norton Utility data file that is easily regenerated.
ECHO Selected Hotshot Files > Con	Tell the user which files are next.
FILEATTR C:\HOTSHOT\HS.CFG /A-	Hotshot updates this file each time it is run, but does not need the new version to run properly.
ECHO Deleting PC-Link Error File>Con	Tell the user which files are next.
DEL \PCLINK*.ERR	Delete old error messages
ECHO Deleting PC-Link JUNK*.* Files > Con	Tell the user which files are next.
DEL \PCLINK\JUNK*.*	Delete old junk files. When I need to save a file temporarily, I use the name junk so I know I can erase it later.
CTTY CON	Turn the console back on.
ECHO **ALL CLEARED**	Tell the user the batch file is finished.
CD\SYSLIB	Change to the DOS library.

sages, and I pipe the ECHO statements to Con in order to put intelligent messages on the screen.

While CTTY NUL is in effect, the keyboard is essentially disconnected. If you need to get input from the keyboard, you can bypass the CTTY NUL with piping. For example,

    PAUSE < CON

would accept a single keystroke from the keyboard for the PAUSE command. You can use this with programs designed to take input from the keyboard for an ErrorLevel test, as Fig. 13-38 shows. Notice that I redirect the prompt first.

Batch File Line	Explanation
`@CLS`	Clear the screen. The @ preceding the CLS command turns off command-echoing for that single line.
`@CTTY NUL`	Use NUL as the console. This turns off the screen and the keyboard. This command is preceded by an @ because screen echoing is in effect until after this command is issued.
`REM CTTYKEY.BAT`	Remark giving the name of the batch file.
`ECHO Press 1 2 3 or 4 > CON`	Pipe text to the screen when the screen is otherwise turned off by the CTTY NUL command..
`BE ASK " " 1234 < CON`	Obtain a keystroke from the keyboard when the keyboard is otherwise turned off.
`CTTY CON`	Return control to the keyboard and screen.

13-38 CTTYKEY.BAT, which is structured to allow you to use the keyboard with CTTY NUL in effect.

Because the console isn't active, Ask can't display the prompt itself. In addition, if you press an invalid key, Ask can't sound the bell to warn you.

A word of caution

Because of the way DOS works, you should never use the CTTY NUL command while loading memory-resident programs. Consider the batch file with the following lines:

```
CTTY NUL
TSR
CTTY CON
```

This batch file segment turns off the console, loads a memory-resident program, and turns the console back on. When the TSR program loads, terminates, and stays resident, DOS clears the file buffers and file handles used by the memory-resident program, but not the file handle it used in the CTTY NUL command. Thus, this batch file segment needlessly uses one file handle. You have the same problem if you try to hide the TSR messages by loading it with the command:

```
TSR>NUL
```

DOS has a limited number of file handles, so you should avoid using either method when loading memory-resident programs. In the best case, you could end up trying to run a program and get a *Not enough file handles* error message. In the worse case, you wouldn't get this error message until you try to save your data. In that case, you'd lose all your work.

Running commands inside a batch file

While exploring the different things you can do with batch files, I discovered how to enter commands that run inside a batch file. One time you might have a DIR command that runs inside a batch file, and the next time you might run a CHKDSK command inside the same batch file.

MIDDLE1.BAT in Fig. 13-39 shows the simplest way. You just enter the commands on the command line. MIDDLE1.BAT limits you to nine commands, a

Batch File Line	Explanation
`@ECHO OFF`	Turn command-echoing off.
`REM MIDDLE1.BAT`	Remark giving the name of the batch file.
`ECHO Normally there would be` `   commands here`	Documentation message.
`%1`	Use the first replaceable parameter as a command. Once the batch file runs out of replaceable parameters, the remaining lines will be treated as blank lines and will have no impact of the batch file. Therefore, unlike the IF tests, these lines do not need (and could not run with) parentheses around the replaceable parameters.

`%2`
`%3`
`%4`
`%5`
`%6`
`%7`
`%8`
`%9`
	Use the remaining replaceable parameters as commands.

`ECHO Normally there would be` `   more commands here`	Documentation message.

13-39 MIDDLE1.BAT, which lets you enter up to nine commands to run inside the batch file.

reasonable number given the 127-character limit of the command line. If there are less than nine commands, the extra replaceable parameters are treated as a blank line. MIDDLE2.BAT in Fig. 13-40 improves on MIDDLE1.BAT slightly by using the SHIFT command. It will let you run more than nine commands if you can fit them all on the 127-character command line.

MIDDLE3.BAT in Fig. 13-41 makes the biggest improvement of all. It stops in the middle and lets you create a batch file interactively with the COPY CON

Batch File Line	Explanation
`@ECHO OFF`	Turn command-echoing off.
`REM MIDDLE2.BAT`	Remark giving the name of the batch file.
`ECHO Normally there would be     commands here`	Documentation message.
`:TOP`	Label marking the top of the loop.
`IF (%1)==() GOTO END`	Once the replaceable parameters are exhausted, exit the loop.
`%1`	Run the replaceable parameter as a command.
`SHIFT`	Move all the replaceable parameters down one level.
`GOTO TOP`	Continue at the top of the loop.
`:END`	Label marking the (near) end of the batch file.
`ECHO Normally there would be     more commands here`	Documentation message.

13-40   MIDDLE2.BAT, which lets you enter as many commands to run inside the batch file as will fit on the 127-character command line.

Batch File Line	Explanation
`@ECHO OFF`	Turn command-echoing off.
`REM MIDDLE2.BAT`	Remark giving the name of the batch file.
`ECHO Normally there would be     commands here`	Documentation message.
`:TOP`	Label marking the top of the loop.
`IF (%1)==() GOTO END`	Once the replaceable parameters are exhausted, exit the loop.
`%1`	Run the replaceable parameter as a command.
`SHIFT`	Move all the replaceable parameters down one level.
`GOTO TOP`	Continue at the top of the loop.
`:END`	Label marking the (near) end of the batch file.
`ECHO Normally there would be     more commands here`	Documentation message.

13-41   MIDDLE3.BAT, which lets you enter commands to run inside the batch file as the batch file is running.

command. It echoes the commands necessary to tell DOS to stop recording the keystrokes into the batch file. When it finishes running, it deletes the temporary batch file.

Advanced batch file branching

Figure 13-41 illustrates how you can use the COPY CON command to create a batch file "on the fly," and use that batch file to run different commands in the middle of the file. In an earlier chapter, I showed you a batch file called RETURN.BAT (reproduced in Fig. 13-42) that combines the COPY command with DOS piping to construct a unique batch file each time RETURN.BAT is run. It turns out that the techniques represented by the batch files in Figs. 13-41 and 13-42 give you extreme power to branch batch files and perform noncase-sensitive comparisons.

Batch File Line	Explanation
`@ECHO OFF`	Turn command-echoing off.
`REM RETURN.BAT`	Remark giving the name of the batch file.
`COPY C:\BAT\RETURN C:\BAT\RETURNTO.BAT`	Copy the file RETURN to the file RETURNTO.BAT. RETURN contains the line CD\ and nothing more.
`CD >> C:\BAT\RETURNTO.BAT`	Pipe the current subdirectory to RETURNTO.BAT. If the current subdirectory were \BAT, the last two lines would result in RETURNTO.BAT containing the line CD\BAT.

13-42 RETURN.BAT, which constructs a batch file to return you to the current subdirectory.

Begin by considering an accounting batch file. Part of this file performs a monthly closing that takes two hours. This closing can wait, however, so you want the batch file to give the user the option of skipping the closing. What can you do?

You can require the user to enter a command line switch when he starts the batch file if he wants to skip the closing. This places the largest burden on both the user and the batch file author. The user has to remember to enter a command to skip the closing on the first. If he forgets, the computer processes the closing for two hours. The batch file author has to test for the command line switch. Assuming the switch is *skip*, the author has to, at the minimum, test for *skip*, *Skip*, and *SKIP*, and what if you allow the user to enter either *skip* or *yes*?

You can remind the user that it's time for a closing and ask him if the batch file should skip that. To do this, use an ErrorLevel test like InKey. This test limits the user to a single character response to a question like *Perform monthly closing? (Y/N)*, and the batch file author has to test for only two possible ErrorLevel values. A single character is enough for this case, but might be confusing and difficult to test for when there are a number of valid responses.

The first extension to batch file branching is to run a batch file with the name of the user's response to a question. This avoids the case problem completely by making the test completely case insensitive, since you can CALL a batch file using any mixture of upper- and lowercase. In fact, it avoids having to perform any testing at all in the batch file; however, it requires that your users enter a valid response to the prompt. If they do not, then the batch file as presented, fails.

BRANCH.BAT in Fig. 13-43 illustrates the technique. BRANCH.BAT uses COPY CON to capture the user's response in a file. The file HOLDING contains

Batch File Line	Explanation
`@ECHO OFF`	Turn command-echoing off.
`REM BRANCH.BAT`	Remark giving the name of the batch file.

`ECHO Do you with to run the monthly`
`ECHO closing now? (Takes 2 hours)`
`ECHO Acceptable responses are:`
`ECHO Yes, No`
`ECHO Enter a space FIRST`
`ECHO Case does not matter`
`ECHO Press the F6 key and the`
`ECHO return key after entering`
`ECHO your response.`
	Warn the user that this batch file takes a long time to run.

`COPY CON JUNK`	Create a file called JUNK to store the user's response. When the user presses F6, DOS stops recording information in this file and the batch file continues. Notice this lacks any error checking.
`COPY HOLDING+JUNK RESPONSE.BAT`	Combine the contents of a holding file called HOLDING with the file the user just created in the batch file called RESPONSE.BAT. The user's response will then function as a replaceable parameter.
`CALL RESPONSE`	Call the batch file created in the step above. The batch file runs the second application.

13-43 BRANCH.BAT, which constructs a batch file that calls another batch file, based on user response.

the CALL command and then an end-of-file marker. After the user enters his response, DOS file concatenation is used to combine the two into a single file containing the CALL command, followed by the response. The batch file calls this file, which in turn calls the batch file corresponding to the user's response. If your version of DOS doesn't support CALL, you can construct this file using the COMMAND/P and EXIT trick discussed earlier in this book. (I leave that to the reader as an incentive to upgrade your DOS.) As the author, you have to write batch files corresponding to all reasonable alternatives. In this case, that would be YES.BAT and NO.BAT.

This technique raises a couple of problems. The most obvious problem is forcing the user to enter only valid responses. For example, this method would fail if the user entered *Yeah* in response to the prompt. A second problem is the user can enter more than one command while constructing the batch file. If that second command is a batch file, it will run, and control will never pass back to the original batch file because there won't be a CALL in front of it.

There's no way to prevent this other than constructing very clear prompts for the user. Do note that if the user adds extra spaces or Returns, it won't affect the batch file. A third problem with this method is it can really clutter up your hard disk because every response needs a batch file. Finally, the need for one batch file per response also means that, if two different batch files need a response of Yes where YES.BAT does something different for each one, you're going to have to put them in separate directories and keep track of that (because you can no longer just CALL YES, but rather have to CALL C: \ SET1 \ YES.

The second technique uses a very similar method, but the user's response is placed in the environment rather than being used as a command to run a batch file. That eliminates the clutter of the above method, but at the expense of reintroducing case-sensitive responses. BRANCH2.BAT in Fig. 13-44 illustrates this. HOLDING2 contains the line SET RESPONSE=, with no Return. This gets combined with the user's response to form a command that sets the response variable into the environment. Because called batch files share the environment with the parent batch file, this change to the environment is permanent. However, you can't use this method prior to DOS 3.3 because a batch file called with COMMAND/P doesn't share a common environment with its parent. Rather, it gets its own copy after the EXIT command.

Technically, the called batch file doesn't get a copy of the environment; only .COM and .EXE program files get a copy of the environment. However, the command to "trick" a called batch file prior to DOS 3.3 is COMMAND/P. When followed by the batch file name, it runs COMMAND.COM, which is a program that gets a copy of the environment. The EXIT command then unloads both COMMAND.COM and its copy of the environment.

Note that this test is case sensitive and you can have a problem if the user enters a space before the response. This method shares many problems with an

Batch File Line	Explanation
`@ECHO OFF`	Turn command-echoing off.
`REM BRANCH2.BAT`	Remark giving the name of the batch file.

`ECHO Do you with to run the monthly`
`ECHO closing now? (Takes 2 hours)`
`ECHO Acceptable responses are:`
`ECHO Yes, No`
`ECHO Enter a space FIRST`
`ECHO Case does not matter`
`ECHO Press the F6 key and the`
`ECHO return key after entering`
`ECHO your response.`
	Warn the user that this batch file takes a long time to run.

`COPY CON JUNK`	Create a file called JUNK to store the user's response. When the user presses F6, DOS stops recording information in this file and the batch file continues. Notice this lacks any error checking.
`COPY HOLDING2+JUNK RESPONS2.BAT`	Combine the contents of a holding file called HOLDING with the file the user just created in the batch file called RESPONSE.BAT. The user's response will then function as a replaceable parameter.
`CALL RESPONS2`	Call the batch file created in the step above. The second batch file places the user's response into the environment.

13-44 BRANCH2.BAT, which is similar to BRANCH.BAT in Fig. 13-43, except it places the user's response in the environment.

ErrorLevel test; however, it avoids one problem with ErrorLevel tests because it allows responses longer than one character.

Tidy cleanups

Some of the techniques in this book create temporary files the batch file should delete before terminating. Still others create entire temporary batch files that need to be deleted. Sometimes, when you delete a batch file that's running, you get the DOS *Batch file missing* error message. However, this isn't always the case. A batch file that ends with an end-of-file (EOF) marker on the last line all by itself or without an EOF marker, will give the extra line. A batch file that has the EOF marker on the last command line following a command won't.

DOS executes batch files one line at a time. In addition, it reads in only one line at a time. When DOS reads in the DEL MISSING.BAT line from the batch file in Fig. 13-45, it sets a flag to tell itself that there's another line to run. When it goes

Batch File Line	Explanation
@ECHO OFF	Turn command-echoing off.
REM MISSING1.BAT	Remark giving the name of the batch file.
DEL MISSING1.BAT	Delete the batch file to illustrate that DOS will give an error message.
DIR	This command is never executed because the batch file is deleted on the above line.

13-45 MISSING1.BAT, which deletes itself and then issues an error message.

back to read that line, however, the batch file has been erased—hence, the error message. When DOS reads the same line from the batch file in Fig. 13-46, it sets a flag to tell itself there are no additional lines in the batch file, and therefore doesn't try to read another line. That's why there's no error message in Fig. 13-46.

Batch File Line	Explanation
@ECHO OFF	Turn command-echoing off.
REM MISSING2.BAT	Remark giving the name of the batch file.
DEL MISSING2.BAT^Z	This line deletes the batch file. The ^Z indicates that this line is followed immediately by an end-of-file marker. As a result, DOS does not issue an error message when this batch file deletes itself.

13-46 MISSING2.BAT, which deletes itself but doesn't issue an error message because of an EOF marker at the end of the file.

This blank line at the end of a batch file is the reason some batch files terminate with several DOS prompts on the screen. The blank line acts the same as pressing Enter at the DOS prompt. When one batch file calls another, you can actually end up with more than one extra DOS prompt on the screen. This can be especially important to users with dual floppy-disk drive systems. Some programs you load require you to swap disks during operation. As a result, you might have a different disk in the computer when you exit the program than the one containing the batch file that started the application. Under most versions of DOS, the computer will prompt you for the disk containing the batch file, which is annoying at best. A few versions will give you a *Batch file missing* error message. That could scare new users. By making sure the last line of the batch file contains the command to load the program followed by an EOF marker, you can avoid this problem.

This can be an annoying problem because many editor programs don't give you a lot of control over where the EOF marker is placed. Still other editors don't use an EOF marker because DOS doesn't require one. Many of these same editors will allow you to manually add an EOF marker by typing in an ASCII 26 by holding down the Alt and Shift keys and typing 026 on the number pad (the numbers at the top won't work). The program will probably allow you to continue typing after the ASCII 26, but you shouldn't do that. DOS will ignore anything after an ASCII 26, so you won't see how typing the file to the screen and running any batch commands after the ASCII-26 won't run. While DOS doesn't need an EOF marker, it does treat that character as the end of the file and won't process beyond it.

Selecting a working filename

A number of the batch file examples in this book create one or more working files while they run. On my system, I generally use the filename JUNK, with the understanding that any file on my system with the name JUNK*.* is subject to erasure at any time. If you're not willing to do that, then you can have your batch file cycle through several names and select a name that's not currently in use. FINDFREE.BAT in Fig. 13-47 illustrates this. It cycles through 25 names, looking for one that's not being used. If more than one are free, it uses the last one it finds. You would want to vary the number for your system so the batch file doesn't spend too much time cycling through the names, but yet has a high probability of finding a free name.

Batch File Line	Explanation
`@ECHO OFF`	Turn command-echoing off.
`REM FINDFREE.BAT`	Remark giving the name of the batch file.

`FOR %%J IN (1 2 3 4 5 6 7 8 9`
`10 11 12 13 14 15 16 17 18`
`19 20 21 22 23 24 25) DO IF`
`NOT EXIST JUNK%%J SET`
`FILE=JUNK%%J`
	Cycle through twenty five names (JUNK1 to JUNK25) and set an environmental variable equal to the name of each one that does not exist. Each nonexistent file will overwrite the last resulting in only one name in the environment.

`ECHO Working File is %FILE%`	Message to tell the user the name of the file that was selected.

13-47 FINDFREE.BAT, which will cycle through 25 names looking for an unused one.

Saving disk space with environmental variables

Some batch files end up being very long. For example, CHECKER2.BAT on the disk contains 12,826 bytes. When a batch file has a single command repeated a number of times, you can shorten the batch file by storing that command as an environmental variable and then replacing the command with %VARIABLE% in the batch file. Figure 13-48 shows SAVESPACE.BAT. This batch file is identical in function to CHECKER4.BAT, but contains only 6,477 bytes, a savings of almost 50 percent.

Batch File Line	Explanation
`@ECHO OFF`	Turn command-echoing off.
`REM SAVESPACE.BAT`	Remark giving the name of the batch file.

`SET E=IF ERRORLEVEL`
`SET N=IF NOT ERRORLEVEL`
`SET O=ECHO`
	Set three environmental variables that will be used to shorten the batch file lines.

`%E% 255        %O% 255`	When DOS expands the environmental variables, this line becomes IF ERRORLEVEL 255 ECHO 225.
`%E% 254 %N% 255 %O% 254`	When DOS expands the environmental variables, this line becomes IF ERRORLEVEL 254 IF NOT ERRORLEVEL 255 ECHO 254.
`%E% 253 %N% 254 %O% 253`	When DOS expands the environmental variables, this line becomes IF ERRORLEVEL 253 IF NOT ERRORLEVEL 254 ECHO 253.
The batch file continues in a similar fashion for 253-2	
`%E%   1 %N%   2 %O%   1`	When DOS expands the environmental variables, this line becomes IF ERRORLEVEL 1 IF NOT ERRORLEVEL 2 ECHO 1.
`%E%   0 %N%   1 %O%   0`	When DOS expands the environmental variables, this line becomes IF ERRORLEVEL 0 IF NOT ERRORLEVEL 1 ECHO 0.

13-48   SAVESPACE.BAT, which illustrates how to save disk space with environmental variables.

Of course, using this method makes it more difficult to debug the batch file, makes the batch file run somewhat slower, and requires additional environmental space. Therefore, you should use this only when space is very much at a premium on your system.

Making ErrorLevel easier to use

The DOS ErrorLevel has two significant problems:

- Running any .EXE or .COM program resets the ErrorLevel. That makes it difficult to make multiple tests when you need to run programs based on the value of those tests.
- The test is a greater than or equal to test. That means the logic to use the test is much more complex than it needs to be.

The solution to these two problems is to convert the ErrorLevel value to a numeric variable and then use that numeric variable. SAVE-ERR.BAT in Fig. 13-49 does

Batch File Line	Explanation
`@ECHO OFF`	Turn command-echoing off.
`SET ERROR=`	Reset the environmental variable to nul.
`REM SAVE-ERRORLEVEL.BAT`	Remark giving the name of the batch file.
`FOR %%J IN (0 1 2) DO IF ERRORLEVEL %%J00 SET ERROR=%%J`	Find out if a) ERRORLEVEL>200 b) ERRORLEVEL>100 c) ERRORLEVEL>0
`IF %ERROR%==2 GOTO 2`	Jump to a special section if the ERROR-LEVEL is 200 or larger. This is required because the maximum ERRORLEVEL is 255 and DOS does not handle ERRORLEVEL tests for numbers over 255 in a manner that will work with this batch file. When testing ERRORLEVEL 260 (for example) DOS subtracts increments of 256 until the number is less than 256, or 4 in this example.
`FOR %%J IN (0 1 2 3 4 5 6 7 8 9) DO IF ERRORLEVEL %ERROR%%%J0 SET ERROR=%ERROR%%%J`	As complex as this looks, DOS understands it. If the value of ERROR was 1 coming into this test and the FOR loop is on 6, the test line reads: IF ERRORLEVEL 160 SET ERROR=16 This test sets the value of the tens digit.

13-49 SAVE-ERR.BAT, a batch file that can save the ErrorLevel setting in the environment.

13-49 Continued

Batch File Line	Explanation
FOR %%J IN (0 1 2 3 4 5 6 7 8 9) DO IF ERRORLEVEL %ERROR%%%J SET ERROR=%ERROR%%%J	This test sets the value of the ones digit.
GOTO END	Jump to the end of the batch file.
:2	This marks the beginning of the section that handles ERRORLEVEL greater than or equal to 200.
FOR %%J IN (0 1 2 3 4 5) DO IF ERRORLEVEL %ERROR%%%J0 SET ERROR=%ERROR%%%J	Test for the tens digit. Since the maximum ERRORLEVEL value is 255, the test does not need to exceed 5.
IF %ERROR%==25 GOTO 25	If the ERRORLEVEL is 250 or larger, jump to a special section because the batch file needs to test only to five.
FOR %%J IN (0 1 2 3 4 5 6 7 8 9) DO IF ERRORLEVEL %ERROR%%%J SET ERROR=%ERROR%%%J	Test for the ones digit.
GOTO END	Exit the batch file.
:25	Label marking the section of the batch file to testing ERRORLEVEL values greater than or equal to 250.
FOR %%J IN (0 1 2 3 4 5) DO IF ERRORLEVEL %ERROR%%%J SET ERROR=%ERROR%%%J	Test for the ones digit.
:END	Label marking the end of the batch file.

just this. As you can see by reading over the code, the process is complex. Unfortunately, the command SET ERROR=%ERRORLEVEL% doesn't work. CHECKER5.BAT in Fig. 13-50 shows how much easier ErrorLevel tests are when the ErrorLevel value is converted to a numeric value.

Summary

This chapter has shown you a number of "tricky" things you can do with batch files. I hope that, while reading it, you were inspired to write your own advanced batch files.

Batch File Line	Explanation
`ECHO OFF`	Turn command-echoing off.
`REM CHECKER5.BAT`	Remark giving the name of the batch file.
`CALL SAVE-ERR.BAT`	Call another batch file that stores the value of ERRORLEVEL in the environment in the environmental variable ERROR.
`IF %ERROR%==255 ECHO 255`	Since this line tests an environmental variable rather than ERRORLEVEL, it is an equality test.
`IF %ERROR%==254 ECHO 254`	Test for an ERRORLEVEL of 254.
The Batch File Continues In A Similar Fashion For 253-2	
`IF %ERROR%==001 ECHO    1`	Test for an ERRORLEVEL value of 1. Note that SAVE-ERR.BAT stores three digits for each ERRORLEVEL value.
`IF %ERROR%==000 ECHO    0`	Test for an ERRORLEVEL value of 0.

13-50 CHECKER5.BAT, a batch file that uses SAVE-ERR.BAT, shown in Fig. 13-49, to make testing the ErrorLevel easier.

14
CHAPTER

The DOS environment

Using the DOS environment, you can create a set of variables that can be accessed by any batch file and by any program. This environment is useful for passing parameters between programs and batch files, and for supplying batch files with often used information without having to enter it on every command line.

In spite of these advantages, the DOS environment is under-utilized. There are a couple of reasons. First, it's poorly documented. In fact, the *%variable%* feature was undocumented until just recently. While undocumented, it works with DOS 2.0 and later. A second limitation is that space is limited. A long path statement and a complex prompt can fill up your environment! Don't worry, this chapter will show you how to expand the size.

A final problem is that programs have access only to a copy of the environment, not the original. So a program can use the environment as temporary storage or as a source of direction, but it can't use it to pass information to other programs. While programs (.COM and .EXE files) have access only to a copy of the environment, batch files have access to the original. So these limitations don't apply to batch files.

What is it?

The DOS environment is a section of RAM (Random Access Memory) called the master environment block that DOS sets aside for specific information. Three pieces of information are always stored in the environment. They are:

- The location of COMMAND.COM
- The PATH, if one has been set
- The PROMPT, if it's been changed from the default

You can see the contents of your environment with the command SET followed by an Enter. A copy of my environment is shown in Fig. 14-1. Note that some of the information is so wide that it wraps to a second line of the screen.

This original copy of the environment is "owned" by COMMAND.COM, and COMMAND.COM is the only program that can modify its contents. Users can modify its contents from the DOS prompt and batch files can do the same, but other programs can't generally modify this original environment. Any time you run a program, that program gets a copy of the environment from the COMMAND.COM if it's run from the DOS prompt, and from another program if you shell out of one program to run another.

```
C:\WORD\BOOK>set
COMSPEC=C:\COMMAND.COM
PATH=C:\;C:\BAT;C:\SYSLIB;C:\WORD;C:\NORTON;C:\SIDEKICK;C:\W
ORDSTAR;E:\WINDOWS;E
:\PAGEMAKER;E:\BALER;C:\DBASE;H:\;C:\RIGHTWRI
LIB=E:\baler
BALER=E:\baler
TEMP=E:\PAGEMAKE\MOUSE\cpanel
DBPATH=C:\INFORMIX;
INFORMIXDIR=C:\INFORMIX
PROMPT=$p$g

C:\WORD\BOOK>
```

14-1 A copy of my environment.

This has important implications for memory-resident (TSR or terminate-and-stay-resident) software. When you load the TSR software, it gets a copy of the environment from COMMAND.COM; however, that copy is static. If you update the original environment with a SET command, the copies of the environment that are attached to TSR software aren't updated. This can create problems if the TSR software depends on environmental variables to function properly.

When a program terminates, its copy of the environment is also terminated. Any changes to the environment made to that copy are lost forever. For example, if you're running Lotus 1-2-3 and you use the /System to shell to DOS to change your prompt, the new prompt will be lost as soon as you return to Lotus. (Lotus loads a second copy of COMMAND.COM to let you shell out. That copy of COMMAND.COM has an environment attached and your new prompt is stored there. Use the EXIT command to return to Lotus—that EXIT command unloads this copy of COMMAND.COM and terminates its environment.)

The SET command

DOS stores each piece of information in the environment as a string. As you'll see later, this allows you to enter absolutely anything you want into the environment. The general syntax for placing information into the environment is:

SET *variable* = *value*

The only space should be between the SET and the variable name. DOS will actually accept other spaces, for example, before or after the equal sign. These are treated as part of the variable name or the value, however, and make working with them difficult. The command:

SET TEMP = C: \ JUNK

will actually create a variable named TEMP(space), which contains the value (space)C: \ JUNK. You can avoid a lot of problems by avoiding extra spaces in the SET command.

The keywords COMSPEC, PATH, and PROMPT have special meaning DOS. These are the ways you change default values in the environment. The general syntax for these is:

SET PROMPT = *value*

SET COMSPEC = *value*

SET PATH = *value*

but DOS allows you to drop the SET in front of them. Warning: changing COM SPEC is dangerous and can cause your computer to lock up. If the command isn't just right, you'll get the dreaded *Cannot load COMMAND, system halted* error message, which means you need to reboot. You must change COMSPEC to increase the environment, and this chapter shows how to do that safely. When experimenting, make sure to save everything first.

In addition to the three entries DOS places into the environment automatically, DOS allows you to store your own information in the environment. This custom information can be accessed by programs and accessed and modified by batch files. The GOHOME.BAT batch file in Fig. 14-2 always moves you to a default directory defined at the beginning of the session. You set or change the home subdirectory with the command SET HOME=C: \ SUBDIRECTORY. By setting HOME at the beginning of the session, I can readily move batch to HOME. Unlike a hardwired batch file, I can change HOME "on the fly" as my needs change. You can remove a variable from memory with the:

SET VARIABLE =

command. Be sure not to enter any spaces after the equal sign, or you'll SET the

Batch File Line	Explanation
REM GOHOME.BAT	Remark giving the name of the batch file.
IF NOT (%HOME%)==() CD\%HOME%	If the environmental variable HOME has been set, change to that subdirectory.

14-2 GOHOME.BAT, which allows the user to automatically move to the home directory.

variable equal to spaces. You can verify that the variable was removed by entering the SET command by itself.

SET PROMPT

The default DOS prompt is a C>, which tells you almost nothing. The C indicates the default drive. You can use the PROMPT command, however, to change the DOS prompt to a wide range of prompts. The PROMPT command is normally just used in the AUTOEXEC.BAT file. When used by itself, PROMPT resets the prompt to C>.

Any printable character string can be included in the PROMPT command. In fact, one of the first tricks most computer users learn is to include their name or company name in the prompt. Special characters can be included in the prompt with the commands in Table 14-1. Any other character following a dollar sign is

Table 14-1 Metacharacters to use in the PROMPT command.

Command	Action
$$	Display a dollar sign
$t	Display the time
$d	Display the date
$p	Display the current subdirectory
$v	Display the DOS version
$n	Display the current drive
$g	Display a greater than sign
$l	Display a less than sign
$b	Display a vertical bar
$q	Display the equal sign
$h	Display a backspace (thus deleting the prior character)
$e	Include an escape (Useful when ANSI.SYS is loaded)
$_	Include a carriage return and line feed

ignored. The most popular prompt is:

SET PROMPT = pg

This commands adds the current subdirectory to the default disk display. It's important to remember that any prompt you develop is stored in the environmental space, along with the path and set variables. A long prompt combined with a long path and a set variable might require you to expand your environmental space, as explained later in this chapter.

SET COMSPEC

COMSPEC is short for SET COMmand SPECification. It tells DOS where to find COMMAND.COM when it's overwritten by a program. DOS takes up a lot of memory. When your computer is short of memory, either because it has less than 640K or you have a lot of memory-resident software, this can be a problem. The lack of memory might prevent some programs from being run or limit the size of others. DOS solves this problem by making part of itself provisionally resident (or transient) in memory. You need this part to enter DOS commands, but not to run application programs. If a program needs this space, it can overwrite the transient portion of DOS.

When you exit an application program that's overwritten the transient portion of DOS, DOS is less than complete. If you were to use this version, you wouldn't be able to enter most internal commands. DOS replenishes itself by rereading portions of COMMAND.COM into memory. (Note: This is why COMMAND.COM isn't a hidden file like the other two system files.) Usually, DOS reloads itself from the drive it booted from. Using:

SET COMSPEC = C: \ COMMAND.COM

you can force DOS to reload itself from some other place. You can also change COMSPEC using the SHELL command in the CONFIG.SYS file. Many RAM-disk users copy COMMAND.COM to their RAM disk and then use the SET COMSPEC command to reload COMMAND.COM from the RAM disk. This is noticeably faster than reloading from disk.

Note: While available in DOS series 2, the SET COMSPEC command doesn't work reliably in versions of DOS prior to 3.0.

SET PATH

There are four types of commands DOS will accept: internal commands, .EXE program names, .COM program names, and batch file names (.BAT). Every time DOS receives a command, it first checks to see if the command is an internal command, like ERASE. If so, it executes it. If the command isn't an internal command, DOS next checks the current subdirectory for an .EXE file by that name, then a .COM file, and finally a .BAT file. If DOS finds a program with the correct name, it executes that program. If DOS doesn't file in the current directory, it searches the path for a .COM, .EXE, or .BAT file. If DOS finds a program in the path with the correct name, it executes that program. Otherwise, DOS returns the *Bad command or filename* error message. The hierarchy of DOS commands is shown in Fig. 14-3.

Internal Command	(DOS commands)
.COM	(Program in current subdirectory)
.EXE	(Program in current subdirectory)
.BAT	(Batch File in current subdirectory)
C:\FIRST\.COM	(Program)
C:\FIRST\.EXE	(Program)
C:\FIRST\.BAT	(Batch File)
C:\SECOND\.COM	(Program)
C:\SECOND\.EXE	(Program)
C:\SECOND\.BAT	(Batch File)
C:\THIRD\.COM	(Program)
C:\THIRD\.EXE	(Program)
C:\THIRD\.BAT	(Batch File)

14-3 The hierarchy of DOS commands if PATH = C: \ ;C: \ FIRST;C: \ SECOND;C: \ THIRD.

So the path is nothing more than a list of subdirectories for DOS to search when a program isn't in the current subdirectory. The syntax is:

PATH = C: \ ;*subdirectory1;subdirectory2;...;lastsubdirectory*

so, if your path is:

PATH = C: \ ; \ SYSLIB; \ DATABASE; \ WORDPROCESSOR

then DOS will search only those subdirectories on the default disk. This is normally what you want. However, if you're working on the A drive, then the path is really:

PATH = C: \ ;A: \ SYSLIB;A: \ DATABASE;A: \ WORDPROCESSOR

because A is the default drive. So you're better off specifying the full path, like this:

PATH = C: \ ;C: \ SYSLIB;C: \ DATABASE;C: \ WORDPROCESSOR

A problem is that the PATH command can contain only the same 127 characters as other DOS commands. Before DOS 3.0, there was simply no way to have a path longer than 127 characters. While DOS 3.0 retained the 127-character command line limit, it introduced the Substitute command. The SUBST command allows you to substitute a drive letter for a subdirectory. So:

SUBST D: C: \ SYSLIB \ LEVEL1 \ LEVEL2

allows you to use D: anywhere you would have used C: \ SYSLIB \ LEVEL1 \ LEVEL2. Your PATH command can now be:

PATH = C: \ ;D: \

instead of:

PATH = C: \ ;C: \ SYSLIB \ LEVEL1 \ LEVEL2

This makes the command shorter, as well as easier to read. Generally speaking, you won't have set the path before using the SUBST command. Therefore, either SUBST.EXE must be in the root directory or you must change to the directory containing it before you issue the SUBST command. If you had the SUBST.EXE file in the C: \ SYSLIB directory, you would first change to that directory with the following command:

CD \ SYSLIB

and then give your SUBST command, for example:

SUBST D: C: \ SYSLIB \ LEVEL1 \ LEVEL2

If you enter the PATH command with nothing after it, DOS displays the current path. If you enter PATH followed by a semicolon DOS resets the path to nothing. This causes DOS to search only the default directory for programs and batch files. If you specify a path incorrectly, DOS won't find the error until it needs to search the path. If you enter an invalid directory in the path, DOS ignores that entry.

Using SET variables in batch files

As explained above, SET variables are variables you've placed into the environment with the SET command, or that DOS has placed in the environment with a default value. A batch file can use these variables by adding a percent before and after their name. This is illustrated in Fig. 14-4.

This is a very simple password system that will stop only new users. By typing the batch file, a user can see the commands needed to run the program without the batch file. At least typing the batch file doesn't show the password.

Default SET entries can also be used in batch files. For example, Fig. 14-5 shows a batch file that will set the prompt to pg if no prompt has been set. If a PROMPT command has already been given, the prompt will be unchanged.

Batch File Line	Explanation
`ECHO OFF`	Turn command-echoing off.
`REM PASSWORD.BAT`	Remark giving the name of the batch file.
`IF (%1)==() GOTO NOPASS`	If the user did not enter a password on the command line, jump to an error-handling routine.
`IF (%PASSWORD%)==() GOTO NOTSET`	If the environmental variable PASSWORD is blank, jump to an error-handling routine.
`IF NOT %1==%PASSWORD% GOTO NO`	If the user's password does not match the one stored in the environmental variable, jump to an error-handling routine.
`PROGRAM` `GOTO END`	If the user's password matches the environmental variable, run the program and then exit the batch file.

`:NOPASS`
`ECHO You must enter a password.`
`ECHO See manual for syntax.`
`GOTO END`
	If the user did not enter a password, explain the problem and exit the batch file.

`:NOTSET`
`ECHO Password not set.`
`ECHO Call system operator.`
`GOTO END`
	If the password has not been set, explain the problem to the user and then exit the batch file.

`:NO`	Label marking the beginning of the section for handling an incorrect password.
`ECHO INCORRECT PASSWORD` `ECHO LOCKING SYSTEM`	Explain the problem.
`PAUSE>NUL`	Simulate a locked computer by pausing execution and piping the DOS message to NUL. Pressing any key will restart the batch file and allow the user to continue using the computer. The computer could be completely locked up with a CTTY NUL command followed by a PAUSE command. Using this method, the user would have to reboot the computer to use it again.
`GOTO END`	Exit the batch file if the user presses a key to restart the batch file.
`:END`	Label marking the end of the batch file.

14-4 PASSWORD.BAT, a batch file to implement a simple password system.

Batch File Line	Explanation
ECHO OFF	Turn command-echoing off.
REM NEWPROMPT.BAT	Remark giving the name of the batch file.
IF NOT (%PROMPT%)==() GOTO END	If the prompt already have a value, then exit this batch file without resetting the prompt.
SET PROMPT=pg	Reset the prompt.
:END	Label marking the end of the batch file.

14-5 NEWPROMPT.BAT, a batch file that makes setting the system prompt a little easier.

Increasing the size of the environment

Most Microsoft compilers use one or several SET variables to point to their libraries. In fact, a couple of them use the same variables to point to different libraries! I once got a frantic call from a developer using two Microsoft products. He didn't know how to deal with this problem. I told him to construct two batch files, one to start each compiler. He could then have each batch file custom set the variables for that compiler. He called me back even more frantic because it wouldn't work. I had him type in SET at the DOS prompt and read the contents back to me. It turned out that he hadn't expanded the environment and, with his long path and prompt, there just wasn't enough room to store all the information he was trying to shove into the environment. I walked him through the procedure to expand the environment and everything worked properly.

The default size of the environment is 160 bytes. That means it can store 160 characters. This 160-character storage space must store the COMSPEC value, the PATH, the PROMPT, and any variables you want to enter. If this isn't enough room, you need to expand the environment.

There's an additional consideration when you're deciding on the size of the environment. Each program gets a full copy of the environment. That means that every memory-resident program gets a full copy of the environment. If you expand the environment to 2K and you load six memory-resident programs, then each memory-resident program will get a 2K copy of the environment. The result is that the 2K original environment and its six copies now occupy 14K.

Users of DOS 3.0 and later have it easy. For them, adding one of the following lines as the first line of their CONFIG.SYS file will expand the environment:

Version 3.0   SHELL = C: \ COMMAND.COM /E:*xx* /P
Version 3.1   SHELL = C: \ COMMAND.COM /E:*xx* /P
Version 3.2   SHELL = C: \ COMMAND.COM /E:*yyyyy* /P

Version 3.3   SHELL = C: \ COMMAND.COM /E:*yyyyy* /P
Version 4.0   SHELL = C: \ COMMAND.COM /E:*yyyyy* /P
Version 5.0   SHELL = C: \ COMMAND.COM /E:*yyyyy* /P

If you're running off floppy disks, then change the C: \ to an A: \ . The *xx* is a number between 10 and 62. It represents the number of 16-byte segments to use for the environment. So a 20 gives you a 320-byte environmental space. The maximum value is 992 bytes, which is an *xx* of 62. Beginning with version 3.2, you can create a much larger environment. The *yyyyy* can be a number from 160 to 32,768. This allows an environmental space up to 32K! The /P is required to force COMMAND.COM to automatically run the AUTOEXEC.BAT file. Because the SHELL command is in the CONFIG.SYS file and the CONFIG.SYS file is processed prior to the AUTOEXEC.BAT file, without the /P switch the AUTOEXEC .BAT file will be bypassed.

The above SHELL statements use the /E and /P switches. These aren't SHELL switches; rather, they're COMMAND.COM switches. The full set of switches are:

/C   This tells COMMAND.COM to run the command listed after the /C switch. This is used to trick COMMAND.COM into running a subroutine batch file by giving the batch file name after the /C and having the last command in the batch file be an EXIT to unload that copy of COMMAND.COM.

/D   This causes COMMAND.COM not to run the AUTOEXEC.BAT file. It's used in conjunction with the /P switch, below.

/E   This switch, which changes the environment size, first appeared in DOS 3.0, but it wasn't documented until DOS 3.1. Also, it works differently in DOS 3.0 than it did in later versions.

/F   This switch first appeared in DOS 3.1. It causes DOS to automatically respond with a *Fail* anytime it displays the *Abort, retry or fail* or *Abort, ignore, retry or fail* error message. You'll still see the error message on the screen, along with DOS's response.

/P   This tells COMMAND.COM to load in permanent mode, which causes COMMAND.COM to set a couple of switches internally. One switch causes it not to unload when you issue an EXIT command. Another switch causes it to run the AUTOEXEC.BAT file after loading.

Note that you're required to put the .COM extension on the end of COMMAND .COM. And these changes won't take effect until you reboot. Make sure you have a bootable system disk in case you make a mistake. Some mistakes will hang the computer. If this happens, reboot from the floppy disk and switch over to the hard disk to edit the problem CONFIG.SYS. As a precaution, you should make a copy of your CONFIG.SYS file before trying this change.

If you use DOS version 2, then you must change the COMMAND.COM program in order to increase the environment. The example shown in Fig. 14-6 expands the environment to 992 bytes. DOS version 2 includes a routine that limits the environment to a maximum of 992 bytes, regardless of how COMMAND .COM is patched. It expands the environment in 16-byte increments. If you enter an odd increment, it's rounded up to the nearest 16 bytes.

Command	Explanation
A:<Return>	Log onto the A drive. The modification will be made to a floppy disk (formatted as a system disk) and later transferred to the hard disk once the change is tested.
DEBUG COMMAND.COM	DOS command to start DEBUG (a DOS program editor) and edit COMMAND.COM.
-	The dash is the DEBUG prompt. When you see a dash, DEBUG is waiting for a command.
-s 100 L 1000 bb 0a 00	This is the command to search for the part of COMMAND.COM that stores the size of the environment. That location will be different on different versions of DOS. NOTE: This command is case sensitive. You must enter the command exactly as shown. Also, the 0s are zeros and not letters.
XXXX:YYYY	When DEBUG finds the correct string, it will display this information as two numbers separated by a colon. The numbers are in hexadecimal so they might also contain letters. That is ok. You will be using the second number.
-e YYYY bb 3e 00	This is the DEBUG command to edit COMMAND.COM so it will allocate more space for the environment. The 0a 00 two lines above was the default 160 bytes in hexadecimal. This command changes that to 992 bytes (3e 00 in hexadecimal.) NOTE: Do not use YYYY. Replace the YYYY with the second number from the line above. Do not enter YYYY.
-w	Write the change to disk. You should see the message "Writing ZZZZ bytes" where ZZZZ will be a number.
-q	Quit DEBUG. Now reboot from the floppy disk and test it for proper operation.

14-6 The commands to patch COMMAND.COM in order to enlarge the environmental space for DOS version 2.

To edit the COMMAND.COM program, you'll use Debug. DEBUG.COM is a program editor that comes with DOS. The first step is to format a floppy disk as a system disk. The changes will be made to this disk, even if you have a hard disk. Once you are sure that everything works, you can copy COMMAND.COM from the modified floppy disk to your hard disk. After formatting a system disk (FORMAT /S), copy DEBUG.COM to the floppy. Finally, change over to the A drive and perform the steps in Fig. 14-6.

Note: I've tested this patch on IBM's PC DOS versions 2.0 and 2.1 and Compaq's MS DOS versions 2.0 and 2.1. While it should work on most compatibles, some vendors rewrite parts of COMMAND.COM for specific purposes. It's possible that this could prevent the patch from working. If you have trouble, check with the manufacturer of your computer or upgrade to a series 3 version of DOS, where you won't have this problem.

After you patch COMMAND.COM, reboot from the new floppy disk and run the batch file TESTENVI.BAT shown in Fig. 14-7. If the environment is expanded, the patch worked and you can copy COMMAND.COM to other floppy disks or to your hard disk. Otherwise, you need to reformat the disk and try again,

Batch File Line	Explanation
ECHO OFF	Turn command-echoing off.
REM TESTENVI.BAT	Remark giving the name of the batch file.
ECHO Use this variable to test your ECHO environment. The last line in ECHO this batch file will display ECHO the environment. Count the ECHO characters you see before the ECHO variable 1. Be sure to count ECHO the variable names and the equal ECHO sign. Then add 50 for each ECHO numeric variable except the last. ECHO Since the last variable may have ECHO been cut short, you must count ECHO those characters. The resulting ECHO number is the current size of the ECHO environment. ECHO NOTE: If you see all 19 ECHO variables, then your environment ECHO is too large to measure using ECHO this batch file.	Documentation remarks.

14-7   TESTENVI.BAT, a batch file to test the success of the COMMAND.COM patch in Fig. 14-6.

14-7 Continued

Batch File Line	Explanation
SET 1=12345678901234567890123456789 0123456789012345678	Define an environmental variable. Including the SET 1= this line contains 50 characters.
SET 2=12345678901234567890123456789 0123456789012345678	Define an environmental variable.
The batch file continues in similar fashion for variables 3-18.	
SET 19=12345678901234567890123456789 012345678901234567	Define an environmental variable.
SET	Display the contents of the environment.

contact the manufacturer for information on how to patch his version of COM-MAND, or upgrade to a series 3 or later version of DOS.

Summary

This chapter has presented a discussion of the usefulness of the DOS environment and explained how to expand the DOS environment by patching COMMAND .COM (in version 2 of DOS) or by including the SHELL command in your CONFIG.SYS file. Most of the sample batch files are on the disk.

15
CHAPTER

Modifying DOS

This chapter will show you how to modify several DOS files in order to customize the way DOS works. The illustrations show the modifications being made with The Norton Utilities. Any other similar product should work as well. The purpose of this chapter is to illustrate how to customize DOS, not to explain how to use The Norton Utilities. I'll leave that task to its manual.

A word of warning

Modifying DOS files is never risk free. If you make a mistake, it's possible that you won't be able to boot off your disk. Less serious problems are also possible. One common one results from someone booting from a floppy disk with DOS installed. Because that disk will most likely be an unchanged version of DOS, your carefully constructed modifications won't work. You can reduce the risk of these problems with three simple steps:

1. Before you begin, make a backup of the hard disk.
2. Before you begin, prepare a bootable floppy disk that contains every file you'll need in order to return the system to its original state if you make a mistake. These files should include a copy of the files you're modifying, a text editor, and your restore program.
3. As soon as you finish modifying a file, reboot the file and try various DOS operations to make sure they work properly. If they don't, the changes you made will be fresh in your mind so you can correct them.

With these precautions in mind, any knowledgeable user should be able to make these modifications with little difficulty.

Your AUTOEXEC.BAT and CONFIG.SYS files

The current trend in software is to have the installation program do everything for you. Generally, you type INSTALL and the software installation program will:

1. Create a directory for the software files.
2. Copy all the files to this directory.
3. Add the directory to your path statement in your AUTOEXEC.BAT file.
4. Change the FILES= and BUFFERS= statements in your CONFIG.SYS file.

It's the last two steps that I object to, especially when the package modifies these files without first asking permission. If your path statement is like that of most users, it's already near the 127-character DOS limit. Blindly tacking on another subdirectory can cause you to exceed this limit. You probably won't even know there's a problem until you reboot the computer. On some models under certain version of DOS, a path that's too long will cause the computer to mysteriously lock up with no warning.

The problem is even worse with memory-resident software. Most memory-resident software on the market expects to either be loaded first or last. When that software installs itself, it will add itself as either the first or last line in your AUTOEXEC.BAT file. If the new software conflicts with existing software, you end up with an AUTOEXEC.BAT file that locks up your computer. Again, you have no indication that the new software is the problem or how to correct the problem.

Some software automatically modifies your CONFIG.SYS file or adds device drivers. Changing a BUFFERS= or FILES= statement is no big deal. You can always edit the file and return it to its original value. A new number won't do any damage. And if you have reasonable values (BUFFERS=20 and FILES=20), as a general rule, the installation software won't change the values.

Adding device drivers is another matter. Device drivers can cause all the memory problems of memory-resident software, with the additional drawback that they're loaded so early in the boot process you can't use Ctrl−Break to stop their loading. Fortunately, device driver conflicts are uncommon.

Because I can't stop self-installing software from modifying my AUTOEXEC.BAT and CONFIG.SYS files, I decided to prevent it by using DOS. There are three ways to protect your AUTOEXEC.BAT file and two ways to protect your CONFIG.SYS file.

The easiest way to protect your AUTOEXEC.BAT file is with a single line in the AUTOEXEC.BAT file that calls a second batch file. This second batch file serves as your "real" AUTOEXEC.BAT file. This method has the advantage that you can examine your "fake" AUTOEXEC.BAT file after installing software to see how it was modified. You can then incorporate those changes into your "real"

AUTOEXEC.BAT file if you think they would be useful. The drawback is that you must recreate your one-line fake AUTOEXEC.BAT each time it's modified by installing software. Because the CONFIG.SYS file has no command to call another file, this method can't be used on the CONFIG.SYS file.

Read only

Every file has four attributes that DOS tracks:

Archive This flag indicates if the file has changed since the last time it was backed up.

System This flag indicates that the file is a special DOS file. This attribute is sometimes assigned to special files by various forms of copy protection.

Hidden This flag indicates a file that you don't see when you perform a directory. These are generally special DOS files. This attribute is sometimes assigned to special files by various forms of copy protection.

Read only This flag indicates a file that can be read by any program, but can't be modified.

By making the AUTOEXEC.BAT and/or CONFIG.SYS files read only, you can prevent installation programs from modifying them. If you have DOS 3.0 or later, you can make a file to read only with the following command:

    ATTRIB +R AUTOEXEC.BAT

This method has one drawback. Some software installation programs will crash when they try to modify the AUTOEXEC.BAT or CONFIG.SYS file and fail. The only way to install those programs is to remove the read-only protection and reinstall them normally.

Changing DOS

The Norton Utilities allow you to edit any file, so it's a good program to use in order to edit your DOS files. When you're editing a file, you'll see hexadecimal values on the left side of your screen and ASCII values on the right. You can make changes on one side, and they'll be reflected on the other side.

DOS must know which file to load as the CONFIG.SYS file and which file to load as the AUTOEXEC.BAT file. This isn't automatic; the names are stored in DOS. You could change the name of CONFIG.SYS to START1.SYS. If you then change the name in the DOS code, DOS would treat START1.SYS as CONFIG.SYS. You could rename AUTOEXEC.BAT as START-UP.BAT and change the DOS code, and START-UP.BAT would function as your AUTOEXEC.BAT file.

If you make these changes, the CONFIG.SYS and AUTOEXEC.BAT file-names will have no special meaning to your modified version of DOS. As a result, when installation software creates or modifies the CONFIG.SYS or AUTOEX-EC.BAT file, it won't change how the system works.

One special note: START1.SYS and START-UP.BAT have the same number of letters in their names and extensions as do CONFIG.SYS and AUTOEXEC .BAT. This is important. You can use any names and extensions you like, but they must have *exactly* the same length as the ones they're replacing.

Because CONFIG.SYS is loaded and processed prior to loading the command processor, its name is stored in the IBMBIO.COM (or equivalent MS-DOS) file. Edit this file. Scroll through the file until you see the ASCII text *CON-FIG.SYS* on the right side of the screen. This is shown in Fig. 15-1. Move the

15-1 Screen display of patching IBMBIO.COM to get configuration information from a file other than CONFIG.SYS.

cursor to the ASCII file and replace *CONFIG.SYS* with the name of the file you've selected. Remember:

- The name must have six characters.
- The name must be typed over top of *CONFIG*.
- The extension must have three characters.
- The extension must be typed over the *SYS*.

Save your modified file and exit The Norton Utilities. This change will take effect the next time you reboot the computer.

The AUTOEXEC.BAT file is processed after the command processor is loaded, so its name is stored in COMMAND.COM. Edit this file. Scroll through the file until you see the ASCII text *AUTOEXEC.BAT* on the right side of the screen. This is shown in Fig. 15-2. Move the cursor to the ASCII file and replace

15-2 Screen display of patching COMMAND.COM to change the name of internal commands.

AUTOEXEC.BAT3 with the name of the file you've selected. Remember:

- The name must have eight characters.
- The name must be typed over *AUTOEXEC*.
- The extension must have three characters. It doesn't have to be *BAT*, but if it has a BAT extension you can run it from the DOS prompt.
- If you choose to change it, the extension must be typed over top of *BAT*.

Save your modified file and exit The Norton Utilities. This change will take effect the next time you reboot the computer.

If you're so inclined, these changes can be made using the Debug program that comes with your DOS disk. Figure 15-3 shows how to do this using Compaq DOS 3.2. Other versions of DOS should work similarly.

COMMAND	MEANING
DEBUG IBMBIO.COM	Edit IBMBIO.COM. DEBUG.COM must be in the current directory or in your PATH. Note that Debug will edit IBMBIO.COM even though it is a hidden file.
-RCX	Debug command to display the length of the file.
CX 406A :	Debug responding with length of file in hexadecimal. Press return again at the colon prompt to return to the dashed Debug prompt. The size of the file (406A) will vary depending on the version of DOS you are modifying.
-S 100 406A "CONF"	Command telling Debug to search for the text CONF. Be sure to replace the 406A with the number from the RCX command.

15-3 The steps to modify IBMBIO.COM using Debug.

15-3 Continued

COMMAND	MEANING
420E:3F11	Debug response telling you where the text was located. Ignore the first four numbers, we will use the 3F11. Remember to replace 3F11 with the number you got.
-E 3F11 "START.SYS"	Edit the file and replace CONFIG.SYS with START1.SYS. Be sure to replace 3F11 with the number you got.
-D 14B1	Display the changes to make sure you did not make a mistake. Be sure to replace 14B1 with the number you got.
-W	Write your changes to disk. Before the W command, nothing has been on the disk. Quitting without saving will discard all your changes if you make a mistake.
-Q	Quit Debug. Will not prompt you to save.

Changing commands

The same technique can be used for an even more powerful purpose. DOS stores the name of all its internal commands in the COMMAND.COM file. The name of these commands can be changed, just like the CONFIG.SYS and AUTOEXEC .BAT filenames were. The new command names must also be the same length as the existing command name. In addition, the name must not conflict with other command names and must not contain illegal characters. The commands to modify COMMAND.COM with the Debug program are shown in Fig. 15-4.

COMMAND	MEANING
DEBUG COMMAND.COM	Edit COMMAND.COM. DEBUG.COM must be in the current directory or in your PATH.
-RCX	Debug command to display the length of the file.
CX 5D2F :	Debug responding with length of file in hexadecimal. Press return again at the colon prompt to return to the Debug prompt. The size of the file (5D2F) will vary depending on the version of DOS you are modifying.
-S 100 5D2F "AUTO"	Command telling Debug to search for the text AUTO. Be sure to replace the 5D2F with the number you got from the RCX command.
6880:14B1	Debug response telling you where the text was located. Ignore the first four numbers, and use the 14B1. Remember to replace 14B1 with the number you got.

15-4   The steps to modify COMMAND.COM using Debug.

15-4 Continued

COMMAND	MEANING
`-E 14B1 "STARTUP.BAT"`	Edit the file and replace AUTOEXEC.BAT with START-UP.BAT. Be sure to replace 14B1 with the number you got.
`-D 14B1`	Display the changes to make sure you did not make a mistake. Be sure to replace 14B1 with the number you got.
`-W`	Write your changes to disk. Before the W command, nothing has been on the disk. Quitting without saving will discard all your changes if you make a mistake.
`-Q`	Quit Debug. Will not prompt you to save.

If you're a network coordinator, you can reduce your problems by changing the names of the DEL and ERASE commands to something people aren't likely to use, like XXX and XXXXX. You can then enforce file security by requiring users to submit a list of files to be erased to you. You could then erase them with the XXX command.

If you're just trying to prevent common mistakes, you can replace DEL, ERASE, and other troublesome commands with batch files. These batch files can be very powerful.

Consider the batch file called DEL.BAT in Fig. 15-5. Because the DEL command was renamed to XXX, there's no internal command named DEL, so it's a valid batch file name. This batch file is much more useful than the naked DEL command.

Batch File Line	Explanation
`ECHO OFF`	Turn command-echoing off.
`REM DEL.BAT`	Remark giving the name of the batch file.
`:TOP`	Label marking the top of a loop.
`IF (%1)==() GOTO NO-FILES`	Quit if a replaceable parameter is not entered. Notice that the commands inside the subroutine are indented.
`IF %1==*.* GOTO NOT-OK`	A replaceable parameter of *.* is considered an error and the batch file jumps to a section to handle that error.
`DIR %1/W`	Display all the files that are selected for deleting.
`ECHO YOU ARE GOING TO ERASE THESE FILES - IS THAT OK (Y/N)`	Tell the user what is happening.

15-5 DEL.BAT, a batch file to alter the internal command names recognized by COMMAND.COM.

Batch File Line	Explanation
CHECK KEYPRESS	Use the Check program to get a response from the user.
REM CHECK FOR AN ASCII VALUE GREATER THAN y	Documentation remark.
IF ERRORLEVEL 122 GOTO SKIP	If the ERRORLEVEL is above y, assume a key other than y was selected and skip these file.
REM CHECK FOR ASCII=y	Documentation remark.
IF ERRORLEVEL 121 GOTO KILL	Now, a value greater than or equal to 121 is a y and the batch file skips to a section to delete the files.
REM CHECK FOR AN ASCII VALUE BETWEEN Y AND y	Documentation remark.
IF ERRORLEVEL 90 GOTO SKIP	If the ERRORLEVEL value is equal to or over 90 (actually 90-120 from above) then either the key was a y or a key with an ASCII value higher than Y. Since y has already been handled and the files are not deleted for the other possible values, the batch file skips the deleting.
REM CHECK FOR ASCII=Y	Documentation remark.
IF ERRORLEVEL 89 GOTO KILL	If the value is greater than or equal to 89 now, then it is a Y and the batch file jumps to the section that deletes the files.
REM FOR AN ASCII VALUE LESS THAN Y	Documentation remark.
IF ERRORLEVEL 0 GOTO SKIP	None of the remaining values are acceptable for deleting so the batch file skips the files.
:KILL	Section of the batch file that deletes the file. Notice that this subroutine (and the remaining ones) are also indented.
XXX %1	Delete the files. For this batch file to work, you must modify COMMAND.COM so the internal DEL command is renamed to XXX. The book explains how to do this.

15-5   Continued

Batch File Line	Explanation
GOTO END	Exit after deleting the files. By using a SHIFT command and a GOTO TOP command, this batch file could delete more than one set of replaceable parameters at a time.
:NO-FILES	Error subroutine for when the user does not enter a file specification.
ECHO NO FILES SPECIFIED	Tell the user what happened.
GOTO END	Exit the batch file.
:NOT-OK	Error subroutine for when the user enters *.* as the files to erase.
ECHO DEL *.* NOT ALLOWED	Tell the user what is wrong.
GOTO END	Exit the batch file.
:SKIP	Error subroutine for when the user does not answer Y or y when ask about deleting the files.
ECHO %1 NOT ERASED	Tell the user what happened.
GOTO END	Exit the batch file
:END	Label marking the end of the batch file.

Conclusion

Keep in mind that, when you change the name of files or commands inside DOS, it's easy to make mistakes. Have the files handy that you'll need to correct any problems. In addition, remember that your changes won't be in effect if someone boots off another copy of DOS, and that you'll have to make these changes each time you upgrade DOS. Most of the example batch files in this chapter are on the disk.

Part 5
Reference

16
CHAPTER

Quick reference list

In the first section of this book, I introduced batch file commands and features in a tutorial manner—one at a time, in an order designed to make them easy to learn. While useful for learning batch file programming, this method is far less useful for quick reference.

This section covers each DOS command, feature, variable, files, etc., by itself, in alphabetical order, with the DOS version of when it was introduced (if applicable) beside it. You should use this section as a quick reference, after reading the first four chapters of the book. If you need a more complete explanation of anything listed here, consult your DOS manual.

%0 through %9

When you start a batch file, you can pass its information by typing that information after the name of the batch file and before pressing Enter. Each piece of information must be separated by a space or a comma. The name of the batch file becomes %0. The first piece for information becomes %1, the second becomes %2, and so on. If more than nine pieces of information are passed to the batch file, the SHIFT command (explained later in the list) must be used to process the additional information. DOS restricts the command line to 127 or less characters. This, plus the requirement to separate each piece of information, restricts the amount of information that can be passed to a batch file.

Batch file SHOWPARA.BAT in Fig. 16-1 illustrates this feature. The %0 − %9 variables are automatically replaced with the values passed on the command line, and the extra values are ignored.

Batch File Line	Explanation
`@ECHO OFF`	Turn command-echoing off.
`REM SHOWPARA.BAT`	Remark giving the name of the batch file.
`ECHO %0 %1 %2 %3 %4 %5 %6 %7 %8 %9`	Echo the first ten replaceable parameters.

16-1   SHOWPARA.BAT, which illustrates the use of replaceable parameters.

%%j (2.0)

A DOS variable for use with the FOR command. For an example, see FOR in the list.

%variable% (2.0)

Batch files can use the SET variables by surrounding the name of the variable with percent signs. If the variable is NAME, then a batch file can access it with %NAME%.

: (2.0)

The colon is used in a batch file to assign a name. It is followed by a single-word name. You can then use the GOTO command to jump to that name for processing. Figure 16-2 shows an example.

Batch File Line	Explanation
`REM SHOWGOTO.BAT`	Remark giving the name of the batch file.
`GOTO END`	Jump to the label END.
`ECHO THIS LINE WILL NEVER BE` `     PROCESSED BY THIS BATCH FILE`	Since the GOTO command above caused the batch file to jump to the label END, this line is never processed.
`:END`	Label marking the (near) end of the batch file.
`ECHO THE END`	Tell the user the batch file has finished.

16-2   SHOWGOTO.BAT, which shows how to assign a name with a colon that a GOTO statement can then access.

^Z

When creating batch files by copying them from the console (e.g., COPY CON: BATCH.BAT) you tell DOS to finish recording your keystrokes by pressing either the F6 key or Ctrl−Z (^Z) followed by an Enter.

>NUL

This is a way to keep some DOS messages from showing. It uses DOS piping to route the message to NUL. NUL is DOS's version of oblivion. Note that the batch file in Fig. 16-3 doesn't display the DOS message *1 File(s) copied* when it runs. That's because the message was routed to NUL. It's also possible to route the messages to the printer using >PRN.

Batch File Line	Explanation
`@ECHO OFF`	Turn command-echoing off.
`REM SHOWNUL.BAT`	Remark giving the name of the batch file.
`COPY *.DOC *.BAK > NUL`	Copy files and pipe the DOS error messages to NUL.

16-3 SHOWNUL.BAT, a batch file that shows how you can send unwanted messages to oblivion, or *NUL*.

When you're copying files in a batch file with echo turned off, the user is often unaware that files are being copied. As a result, he can become confused when he sees a *1 file copied* message. By routing the message to NUL, e.g.,

COPY C: \ SUB1 \ FILE1 C: \ SUB2 \ FILE1.BAK/V > NUL

you can prevent any confusion. You must be careful when you do this, however. DOS commands are inconsistent about how they display error messages. Some commands will force the error message to the screen even with output redirected, while others will send the error message along with the other messages when output is redirected. For example, if you try to copy a file that doesn't exist, the error message will be piped to the alternative device and nothing will be displayed on the screen. If you try to rename a file that doesn't exist, the error message will be displayed on the screen but not redirected to an alternative device.

If you're concerned about error messages, you should redirect output to a log file instead of NUL. To do that, you would change the command above to:

COPY C: \ SUB1 \ FILE1 C: \ SUB2 \ FILE1.BAK/V >> ERRORS.TXT

Note the use of >> instead of >. That saves all the messages, not just the current error message. Of course, you'll need to periodically erase this file or it will gradually become very large. Whenever you think there was an error but nothing is displayed on the screen, you can examine ERRORS.TXT to see exactly what the error message was.

<

The less-than symbol (<) is used to direct standard input into a program. Specifically, input that would usually come from the keyboard is redirected to come from a file. For example, if your version of DOS requires a Return after the user answers Y to a prompt, you could create a file called YES.TXT that contains a Y followed by a Return. You could then delete all your files without answering a prompt with the following command:

```
DEL *.* < YES.TXT
```

Of course, it's more work to create YES.TXT than it is to answer the prompt. However, this technique can be used within batch files to reduce the control the user has over the batch file.

The < redirect has more uses than just answering prompts. Many magazines show you how to create short .COM programs using a DOS Debug program. They usually direct you to create a "script" file for Debug containing the proper commands. After you're sure the script file is correct, you actually create the .COM file with the command:

```
DEBUG < SCRIPT
```

This command runs Debug, which actually creates the .COM file. It also causes Debug to get all its inputs from the script file.

+

The addition sign (+) is the DOS appending command. The command:

```
COPY FILE1 + FILE2 + FILE3 FILE4
```

causes the files FILE1, FILE2, and FILE3 to be copied into a single file named FILE4. Note that DOS will respond with a *1 file(s) copied* message.

@ (3.3)

Beginning with DOS 3.3, you can precede any command with an "at" symbol (@) to turn off echoing for that line, even if the default is ECHO ON. Many users put @ECHO OFF as the first line of their batch files so nothing is echoed to the screen.

ANSI.SYS (2.0)

ANSI.SYS replaces the screen and keyboard handling of DOS with more powerful routines. ANSI.SYS allows keyboard remapping and improves screen handling. The syntax is difficult, but ANSI.SYS can remap any key to any other set of keystrokes. ANSI.SYS can also use special keystrokes to control such screen functions as setting the screen colors.

APPEND (3.3)

The PATH command is limited because it only searches for .COM, .EXE, and .BAT files. The APPEND command works like an expanded PATH because it searches for any type of file. This command creates a new problem, however, with certain older programs like WordStar. WordStar will find the old version of a data file based on the APPEND path, but will save the modified file in the current directory. Depending on if the application deletes the old version (WordStar does), you can end up with a file that's been moved or two versions of a file.

ASSIGN (2.0)

This command reroutes references from one disk drive to another. Only one ASSIGN can be in effect at any time, but a single assignment can assign multiple drives, for example, ASSIGN C=D D=C. ASSIGN alone cancels any existing assignment.

ATTRIB (3.0)

ATTRIB allows you to change the read-only and archive attributes of a file.

AUTOEXEC.BAT

This is a special batch file that's automatically executed each time you reboot the computer. In addition to the normal batch file restrictions, the AUTOEXEC.BAT must be in the root directory of the boot disk.

AUX

AUX is the first communication port. This keyword is the same as COM1.

BACKUP (2.0)

This is a method of storing all your hard disk files on floppies. They must then be replaced on the hard disk with the RESTORE program. BACKUP is very slow and there are many commercially available programs that are much faster. BACKUP returns ErrorLevel values that can be used by a batch file. These are listed in Table 16-1.

The BACKUP program underwent a major revision for DOS 3.0 and again for DOS 3.2. That divides backups into three categories: prior to DOS 2.0, DOS 3.0 and 3.1, and DOS 3.2 and later. A backup disk produced in one of these three categories can't be used by the RESTORE program in another category.

If you need to make a backup before you reformat your hard disk to upgrade to a newer version of DOS, the steps you need to perform are as follows:

Table 16-1 BACKUP ErrorLevel values.

Value	Meaning
0	Normal completion.
1	No files were found.
2	There was a file sharing conflict.
3	User terminated the restore process with a Ctrl-Break or a Ctrl-C.
4	The restore process terminated because of an error.

1. Boot off a floppy disk containing the version of DOS to which you're upgrading (because most DOS programs check the version of DOS they're running under and will run only under the one version for which they're written).
2. Make at least one backup of the hard disk using the BACKUP program that comes with the version of DOS to which you're upgrading.
3. Reformat the hard disk.
4. Use the RESTORE program that comes with the new version of DOS to restore the hard disk. Make sure you don't restore any of the DOS programs from the backup. This includes the hidden files and COMMAND .COM.

You can avoid these problems with a shareware program called Restore 5.1. Restore 5.1 will restore DOS backups from any DOS version to a computer running any DOS version. To obtain a copy of Restore 5.1, send a blank formatted disk and $15.00 to the author. The address and phone number are:

CANADIAN MIND PRODUCTS
Suite 162
1020 Mainland Street
Vancouver, B.C.
Canada V6B 2T4
(604) 684-6529.

You should note that not all DOS version upgrades require you to reformat the hard disk. You have to do this only if the cluster size for the new version of DOS is different from the old version or if you're upgrading to DOS 4.0. If you don't need to reformat the hard disk, the steps are as simple as booting off the new DOS disk and doing the following:

1. Type SYS C: at the DOS command line.
2. Type COPY COMMAND.COM C:
3. Replace the old DOS programs with new DOS programs.

Your dealer can help you decide if you have to reformat the hard disk. If reformatting the hard disk is optional, he can explain the benefits to you.

BREAK (2.0)

The BREAK command controls how often DOS will check for Ctrl−Break. The default is OFF, which causes DOS to check during output or input processing. BREAK ON causes DOS to check more often.

BUFFERS (2.0)

This is a CONFIG.SYS command that controls how much memory DOS allocates to storing copies of data it reads from or writes to a disk.

CALL (3.3)

CALL temporarily turns the processing over to one batch file from within another batch file. When the called batch file terminates, control is passed back to the calling batch file. The called batch file must have an extension of .BAT.

CHCP

This command displays or changes the active code page.

CHDIR (2.0)

This command is used to change directories. You can also use the shorter CD command.

CHKDSK (1.0)

CHKDSK is a DOS program that examines the entire disk for certain types of errors. Specifically, it checks the directory structure and makes sure the structure of the disk matches the file allocation table (FAT). It also reports the number of files, and the space used and available. It can also be used to correct certain errors in the FAT if used with the /F (fix) option.

Many computer users think that CHKDSK checks the entire disk for problems. This is incorrect. CHKDSK only checks the file allocation table for logical consistency. The disk itself can have many problems that CHKDSK won't spot. That is why disk checking programs like Disk Technician Advanced take much longer than CHKDSK to run. The errors CHKDSK does spot are:

Lost clusters   CHKDSK follows all the chains in the FAT to make sure they have an associated directory entry. Those that don't are called lost clusters because they've lost their directory entry. CHKDSK can convert these to files that it places in the root directory with the names FILE0000.CHK, FILE0001.CHK, and so on.

Invalid subdirectory entries   This is a subdirectory that's not attached to a parent directory. CHKDSK can convert this to a file. When it does that, all the files that were in that subdirectory are lost clusters because they no longer have a directory entry.

Cross-linked files   These are two or more file allocation table chains that merge into a common cluster. At least one of these files is damaged because two files can't legally share a cluster. CHKDSK won't correct this problem—it just points it out. To correct it, note the names of the files involved, copy them to new names, and then delete the old names. Because at least one of these new files is damaged, you must manually examine each one to see if it's still usable.

Allocation error   This is when the size stored in the directory doesn't match the number of clusters. For example, if a directory is 1,000 bytes, CHKDSK expects to find two 512-byte clusters in the file chain. CHKDSK changes the length in the directory to match the number of clusters it finds.

Invalid cluster   This happens when a file chain points to a cluster that's marked in the file allocation table as being empty.

Although CHKDSK attempts to correct many of the errors it spots, its corrections need to be checked by a knowledgeable user to make sure the actions it took resulted in usable files.

CLS (2.0)

The CLS command clears the screen.

COM

COM1 is the first communication port, COM2 is the second, and so on. This DOS designation is useful for directing output with the MODE command or DOS piping.

COMMAND (1.0)

This command loads COMMAND.COM as a secondary command processor. The complete syntax is:

    [drive] [path] COMMAND [drive2] [path2] [/E:xxxxx] [/P] [/C string]

The [*drive*] and [*path*] specify the location of COMMAND.COM. They aren't required if COMMAND.COM is in the path. The [*drive2*] and [*path2*] specifications tell the second COMMAND.COM where to look for the transient portion of COMMAND.COM if it's been overwritten. This is exactly like the COMSPEC command for the original COMMAND.COM. The /E:*xxxxx* increases the environmental space by the specified amount. The optional /P switch forces this COMMAND.COM to remain in memory until the system is rebooted so the EXIT command won't work. The optional /C switch passes the string that follows as a command to the second COMMAND.COM. This command can be a batch file.

The second COMMAND.COM gets a copy of the environmental space from the original COMMAND.COM. Modifications to the environmental space of the second COMMAND.COM don't affect the environmental space of the original COMMAND.COM. Loading a second copy of COMMAND.COM is an excellent way to test batch files that access the environmental space because the original environmental space isn't affected.

COMP (1.0)

This command compares two files and reports any differences.

COMSPEC (2.0)

The COMSPEC command is used to specify where COMMAND.COM will look to reload its transient portion when it is overwritten. The syntax is:

```
COMSPEC = C: \ COMMAND.COM
```

This is a specialized command that isn't needed during normal DOS operation. The default when it isn't specified is the location where the original COMMAND.COM was loaded.

CONFIG.SYS

CONFIG.SYS is a special file used by DOS to configure the system. Most of the commands are unique to the CONFIG.SYS file, and are listed in Table 16-2.

COPY (1.0)

COPY is used to duplicate data between two DOS devices. The most common two are files. However, COPY can also be used with the PRN, NUL, and CON devices.

Table 16-2 A summary of CONFIG.SYS commands.

Command	Meaning
DEVICE =	Expands DOS to handle equipment not directly supported by DOS.
ANSI.SYS	Replaces DOS screen and keyboard handling with more powerful routines.
VDISK.SYS	Uses part of RAM as an electronic disk drive.
DISPLAY.SYS	Defines an external drive as a logical drive.
DRIVER.SYS	Used for displaying character sets from other countries.
PRINTER.SYS	Used for printing character sets from other countries.
BREAK = ON/OFF	Used to control when DOS checks for a Ctrl-Break.
SHELL =	Used to expand the environment and to define an alternate command processor to replace COMMAND.COM.
BUFFERS = #	Used to allocate space for disk caching.
FILES = #	Controls how many files the system can open at one time.
LASTDRIVE =	Used to control how many disk drives DOS appears to have.
COUNTRY =	Controls how the date and time are displayed.

COUNTRY (3.0)

This is a CONFIG.SYS command for controlling how the date and time are displayed. The COUNTRY codes are given in Table 16-3.

Table 16-3 Code values for the COUNTRY command.

Country	Code	KEYBxx
United States	001	US
Canada (French)	002	CF
Latin America	003	LA
Netherlands	031	NL
Belgium	032	BE
France	033	FR
Spain	034	SP
Italy	039	IT
Switzerland	041	SF, SG
United Kingdom	044	UK

Table 16-3 Continued

Country	Code	KEYBxx
Denmark	045	DK
Sweden	046	SV
Norway	047	NO
Germany	049	GR
Australia (English)	061	----
Japan	081	----
Korea	082	----
People's Republic of China	086	----
Taiwan	088	----
Asia (English)	099	----
Portugal	351	PO
Finland	358	SU
Arabic	785	----
Hebrew	972	----

CTTY (2.0)

This command is used to redirect DOS input and output to an alternative device.

DATE (1.0)

The DATE command is used to enter or change the date in DOS. Depending on the version of DOS, the DATE command can also change the date stored in the hardware clock.

Debug (1.0)

Debug is a program editor primarily aimed at advanced programmers editing .EXE and .COM program files. It can also be used to examine aspects of a program while it's running and to create simple programs.

DEL (1.0)

DEL is a DOS command for removing a file or files from a disk.

DEVICE (2.0)

This is a CONFIG.SYS command for attaching device drivers to DOS.

DEVICEHIGH (5.0)

This command loads device drivers into high memory. This command requires an 80386 or 80486 and EMM386.EXE loaded before you use it.

Device drivers

These are programs that allow unusual devices (like a mouse) to communicate with DOS.

DIR (1.0)

DIR will display a list, or directory, of files on a disk or in a subdirectory. DOS 5.0 added the ability to display sorted directories.

DISKCOMP (1.0)

This is a DOS program that compares two floppy disks.

DISKCOPY (1.0)

This is a DOS program you can use to make an exact copy of one disk onto another disk.

DO (2.0)

The DO command doesn't achieve anything by itself. It's used as a separator in the FOR command, and indicated that what follows is a DOS command. The batch file in Fig. 16-4 illustrates using the DO command with the FOR command to delete all .BAK files. The command DEL %%h is carried out for each file matching the command IN (*.BAK), so every .BAK file is deleted.

Batch File Line	Explanation
`REM FOR-BAK.BAT`	Remark giving the name of the batch file.
`DIR *.BAK`	Perform a directory of the *.BAK files. If the user might potentially want to abort the erasure, the batch file would need a warning and a PAUSE command to give the user a chance to press Control-Break.
`FOR %%h IN (*.BAK)` `   DO DEL %%h`	Delete the files one at a time using a FOR loop. Of course, this is just for illustration--normally you would use DEL *.BAK to delete all the files.
`DIR *.BAK`	Perform a directory of all .BAK files.

16-4   FOR-BAK.BAT, a batch file that uses the FOR DO statement to erase all .BAK files.

DOS-HIGH (5.0)

This command loads DOS into high memory and maintains the links necessary to load memory-resident software in high memory.

DOSKEY (5.0)

A small (4K) memory-resident program that saves and recalls commands entered on the command line. It also allows command aliasing, where a shorter name replaces a long command.

DRIVPARM

DRIVPARM modifies the parameters for an existing drive.

ECHO (2.0)

The ECHO command has two different functions. The first function is to switch certain DOS messages on and off. When used this way, the ECHO command has three possibilities:

```
ECHO ON
ECHO OFF
ECHO
```

When ECHO is on, DOS displays all batch file commands as they execute. When ECHO is off, DOS doesn't display most batch file commands as they execute. ECHO by itself tells DOS to display the status of ECHO. The batch file SHOWE-CHO.BAT in Fig. 16-5 illustrates the ECHO command. The default for DOS is ECHO ON. That means that ECHO will be on every time you run a batch file unless you turn it off with an ECHO OFF command. Specifying ECHO OFF in one batch, however, doesn't affect its state in the next batch file. DOS returns ECHO to on after every batch file.

The second use of the ECHO command is to display a message on the screen. ECHO displays its message, even when ECHO is turned off. The batch file in Fig. 16-6 illustrates using ECHO to send a message to the screen. When ECHO is on, the message is displayed twice—once when DOS echoes the batch file command, and a second time when DOS carries out the command and displays the message. When ECHO is off, the message is displayed only once—when DOS carries out the command.

Batch File Line	Explanation
REM SHOWECHO.BAT	Remark giving the name of the batch file. Since command-echoing is on, it will show on the screen.
ECHO	This command will display the status of echo.
DIR	Perform a directory. Since echoing is on, more information than usual will show on the screen.
COPY CHAPTER4.DOC *.BAK	Copy a file. Since echoing is on, more information than usual will show on the screen.
@ECHO OFF	Turn command-echoing off.
DIR	Perform a directory. Notice that the DIR command does not show on the screen.
COPY CHAPTER4.DOC *.BAK	Copy a file. With command-echoing off, the command does not show on the screen. However, all DOS messages still show on the screen.

16-5 SHOWECHO.BAT, a batch file that illustrates the ECHO command.

Batch File Line	Explanation
REM ECHOMESS.BAT	Remark giving the name of the batch file. Since echoing was not turned off, this will show on the screen.
ECHO	Display the status of echo.
ECHO This is a typical message	Display a message. Since echoing is still on, DOS will display this message twice.
ECHO OFF	Turn command-echoing off.
ECHO This is a typical message	Display a message. Since echoing is off, DOS will only display this message once.

16-6 ECHOMESSAGE.BAT, another batch file that illustrates the ECHO command.

EDIT (5.0)

This command runs the excellent editor added to DOS 5.0. See appendix A for more information.

EDLIN (1.0)

EDLIN is a simple line editor supplied with DOS.

EMM386 (5.0)

EMM386 loads as a device driver in the CONFIG.SYS file to perform memory management on 80386 and 80486 computers. It will also run from the command line (if loaded in the CONFIG.SYS file) to display information about the status of memory.

ERASE (2.0)

This is a DOS command to remove files from a disk or subdirectory.

ErrorLevel

ErrorLevel is one of both the most useful and least used batch commands. It allows a program to terminate and pass a one-byte value through DOS back to the calling program. This value can then be accessed from a batch file with the ERRORLEVEL batch command.

Programs can use ErrorLevel to report back to a batch file if they were successful in their execution. The batch file can then use that information to decide what to do next. In addition to a few DOS commands, some after-market products, especially compilers, support ErrorLevel. This support allows a batch file to compile a program and then go through the time-consuming linking only if the compiling was successful. For example, the batch file in Fig. 16-7 will compile a Clipper program and then link the compiled .OBJ file only if the compiling was successful.

Batch File Line	Explanation
REM CLIPPER.BAT	Remark giving the name of the batch file.
CLIPPER %1	Use Clipper to compile the filenamed in the %1 replaceable parameter. Notice there is no testing to make sure a replaceable parameter was entered or that the file exists.
IF NOT ERRORLEVEL 1 PLINK86 %1 LIB	If the ERRORLEVEL is less than one (e.g., zero) then Clipper finds a %1 file and compiles it successfully, so use Plink to link the file.

16-7 CLIPPER.BAT, which will compile a Clipper program, and then link it only if the compilation was successful.

The one-byte value assigned to ErrorLevel is retained until another number is assigned to replace it or until another .COM or .EXE program is run. This allows multiple tests on ErrorLevel, as required. The ErrorLevel test isn't a straightforward test. The following:

ERRORLEVEL 7

isn't a test for ERRORLEVEL=7, rather it's a test for ERRORLEVEL > =7. Any number greater than or equal to seven will return a true value for this test. So you need to test for the highest possible ErrorLevel first, then the next highest, and so on. Not only must you test for the highest values first, you must branch out of the testing as soon as the test is true. Because the ErrorLevel test is a greater than or equal test, if it passes at seven, it will pass at six, at five, at four, and so on.

EXE2BIN (1.1)

EXE2BIN is a program used to convert some types of .EXE programs to binary format. It's generally used only by programmers.

EXIST (2.0)

The EXIST keyword can be combined with the IF command to test files that exist in the current subdirectory or on the current disk, and take appropriate action. See IF for an example.

EXIT

This allows you to leave a secondary command processor when one is loaded. EXIT has no effect if COMMAND.COM is loaded as the second command processor with the /P switch.

External commands

There are two types of DOS commands: internal and external. Internal commands are those that are loaded into memory when the computer boots, like DIR. No program is required in order to get a directory. External commands are those that run a program from disk, like FORMAT. External commands require a program by that name in the default subdirectory or in the path.

FASTOPEN (3.3)

Large hard disks have created a special problem for DOS. It has to weed through larger and larger hard disks to find the files you request. That takes time. DOS 3.3 overcomes this problem with the FASTOPEN command. It stores the directory location of the files you've used recently in memory. This speeds up searching for files the second time you run a program or load a file. This is especially important because DOS 4.0 allows you to create very large hard disks.

Under certain conditions, however, FASTOPEN can lead to a very disconcerting error message. When you run a disk optimizer, it changes the location of files on the hard disk. The optimizer does its work in such a way that FASTOPEN won't record the change. As a result, you can get a *File does not exist* error message when FASTOPEN tries to help DOS open a file you've run before. The file still exists, but not in the location FASTOPEN thinks it is. As a result, you should always reboot to clear out FASTOPEN after optimizing your hard disks.

FC (2.0 MS-DOS only)

FC compares two files, just like COMP. FC, however, will set the DOS ErrorLevel to 1 if the files don't match, and FC has a number of switches to control its operation. Those switches are shown in Table 16-4. FC comes only with MS-DOS and not PC-DOS. In addition, not all versions of MS-DOS include FC.

Table 16-4 FC switches.

Switch	Function
A	Abbreviates the method used to display differences.
B	Performs a binary comparison.
C	Ignores cases for letters.
L	Performs an ASCII comparison, the default.
N	Displays line numbers in an ASCII comparison.
T	Treats tabs as a single character.
W	Treats all combinations of spaces and tabs as a single character.
#	Sets the number of lines FC can compare. The default is 100.

FCBS (3.0)

This controls the maximum number of file control blocks that can be simultaneously open. The format is:

    FCBS = x,y

with x being a range from 1 to 255. It's the number of FCB-opened files that can be open at any one time. The default value is 4. The variable y can be a range from 0 to 255. This is the number of FCB-opened files to be protected from automatic closure. The default is 0. Generally, the default values are acceptable.

FDISK (2.0)

FDISK is the second step to setting up a hard disk. (The first step is a low-level format, usually performed by the manufacturer.) FDISK partitions the hard disk into logical drives. Unless your drive is over the DOS 32-Meg limit or you'll be using another operating system, you generally create only one partition. The final step is running FORMAT.COM to do a high-level format.

FILES (2.0)

The FILES command is a CONFIG.SYS command that controls how many files the entire system can have open. The maximum number of files that a processor can have open is 20, assuming the FILES command allows 20. This twenty includes five predefined files, input, output, error, auxiliary, and printer. Several major programs, like dBASE III, require FILES=20. So include the command:

    FILES = 20

in your CONFIG.SYS and forget it.

FIND (2.0)

This is a DOS filter used to locate text matching a criteria. For example:

    DIR | FIND "DIR"

would display only those files containing a DIR, which are the subdirectories. The DIR command performs a normal directory. The | pipes the result of the directory to the FIND program. FIND checks each line to see if it contains a DIR. If it does, that line is displayed to the screen, otherwise, it's discarded. The match must be exact. *DIR* doesn't match *dir*. FIND has three switches, as shown in Table 16-5.

Table 16-5 FIND switches.

Switch	Function
C	Causes FIND to display only the total number of lines matching the criteria.
N	Causes FIND to display the line number along with the text for any line matching the criteria.
V	Reverses the search, causing FIND to display any line that does not contain the criteria.

FOR (2.0)

The FOR command is used to cause DOS to loop through a series of files and perform a single action on those files. There are two forms of the command. The first takes a list of files:

    FOR %%h IN (CHAPTER1.BAK CHAPTER2.BAK) DO ERASE %%h

and the second uses DOS wildcards to calculate all applicable files:

    FOR %%j IN (*.BAK) DO DEL %%j

These two formats can't be mixed. In general, the command is:

    FOR %%variable IN (file set) DO command

The FOR command must be all on one line. FOR commands can't be nested, so only one FOR command can be used on each line. The *%%variable* must be a single character, for example % %A through % %Z. In addition, you must use the same case for each FOR command. You can also use the FOR command from the DOS prompt without a batch file. The only change is that the % %*variable* must be changed to a %*variable*. The batch file in Fig. 16-4 illustrates using FOR to delete all .BAK files.

Note that DOS replaces the % %h with %h when it displays it on the screen. This is how you would enter the command from the DOS prompt without a batch file. When DOS sees a %*variable*, it always replaces it with its value. A % %*variable*, on the other hand, tells DOS to use %*variable* and not to replace it with a specific value.

FORMAT (1.0)

FORMAT prepares a disk for use. On a floppy disk, it does a low-level format, partitions the disk, and does a high-level format. On a hard disk, FORMAT does only a high-level format.

GOTO (2.0)

The GOTO command is exactly the same in a batch file as it is in BASIC. It transfers control from the current line in the batch file to the line following the name that comes after the GOTO command. The name line must begin with a colon and be directly followed by a name. Figure 16-2 shows an example of a batch file using the colon to assign a name, and a GOTO statement to jump to the name. The GOTO command is useful to control batch file program flow based on ErrorLevel or on replaceable parameters.

GRAFTABL (3.0)

This is a DOS memory-resident program to establish the extended ASCII characters for graphics mode.

GRAPHICS (1.0)

This is a DOS memory-resident program that allows you to print graphics on some dot-matrix printers.

IF

The IF command allows conditional execution of DOS commands. The ErrorLevel section, earlier, illustrates using IF, with the ErrorLevel set by the Clipper compiler, for the batch file to decide if it should link the .OBJ file. The IF command can be used to test replaceable parameters. Figure 16-8 shows a batch file that tests a replaceable parameter.

Batch File Line	Explanation
REM SHOWIF.BAT	Remark giving the name of the batch file.
ECHO OFF	Turn command-echoing off.
IF %1==A First parameter was an A	If the user entered a capital A, echo that fact to the user. As explained in the text, this batch file will not operate properly when the user does not enter a replaceable parameter on the command line.
NOT %1==A ECHO First parameter was not an A	If the user did not enter a capital A, echo that fact to the user.

16-8 SHOWIF.BAT, a batch file that uses the IF command to test a replaceable parameter.

Unfortunately, DOS isn't very smart in making these comparisons, as shown in the batch file in Fig. 16-8. When run, DOS replaces %1 with the first parameter, which is nothing in this case. DOS then tries to compare nothing to something and can't. DOS then reports an error. The solution to this minor dilemma is simple. Simply surround the comparison with a set of symbols so DOS will compare something to something. I always use parentheses, shown in Fig. 16-9. The comparison now proceeds just as you would expect.

Batch File Line	Explanation
REM SHOWIF2.BAT	Remark giving the name of the batch file.
ECHO %1	Echo the first replaceable parameter entered on the command line.
IF (%1)==(A) ECHO First parameter was an A	If the user entered a capital A, echo that fact to the user. Notice that rather than testing the to see if the replaceable parameter was blank first, this batch file just adds parentheses around all the tests.
IF NOT (%1)==(A) ECHO First parameter was not A	If the user did not enter a capital A, echo that fact to the user.

16-9 SHOWIF2.BAT, a batch file that attempts to test a null parameter.

The IF command can also be combined with the EXIST keyword to take appropriate action if a file exists on the current drive or subdirectory, for example, the batch file in Fig. 16-10.

Batch File Line	Explanation
REM SHOWIF3.BAT	Remark giving the name of the batch file.
DIR *.BAK	List all the *.BAK files.
IF EXIST *.BAK DEL *.BAK	If any *.BAK files exist, delete them.
DIR *.BAK	List all the *.BAK files to confirm they were deleted.
IF EXIST *.BAK DEL *.BAK	Run the IF test again to show the batch file does not execute this line when no *.BAK files exist.
IF NOT EXIST *.BAK ECHO No backup files to delete	If no *.BAK files exist, tell the user that.

16-10 SHOWIF3.BAT, which uses IF EXIST to take a certain action if a file exists on the current drive and/or subdirectory.

IN (2.0)

Like the DO command, IN does nothing by itself and is used as a separator. It separates the variable name from the list of files. For an example, see FOR.

INSTALL (4.0)

INSTALL executes a memory-resident program while processing the CONFIG.SYS file.

Internal commands

See External commands.

JOIN (2.0)

JOIN is used to combine a drive and all its files into the empty subdirectory of another drive. This command is useful to prevent having to switch between drives to access information, and for making backups of multiple drives with an inflexible backup program.

KEYBxx (3.0)

This is a DOS memory-resident program to remap the keyboard for certain other countries. Values for *xx* are given in Table 16-3.

LABEL (3.0)

LABEL is a program to change (or add) a volume label to a disk.

LASTDRIVE (3.0)

This CONFIG.SYS command controls how many disk drives DOS appears to have. It sets only an upper limit; DOS still tracts the correct number. The syntax is:

```
LASTDRIVE=D
```

Note there's no colon after the drive letter. Remember that LASTDRIVE must leave room for any RAM disks you set up—as well as any unusual disk or tape drives added as device drivers, any hard disks that have been partitioned into more than one drive, and any "fake" drives set up with the SUBST command.

LINK (1.0)

This is a DOS command to connect a compiled program with its libraries. It's generally used only by programmers.

LOADHIGH (5.0)

This command loads a program into high memory. It requires EMM386.EXE loaded in the CONFIG.SYS file.

LPT

LPT1 is the first printer port. LPT1 is the same as PRN. LPT2 is the second printer port, and so on. This keyword is useful for directing output with the MODE command, and for DOS piping.

MEM (4.0)

MEM displays the amount of memory.

MIRROR (5.0)

MIRROR loads a memory-resident program that stores the information on each erased file that UNDELETE uses to unerase a file. It also creates a file that UNFORMAT uses to unformat a disk.

MKDIR (2.0)

The shortened form is MD. It created a new subdirectory off the current subdirectory.

MODE (1.0)

This is a DOS program that controls some printer operations, communications ports, and the screen.

MORE (2.0)

This is a DOS program to capture DOS output going to the screen and display it one screen at a time. The syntax for use with a directory is:

DIR | MORE

NLSFUNC (3.3)

NLSFUNC can be used in either the CONFIG.SYS file or from the command line to support country-specific information and code page switching.

NOT (2.0)

The NOT command is used to reverse a DOS decision. If the IF EXIST statement is true, then the IF NOT EXIST statement is false. If the IF EXIST statement is false, then the IF NOT EXIST statement is true. Figure 16-11 shows an example of a batch file using the NOT command.

Batch File Line	Explanation
`REM SHOWNOT.BAT`	Remark giving the name of the batch file.
`IF EXIST *.BAK ECHO There are` `backup files`	Check for *.BAK files and tell the user if they exist.
`IF NOT EXIST *.BAK ECHO There are` `no backup files`	Check for *.BAT files not existing and tell the user if there are not any. Between this and the prior line, the user will know if any *.BAK files exist.
`DEL *.BAK`	Delete any *.BAK files. If none exist, DOS will display a "File not found" error message. The batch file could prevent this by using an IF test.

`IF EXIST *.BAK ECHO There are`
`backup files`
`IF NOT EXIST *.BAK ECHO There are`
`no backup files`
	Just for illustration, again check for any *.BAK files and tell the user the results.

16-11 SHOWNOT.BAT, a batch file that uses the NOT modifier in an IF EXIST test.

NUL

NUL is the DOS version of oblivion. It's used in conjunction with DOS piping to keep most DOS messages from appearing on the screen. NUL is useful when you want to hide something from the user.

PATH (2.0)

DOS accepts four types of commands: internal commands, .EXE program names, .COM program names, and .BAT filenames. When DOS receives a command, it first checks to see if that command is an internal command, like ERASE. If so, it executes that command. If not, DOS next checks the current subdirectory for a .COM file by that name, then a .EXE file, and finally a .BAT file. If DOS finds a program with the correct name, it executes that program. If it doesn't find a program in the current directory, DOS searches the path for a .COM, .EXE, or .BAT file. If DOS finds a program in the path with the correct name, it executes that program, otherwise, it returns the *Bad command or filename* error message. These commands are shown in Fig. 16-12.

Internal Command	(DOS commands)
.COM	(Program in current subdirectory)
.EXE	(Program in current subdirectory)
.BAT	(Batch File in current subdirectory)
C:\FIRST\.COM	(Program)
C:\FIRST\.EXE	(Program)
C:\FIRST\.BAT	(Batch File)
C:\SECOND\.COM	(Program)
C:\SECOND\.EXE	(Program)
C:\SECOND\.BAT	(Batch File)
C:\THIRD\.COM	(Program)
C:\THIRD\.EXE	(Program)
C:\THIRD\.BAT	(Batch File)

16-12   The hierarchy of DOS commands if PATH = C: \ ;C: \ FIRST;C: \ SECOND;C: \ THIRD.

So the path is nothing more than a list of subdirectories to be searched when a command isn't located in the current subdirectory. The syntax is:

PATH = C: \ ;*subdirectory1;subdirectory2;...;lastsubdirectory*

Although you're better off to specify the full path, like this:

PATH = C: \ ;C: \ SYSLIB;C: \ DATABASE;C: \ WORDPROCESSOR

A problem is that the PATH command is limited to the same 127 characters as other DOS commands. This can be overcome with the SUBST command.

If you enter the PATH command with nothing after it, DOS displays the current path. If you enter PATH; DOS resets the path to nothing. This causes DOS to search only the default directory for programs and batch files. If you specify a path incorrectly, DOS won't find the error until it needs to search the path. If you enter an invalid directory in the path, DOS ignores that entry.

The PATH command is really a SET variable. The difference is that you don't have to start the command with a SET, although you could. Like other SET variables, the path is accessible to a batch file with the variable name %PATH%. So a batch file could add the E drive to the path with the command:

PATH = %PATH%;E: \

Like other SET variables, this wouldn't work from the command line.

PAUSE (1.0)

PAUSE suspends the batch file, displays the message *Strike a key when ready...*, and waits for the user to strike almost any key. The *Strike a key when ready...* message can be piped with DOS piping, making the user think the computer has locked up. The message, by the way, really means strike any key except Caps Lock, NumLock, ScrollLock, Ctrl, Alt, or Shift.

The PAUSE command is useful for two reasons. First, it gives the user a chance to switch disks when that's required. Second, it gives the user a chance to hit Ctrl−Break and stop the batch file if the next action is potentially destructive. The key pressed by the user isn't passed on to the batch file, so you can't branch based on the key pressed. Figure 16-13 shows a batch file with a PAUSE command in it.

Batch File Line	Explanation
REM SHOWPAUS.BAT	Remark giving the name of the batch file.
DIR	Perform a directory.
PAUSE	Pause the batch file and wait for the user to press a key.
ECHO FINISHED	Tell the user the batch file is finished.

16-13 SHOWPAUSE.BAT, a batch file that uses the PAUSE command.

Piping (2.0)

The piping features of DOS are very similar to analogous UNIX features. They aren't well understood because there was no similar features in CP/M—an operating system for earlier computers and from which many of the features of DOS are derived.

Data redirection is a simple concept in which data or output from one program is made available to another program. The > is a DOS piping command. It's used to route DOS messages to alternative locations.

When the alternative location is a file, > piping causes the file to be overwritten if it exists. For this reason, you must be very careful when using a > in a batch file. You should always test first, using an IF EXIST statement, before piping to a file. If the file exists, you can issue an error message and stop, rename the existing file, or pipe to an alternative file—after checking to make sure it doesn't exist.

The >> is another DOS piping command. It's used to route DOS messages to alternative locations. When the alternative location is a file, >> piping causes the messages to be appended to the end of the existing file.

The | symbol (pipe) is the third DOS piping command. Instead of creating a permanent file like > or >>, | creates a temporary file that's read and erased by the following program. A common use is in the command:

    DIR|MORE

The above command will create two temporary files, with names like 0E2B008 and 0E2B00E, to feed data from the DIR command to the MORE program. Note that MORE.COM must be in the current directory or in the path. When MORE is finished, it erases these two temporary files. The names of the two temporary files change, depending on what time and date you use the | to pipe data. Another use of | is to pipe data into a program that it needs to run . For example:

    ECHO Y|DEL *.*

will erase all the files in the current directory without asking, in most versions of DOS. That's because the DEL command requires you to confirm the deletion when you're deleting all the files, but that confirmation is piped into the DEL command using the ECHO Y command first.

PRINT (2.0)

PRINT is a DOS memory-resident program that prints ASCII files on a printer in the background while the computer is performing another task.

PRN

PRN is another name for LPT1.

PROMPT (2.0)

The default DOS prompt is a C>, which tells you almost nothing. The C indicates the default drive. You can use the PROMPT command to change the DOS prompt, and there are a wide range of prompts. The PROMPT command is normally used just in the AUTOEXEC.BAT file. When used by itself, PROMPT resets the prompt to C>.

Any printable character string can be included in the prompt, although some characters require special coding to be included. These are illustrated in Table 16-6. Any character not in this list that follows a dollar sign is ignored. The batch file in Fig. 16-14 develops the prompt I use.

Table 16-6   Metacharacters you can use in the PROMPT command.

Command	Action
$$	Display a dollar sign
$t	Display the time
$d	Display the date
$p	Display the current subdirectory
$v	Display the DOS version
$n	Display the current drive
$g	Display a greater than sign
$l	Display a less than sign
$b	Display a vertical bar
$q	Display the equal sign
$h	Display a backspace (thus deleting the prior character)
$e	Include an escape (Useful when ANSI.SYS is loaded)
$_	Include a carriage return and line feed

Batch File Line	Explanation
REM PROMPT1.BAT	Remark giving the name of the batch file.
PROMPT Ronny Richardson 999-99-9999$_$p$g	Change the prompt to my Social Security number along with the drive and subdirectory.

16-14   PROMPT1.BAT, which sets the prompt in the batch file.

It's important to remember that any prompt you develop is stored in the environmental space, along with the path and set variables. A long PROMPT command, combined with a long path and set variables, might require you to expand your environmental space.

QBASIC (5.0)

This is a new interpretive BASIC that's very similar to the QuickBasic compiler.

REBUILD (5.0)

The REBUILD command unformats a disk that's been formatted.

RECOVERY (2.0)

This is a program to check files for damage and to rebuild a damaged disk directory. The program is limited and often causes more damage than it will correct.

REM (1.0)

The REM command is used to document the batch file. If ECHO is off, the remarks won't show on the screen when the batch file is running. The REM lines have no impact on the functioning of a batch file. Blank remark lines can be used to space out the batch file in order to improve readability. They will slightly slow down the batch file. Beginning with DOS 4.0, remarks can also be used in the CONFIG.SYS file.

REN (1.0)

This is short for RENAME, which changes the name of a file or group of files.

Replaceable parameters

See %0 – %9.

REPLACE (3.2)

This command is used to update files that already exist, or add new files to a directory. REPLACE sets ErrorLevel values that can be used by batch files. These values are listed in Table 16-7.

Table 16-7 REPLACE ErrorLevel codes.

Code	Meaning
0	Normal completion.
1	Ctrl-Break or Ctrl-C used to abort or an "Abort, Retry or Ignore" prompt was displayed and the user selected Abort.
2	File not found.
3	The specified path was not found or the specified path was too long.
5	Access to the file was denied by the operating system.
8	Insufficient memory to complete the process.
11	An error on the command line, for example, using an invalid parameter.
15	An invalid drive was specified.
25	An invalid version of DOS is being used.

RESTORE (2.0)

This is a program to recover hard disk files stored on floppies with the BACKUP program. RESTORE returns ErrorLevel values that can be used by a batch file. These values are listed in Table 16-8. See BACKUP for more on RESTORE.

Table 16-8 RESTORE ErrorLevel codes.

Value	Meaning
0	Normal completion.
1	No files were found.
2	There was a file sharing conflict.
3	The user terminated the restore with a Ctrl-Break or a Ctrl-C.
4	The restore process terminated because of an error.

RMDIR (2.0)

The short form for this command is RD. It removes an empty subdirectory from a disk.

SELECT (3.0)

This sets the keyboard, date, and time formats.

SET (2.0)

The SET command has two functions. By itself, it displays the contents of the DOS environment. When used with a variable, it stores the value of that variable in the DOS environment. The batch file in Fig. 16-15 is used to set the variable TEMP into the environment.

Batch File Line	Explanation
`@ECHO OFF`	Turn command-echoing off.
`REM SHOWSET.BAT`	Remark giving the name of the batch file.
`SET`	Display the environment.
`SET TEMP=Variable used by a program`	Place an environmental variable into the environment. If the environment has not been expanded, the entire contents might not fit.
`SET`	Display the environment now that the new variable has been added.

16-15 SHOWSET.BAT, which shows modifying the environment with the SET command.

It's important to remember that any variables you set are stored in the environmental space, along with the path and prompt. A long prompt combined with a long path and SET variable might require you to expand your environmental space.

Batch files can use the SET variable for branching, by using the name surrounded by percent signs. If a variable is set with the name TEMP, then a batch file can access it with %TEMP%. Also, a SET variable can be removed from the environment with the:

```
SET TEMP=
```

command. This command can be issued from a batch file or from the DOS prompt. It releases the variable and frees up the environmental space used to store that variable.

SETVER (5.0)

This command causes DOS to "lie" to a program about the version of DOS running. That way, you can run programs under DOS 5.0 that require a different version of DOS.

SHARE

SHARE is a program that allows network users to install file-sharing and file-locking routines. DOS version 4 also requires it for hard disks over 32 Megs. This requirement was removed in DOS 5.0.

SHELL (2.0)

This is a CONFIG.SYS command used to expand the DOS environment, change where DOS looks for COMMAND.COM, and load a different command interpreter. The syntax is:

```
SHELL = C:\COMMAND.COM
```

SHIFT (2.0)

The SHIFT command is used to assign all replaceable parameters a new variable number that's one lower than the prior number. %0 is dropped, %1 becomes %0, %2 becomes %1, and so on. If more than nine replaceable parameters are entered, the next unused parameter becomes %9. The SHIFT command can be used as many times as required. An example of a batch file using the SHIFT command is shown in Fig. 16-16.

Batch File Line	Explanation
`REM SHOWSHIF.BAT`	Remark giving the name of the batch file.
`ECHO %0 %1 %2 %3 %4 %5 %6 %7 %8 %9`	Display the first ten environmental variables in order.
`SHIFT`	Move all the environmental variables down one level.

`ECHO %0 %1 %2 %3 %4 %5 %6 %7 %8 %9`
`SHIFT`
`ECHO %0 %1 %2 %3 %4 %5 %6 %7 %8 %9`
`SHIFT`
`ECHO %0 %1 %2 %3 %4 %5 %6 %7 %8 %9`
`SHIFT`
	Display the first ten environmental variables in order to move all the environmental variables down one level--three times.

`ECHO %0 %1 %2 %3 %4 %5 %6 %7 %8 %9`	Display the first ten environmental variables in order.

Fig. 16-16 SHOWSHIFT.BAT, which shows the use of the SHIFT command.

SORT (2.0)

This is a DOS filter, like MORE. It rearranges lines of data into alphabetical order and can also be used in stand-alone mode to sort a file. To obtain a sorted directory, enter:

```
DIR | SORT
```

The DIR produces a directory, and the | symbol pipes the output to the SORT program, which sorts it.

The SORT command has two switches, /# and /R. The /# causes SORT to sort each line beginning with the text in number column specified by #. The /R causes a reverse sort, where B comes before A. So

```
DIR | SORT/R/ + 10
```

would produce a directory sorted in reverse order based on the extension, which begins in column ten. The /R must come before the /# or SORT will ignore it. In earlier versions of DOS, text is sorted by ASCII number, so ZEBRA comes before aardvark. This is corrected beginning with DOS 3.0.

STACKS (3.2)

The stack is the memory DOS uses to save information when processing is interrupted. The stack also acts as a temporary storage area while DOS is running a program. Because DOS sometimes needs to process simultaneous interrupts, it sets up a fairly large stack. The default is nine 128-byte areas. Some programs assume the stack will be large enough for all their needs and just use it as required. Sometimes a complex task, however, can result in a situation where the stack isn't large enough. If that ever happens, you have to increase the size of the stack. The command syntax is:

```
STACKS = x,y
```

where x is the number of stack frames and y is their size. The variable x can vary from 8 to 64 and the default is 9, and y can vary from 32 bytes to 512 bytes and 128 bytes is the default. You should change from the default values only if you receive a *Fatal internal stack failure, system halted* error message.

SUBST (3.1)

This command substitutes a drive letter for a subdirectory. This shortens path statements and allows older programs that don't support directories (like Word-Star 3.3) to be used on a hard disk. The correct syntax is:

```
SUBST D: C: \ SYSLIB \ LEVEL1 \ LEVEL2
```

You can use D: anywhere you would have used C: \ SYSLIB \ LEVEL1 \ LEVEL2, including a path statement. Generally speaking, you won't set a path before using the SUBST command. Therefore, either SUBST.EXE must be in the root directory or you must change to the directory containing it before you issue the SUBST command.

SYS (1.0)

The SYS command is used to transfer the two DOS hidden files to another disk.

TIME (1.0)

The TIME command is used to enter or change the time known to DOS. Depending on the version of DOS, the TIME command can also change the time stored in the system clock.

TREE (2.0)

TREE can display a complete directory map.

TRUENAME (4.0)

This is an undocumented command that cuts through all the drive substitutions and assignments, and gives the true name and location of a file. While undocumented, the command continues to work in DOS 5.0.

TYPE (1.0)

TYPE allows you to display the contents of an ASCII file on the screen. It's identical to specifying:

```
COPY file CON
```

If you use TYPE to display a binary (program) file, you'll see a lot of funny characters on the screen and the computer will beep a lot. All this happens because DOS has trouble displaying binary codes and interprets some of them as the command to ring the bell.

Note that you can't use wildcards in conjunction with the TYPE command. However, you can use the interactive version of the FOR batch command as follows:

```
FOR %j IN (*.DOC) TYPE %j
```

USER

Some older versions of DOS include the keyword USER. Where it's available, it's a direct replacement for CON. Because it has no advantage over CON and CON is always available, however, you should use CON wherever possible.

UNDELETE (5.0)

UNDELETE is a utility like the unerase program in the Norton Utilities that recovers an erased file.

UNFORMAT (5.0)

The UNFORMAT command recovers a formatted disk.

VER (2.0)

VER displays the current version of DOS in use.

VERIFY (2.0)

The VERIFY command is used to control whether or not DOS checks data once it's written to disk.

VOL (2.0)

VOL is used to display a disk volume label.

XCOPY (3.2)

This is a more powerful version of the COPY command. The main differences are that XCOPY loads as many files into memory as it can before writing to the target disk, and XCOPY can copy based on the archive flag and date. XCOPY returns ErrorLevel values that can be used in batch files. Those values are shown in Table 16-9.

Table 16-9   XCOPY ErrorLevel codes.

Code	Meaning
0	Normal completion.
1	No files were found to copy.
3	User pressed Ctrl-Break or Ctrl-C to stop the copy or answered Abort to the "Abort, Retry, or Ignore" error message.
4	General error. (Any error not listed above.)

17
CHAPTER

Summary table

Command	Syntax Description	Version of DOS Added	Internal or External
APPEND	Establishes a "path" for files other than .COM, .EXE, and .BAT. Useful with .COM, .EXE, and .BAT. Useful with older programs that do not support subdirectories.	3.3	External
ANSI.SYS	DEVICE=ANSI.SYS in CONFIG.SYS file A program to extend control over the screen.	2.0	External
ASSIGN	ASSIGN B=A Reassigns drive letters so one drive appears to be another drive. Useful with inflexible programs that expect data to be on a specific drive.	2.0	External
ATTRIB	ATTRIB [+R][-R][+A][-A] *file* Change read only and archive flag of files. Enhanced in DOS 3.3 to process subdirectories as well as files.	3.0	External

Command	Syntax Description	Version of DOS Added	Internal or External
BACKUP	BACKUP C:*path**files* A: [/S][/M][/A][/D] Make copy of files on a hard disk to floppy disks. Files must be RESTOREd to be useful. DOS 3.0 adds the ability to automatically format disks while performing a backup, and the ability to backup files modified after a certain date. Backups created prior to DOS 3.0 are not compatible with later RESTORE programs. Backups created prior to DOS 3.2 are not compatible with later RESTORE programs. Beginning with DOS 3.3, BACKUP will format disks if the /F option is included. Also, only two files are created on each disk, CONTROL.xxx and BACKUP.xxx, where xxx is the disk number. Using this method, BACKUP is about one-third faster than prior versions. DOS 3.3 also adds a /T option to backup files modified after a specified date, and a /L option to create a log file to store the names of the backed-up files. Performance was also greatly improved. Beginning with DOS 4.0, BACKUP will format disks that need it automatically without using a command-line switch.	2.0	External
BASIC	BASIC Programming language built into ROM memory on IBM computers. Other brands do not generally support a ROM-based Basic program. Enhanced in DOS 3.3 to be more compatible with BASICA.	1.0	Internal
BASICA	BASICA *filename* A programming language, more advanced than BASIC. Many clones will name this program BASICA or GWBASIC. DOS 1.05 removed major bugs.	1.0	External
BREAK	BREAK [=ON] [=OFF] Controls how often DOS checks for a Ctrl-Break from the keyboard. Can be used either as a DOS command or in the CONFIG.SYS file.	2.0	Internal

Command	Syntax Description	Version of DOS Added	Internal or External
BUFFERS	BUFFERS=# Include in CONFIG.SYS file. Enhanced in DOS 3.3 so default is tied to the machine's configuration. Enhanced in DOS 4.0 so it can read additional sectors and use expanded memory.	2.0	Internal
CALL	CALL *batch file* Runs a second batch file from within a first batch file. When the second batch file finishes, control automatically passes back to the first batch file. Since this does not load a second copy of COMMAND.COM, any changes the second batch file makes to the environment are passed back to the first batch file (and DOS) when the second batch file terminates.	3.3	Internal
CD or CHDIR	CD *directory* Change subdirectories.	2.0	Internal
CHCP	CHCP *nnn* Displays or changes the active code page.	3.3	Internal
CHKDSK	CHKDSK [/F] [/V] A program that checks subdirectories and files against their file allocation table entries. DOS 2.0 made the corrective action (/F) optional.	1.0	External
CLS	CLS Clears the screen.	2.0	Internal
COMMAND	COMMAND *path* [/E:XX] /C *string* Loads a second command processor. Beginning with DOS 3.0, optionally expands the environment. (This was not documented until DOS 3.1.) You add it to the CONFIG.SYS file. In DOS 3.3, the Fail option was added to critical error messages to allow easier stopping of certain processes.	1.0	External

Command	Syntax Description	Version of DOS Added	Internal or External
COMP	COMP *file set 1 file set 2* Compares the contents of two sets of files to see if they are the same. Beginning with DOS 2.0 adds the use of wildcards.	1.0	External
COMSPEC	COMSPEC= Include in CONFIG.SYS file. Defines an alternate path to COMMAND.COM.	2.0	Internal
COPY	COPY *drive:\path\file drive:\path\file* [/A][/B][/V] Copy files from one location to another. DOS 2.0 added binary (/b) copying and verification (/v) while copying.	1.0	Internal
COUNTRY	COUNTRY=# Include in CONFIG.SYS file. Added as internal command in DOS 3.0 and changed to external command in DOS 3.3.	3.0/3.3	Internal/External
CTTY	CTTY *device* Use remote terminal in place of console.	2.0	Internal
DATE	DATE Set system date. External command prior to DOS 1.1 Beginning with DOS 3.3, it also sets the time in the CMOS clock.	1.0	Internal
DEBUG	DEBUG *file* Examine and modify files, memory, or disk contents.	1.0	External
DEL	DEL *files* /P Remove files from a disk. /P (prompt before erasing each file) was added in DOS 4.0.	1.1	Internal
DEVICE	DEVICE=*driver* Attach a device driver to DOS. Include in CONFIG.SYS file.	2.0	Internal
DEVICEHIGH	DEVICEHIGH *driver* Loads device drivers into high memory. Requires a 80386SX, 80386 or 80486 computer and EMM386 loaded first.	5.0	Internal

Command	Syntax Description	Version of DOS Added	Internal or External
DIR	DIR [PATH] *files* [/P][/W] [/O*option*] List files on a disk or in a subdirectory. DOS 2.0 added a volume label and time to the directory display. Note that DIR handles wildcards differently from other programs. Specifically, DIR * will display the same files as will DIR *.* while other programs require the full file specification. This can cause some confusion when a batch file uses the DIR command to display files and then the DEL command to delete them. DOS 5.0 added the option to sort the display with the /O option. Sorting methods are name, extension, date, and size. The normal sort is smallest to largest and can be reversed by preceding the switch with a negative sign.	1.0	Internal
DISKCOMP	DISKCOMP *drive drive* [/1][/8] Compare two floppy disks to see if they are the same.	1.0	External
DISKCOPY	DISKCOPY *drive drive* [/1] Make an exact copy of one disk on second disk.	1.0	External
DISPLAY.SYS	DEVICE=DISPLAY.SYS Device driver for displaying the character sets from other countries on the screen.	3.3	External
DO	FOR %J IN (*.*) DO *command* Part of the FOR command.	2.0	Internal
DOS	DOS=[HIGH/LOW] [UMB/NOUMB] DOS=HIGH loads most of DOS into high memory. The UMB option keeps certain links open, allowing memory resident software to be loaded into free high memory. This requires a 80286 or higher processor.	5.0	Internal
DOSKEY	DOSKEY /reinstall /bufsize= /dmacs /dhist macro= [insert/overstrike] Loads a small (4K) program to recall prior commands and allow command alaising. Options include: Loading more than one copy. Changing the buffer size. Listing the macros. Listing the available commands. Defining a macro. Altering the default insert/overstrike mode for editing.	5.0	Internal

Command	Syntax Description	Version of DOS Added	Internal or External
DRIVER.SYS	DEVICE=DRIVER.SYS /D[/C][/F:f][/H:hh][/N][/S:ss][/T:tt] Gives new names to logical devices.	3.2	External
DRIVPRAM	DRIVPRAM /d:*number* /c /f:*factor* /h:*heads* /i /n /s:*sectors* /t:*tracks* Modifies the parameters used for an existing drive.	3.2	Internal
ECHO	ECHO *on off message* Display a message on the screen.	2.0	Internal
EDIT	EDIT *filename* Runs the excellent ASCII editor included with DOS 5.0. This editor is very much like the editor built into Quickbasic.	5.0	External
EDLIN	EDLIN *file* Simple ASCII file editor. Major improvements were introduced with DOS 2.0.	1.0	External
EMM386	EMM386 [on/off/auto] [w=on/off] This is the DOS 5.0 memory manager for 80386SX, 80386, and 80486 computers. It simulates expanded memory using extended memory and it allows the loading of device drivers and memory-resident software in high memory. It also enables and disables support for the Weitek coprocessor.	5.0	External
ERASE	ERASE *files* /P Remove files from a disk. /P (prompt before erasing each file) was added in DOS 4.0.	1.0	Internal
ERRORLEVEL	IF ERRORLEVEL # DO *command* Batch file command for reading ERRORLEVEL as set by other programs.	2.0	Internal
EXE2BIN	EXE2BIN *files files* Convert .EXE files to binary format. (Not all files can be converted.)	1.1	External
EXIST	IF EXIST *.* command Batch file command for testing if a file is present. Part of IF statement.	2.0	Internal

Command	Syntax Description	Version of DOS Added	Internal or External
EXIT	EXIT Removes the most recently loaded COMMAND.COM from memory. Has no impact if only one copy is in memory.	2.0	Internal
FASTOPEN	FASTOPEN drive:=*xx,yy* The FASTOPEN command remembers where files are located on a disk once you use them once. That makes repeated access to the files much faster. The drive is the drive to use FASTOPEN on, it should be a hard disk. The xx is the number of files and subdirectories to retain in memory. The range is 10-999 and the default is 34. The yy is the number of continuous space buffers for the files identified. This is omitted if you specify a drive letter but no value for xx; otherwise, its default is 34. FASTOPEN can use a /X switch to perform its functions in expanded memory beginning with DOS 4.0. FASTOPEN does not adjust the location it has for files if you run a disk optimizer. Therefore, you must reboot after optimizing or DOS will not be able to find files when you have used the files before and FASTOPEN tries to help DOS locate those files.	3.3	External
FC	FC *file1 file2* [/A/B/C/L/LB#/N/T/W/#] Compares two files and reports on any differences. Also sets the DOS ERRORLEVEL to one if the files are different.	2.0	External (MS DOS Only)
FCBS	FCBS=# Controls the maximum number of File Control Blocks that can be simultaneously open. Include in CONFIG.SYS file.	3.0	Internal
FDISK	FDISK Initializes and partitions a hard disk. Required before FORMATting a hard disk. Beginning in DOS 3.3, it supports multiple DOS partitions.	2.0	External
FILES	FILES=# Controls how many files the entire system can have open at once. Include in CONFIG.SYS file.	2.0	Internal
FIND	FIND [/V][/C][/N] "*string*" A filter for locating lines that contain a specific set of ASCII characters. Must be an exact match, including case. Generally used with DOS piping commands.	2.0	External

Command	Syntax Description	Version of DOS Added	Internal or External
FOR	FOR %%j IN (SET) DO *command* Loop through items in (SET) and perform the command once per item. Generally used in batch file although it can also be used from the command line. When used from the command line, only one percent sign is used.	2.0	Internal
FORMAT	FORMAT *drive* [/S][/1][/8][/V][/N][/4] A program to prepare a diskette or hard disk for use. On a floppy disk, FORMAT performs a low-level formatting, a partitioning, and a high-level format. On a hard disk, FORMAT performs only the high-level formatting. FDISK performs the partitioning. DOS contains no low-level formatting. Must be included with the drive or performed at factory. DOS 2.0 added a volume label (/v). DOS 3.2 added protection to prevent accidentally formatting a hard disk. You must include the drive letter to format the default drive. In addition, you must enter the volume label to format a hard disk.	1.0	External
GOTO	GOTO *label* Batch file looping command.	2.0	Internal
GRAFTABL	GRAFTABL Memory resident program to load high-order characters into memory for graphic mode.	3.0	Internal
GRAPHICS	GRAPHICS Memory resident program to allow screen-print to print graphic screens. Beginning with DOS 3.3, it is compatible with thermal and LCD printers.	2.0	External
IF	IF [NOT] *condition command* Batch command to conditionally execute commands.	2.0	Internal
IN	FOR %J IN (*.*) DO *command* Part of the FOR command.	2.0	Internal

Command	Syntax Description	Version of DOS Added	Internal or External
INSTALL	INSTALL=*drive:\path\file* Runs a memory resident program while processing the CONFIG.SYS file. Only a few memory resident programs, like SHARE, can be run this way.	4.0	Internal
JOIN	JOIN *path* [/D] A command to treat all the files in one drive or subdirectory as though they were in another.	3.1	External
KEYB??	KEYB[FR][GR][IT][SP][UK] A memory resident program to change the keyboard translation and date and time formats for other countries.	3.0	External
LABEL	LABEL *drive label* Enter or change a volume label.	3.0	External
LASTDRIVE	LASTDRIVE= CONFIG.SYS command to specify the last drive. This command may be unnecessary in DOS 3.1 and higher. In these versions, the default last drive is E. If you specify a LASTDRIVE, you add 2K of overhead to DOS.	3.0	Internal
LINK	LINK Run the LINK program. Generally only used by programmers.	1.0	External
LOADHIGH	LOADHIGH *drive:\path\file* Loads a memory resident program into high memory. This requires a 80386SX or higher processor.	5.0	Internal
MD or MKDIR	MD [*drive*] *name* Create a subdirectory.	2.0	Internal
MEM	MEM [/program] [/debug] Displays the amount of memory a system has quickly, without having to run the slower CHKDSK. It can also display the programs and internal drivers loaded into memory.	4.0	External
MIRROR	MIRROR [drives:] [/t drives[-entries]] [/1] [/u] Records information on disks that undelete and rebuild use to recover deleted files or formatted disks.	5.0	External

Command	Syntax Description	Version of DOS Added	Internal or External
MODE	MODE [LPT1=COM] A program that controls the screen, printer, speed, display, and other important functions. Exact usage will depend on the brand of computer and the version of DOS in use. Major improvements made in DOS 1.1. DOS 3.3 adds support for COM3 and COM4 and transfer rates up to 19.2 Kbps.	1.0	External
MORE	DIR | MORE Program to scroll data to the screen one screen full at a time.	2.0	External
NOT	IF NOT Batch file command for reversing a DOS decision. If the IF test is true, then the IF NOT test is false.	2.0	Internal
NLSFUNC	NLSFUNC *filename* Used in either the CONFIG.SYS file or from the command line to support country-specific information and code-page switching.	3.3	External
PATH	PATH=C:\;B:\;A:\;*path* Control what drives and subdirectories DOS searches for programs and batch files.	2.0	Internal
PAUSE	PAUSE Batch file command to suspend execution until a key is pressed.	1.0	Internal

PRINT	PRINT *drive*:*path**file* [/D:*device*] [/B:*buffer size*]
	    [/U:*busyticks*] [/M:*maximum ticks*]
	    [/S:*time slice*] [/Q:*queue size*] [/T] [/C] [/P]
	
	Memory resident program to print ASCII files in background while computer doing something else.
	
	DOS 3.0 changes the way PRINT gets CPU time for printing.
		2.0	External

PRINTER.SYS	DEVICE=PRINTER.SYS Device driver for changing the printer character set to a set for another country.	3.3	External
PROMPT	PROMPT=NEW PROMPT Command to change the DOS prompt.	2.0	Internal
QBASIC	QBASIC *file* [/b] [/nohi] [/b] [/*editor*] [/g] [/mbf] Loads interpretive Quickbasic.	5.0	External

Command	Syntax Description	Version of DOS Added	Internal or External
RD or RMDIR	RD *drive:\subdirectory* Command to remove an empty subdirectory.	2.0	Internal
RECOVER	RECOVER *drive:\path\files* Command to rescue files from disk with bad sectors. WARNING: This command has the potential to do a lot of damage and should only be used by experienced users and only after making a complete backup.	2.0	External
REM	REM *text* Batch file command to enter remarks in a batch file. Nothing after REM is executed.	1.0	Internal
REN or RENAME	REN Old New Command to change the name of files.	1.1	Internal
REPLACE	REPLACE *drive:\path\files drive:\path\files* [/A][/D][/P][/R][/S][/W] Selectively replace files on a target drive or subdirectory with files of the same name from a different drive or subdirectory.	3.2	External
RESTORE	RESTORE *drive:\path\files* [/S][/P] Replace files on a hard disk with those created on floppy disks during a BACKUP. Version 3.3 of DOS adds many new features. /B:*date*, /A:*date*, /E:*time*, and /L:*time* switches to restore files modified before or after a specified date and time. A /M switch restores files modified or deleted since the last backup. A /N switch restores the files that have been deleted since the last backup. Major enhancements made with DOS 3.0. Backups created prior to DOS 3.0 are not compatible with later RESTORE programs. Backups created prior to DOS 3.2 are not compatible with later RESTORE programs.	2.0	External
SELECT	SELECT [A:/B:] *drive:\path* AAA BB A program to pick alternate keyboard and time formats for different countries.	3.0	External
SET	SET *name=string* A command to enter or delete variables from DOS environment.	2.0	Internal

Command	Syntax Description	Version of DOS Added	Internal or External
SETVER	SETVER *drive*:*path**file version number* Causes DOS to "lie" about its version number to the specified program. That way, programs that require a specific DOS version can run under DOS 5.0. This command requires a DEVICE=*drive*:*path*\\SETVER.EXE statement in CONFIG.SYS file.	5.0	External
SHARE	SHARE *drive*:*path**files* [/L:*locks*] A memory resident program that controls file sharing on a network.	3.0	External
SHELL	SHELL= CONFIG.SYS command to replace COMMAND.COM with alternate command processor or to expand the DOS environment.	2.0	Internal
SHIFT	SHIFT A batch file command to make additional replaceable parameters available to DOS.	2.0	Internal
SORT	SORT [/R][/+*n*] A program that rearranges text into ASCII order. Generally used with DOS piping commands.	2.0	External
STACKS	STACKS=*x,y* Include in CONFIG.SYS to change the number stack frames used to process hardware interrupts and their size. Enhanced in DOS 3.3 so the default is tied to the machine's configuration.	3.2	Internal
SUBST	SUBST *drive*:*path drive* [/D] A command to treat a subdirectory as a drive.	3.1	Internal
SYS	SYS DRIVE Move the hidden system files to a drive.	1.0	Internal
TIME	TIME Set DOS time. External prior to DOS 1.1. Beginning with DOS 3.3 it also sets the CMOS clock.	1.0	Internal
TREE	TREE *drive* [/F] Displays the tree structure of a drive.	2.0	External

Command	Syntax Description	Version of DOS Added	Internal or External
TRUENAME	TRUENAME *File* Displays the true name of a file. For example, if you enter the command ASSIGN A=B then the command TRUENAME B:FILE where file is actually on the A drive, the response will be A:FILE. The command is not documented.	4.00	Internal
TYPE	TYPE *drive:\path\file* Display an ASCII file to the screen.	1.0	Internal
UNDELETE	UNDELETE *file list* [/dt] [/dos] [/all] Unerase the specified files.	5.0	External
UNFORMAT	UNFORMAT [drive] [/j] [l] [/test] [/p] Unformats a hard disk.	5.0	External
VDISK.SYS	DEVICE=*drive:\path*\VDISK.SYS *size sector siz directory entries* DOS command to create an electronic drive. DOS 2.0 manual contained source code.	3.0	External
VER	VER Display the DOS version number.	2.0	Internal
VERIFY	VERIFY [ON][OFF] Control whether DOS checks data after it writes to disk.	2.0	Internal
VOL	VOL *drive* Display the volume label.	2.0	Internal
XCOPY	XCOPY *drive:\path\files drive:\path\files* [/A][/E][/M] [/P][/S][/V][/W] Advanced copy command. Unlike the COPY command, XCOPY sets the DOS ERRORLEVEL when it terminates.	3.2	External

A
APPENDIX

Editing batch files

You can edit batch files in two basic ways: with a word processing program, like WordStar, or with a batch file editing program, like EDLIN (and the upgraded program in DOS 5.0 called EDIT).

End-of-file markers

One of the biggest problems of editing a batch file with a word processor is generating end-of-file markers. Traditional word processors, like WordStar, use the ASCII character Ctrl−Z (^Z), which has an ASCII value of 26 and a hexadecimal value of 1A, to mark the end of a file. That means that the ^Z is generally the last character in the files they create. This isn't required under DOS, rather it's a holdover from CP/M. (CP/M, or Control Program for Microcomputers, was a popular 8-bit operating system that was widespread prior to the introduction of the IBM PC.)

Under CP/M, files were always stored in blocks of 128 bytes, regardless of their actual size. The CP/M directory stored only the number of 128-byte blocks used by the file, not its actual size. The end-of-file marker was placed at the end of the file in the last block to point out where the file stopped and useless information began.

Under DOS, the actual size of the file is stored in the directory. So a program can determine from the directory where a file stops and useless information begins. However, many programs still place an end-of-file marker at the end of the file. These programs can become confused when the end-of-file marker is missing. Using COPY CON to create a batch file doesn't add an end-of-file marker to the file because DOS knows that one isn't needed.

WordStar, and other word processors, have problems with files that don't have end-of-file markers. WordStar displays a string of NULs, ^@^@^@^@^@^@

^@^@^@^. You can delete this line and WordStar will add an end-of-file marker. If you try to move the cursor around on this line, however, the computer will "hang." With WordStar, you must either avoid this line or immediately move the cursor to it and delete it using Ctrl−Y.

Microsoft Word displays the missing end-of-file marker as a series of right arrows. Word has no problem deleting these characters or leaving them in the file. The presence or absence of an end-of-file marker has no effect on the operation of a batch file.

End-of-file markers can cause another type of problem when you use DOS piping (> >) to append data to a file, and the file already has an end-of-file marker. While many programs don't require an end-of-file marker, most programs recognize that it marks the end of the file.

You can see this for yourself. The included disk contains a file called EOF.TXT that ends with several end-of-file markers and a file without the end-of-file markers called NO-EOF.TXT. Issue the following at the DOS prompt:

```
TYPE EOF.TXT
TYPE NO-EOF.TXT > > EOF.TXT
TYPE EOF.TXT
```

As you can see, it appears that EOF.TXT didn't receive the text that was piped to it. In fact it did. The problem is that DOS stops processing the file when it hits that end-of-file marker. This problem is much easier to prevent than it is to cure. To prevent the problem, you can use the COPY command to strip out the end-of-file markers from a text file before piping to it. The syntax is:

```
COPY EOF.TXT/A EOF-GONE.TXT/B
```

The /A tells DOS to stop copying when it hits the first end-of-file marker. As a result, this can't be used to strip the end-of-file markers from the middle of the file you just created. It would stop copying when it hit the first end-of-file marker. The /A option should be used with care. It can damage programs and some data files. The /B tells DOS not to write an end-of-file marker to the file after copying. Now you can pipe to EOF-GONE.TXT without any problem. Of course, you could delete EOF.TXT and rename EOF-GONE.TXT to the EOF.TXT name.

Reclaiming a file with an end-of-file marker in the middle of it is more difficult. Since most programs stop processing a file at the first end-of-file marker, they're useless for reclaiming the file. The only program I know of that will ignore the end-of-file markers is the Norton Utilities file editor. Because it was written to recover erased data, it shows you every single character on the disk.

Figure A-1 shows a shot of the Norton Utilities editing EOF.TXT after NO-EOF.TXT was piped to it. The Norton Utilities splits the screen in half. On the right side you see the ASCII contents of the file and on the left side you see the identical part of the file in hexadecimal. At the beginning, on the right you see

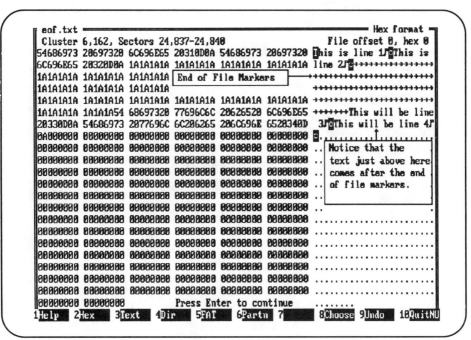

```
eof.txt ═══════════════════════════════════════════════ Hex format ═
Cluster 6,162, Sectors 24,837-24,840                   File offset 0, hex 0
54686973 20697320 6C696E65 20310D0A 54686973 20697320 This is line 1␍␊This is
6C696E65 20320D0A 1A1A1A1A 1A1A1A1A 1A1A1A1A 1A1A1A1A line 2␍␊↔↔↔↔↔↔↔↔↔↔↔↔↔↔
1A1A1A1A 1A1A1A1A 1A1A1A1A ┌─────────────────┐ ↔↔↔↔↔↔↔↔↔↔↔↔↔↔↔↔↔↔↔↔↔↔
1A1A1A1A 1A1A1A1A 1A1A1A1A │ End of File Markers │ ↔↔↔↔↔↔↔↔↔↔↔↔↔↔↔↔↔↔↔↔↔
1A1A1A1A 1A1A1A1A 1A1A1A1A └─────────────────┘ ↔↔↔↔↔↔↔↔↔↔↔↔↔↔↔↔↔↔↔↔↔↔↔
1A1A1A1A 1A1A1A54 68697320 77696C6C 20626520 6C696E65 ↔↔↔↔↔↔↔This will be line
20330D0A 54686973 2077696C 6C206265 206C696E 6520340D 3␍␊This will be line 4␍
0A000000 00000000 00000000 00000000 00000000 00000000 ␊......................
00000000 00000000 00000000 00000000 00000000 00000000 ..┌─────────────────┐
00000000 00000000 00000000 00000000 00000000 00000000 ..│ Notice that the │
00000000 00000000 00000000 00000000 00000000 00000000 ..│ text just above here│
00000000 00000000 00000000 00000000 00000000 00000000 ..│ comes after the end │
00000000 00000000 00000000 00000000 00000000 00000000 ..│ of file markers. │
00000000 00000000 00000000 00000000 00000000 00000000 ..└─────────────────┘
00000000 00000000 00000000 00000000 00000000 00000000 ......................
00000000 00000000 00000000 00000000 00000000 00000000 ......................
00000000 00000000 00000000 00000000 00000000 00000000 ......................
00000000 00000000 00000000 00000000 00000000 00000000 ......................
00000000 00000000 00000000 00000000 00000000 00000000 ......................
00000000 00000000 00000000 00000000 00000000 00000000 ......................
00000000 00000000      Press Enter to continue      ........
1Help  2Hex  3Text  4Dir  5FAT  6Partn  7       8Choose 9Undo  10QuitNU
```

A-1 Using the Norton Utilities to view EOF.TXT after NO-EOF.TXT was piped to it.

the contents of EOF.TXT before the piping and on the left you see a series of 1As. An end-of-file marker is hexadecimal 1A. Next, on the right you see the data that was piped from NO-EOF.TXT. Finally, you see data remaining from prior files that was never overwritten. By replacing the 1As with 00s, you can remove the end-of-file markers for the file. After saving the file and exiting to DOS, you can use the file without problem and all the data will be there.

EDIT.COM In DOS 5.0

Every version of DOS prior to DOS 5.0 included EDLIN, the absolutely terrible line editor, as the only means of editing a DOS text file like a batch file. DOS 5.0 still includes EDLIN, but it also includes a very powerful editor called EDIT.

EDIT looks and feels like a cross between a Windows program and the QuickBasic editor. It's a full-screen editor that uses pull-down menus, as shown in Fig. A-2. The entire program supports a mouse. There's even a "mouse elevator" on the right side of the screen for rapid movement around files. No matter what you're doing in EDIT, context-sensitive help is available, as shown in Fig. A-3.

The reason EDIT feels so much like the QuickBasic editor is because EDIT .COM is a small program that performs some minor configurations and then loads the runtime QuickBasic editor. EDIT has four menus: File, Edit, Search, and Options. The File menu has the normal options to load and save files. The Edit menu has the following four options:

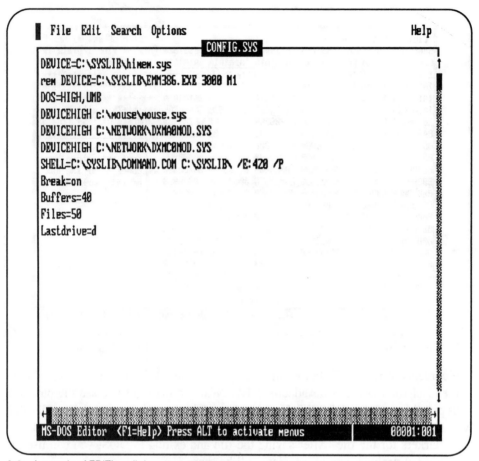

File Edit Search Options   Help

```
                        ┌─────────CONFIG.SYS─────────┐
DEVICE=C:\SYSLIB\himem.sys                                      ↑
rem DEVICE=C:\SYSLIB\EMM386.EXE 3000 M1                         █
DOS=HIGH,UMB
DEVICEHIGH c:\mouse\mouse.sys
DEVICEHIGH C:\NETWORK\DXMA0MOD.SYS
DEVICEHIGH C:\NETWORK\DXMC0MOD.SYS
SHELL=C:\SYSLIB\COMMAND.COM C:\SYSLIB\ /E:420 /P
Break=on
Buffers=40
Files=50
Lastdrive=d


                                                               ↓
MS-DOS Editor  <F1=Help> Press ALT to activate menus      00001:001
```

A-2   A sample of EDIT's pull-down menu system.

Cuts   This cuts the highlighted text out of the document into the scrap.

Copy   This copies the highlighted text to the scrap without disturbing the high-lighted text.

Paste   This copies the text in the scrap to the document at the cursor position. It doesn't disturb the contents of the scrap, so you can make multiple copies.

Clear   This clears the contents of the scrap.

And the Search menu has three options:

Find   This lets you locate the next occurrence of text.

Repeat Last Find   This lets you find the next occurrence of text after searching once.

Change   This lets you perform a search and replace on text.

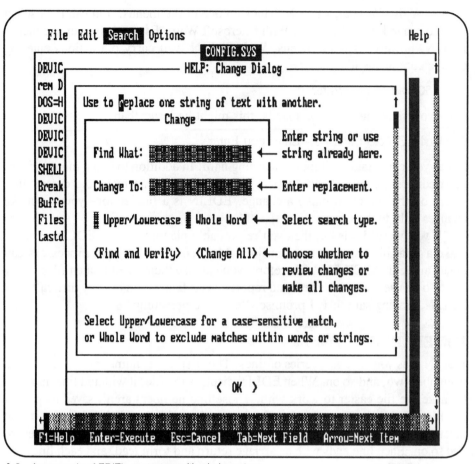

A-3 An example of EDIT's context-sensitive help system.

The Options menu lets you change the path to the help file and change the colors displayed on the screen. EDIT allows you to edit files as large as will fit into memory. I've successfully used it to edit files as large as 250K without any problems. All in all, it's a fantastic replacement for EDLIN.

The EDLIN editor

Most computer books have a chapter covering the EDLIN editor. Writing about EDLIN is popular because it comes with DOS, so everyone has a copy. If you need to explain how to edit a file, you can use EDLIN commands and most of the people you're talking to will have access to the program. If you use WordStar commands (for example) not all your listeners will have WordStar.

In spite of this advantage, EDLIN is poorly understood. And with good reason. EDLIN has two major disadvantages over word processing programs— EDLIN is command driven and it's a line editor. Most word processors are menu driven. With WordStar, Ctrl—K brings up one of the menus. You can then select your command from the menu. With Microsoft Word, Escape brings up the menu. EDLIN, however, has no menus. With EDLIN, you carry out actions entering cryptic commands like:

1,50R*old* ^Z *new* Enter

Once you've learned the commands, this might be faster than

Ctrl—Q A*old* Enter *new* Enter ngu Enter

But as you can imagine, it makes learning hard. In addition to being menu driven, most editors are full-screen editors. That means you can move the cursor anywhere on the screen to make a change. EDLIN is a line editor—you can make changes only to the current line.

If you've read this far, then you're probably planning to use EDLIN. Let me make a final plea for you to reconsider. Most commercial word processors can create and edit ASCII files. Therefore, you can use them to edit batch files. They can also be used to write letters and reports, tasks that would be very difficult with EDLIN. Having said that, I promise, "no more preaching."

How EDLIN views your files

EDLIN sees your file as a series of lines. The first line is number one, the second is number two, and so on. When EDLIN displays the file, it will add line numbers to make the file easier to work with. Those line numbers aren't saved as part of the file. The lines are renumbered after you've added or deleted lines. If you delete line six, then line seven becomes line six, line eight becomes line seven, and so on. Each line ends with a carriage return and form feed, and each line consists of ASCII text.

EDLIN keeps track of only the current line, the line you're currently working on. When you list a file, EDLIN marks the current line with an asterisk (*). When you give EDLIN a command, you can tell it to apply that command to the current line, or you can specify a set of line numbers.

Like most contemporary word processors, EDLIN has a built-in safety feature. When you edit a file, the first thing it does is make a copy of that file with a .BAK (backup) extension. That way, if you make a mistake while editing, you can always go back to the old version. Each time you save the file, the version you saved the last time replaces the .BAK version. So you always have the version you're editing, the version you last saved, and the second-to-last version you saved.

Using EDLIN

Using EDLIN requires that EDLIN.COM be in the current directory or in the search path. To edit a file, enter the following at the DOS prompt:

EDLIN *filename.extension*

If EDLIN doesn't find the specified file, it will report *New file* to indicate that you're creating a file. If EDLIN finds the file and it will fit into memory, it will respond with an *End of input file* message. If EDLIN finds the file and the entire file won't fit into memory, it will respond with no message. You can still work on the file, just not all at once. When EDLIN is ready to accept commands, it gives you an asterisk as a prompt.

When you've finished using EDLIN, you can use the E command (End) to quit and save your work. You'll then be returned to the DOS prompt. The E command saves your work and copies the last version to the .BAK file. You can quit without saving your changes with the Q (Quit) command. To keep you from accidentally losing data, EDLIN will verify that you really want to quit, with an *Abort edit? (y/n)* message. Unless you answer Y, EDLIN won't quit without saving.

You've probably noticed that both these commands are single letters. In fact, all EDLIN commands are single letter commands. The Edit and Quit commands affect the whole file, so it wouldn't make sense to include parameters. Other commands require additional information. The most common piece of information is which lines the command should affect. There are five ways to specify a line number:

- Leave it blank. In this case, EDLIN usually uses the current line.
- Enter a period. This causes EDLIN to always use the current line.
- Give it a specific line number, like 12. If the number is too big, EDLIN uses the last line in the file or in memory.
- Enter a pound sign (#), which forces EDLIN to use the last line in the file or in memory.
- Enter a +10, which causes EDLIN to use the line ten lines after the current line. You can also use a −10. Of course, the 10 can be replaced with any number.

EDLIN isn't automatically in Insert mode when you start. You must use the I (Insert) command to go into the Insert mode. The syntax is #I, where # is the line where you want to begin inserting lines. If you leave off the #, the current line is used. As you enter text and press Enter, additional lines are added automatically.

While you're entering lines, you can't enter EDLIN commands. To stop entering lines and return to the command prompt (*), press Ctrl−C or Ctrl−Break. You should use these key combinations only after you've pressed Return for the last line you'll be entering. If you press Ctrl−C in the middle of a line, that line is discarded.

Because you can't see much of the file on the screen, you need some way to view the entire file. This is the L (List) command. The full syntax is #,##L where # is the first line to list and ## is the last line to list. If you leave out the line numbers, L lists 23 lines with the current line in the middle. If you enter #,L or #L, then EDLIN lists 23 lines starting with the line number you specify. If you enter, ##L then EDLIN lists 23 lines with the specified line in the center.

To erase a line, use the D (Delete) command. The full syntax is #,##D where # is the first line to delete and ## is the last line to delete. Entering just D deletes the current line. Remember that when you delete lines, the remaining lines are renumbered.

To edit an existing line, just enter the line number of the line to edit. EDLIN displays the line with a blank line below it with the same number. Edit the line exactly like you edited the last command you entered at the DOS prompt. Pressing the right arrow or F1 once restores the next character. Pressing F3 restores the remaining portion of the line. Pressing the left arrow moves you back one character. Insert lets you insert characters and Delete deletes a character. Press Enter when you're finished editing. Remember that only the portion of the line showing when you press Enter is retained.

To search through a file to find text, enter #,##S*text*, where # is the first line to search, ## is the last line to search, and *text* is what you're looking for. If # is left off, then EDLIN starts on the line after the current line. If ## is left off, then the search continues to the end of the file or the end of the file in memory. If text is left off, then EDLIN uses the last thing you searched for.

EDLIN reports only exact matches, so Ronny doesn't match RONNY. If EDLIN finds text, then that line is made the current line and displayed, although you remain in the command mode. If the text isn't found, then EDLIN displays a *Not found* message.

EDLIN can replace every specific occurrence of text with a new set of text using the R (Replace) command. The specific syntax is #,##R*old*^Z*new*, where # is the first line to replace. ## is the last line to replace, *old* is the old text and *new* is the replacement text. The ^Z is part of the command and is used to separate the old and new text. This version of the Replace command is automatic. Each occurrence of old text is replaced with new text automatically. You can also verify each replacement by adding a question mark before the R.

When a file is too big to fit into memory, EDLIN has two commands to allow you to edit these files. The W (Write) command is used to move part of the front of the file out of memory and onto disk. The specific syntax is #W, where # is the number of lines to move to disk. If you leave off the #, then EDLIN will move enough lines to disk to free up 25% of the memory. After a Write operation, the remaining lines are renumbered from one, so line one is no longer the first line in the file.

More lines can be brought into memory with the A (Append) command. The specific syntax is #A, where # is the number of lines to bring into memory (if they'll fit). If all the lines you request won't fit, then EDLIN brings in only enough to fill 75% of the available memory. If the Append command reads in the entire file, then EDLIN responds with the *End of input file* message.

2.0 commands

Beginning with DOS 2.0, several more commands were added to EDLIN. The C (Copy) command is used to make a copy of existing lines. The specific syntax is *#,##,###,####*C. *#* is the first line of the copy. *##* is the last line of the copy, *###* is the line number to place the copy before, and *####* is how many copies to make. So 1,3,7,2C would make two copies of lines 1-3 and place them just before line seven.

You can move text around using the M (Move) command. The specific syntax is *#,##,###*M, with *#* being the first line to move, *##* the last line to move, and *###* the line number of the new location.

You can merge another file into the current file using the T (Transfer) command. The specific syntax is *#*T*filename*, with *#* being the line number where the file is to go and *filename* being the name of the file to merge. The merging file is unaffected.

The final command is P (Page). It's almost like the List command. The only difference is that the Page command makes the last line list the current line, while the List command doesn't change the current line.

You're probably beginning to see that using EDLIN is far more complex than using most word processors. To make matters worse, EDLIN has only two minor advantages over other word processors—it automatically creates ASCII files and it's just 8K big. Other than its small size and ability to create ASCII files, EDLIN has little to recommend it.

Summary

Some of the major points of this appendix are the following:

- When using word processing programs to edit batch files, you'll most likely have problems with end-of-file markers.
- The DOS 5.0 Edit program uses pull-down menus that work with either the keyboard or mouse, and it feels very much like the QuickBasic editor.
- There are many commands you need to know when using EDLIN, including End, Quit, Insert, List, Delete, Search, Replace, Write, Append, Copy, Move, Transfer, and Page. You use the first letter of these commands at the command (*) prompt.
- There are five ways to enter a line number in EDLIN: Leave it blank, enter a specific line number, or use one of the three following symbols: a period, a pound, a plus, or a minus sign.

B
APPENDIX

DOS redirection

Normally, you enter input from the keyboard and output goes to the screen, printer, or disk drive. This input and output is often called I/O. DOS has the ability, however, to redirect I/O to and from nonstandard locations. This is called *redirection*, or *piping* for short.

All of the piping features of DOS were introduced in DOS 2.0, and are very similar to analogous UNIX features. They aren't well understood, however, because there were no similar features in CP/M, an operating system for earlier computers and from which many of the features of DOS are derived. There are four piping symbols. They are:

> This causes output from one location to flow to another location. Many times, it's treated as input by the receiving program. When the alternative location is a file, > piping causes the file to be overwritten if it exists. For this reason, you must be very careful when using a > in a batch file. You should always test first, using an IF EXIST statement, before piping to a file. If the file exists, you can issue an error message and stop, rename the existing file, or pipe to an alternative file—after checking to make sure that file doesn't exist.

>> This is used to route DOS messages to alternative locations. It's the same as the >, except that, when the alternative location is a file, >> piping causes the messages to be appended to the end of the existing file.

< This causes DOS to get its input from the specified device or file.

| Instead of creating a permanent file like > or >>, this creates a temporary file that's read and erased by the following program. A common use is in the command:

DIR|MORE

Another use of | is to pipe data that a program needs to run into that program. For example:

```
ECHO Y|DEL *.*
```

will erase all the files in the current directory without asking, for most versions of DOS. That's because the DEL command requires you to confirm the deletion when deleting all the files, but that confirmation is piped into the DEL command using the ECHO Y command first. Basically, | means that you're using the output of what's on the left as input to what's on the right.

Devices

Generally, piping involves a DOS device. Those devices are the following:

CON Depending on the usage, this is either the screen or the keyboard. When used as the target, it's the screen. When used as the source, CON is the keyboard.

LPT# This is the printer port. LPT1 is the first port and LPT2 is the second port. You can also use PRN to specify the default printer port.

COM# This is the serial port. COM1 is the first port and COM2 is the second. You can also use AUX as the default serial port.

NUL This is an output device that causes any output sent to it to be discarded.

Filename This can be used for either input or output. Any legal filename can be used.

Filters

DOS includes three "filters" you can use to manipulate the data coming out of or going into a pipe. Those filters are:

FIND.EXE Searches each line of a file for specified text.

MORE.EXE This displays one screen of information and pauses until you press any key. Then it displays another screen of information. This continues until all the information has been displayed. MORE can't scroll backwards. The more common usages are:

```
DIR | MORE
TYPE FILE | MORE
```

SORT.EXE This sorts the file (or input) into ASCII order.

Problems

Redirecting can cause problems. The major problem is a "hung" computer. If you use piping to tell a program to get its input from a file, then that file must contain all the input the program requires. If it doesn't, you'll either have to reboot or press Ctrl−Break. Either of these aborts the program you were running. In addition, piping can get around the usual warning. For example, the command:

```
ECHO Y|DEL *.*
```

will delete all your files without asking you if you want to because the ECHO command supplies the necessary response. Those warnings are generally in place for a good reason and it isn't a good idea to avoid them. In addition, piping DOS error messages doesn't always work. Another problem crops up when you specify an invalid pipe. For example:

```
DATE < NUL
PROGRAM < LPT1
```

In the first example, NUL is used as an input device and NUL can never supply input. In the second case, the printer is used for input and, like NUL, it can't supply input. DOS, unfortunately, won't spot either of these problems and the programs or commands will wait forever for a response (or until you press Ctrl−Break or reboot).

Finally, you can destroy data by using pipes improperly. For example, if you wanted to take the data in FILE.DAT and sort it using SORT.EXE, you might issue the command:

```
SORT < FILE.DAT > FILE.DAT
```

This tells DOS to run SORT.EXE and supply it with input from the file FILE .DAT. When SORT.EXE finishes, it's to write the results back to the FILE.DAT file. However, because of the way DOS works, it erases FILE.DAT before sorting, so all the data is lost!

C
APPENDIX

Changes in DOS

DOS has been slowly evolving over the years. The pace of the changes has been slower than for other major programs, probably due in part to the fact that Microsoft is trying to develop two other operating systems: Windows and OS/2.

DOS 4.0 introduced four major changes. DOS 5.0 improved on all of these and borrowed several nice features from programs like Norton Utilities. This appendix reviews the changes in both DOS 4.0 and 5.0.

DOS 4.0

Four major changes face users upgrading to DOS 4.0: a much improved installation program, a DOS shell interface, the ability to use larger hard disks, and support for expanded memory. While these are the major changes, DOS 4.0 has a lot of minor changes as well . . .

Installation

The first change you'll notice with DOS 4.0 is that it has an installation program. Today, installation programs are nothing new to the PC world. In fact, $50 shareware programs and $500 commercial programs have had them for years. However, this is the first version of DOS to have a real installation program. (Some versions of DOS have had a Select program in the past. It would selectively copy new DOS support programs, like FORMAT.COM, over old ones.)

The installation program, also called SELECT like its lesser predecessors, will let you install DOS 4.0 on most hard disks without reformatting. However, if you want to take advantage of partitions greater than 32 Megs, you're going to have to reformat your hard disk. Also, if you're upgrading from a version 2 of DOS, you'll probably want to reformat anyway. Beginning with version 3, DOS began using smaller cluster sizes for many hard disks. Smaller clusters reduce file slack and save space. To take advantage of smaller clusters, you must reformat the hard disk.

During the installation process, DOS requires you to create a boot disk from a blank disk, so plan to have a spare handy. (If you accidently erase COMMAND .COM, you can't boot off the hard disk, and you'll need to have a boot floppy to correct the problem.) After creating this disk, Select prompts you for information such as the keyboard you'll be using, the country format for dates, and the drive to install DOS on. You have the option of updating the existing DOS files on the hard disk or copying all the files to a subdirectory. The Select program gives you three configuration options:

Minimize DOS memory requirements   This leaves the configuration parameters like BUFFERS= and FILES= at their default minimum. It also doesn't load FASTOPEN or ANSI.SYS. Programs also get as much working memory as possible. However, the small BUFFERS= and FILES= values might mean that some programs won't work. In this configuration, DOS requires about 70K. This is about 20K more than DOS 3.3, and that could make a difference with large files. The CONFIG.SYS file will contain the following information:

```
BREAK = ON
FILES = 8
LASTDRIVE = E
SHELL = C: \ DOS \ COMMAND.COM/P/E:256
```

Maximize DOS functions   This installs ANSI.SYS and sets FASTOPEN C: =(150,150). It also sets BUFFERS=25,8. In this configuration, DOS requires about 100K. The CONFIG.SYS file will contain the following information:

```
BREAK = ON
BUFFERS = 25,8
FCBS = 20,8
FILES = 8
LASTDRIVE = E
SHELL = C: \ DOS \ COMMAND.COM/P/E:256
DEVICE = C: \ DOS \ ANSI.SYS/X
INSTALL = C: \ DOS \ FASTOPEN.EXE C: = (150,150)
```

Balance DOS and program memory   This reduces the FASTOPEN and BUFFERS= values. The CONFIG.SYS file will contain the following information:

```
BREAK = ON
BUFFERS = 20
FILES = 8
```

```
LASTDRIVE = E
SHELL = C: \ DOS \ COMMAND.COM/P/E:256
DEVICE = C: \ DOS \ ANSI.SYS
INSTALL = C: \ DOS \ FASTOPEN.EXE C: = (50,25)
```

For some users, the installation program won't create an acceptable set of configuration files. For example, a mouse or external drive might require a device driver, and a cache program usually requires both a device driver and BUFFERS= set to one or two. In addition, the Select program won't configure the configuration files to take advantage of expanded memory. These sorts of changes require that you edit the CONFIG.SYS file, and sometimes the AUTOEXEC.BAT file. Nevertheless, installation is far easier than in the past.

Large hard disk

I used to think that the second most annoying limitation of DOS was the 32-Meg limitation on a single partition of a hard disk. (The 640K limitation of conventional memory is, of course, the most annoying limitation.)

The 32-Meg limitation is very real to users with large database program. You don't need a 32-Meg database, however, to feel the limitation. By the time you go through an associated index file and perhaps an equally sized scratch file for sorting, it's possible to start to feel constrained at 10 Megs. In all fairness to the designers of DOS, anyone trying to work on a database this large with a PC prior to the fast 80386-based computers had severe speed problems that far outstripped the partition limitation.

The reason for this size limitation is two technical aspects of DOS. First, all DOS disks use 512-byte sectors. A sector is the smallest division on a disk. One to sixteen sectors are combined together to form a cluster. The exact number of sectors in a cluster depends on the size of the disk and the version of DOS. A cluster is the smallest disk division that can be assigned to a file. Thus, a disk with 16-sector (8192-byte) clusters allocates 8K to a file containing only one byte. The unused space is called slack.

The second part of the limitation is that DOS stores sector numbers as 16-bit values. As a result, the largest number it could store was 2^{16}, or 65,536. Because each of these represented a 512-byte sector, there was room on the disk for only 65,536 × 512, or 33,554,432 bytes. That's the 32-Meg limitation.

Some nonstandard versions of DOS got around this limitation earlier than DOS 4.0 by increasing the sector size beyond 512 bytes. Any program that works closely with DOS (like the Norton Utilities or a disk optimizer), however, won't work with a nonstandard version of DOS containing large sectors.

DOS 4 eliminates this 32-Meg limitation by having 32-bit sector numbers. As a result, a disk can have 2^{32}, or 4,294,967,296 sectors. Each of these sectors is still 512 bytes, so the largest a hard disk can be under DOS 4.0 is 4,294,967,296

× 512, or approximately 2,199,023,255 Megs. No doubt users will one day fuss about this limitation.

Increasing the size of the hard disk partition caused several other changes in DOS. Every disk has a file allocation table, or FAT. The FAT contains a list of all the clusters and their status. The status can be empty and available to store data, allocated to a file, marked bad, or marked as reserved. (DOS doesn't reserve clusters, but some programs and copy protection schemes do.) The more clusters on a disk, the larger the FAT. In addition, DOS must read the entire FAT into memory while operating.

The FAT is limited to 65,536 cluster entries because clusters are still numbered with 16-bit numbers on a hard disk. This numbering is entirely separate from sector numbering. Each cluster requires 2 bits to mark its status; therefore, the FAT can grow to as large as 65,536 × 2, or 131,072, or 128K. That also means that clusters can grow very large on huge hard disks. Consider the theoretical maximum hard disk of 2,199,023,255 Megs. It can only have 65,536 clusters, so each cluster must be 2,199,023,255/65,536 or 33,554.43 Megs large! Thus, a small batch file would require over 32 Megs of hard disk space.

In practice, DOS 4.0 formats hard disks below 32 Megs with 2K clusters. From 33 to 256 Megs it uses 4K clusters. Beginning with 257 Meg hard disks, it uses 8K clusters.

You might be wondering why the 16-bit numbering was retained in the FAT. The reason is that 80286, 8086, and 8088 processors can handle only 16 bits at a time. (The 80386 can handle 32 bits at a time.) Using 32-bit addressing on a 16-bit machine would drastically slow down the machine. Due to the way the chips are designed, dealing with a single 32-bit number takes much longer than dealing with two 16-bit numbers.

Every DOS disk has a special record called the BIOS parameter block, or BPB, in its first sector. This contains information on the disk, like the location of the bootstrap code, the number of copies of the FAT, the disk number, and so on. Early version of DOS had room for only a 16-bit sector number. (The BPB stores just the total number of sectors on the disk.) Back with DOS 3.2, Microsoft introduced an extended format for the BPB. This extended format has room for a 32-bit FAT number. It also has 4 bytes for a serial number.

There is another reason why clusters are limited to 128 sectors, or 64K. The BPB has only a 1-byte field for the number of sectors per cluster. That limits the number of sectors per cluster to 255. However, convention requires this number to be a multiple of two. Therefore, its maximum value while remaining true to this convention is 128. Thus, the largest hard disk supported under this limitation is actually 64K × 65,536, or 4,194 Megs. And the largest hard disk practically supported under DOS 4.0 is 4 Gigs. Increasing the number of sectors per cluster to 255 raises the limit to 255 × .5K × 65,536, or 8,356 Megs. This limitation can't be exceeded without changing the structure of the BPB, even though other parts of DOS support a larger size.

Some older programs use file control blocks or FCBs to address files. FCBs have room for only an 18-bit number. To address the 32-bit sector numbers introduced in DOS 4.0, the application must use the internal FCBs introduced in DOS 3.0. This also requires loading a DOS program called SHARE.EXE. Thus, it's possible that an older program won't run at all under DOS 4.0.

Each disk formatted under DOS 4.0 gets a unique serial number, which is a hexadecimal number generated with the date and time of the format. The algorithm is fairly complex and the numbers appear random. The serial number isn't used under DOS; in fact, DOS has no support for addressing the serial number. The serial number is intended for OS/2. In the multitasking environment of OS/2, it's critical that a program know if the floppy disk was swapped while another program was running. The unique serial number provides a way to test this. It's interesting to note that even disks created with the DOS 4.0 DISKCOPY program get a unique serial number. However, DOS 4.0 disks that are diskcopied on a system running a lower version of DOS won't get a unique serial number. This could cause problems if a disk is switched under OS/2 for another with the same serial number.

The changes associated with increasing the hard disk partition size, more than any other, impact the user upgrading to DOS 4.0. None of your utilities that access the hard disk directly is going to work. You'll need new versions of unerasing programs, disk optimizers, FAT editors, and so on. The expense of upgrading all your utilities can make the DOS upgrade very expensive indeed. In fact, over nine months after its release, many utilities were still not DOS 4.0 compatible. The problem is especially acute in the shareware market.

At the beginning of this section, I said that "I used to think that the second most annoying limitation of DOS was the 32-Meg limitation on a single partition on a hard disk." After using a 130-Meg hard disk for eight months, I no longer think that 32-Meg partitions are all that bad. The basic problem is that a 32-Meg partition forces you to arrange your data into some sort of logical order. For example, my office machine under DOS 3.3 has a 20-Meg partition for programs and another 20-Meg partition for data. As a result, I need to perform a frequent backup of only the data partition. After all, if something happens to the program partition and I don't have a recent backup, I can restore it from the original distribution disks.

With a single large partition, all the data and programs are mixed up together. Unless your backup program is very flexible, you might not be able to back up only data subdirectories. Personally, I'm currently using Fastback Plus. Fastback limits you to twenty include and twenty exclude subdirectories. So you can back up the entire hard disk and exclude twenty subdirectories, or just list up to twenty subdirectories to back up. With the complex structure that tends to evolve on very large hard disks, this isn't nearly enough entries. In addition, a number of utilities programs are limited to about 200 subdirectories. I don't know how that number came about, but I just finished reviewing a number of DOS shell programs for a book and I frequently ran into that limitation. Depending on how the program works, it will either refuse to run if you have over 200 subdirectories, or run but let you use only the first 200 subdirectories. I'm in the process of purchasing a computer with a 60-Meg hard disk. I plan on formatting it with three smaller partitions (review software, everyday software, and data) and establishing a different backup cycle for each partition.

The DOSShell program

The DOSShell program is a combination menu program and DOS shell. You can add a program to the DOSShell menu by pressing F10 to bring up the program menu and then selecting Add. There are also commands to modify, delete, or copy an existing menu option.

Each menu item has a title that goes in the menu, the commands to start the program, help text that shows up if the user presses F1, and an optional password. DOSShell also provides an unusual way to enter commands. You must enter them all on a single line. You flag each command where you would press Return if you were entering the commands yourself by pressing the F4 key. You can enter a command line up to 500 characters long.

To run a menu option, move the cursor to that option and press Return. DOS Shell doesn't support pressing the first letter of the command. It does, however, support a mouse. You can run an option by moving the mouse cursor to that option and clicking on it twice. DOSShell retains about 4K while running another program.

One of the menu options built into DOSShell is File System. This is a full DOS shell. DOSShell divides the default screen into five parts. At the very top is the menu. Just below this are all the drives available, including substituted drives. You can log onto any two at once. Below that, it divides the major part of the screen in half. On the left you have a graphical tree representation of the hard disk structure. On the right is a list of files in the currently highlighted subdirectory. In addition to the filename and extension, it shows the files size and creation date. To the left of each file is a graphical symbol representing the type of file it is. Programs have one symbol, data files another, and so on. Below that is a single line listing the function keys you can use with the system.

You move the cursor around the files by tagging them by pressing the space bar. The space bar is a toggle and can untag files as well. You can also tag and untag files by clicking on them with the mouse. Once you've tagged the files to operate on, the File menu has options to run the program, print a file, attach a data file type to a program so clicking on the data file will run the program, move a file, copy, delete or rename a file, change attributes, and create a subdirectory.

DOSShell is a very good menu program and an excellent DOS shell with very good mouse support. If I were using DOS 4.0, I wouldn't consider any other menu program or DOS shell, especially because DOS includes DOSShell for free.

Support for expanded memory

Expanded memory, also called EMS for Expanded Memory Specification, is a kludge designed by Lotus, Intel, and Microsoft to get around the 640K DOS limitation on conventional memory. EMS divides memory above 1 Meg into 16K chunks. These 16K blocks of memory are called *pages*. So a 1 Meg EMS memory board would have 64 (1024 ÷ 16) pages, numbered from 0 to 63.

The area between 640K and 1 Meg is reserved for DOS. It's used for things like video display memory. However, DOS doesn't need all this memory, so some of it is available for other uses. The exact amount of memory and its location depend on the system configuration. EMS defines one or more 16K pages of this memory for its own use. The EMS manager then alternately moves requested memory above 1 Meg into these lower memory pages as programs request the contents. This process of swapping memory pages above 1 Meg into pages below 1 Meg is called *bank switching* because banks of memory are being switched around.

DOS 4.0 comes with two device drivers to allow DOS to use EMS memory. These might not work with all vendor's EMS boards, but you can also use the drive that comes with the board. Also note that these drives allow DOS to use only EMS memory. DOS 4.0 can't use extended memory unless you use a program, like 386-to-the-Max, to remap extended memory as expanded memory.

DOS 4.0 comes with three functions that use expanded memory, BUFFERS=, FASTOPEN, and VDISK. You can use these commands as you normally would, or you can use a /X command to force them to use expanded memory. Even though I have the maintenance upgrade to DOS 4, called 4.01, I wasn't able to get the /X parameter to work with the BUFFERS= statement on my true blue IBM Model 70.

Minor changes

Three new commands were added to the CONFIG.SYS file with version 4.0 of DOS. They are:

REM This is short for remark and lets you add comments to your CONFIG.SYS file to document the logic. This is really no big improvement, as I've used REM lines in my CONFIG.SYS file for years. DOS doesn't process any line in the CONFIG.SYS file it doesn't recognize so, prior to the REM command, a REM line just resulted in an *Invalid command* error message.

SWITCHES This tells DOS to use standard keyboard functions, even if an enhanced keyboard is installed. You would use this only if you were running a program that couldn't work with the enhanced keyboard functions.

INSTALL This command allows you to load some DOS memory resident software from the CONFIG.SYS file instead of the AUTOEXEC.BAT file. Regardless of the order of the commands in the CONFIG.SYS file, all device drivers are loaded before any TSR software is loaded with the INSTALL command. The only programs currently supported by the INSTALL command are FASTOPEN.EXE, KEYB.COM, NLSFUNC.EXE, and SHARE.EXE.

MEM This command rapidly shows the amount of conventional, expanded, and extended memory you have and how much is free. There is a /PROGRAM switch to show information on TSR memory usage and a /DEBUG option to show information on device driver memory usage. The information from these two switches is in hexadecimal form, so many users won't understand it.

In addition to these new commands, a /X parameter has been added to the BUFFERS= command, so you can load up to 10,000 buffers in expanded memory. As mentioned previously, I haven't been able to get this to work properly. There have been changes to some of the other commands as well . . .

MODE The MODE command changes its cryptic single-letter switches to English-like switches; however, the old form is still supported so any existing batch files will work without modification.

FORMAT The FORMAT command replaces its cryptic command-line switches for English-like switches (like /F:720 for a 720K disk).

ANSI.SYS ANSI.SYS now lets you set the video mode for up to 50 lines of text (depending on your display), and set the repeat rate for the keyboard.

FDISK In addition to supporting the larger hard-disk sizes, FDISK is easier to use. It displays partition size in megabytes or percentages, not cylinders. It also requires the volume label before deleting a partition.

COMMAND.COM COMMAND.COM has changed the way it processes explicit external commands. Normally when you enter a command, DOS searches for the .COM, .EXE, or .BAT form of that command—in that order. For example, if you have an EXAMPLE.COM and EXAMPLE.BAT program in the same directory, then entering the EXAMPLE command would always run EXAMPLE .COM. Under DOS 4.0, however, you can include the extension in the command to force it to run EXAMPLE.BAT or EXAMPLE.EXE, rather than EXAMPLE .COM. This still doesn't work with internal commands. For example, if you create a batch file called DIR.BAT and enter the command DIR.BAT, you'll get a listing of all the batch files. DOS won't run DIR.BAT.

DEL and ERASE   The DEL and ERASE commands now have a very nice /P switch that will prompt you before deleting each file.

BACKUP   The BACKUP command will now create a .LOG file on the target media and has the /F (format disks as needed) as the default. BACKUP will not back up the three DOS files (IBMBIO.COM, IBMDOS.COM and COMMAND .COM). IBM says this is to make them compatible with OS/2.

TREE   The TREE command now uses nice block graphics to display the graphical structure of the hard disk.

COPY   The COPY command now properly handles the end-of-file (EOF) marker. This corrects a problem with using DOS commands like TYPE with files that have data appended after the EOF marker. The EOF marker is a hold-over from CP/M days that isn't needed at all by DOS or most programs running under DOS. Under CP/M, the operating system stored only the number of clusters in the file. It didn't know where in the last cluster the file ended. That was the purpose of the EOF marker, to flag the physical end of the file. However, DOS stores the actual length of the file so it always knows where the file ends. Therefore, it doesn't need an EOF marker.

Conclusion

One of the things I'm always asking my statistics students is, "But does it pass the *so what* test?" That same question can be applied to DOS. Do the added functions of DOS justify the several hundreds of dollars you're going to have to spend to upgrade DOS and any utilities you use that need a new version for DOS 4.0? The answer to this question is usually No. Depending on your system configuration and usage, you might benefit from the larger partitions. The EMS support is no big deal because it was available elsewhere for some time and, in many cases, only does what a caching program does better. The easy installation is nice but is a one-shot improvement.

The flip side of the question is which version of DOS should you buy if you're purchasing a computer. Here the answer is clearer. DOS 4.0 has only a few minor problems. Incrementally, its improvements justify DOS 4.0 if you're going to buy DOS anyway and are just debating between 3.3 and 4.0. Nothing I've run into in eight months of using it causes me not to recommend it as a primary purchase.

DOS 5.0

DOS 5.0 includes a number of evolutionary changes. Many of these changes are as a result of the influence of Windows 3.0.

More memory

DOS 4.1 and all prior versions of DOS load entirely in the first 640K of memory, the conventional memory area. Because this is also the area in which programs are loaded and executed, DOS has significantly reduced the area available for programs. By DOS 4.01, DOS was laying claim to up to 60K of conventional memory. As programs have become larger and larger and memory resident programs have become more popular, many users lack enough conventional memory to support all the programs they want to run.

On 80286 and above computers, DOS 5.0 addresses this problem by loading much of itself in high memory area, or *HMA*. HMA is the first 64K block of extended memory just above the 1-Meg memory boundary. DOS 5.0 continues to need about 60K, but it loads only 15K in conventional memory while putting the rest in HMA memory.

DOS 5.0 recovers more memory on 80386 and above computers using an improved utility called EMM386. In addition to simulating expanded memory using extended memory, EMM386 can provide access to the upper memory blocks (UMBs). UMBs are the memory between 640K and 1 Meg that isn't being used for other functions. 386Max provides similar access. Using EMM386, you can load device drivers and TSR programs into UMBs—resulting in additional conventional memory for your applications.

You load device drivers into high memory using the DEVICEHIGH= command, and you load TSR software into high memory using the LOADHIGH command either in a batch file or at the command line. DOS 5.0 proved to be less efficient than 386Max on my machine—requiring 41K more of conventional memory than 386Max.

Finally, the kernel that DOS 5.0 is based on has been reduced by about 5K. These reductions came about from code optimization and removing some redundancies in DOS 4.01. This results in DOS 5.0 being only about 6K larger than DOS 3.3, in spite of numerous improvements. Of course, the use of UMBs means that, while DOS 5.0 is larger than DOS 3.3, its demands on conventional memory is smaller.

New utilities

DOS 5.0 adds a number of new utilities to DOS. These aren't new utilities to the computing community as they've been available in other packages for a long time, but including them in DOS makes them available to everyone who upgrades to DOS 5.0. The new utilities are:

Editor Edlin is gone, replaced with a full-screen ASCII editor that has a very QuickBasic-like feel. It uses pull-down menus and supports a mouse.

On-line help Many of the commands and DOS utilities have built-in on-line help. You can access the help by entering a command followed by the /? switch.

Undelete This is just like the Unerase command that's been available in the Norton and Mace utility programs for some time now. When you erase a file, DOS just marks the space as available. If you move to recover the file before the space is reused, you can recover the entire file. Undelete actually works very similarly to the only Quick Unerase utility in the Norton Utilities 4.0. You can run the program without a file specification and it will ask you about every file it finds in the current subdirectory that it can unerase, or you can start it with a file specification in order to limit its search to specific files.

Unformat This lets you recover a hard disk after it's accidently formatted. It doesn't work on floppy disks. Like most utilities of this type, it uses a program to periodically save critical information on the hard disk to a special file that's unaffected by a format, and uses that information to unformat the hard disk.

File transfer DOS 5.0 includes a built-in file transfer program for communicating with and transferring data between other computers using a null-modem cable.

A final note

I'm impressed with the improvements in DOS 5.0 and the extensive beta testing Microsoft has performed on it. I strongly urge anyone with a 80386 or 80486 computer to upgrade for the memory management features, and anyone with a 80286 or above computer to upgrade for the other useful features.

D
APPENDIX

Modifying InKey

InKey has a very nice dual personality. If you simply need a program to use in a batch file to ask the user questions, you can use one of the InKey programs off the disk and not worry about how it works. If that describes how you plan to use InKey, you should probably skip this appendix. However, if you need a specialized program, you can modify InKey to fit your needs. An especially nice feature of InKey is that all you need to construct and modify InKey is the Debug program, which comes with most versions of DOS.

If you plan on modifying InKey, begin by building your own version. In the process of doing that, you can add in your modifications. This appendix describes how to construct InKey and how to modify it.

What InKey does

Before releasing control of the computer to a COM-format user program, DOS first constructs a 256-byte work area in memory called the Program Segment Prefix (PSP). Beginning at offset 81h in the PSP is a replica of the command line that called the program, lacking only the program name itself and any DOS redirection operators that might have been present; the length (in bytes) of the command string appears at offset 80h. InKey simply reaches back into the command-line area of the PSP and writes to the screen whatever it finds there.

There are a few characters that can't be used in an InKey prompt line. The four redirection <, >, |, and > > operators are not allowed. The carriage return is also not allowed because it's the universal command-line terminator in DOS. In addition, the dollar sign ($) isn't allowed. Many of the DOS screen-handling routines require the dollar sign as an end-of-string marker. InKey respects this convention, so any user-embedded $ characters will truncate the prompt.

Constructing InKey

The first portion of InKey is the same for all keyboards and all upshift values. Figure D-1 shows the keystrokes necessary to start the program. After completing the work in Fig. D-1, the program diverges, depending on the keyboard or upshift

Debug Response	Enter	Purpose
	C>DEBUG INKEY.COM	Start Debug and specify file to create.
File not found		Debug message to let you know this is new file.
–		Debug prompt.
–	A 100	Assemble a new program.
xxxx:0100		The xxxx will be different for each computer and is not important. The numbers after the colon are the numbers listed in this figure.
xxxx:0100	JMP 0124	Skip over the data area.
xxxx:0100	DB ' INKEY.COM 3.0 – (C)1987 S. Moore',1A	Copyright notice. (Enter all on one line, not broken.)
xxxx:0124	MOV BX,0080	Point BX to command-line length byte in PSP.
xxxx:0127	CMP Byte Ptr [BX],01	Is there a meaningful string?
xxxx:012A	JBE 0139	If not, go get a keystroke.
xxxx:012C	ADD BL,[BX]	Else point BX to last character of string.
xxxx:012E	INC BX	Next character is the Return.
xxxx:012F	MOV Byte Ptr [BX],24	Change it to end-of-string marker $.
xxxx:0132	MOV AH,09	Select DOS display a string service.
xxxx:0134	MOV DX,0082	Point DX to beginning of string.
xxxx:0137	INT 21	Write the prompt.
xxxx:0139	MOV AH,00	Select BIOS get next keybd char service.
xxxx:013B	INT 16	Wait for the keystroke.
xxxx:013D	CMP AL,00	Is it an extended keycode?
xxxx:013F	JNZ 014F	No, so go process it normally.
xxxx:0141	XCHG AH,AL	Yes, clear AH and prepare to pass it back.
	Find your keyboard in the following figures and continue entering INKEY.COM	

D-1 First part of Debug script for entering InKey.

value you plan on using. Figure D-2 shows the program for a regular keyboard, Fig. D-3 shows it for an enhanced keyboard, and Fig. D-4 shows it for an old Tandy 1000 keyboard. If you're using a custom upshift value—as described later—your program would be similar to these but would use different values. After this, the work to complete the program is the same for all versions. Figure D-5 shows this.

Debug Response	Enter	Purpose
xxxx:0143	ADD AX,007B	Add an "upshift" value to eliminate aliases. You might want to change this.
xxxx:0146	NOP	Keyboard Modification Area.
xxxx:0147	NOP	Keyboard Modification Area.
xxxx:0148	NOP	Keyboard Modification Area.
xxxx:0149	NOP	Keyboard Modification Area.
xxxx:014A	NOP	Keyboard Modification Area.
Go to final InKey figure and finish entering INKEY.COM		

D-2   Second part of Debug script for entering InKey, for traditional PC keyboards.

Debug Response	Enter	Purpose
xxxx:0143	ADD AX,0059	Add an "upshift" value to eliminate aliases. You might want to change this.
xxxx:0146	CMP AX,0080	Is upshifted code valid, e.g. > = 128?
xxxx:0149	JB 0139	No? Reject and go wait for another.
Go to final InKey figure and finish entering INKEY.COM		

D-3   Second part of Debug script for entering InKey, for enhanced IBM keyboards.

Debug Response	Enter	Purpose
xxxx:0143	ADD AX,0048	Add an "upshift" value to eliminate aliases. You might want to change this.
xxxx:0146	CMP AX,0080	Is upshifted code valid, e.g. > = 128?
xxxx:0149	JB 0139	No? Reject and go wait for another.
Go to final InKey figure and finish entering INKEY.COM		

D-4   Second part of Debug script for entering InKey, for Tandy keyboards.

Debug Response	Enter	Purpose
xxxx:014B	MOV DL,7F	Echo as "home plate" character, ASCII 127.
xxxx:014D	JMP 0157	And go spit it out.
xxxx:014F	CMP AL,61	Is it lowercase a or above?
xxxx:0151	JB 0155	If not, let it alone.
xxxx:0153	AND AL,DF	Else force it to uppercase.
xxxx:0155	MOV DL,AL	Echo it as a normal character.

D-5   Final part of Debug script for entering InKey.

D-5 Continued

Debug Response	Enter		Purpose
xxxx:0157	PUSH	AX	Save AX (Int 21 Fn 2 alters AL).
xxxx:0158	MOV	AH,02	Select DOS Display a character service.
xxxx:015A	INT	21	Write character to the screen.
xxxx:015C	POP	AX	Restore the code in AL.
xxxx:015D	MOV	AH,4C	Select Terminate with return code.
xxxx:015F	INT	21	And exit.
xxxx:0161	R CX		Modify register.
0000			Current value of register.
:			Register modification prompt.
:	0061		Write size of .COM file to register.
–	W		Write .COM file to disk.
Writing 0061 bytes			Debug message.
–	Q		Quit Debug.

The Keystroke Reporting Function

An important concept in keystroke retrieval programs is that of aliasing, i.e., the reporting of a keystroke under something other than its actual ASCII identity. Aliasing can be both a desirable and an undesirable phenomenon.

One useful form of aliasing is case insensitivity. In a menu of alphabetized choices, for example, you don't want to have to test each keystroke twice—for both the lowercase and uppercase forms of a character. Removing case sensitivity, however, must be done carefully. Otherwise, undesirable aliases will be introduced. Depending on the strategy you choose, it's possible that the numeric keys wouldn't be reported accurately.

InKey converts lowercase alphabetical characters to uppercase, but lets the rest (almost) pass unaffected. Because anti-aliasing was InKey's main design goal, there are only four characters rendered inaccessible because of aliases, and those are at the very top of the standard ASCII set. The pipe symbol, the tilde, and the braces are reported as their unshifted counterparts: the backslash, grave accent, and square brackets.

Because even a slightly complex batch file might take a few seconds to determine the correct course of action, InKey displays a character to acknowledge the keystroke, so the user isn't tempted to press it again. If the key represents an ASCII character, InKey displays it. For codes below ASCII 32 (the space), the symbol assigned by the IBM PC firmware is displayed, if one exists. The only exceptions are the tab, backspace, carriage return, line feed, and bell. The returned ErrorLevel value is accurate but, rather than displaying the symbol, the cursor obeys the code. If a non-ASCII key is pressed, InKey displays the "home plate" character, ASCII 127.

The second kind of undesirable aliasing has to do with what are called *extended key codes*. The computer's built-in keystroke retrieval services (DOS Interrupt 21h Function 8, and BIOS Interrupt 16h Function 0) report a code for the character the key represents (its ASCII code), as well as a code that represents a number assigned to the key itself, based on its position on the keyboard and the status of the Ctrl, Alt, and Shift keys.

If a key doesn't represent an ASCII character—such as the function keys F1 through F10, or the cursor pad keys—only the extended code is reported. If it happens to coincide with an ASCII character code, there is a potential alias. Thus, the F10 key (extended code 68) could alias as uppercase D (ASCII code 68) and report the same ErrorLevel. To avoid this problem and make available both regular and extended keys, InKey adds a numeric upshift value to extended codes, so they're reported with ErrorLevel values from 128 to 255, where there are no "official" ASCII keyboard characters.

Modification notes

The choice of an upshift value is somewhat critical. To preserve the anti-aliasing feature, it must produce an ErrorLevel code not lower than 128 (hex 80). Because the computer allocates only one byte for a return code (the lower half of the accumulator, register AX), the maximum value of ErrorLevel, code plus upshift, can't exceed 255 (hex FF). With an upshift of 123 (hex 7B), InKey can handle the full range of extended codes supported by the BIOS for both the traditional and early AT 83/84-key keyboards. A full list of extended ErrorLevel codes is given in Tables D-1 through D-3.

Table D-1 Extended keycodes and upshifted ErrorLevel values for an 83/84-key PC keyboard.

Extended Key Code	ERROR-LEVEL	Key	Extended Key Code	ERROR-LEVEL	Key
15	138	Shift-Tab	90	213	Shift-F7
16	139	Alt-Q	91	214	Shift-F8
17	140	Alt-W	92	215	Shift-F9
18	141	Alt-E	93	216	Shift-F10
19	142	Alt-R	94	217	Ctrl-F1
20	143	Alt-T	95	218	Ctrl-F2
21	144	Alt-Y	96	219	Ctrl-F3
22	145	Alt-U	97	220	Ctrl-F4
23	146	Alt-I	98	221	Ctrl-F5
24	147	Alt-O	99	222	Ctrl-F6
25	148	Alt-P	100	223	Ctrl-F7
30	153	Alt-A	101	224	Ctrl-F8
31	154	Alt-S	102	225	Ctrl-F9

Table D-1　Continued

Extended Key Code	ERROR-LEVEL	Key	Extended Key Code	ERROR-LEVEL	Key
32	155	Alt-D	103	226	Ctrl-F10
33	156	Alt-F	104	227	Alt-F1
34	157	Alt-G	105	228	Alt-F2
35	158	Alt-H	106	229	Alt-F3
36	159	Alt-J	107	230	Alt-F4
37	160	Alt-K	108	231	Alt-F5
38	161	Alt-L	109	232	Alt-F6
44	167	Alt-Z	110	233	Alt-F7
45	168	Alt-X	111	234	Alt-F8
46	169	Alt-C	112	235	Alt-F9
47	170	Alt-V	113	236	Alt-F10
48	171	Alt-B	114	237	Ctrl-PrtSc
49	172	Alt-N	115	238	Ctrl-left-arrow
50	173	Alt-M	116	239	Ctrl-right-arrow
59	182	F1	117	240	Ctrl-End
60	183	F2	118	241	Ctrl-PgDn
61	184	F3	119	242	Ctrl-Home
62	185	F4	120	243	Alt-1
63	186	F5	121	244	Alt-2
64	187	F6	122	245	Alt-3
65	188	F7	123	246	Alt-4
66	189	F8	124	247	Alt-5
67	190	F9	125	248	Alt-6
68	191	F10	126	249	Alt-7
84	207	Shift-F1	127	250	Alt-8
85	208	Shift-F2	128	251	Alt-9
86	209	Shift-F3	129	252	Alt-0
87	210	Shift-F4	130	253	Alt-Hyphen
88	211	Shift-F5	131	254	Alt-=
89	212	Shift-F6	132	255	Ctrl-PgUp

Table D-2　Extended keycodes and upshifted ErrorLevel values for an enhanced IBM keyboard.

Extended Key Code	ERROR-LEVEL	Key	Extended Key Code	ERROR-LEVEL	Key
44	---	Alt-Z	112	184	Alt-F9
45	---	Alt-X	113	185	Alt-F10
46	---	Alt-C	114	186	Ctrl-PrtSc

Table D-2 Continued

Extended Key Code	ERROR-LEVEL	Key	Extended Key Code	ERROR-LEVEL	Key
47	---	Alt-V	115	187	Ctrl-left-arrow
48	---	Alt-B	116	188	Ctrl-right-arrow
49	---	Alt-N	117	189	Ctrl-End
50	---	Alt-M	118	190	Ctrl-PgDn
59	131	F1	119	191	Ctrl-Home
60	132	F2	120	192	Alt-1
61	133	F3	121	193	Alt-2
62	134	F4	122	194	Alt-3
63	135	F5	123	195	Alt-4
64	136	F6	124	196	Alt-5
65	137	F7	125	197	Alt-6
66	138	F8	126	198	Alt-7
67	139	F9	127	199	Alt-8
68	140	F10	128	200	Alt-9
70	142	Alt-PrtSc	129	201	Alt-0
71	143	Home	130	202	Alt-Hyphen
72	144	up-arrow	131	203	Alt-=
73	145	Shift-PgUp	132	204	Ctrl-PgUp
74	146	Shift-Home	133	205	Shift-up-arrow
75	147	left-arrow	134	206	Shift-down-arrow
77	149	right-arrow	135	207	Shift-left-arrow
79	151	Shift-End	136	208	Shift-right-arrow
80	152	down-arrow	140	212	Alt-Backspace
81	153	Shift-PgDn	141	213	Ctrl-Tab
83	155	Shift-Del	142	214	Alt-Tab
84	156	Shift-F1	143	215	Alt-Enter
85	157	Shift-F2	144	216	Ctrl-up-arrow
86	158	Shift-F3	145	217	Alt-up-arrow
87	159	Shift-F4	146	218	Alt-left-arrow
88	160	Shift-F5	147	219	Ctrl-7
89	161	Shift-F6	148	220	Ctrl-8
90	162	Shift-F7	149	221	Ctrl-4
91	163	Shift-F8	150	222	Ctrl-down-arrow
92	164	Shift-F9	151	223	Alt-down-arrow
93	165	Shift-F10	152	224	F11
94	166	Ctrl-F1	153	225	F12
95	167	Ctrl-F2	154	226	Ctrl-2 (keypad)
96	168	Ctrl-F3	155	227	Shift-0 (keypad)

Table D-2   Continued

Extended Key Code	ERROR-LEVEL	Key	Extended Key Code	ERROR-LEVEL	Key
97	169	Ctrl-F4	156	228	Ctrl-0 (keypad)
98	170	Ctrl-F5	157	229	Ctrl-Del
99	171	Ctrl-F6	158	230	Alt-Del
100	172	Ctrl-F7	159	231	Ctrl-Ins
101	173	Ctrl-F8	160	232	Alt-Ins
102	174	Ctrl-F9	161	233	Shift-. (keypad)
103	175	Ctrl-F10	162	234	Shift-F11
104	176	Alt-F1	163	235	Shift-F12
105	177	Alt-F2	164	236	Ctrl-. (keypad)
106	178	Alt-F3	165	237	Alt-. (keypad)
107	179	Alt-F4	166	238	Alt-Home
108	180	Alt-F5	172	244	Ctrl-F11
109	181	Alt-F6	173	245	Ctrl-F12
110	182	Alt-F7	182	254	Alt-F11
111	183	Alt-F8	183	255	Alt-F12

Table D-3   Extended keycodes and upshifted ErrorLevel values for Tandy keyboards.

Extended Key Code	ERROR-LEVEL	Key	Extended Key Code	ERROR-LEVEL	Key
44	133	Alt-Z	115	204	Ctrl-left-arrow
45	134	Alt-X	116	205	Ctrl-right-arrow
46	135	Alt-C	117	206	Ctrl-End
47	136	Alt-V	118	207	Ctrl-PgDn
48	137	Alt-B	119	208	Ctrl-Home
49	138	Alt-N	120	209	Alt-1
50	139	Alt-M	121	210	Alt-2
59	148	F1	122	211	Alt-3
60	149	F2	123	212	Alt-4
61	150	F3	124	213	Alt-5
62	151	F4	125	214	Alt-6
63	152	F5	126	215	Alt-7
64	153	F6	127	216	Alt-8
65	154	F7	128	217	Alt-9
66	155	F8	129	218	Alt-0
67	156	F9	130	219	Alt-Hyphen
68	157	F10	131	220	Alt-=
84	173	Shift-F1	132	221	Ctrl-PgUp
85	174	Shift-F2	133	222	F11
86	175	Shift-F3	134	223	F12
87	176	Shift-F4	135	224	Shift-F11

Table D-3 Continued

Extended Key Code	ERROR-LEVEL	Key	Extended Key Code	ERROR-LEVEL	Key
88	177	Shift-F5	136	225	Shift-F12
89	178	Shift-F6	137	226	Ctrl-F11
90	179	Shift-F7	138	227	Ctrl-F12
91	180	Shift-F8	139	228	Alt-F11
92	181	Shift-F9	140	229	Alt-F12
93	182	Shift-F10	141	230	Ctrl-up-arrow
94	183	Ctrl-F1	142	231	Ctrl-- (keypad)
95	184	Ctrl-F2	143	232	Ctrl-5 (keypad)
96	185	Ctrl-F3	144	233	Ctrl-+ (keypad)
97	186	Ctrl-F4	145	234	Ctrl-down-arrow
98	187	Ctrl-F5	146	235	Ctrl-Ins
99	188	Ctrl-F6	147	236	Ctrl-Del
100	189	Ctrl-F7	148	237	Ctrl-Tab
101	190	Ctrl-F8	149	238	Ctrl-/
102	191	Ctrl-F9	150	239	Ctrl-*
103	192	Ctrl-F10	151	240	Alt-Home
104	193	Alt-F1	152	241	Alt-up-arrow
105	194	Alt-F2	153	242	Alt-PgUp
106	195	Alt-F3	155	243	Alt-left-arrow
107	196	Alt-F4	157	244	Alt-right-arrow
108	197	Alt-F5	159	248	Alt-End
109	198	Alt-F6	160	249	Alt-down-arrow
110	199	Alt-F7	161	250	Alt-PgDn
111	200	Alt-F8	162	251	Alt-Ins
112	201	Alt-F9	163	252	Alt-Del
113	202	Alt-F10	164	253	Alt-/
114	203	Ctrl-PrtSc	165	254	Alt-Tab
166	255	Alt-Enter			

Here's how the upshift is calculated. From 255, subtract the highest extended code available:

$$\begin{array}{r} 255 \\ -132 \quad \text{(Ctrl-PgUp)} \\ \hline 123 \end{array}$$

Then subtract the upshift value from 128 to find the lowest code that can be reported:

$$\begin{array}{r} 128 \\ -123 \\ \hline 5 \quad \text{(Shift} - \text{Tab is at code 15)} \end{array}$$

Adapting InKey to accommodate the 101-key IBM Enhanced Keyboard or the older Tandy keyboards (such as the 1000)—and still preserve anti-aliasing—is not difficult. The set of acceptable extended key codes must be restricted by lowering or raising the upshift value, which creates the possibility of aliases on the lower end and exceeding ERRORLEVEL 255 on the upper end. A few additional lines of program code must be introduced to prevent this from happening.

Moreover, the Tandy and IBM keyboards access the "enhancement" keys (such as F11 and F12) in different ways, requiring further modification of InKey's code. IBM added an additional function call (10h) to BIOS Interrupt 16h for the enhancement keys; the Tandy BIOS gets them all from Function 0, which InKey normally uses. The Tandy extended key codes also are markedly different from their IBM counterparts.

Except for very specialized applications, the lowest non-ASCII key likely to be offered the user will be unshifted F1, code 59, so it's probably best to chop off extended keys from the bottom of the range. First, calculate a new upshift value:

IBM Enhanced keyboard	Tandy 1000 keyboard
255	255
−166 (Alt−Enter)	−183 (Alt−F12)
89 (hex 59)	72 (hex 48)

With these upshifts, calculate the lowest codes that will not be rejected:

128	128
− 89	− 72
39	56

The lowest available key for the IBM Enhanced Keyboard will be Alt-Z, code 44; for the Tandy, it will be F1 at code 59. To plug in these new values (which must be in hexadecimal notation):

```
DEBUG INKEY.COM
- E 144 new-upshift-value
```

For the IBM Enhanced Keyboard only, you must also change the Int 16h function call from 0h to 10h:

```
-E 13A 10
```

Finally, you will replace the five NOP instructions beginning at offset 0146 with two program lines that will enforce your new lower bound on extended codes:

```
-A 146
xxxx:0146   CMP AH,80
xxxx:0149   JB 0139
xxxx:014B
```

Though it isn't necessary, you may wish to rename the program before you save and quit, so you'll have both versions:

```
– N new-name.COM
– W
Writing 0061 bytes
– Q
```

Chopping from the bottom of the range is trickier. To calculate the upshift, subtract from 128 the lowest code you wish to report. For example:

$$\begin{array}{r} 128 \\ -\ \ 16\ (\text{Alt}-\text{Q}) \\ \hline 112\ (\text{hex } 70) \end{array}$$

To find the highest reportable code, subtract the new upshift from 255:

$$\begin{array}{r} 255 \\ -112 \\ \hline 143\ (\text{IBM Ctrl}-5\ \text{or Tandy Alt}-\text{Enter}) \end{array}$$

Use DEBUG as before to plug in the new value, being sure to change the IBM function call if necessary. The enforcement code also differs slightly, because you would be checking for an upper bound rather than lower:

```
– A 146
xxxx:0146   CMP AX,FF
xxxx:0149   JA 0139
xxxx:014B
```

Rename the program if you wish, and then be sure to Write before you Quit.

Index

| command, 314
| redirection command, 17, 118, 373, 389
$ chararacter, 118, 389
$$$ files, archival files, 100
%% variables, 48, 314
%0 through %9, 11, 22-25, 16, 313-314, 340
%variable%, 16, 29-33, 314, 330-331
+ command, 316
< redirection command, 17, 118, 316, 373, 389
> redirection command, 17, 118, 373, 389
>> redirection command, 118, 338, 373, 389
>NUL, 315
@ command, 316
0-9 utility, 126
01.BAT, 79
02.BAT, 81
1-LOG.BAT, 271-272
   1.BAT through 6.BAT, 91-92
2-3.BAT, InKey, 123
2THINGS.BAT, 4-5
3COMMANDS.BAT, 267-268
BAT, 31

A
ACCOUNT2.BAT, 32
ADD.BAT, 232-234
aliasing commands (*see* DOSKEY), 325, 353

all-in-one batch files, subroutines, 187-190
allocation errors (CHKDSK), 320
ANSI, 137, 148
ANSI.SYS, 60-61, 73, 137, 148, 316, 349, 384
   DOS.4.0 installation, 378
Answer, 124-125
ANSWER1.BAT, 124
anti-viral batch files, 105-109
   hiding COMMAND.COM, 106-108
   testing critical files (TESTCOMM.BAT), 108-109
   write-protection, 105-106
APPEND, 317, 349
archival files, 95-104
   $$$ files, 100
   BAK files, 99
   commercial program files, 100
   DELOLD.BAT, 102
   DISCARD subdirectory, 101-102
   DOS, 305
   INDEX.BAT, 103
   indexing files, 95, 102-104
   maintaining old files, 95
   OBJ files, 99
   periodic backups, 95, 96-99
   PRN files, 100
   systematic copies, 95, 99-102
   TMP files, 100
ASCII characters/files, 9-10
   locate specific, matching string (FIND), 330, 355, 374

sorting (SORT), 98, 344, 360, 374, 375
type file to screen (TYPE), 90, 266, 345, 361
ASSIGN, 317, 349
ATTRIB, 105-106, 305, 317, 349
attributes, file, 305
AUTOASK.BAT, 84
AUTOBOOT.BAT, 76
AUTOEXEC.001, 78
AUTOEXEC.002, 78
AUTOEXEC.BAT, 55, 66-70, 317, 379
   copying boot files (BOOT.COM), 75-77
   customized, 199
   DOS modification, 304-307
   environmental survey, 77-82
   floppy-disk boot, 83
   memory-resident software, conditional loading, 83
   MODE, 70, 335, 358, 384
   modifying files at installation (ADD.BAT; DOADD.BAT), 232-234
OCCASIONAL.BAT, 210-212
PATH, xviii, 66-68, 141, 150, 290, 291, 293-295, 297, 336-337, 358
PROMPT, 16, 29, 68-69, 290, 291, 292-293, 297, 339-340, 358
Reboot program, 125
repeating batch files (MUL-COPY.BAT), 227-229

AUTOEXEC.BAT (*cont.*)
  replaceable parameter use, 25
  START-UP.BAT, 305-306
  VERIFY, 69-70, 346, 361
AUX, 317

B

background printing (PRINT),
  358
BACKUP, xviii, 4, 41, 317-319,
  350, 385
  ERRORLEVEL use, 45
backup files (*see also* BACKUP)
  archival files, 95-104
  BACKUP-1.BAT, 4
  DOS modification, 303
  replace deleted files with backups (RESTORE), 45, 317-
  319, 341, 359
BACKUP-1.BAT, 4, 43, 96-99
BACKUP-2.BAT, 99
BACKUP-3.BAT, 100
BAK files, archival files, 99
bank switching, 383
BASIC, 350
BASICA, 350
BAT files, 1, 2
Bat2Exec batch file compiler,
  175-177
batch files, 1-10
  %0 through %9 usage, 11, 22-
  25, 16, 313-314, 340
  applications and uses, 2-7
  assign name (: command), 314
  AUTOEXEC.BAT, 317
  BAT files, 1
  branching (*see also*
  BRANCH.BAT;
  RETURN.BAT), 278-281
  breaking loops (BREAK), 49,
  57, 72, 137, 148, 319, 350,
  378
  call batch file within batch file
  (CALL), 229, 319, 351
  clean-up techniques
  (MISSING.BATs), 281-283
  commands running inside batch
  files (MIDDLE.BATs), 276-
  278
  commands, 11-35
  compiler, Bat2Exec, 175-177
  conditional execution (IF), 31,
  39-43, 229, 331-333, 356

EDIT.COM, 365-367
editing techniques, 363-371
EDLIN, 367-371
end-of-file marker (^Z), 314,
  363-365
errors , 49
file-existence testing (EXIST),
  43-44, 328, 354
flow control, 37-51
hiding operation (CTTY), 269-
  270
jump (GOTO), 38-39, 237-239,
  314, 331, 356
looping, 37-51, 356
memory allocation, saving
  space (BIGMENU.BAT), 218-
  221
message display on screen
  (ECHO), 6, 13-20, 138,
  148, 270, 272, 325-326,
  354, 375
naming (FINDFREE.BAT;
  HELP.BAT), 202-205, 283
naming lines for loops, 37
network control
  (NETWORK.BAT), 229-232
read ERRORLEVEL
  (ERRORLEVEL), 33-34, 44-
  47, 327-328, 354
remarks and comments (REM),
  11-13, 65, 72, 340, 359, 383
renaming commands, 3
repeating (MUL-COPY.BAT),
  227-229
replaceable parameters (*see
  also* %0 through %9; SHIFT),
  11, 16, 22-25, 313-314, 340,
  360
reserved names usaged, 168-
  169
reverse DOS decision (NOT),
  47, 358
SET variables, %variable%,
  16, 29-33, 314, 330-331
shortcutting commands using,
  2-3
suppress DOS message display
  (>NUL), 315
suspend execution for keypress
  (PAUSE), 20-22, 337, 358
terminating execution
  (BREAK), 49, 57, 72, 137,
  148, 319, 350, 378

utilities, 126
BATCH.BAT, 9
Batchman commands, 137-152
BEEP, 126, 130-137, 148
BELL.BAT, 19
BIGAPP, configuration of com-
  puter, 79-80
BIGIF.BAT, 42
BIGMENU.BAT, 218-221
BIGSUB.BAT, 187-190
binary files, convert from EXE
  (EXE2BIN), 2, 328, 354
BIOS, 53
boot disks, 54, 83, 378
BOOT.COM, 75-77
bootstrap programs, 54
BRANCH.BAT, 278-281
branching (BRANCH.BAT;
  RETURN.BAT), 278-281
BREAK, 49, 57, 72, 137, 148,
  319, 350, 378
BUFFERS, 57-59, 72, 319, 351,
  379, 383
  DOS 4.0 installation, 378
Builder batch language enhancer,
  164-175

C

CALL, 229, 319, 351
CANCOPY, 137, 148
capitalization (CAPITAL.BAT)
  environmental variables, 239-
  240
  GOTO use, 237-239
  paths, 240-242
CAPSLOCK, 137, 148
case tests CASE.BAT, 261-263
CATALOG.BAT, 216-218
cataloguing floppy disks,
  CATALOG.BAT (*see also*
  REMOVE.BAT), 216-218
CD (*see* CHDIR)
CECHO, 138, 148
CEMM.SYS, 61
CHCP, 319, 351
CHDIR, 86-88, 319, 351
CHECK.BAT, 4
CHECK.COM programs/
  keywords, 111-117
CHECK1.BAT programs, 111-
  117
CHECKERR.BAT, 34, 46, 248-
  253, 285-287

child and parent subdirectories, 87

CHKDSK, 200, 267-268, 319-320, 351

CHECK.BAT , 3-4

CLIPPER.BAT, 47, 327

CLOSE.BAT, 253-256

CLOSE.EXE, 31

CLS, 138, 148, 320, 351

CLW utility, 126

code pages
code-page switching (NLSFUNC), 335, 358
display active code page (CHCP), 319, 351

cold reboots (COLDBOOT), 138, 148, 149

color selections, 138, 148, 149

columns (COLS), 138, 148, 149

COM files, 2, 320-321

COMMAND, 351

command processor (*see also* COMMAND.COM)
load (COMMAND), 351
load COMMAND.COM (COM), 2, 320-321
shell to alternate (SHELL), 63-64, 72, 297-298, 343, 360, 378

COMMAND.COM, 53, 55, 290, 298-300, 384
alternate path (COMSPEC), 29, 291, 293, 297, 321, 352
DOS modifications, 306, 308-311
hiding, anti-viral batch files, 106-108
load (COM), 2, 320-321
replaceable parameter use, 25
running subroutines in DOS, 179-181
shelling to DOS, 191-193
test for viruses (TESTCOMM.BAT), 108-109

commands
batch file, 11-35
Batchman, 137-152
external, xviii, 328, 394
hierarchy of DOS commands, 3
internal, 2, 333
recalling and aliasing (DOSKEY),325, 353
running commands inside batch

files (MIDDLE.BATs), 276-278
running commands occasionally (OCCASIONAL.BAT), 210-212
wildcards, add wildcard support, 266

comments in code (REM), 11-13, 65, 72, 340, 359, 383

communication ports, AUX, 317

COMP, 321, 352

COMPARE, 138, 148, 149

COMPILE.BAT, 33

compiler, Bat2Exec, 175-177

compressed printing (COMPRESS.BAT), 199-200

COMSPEC, 29, 291, 293, 297, 321, 352

CON, 8

conditional command execution (IF), 31, 39-43, 229, 331-333, 356

CONFIG.001, 77

CONFIG.002, 78

CONFIG.SYS, 55, 57-66, 72-73, 297, 321-322, 379
alternate path to COMMAND.COM (COMSPEC), 29, 291, 293, 297, 321, 352
ANSI.SYS, 60-61, 73, 137, 148, 316, 349, 384
BREAK, 49, 57, 72, 137, 148, 319, 350, 378
BUFFERS, 57-59, 72, 351, 379, 383
CEMM.SYS, 61
code-page switching (NLSFUNC), 335, 358
construction guidelines, 73
copying boot files (BOOT.COM), 75-77
country settings (COUNTRY), 59-60, 72, 322, 352
country-specific information (NLSFUNC), 335, 358
customized, 199
device driver attached (DEVICE), 59-60, 72, 323, 352, 378
DISPLAY.SYS, 61, 73, 353
DOS modification, 304-307
DOSHIGH, 72, 325, 353

DRIVER.SYS, 61, 73, 354

EMM386, 73, 326-327, 354, 386

environmental survey, 77-82

file control block number (FCBS), 62, 72, 329, 355, 378

file-opening, maximum number allowable (FILES), 62, 72, 355

floppy-disk boot, 83

hiding COMMAND.COM (NOTUSED.COM), 106

INSTALL, 65, 72, 333, 357, 378, 384

LASTDRIVE, 62-63, 72, 334, 357, 378

modifying files at installation (ADD.BAT; DOADD.BAT), 232-234

PRINTER.SYS, 61, 73, 358

Reboot program, 125

REM, 11-13, 65, 72, 340, 359, 383

repeating batch files (MUL-COPY.BAT), 227-229

run memory-resident program (INSTALL), 357

shell to alternate command processor (SHELL), 63-64, 72, 297-298, 343, 360, 378

stack frames allowable (STACKS), 64-65, 72, 344, 360

START1.SYS, 305-306

SWITCHES, 65, 72, 384

VDISK.SYS, 61, 73, 361, 383

configuration of computer, 53-84
AUTOEXEC.BAT, 55, 66-70, 76
BIGAPP, 79-80
BIOS, 53
COMMAND.COM, 53, 55
CONFIG.SYS, 55, 57-66, 72-73, 297, 321-322, 379
copying boot files (BOOT.COM program), 75-77
customized configurations, 75-84, 199
DOS kernel, 53
environmental survey, 77-82
floppy-disk boot, 83
IBMBIO.COM, 55

configuration of computer (*cont.*)
IBMDOS.COM, 55
memory-resident programs, 71, 77, 83
STARTAPP.BAT, 82
TINYAPP, 79-82
conventions, symbols, usage, xix
COPY, 2, 7-10, 266, 321, 352, 385
COPY CON, 8-10, 363
COUNTRY, 59-60, 72, 322-323, 352
CP/M, 363
CPU, 138, 148, 149
cross-linked files (CHKDSK), 200, 267-268, 319-320, 351
CTTY, 269-276, 323, 352
hiding batch file operations, 269-270
keyboard use with NUL in effect (CTTYKEY.BAT), 275-276
logging computer usage, 270-272
message display, 272-275
CTTYKEY.BAT, 275-276
current date/time (CURRENT.BAT), 205-209
cursors, 139, 141, 151
CURSORTYPE, 139, 149

D

DAILY.COM, 253
DATE, 323, 352
dates, 139, 140, 142, 150, 152, 205-209, 352
DAY, 112, 126, 139, 149
DEBUG, 323, 352
DECLOOP, 141, 151
DEL, 266, 323, 352, 385
DEL.BAT, 309-311
DELOLD.BAT, 102
DEVICE, 59-60, 72, 323, 352, 378
device drivers, 59-60, 324
foreign character sets (DISPLAY.SYS), 61, 73, 353
load (DEVICE), 59-60, 72, 323, 352, 378
load, high memory region (DEVICEHIGH), 324, 352, 386

logical devices, rename (DRIVER.SYS), 61, 73, 354
printing, foreign character sets (PRINTER.SYS), 61, 73, 358
DEVICEHIGH, 324, 352, 386
DIGIT-1/3.BAT, 258-259
DIR, 86, 267, 324, 353
directories and subdirectories, 85-88, 139, 141, 149, 151
adding paths (PATH.BAT), 221-227
change (CHDIR), 86-88, 319, 351
changing/return (RETURN.BAT), 193-196
create (MKDIR), 86, 334, 357
deleting paths (PATH.BAT), 221-227
distributing files on hard disk, 185
editing paths (EDITPATH.BAT), 224-227
find files (FASTFIND.BAT), 200-202
list files (DIR), 86, 267, 324, 353
move files (JOIN), 333, 357
parent and child, 87
path settings (APPEND; PATH), xviii, 66-68, 141, 150, 290, 291, 293-295, 297, 317, 336-337, 349, 358
replace files (REPLACE), 340-341, 359
root directory, 87-88
subdirectory used as drive (SUBST), 67, 344-345, 360
tree structure display (TREE), 8, 86, 345, 360, 385
DIREXIST, 139, 149
DIRSORT, 98
DISCARD.BAT, archival files, 101-102
DISKCOMP, 324, 353
DISKCOPY, 324, 353
disks, floppy (*see* floppy disks)
disks, hard (*see* hard disks)
DISKSPACE, CHECK, 112
DISPLAY, 139, 149
DISPLAY.SYS, 61, 73, 353
DO, 324, 353
DOADD.BAT, 232-234

documentation (*see* remarks or comments)
DOS, 353
appending files (+ command), 316
archive files, 305
AUTOEXEC.BAT files, 304-307
backup files before modification, 303
bootstrap programs, 54
check data after read/write (VERIFY), 69-70, 346, 361
command hierarchy, 3
COMMAND.COM modification, 55, 306, 308-311
CONFIG.SYS files, 304-307
environment (*see* environment)
file attributes, 305
hidden files, 305
IBMBIO.COM, 55, 306-308
IBMDOS.COM, 55
kernel, 53
load to high memory region (DOSHIGH), 72, 325, 353
modifications, 303-311
non-system disk errors, 54
Norton Utilities to modify, 305
piping (> command), 338
POST testing, 53-54
programming language use, 7
read-only files, 305
redirection commands, 316, 373-375
running subroutines, 179-181
shell to alternate command processor (SHELL), 63-64, 72, 297-298, 343, 360, 378
shelling out to DOS, 191-193
start-up procedures, 53-56
START-UP.BAT, 305-306
START1.SYS, 305-306
suppress message display (>NUL), 315
system files, 305
upgrades/modifications to version 4.0, 377-385
upgrades/modifications to version 5.0, 385-387
version numbers, set (SETVER), 343, 360
version numbers, show (VER), 346, 361

DOS 4.0, 377-385
  balance DOS/program memory, 378
  CONFIG.SYS changes, 383-385
  DOSShell program, 382-383
  expanded memory support, 383
  installation, 377-379
  large-capacity hard disk use, 379-382
  maximize DOS functions, 378
  minimize DOS memory requirements, 378
DOS 5.0, 385-387
  Editor utility, 386
  file transfer program, 387
  memory, high memory requirements, 386
  on-line help, 386
  Undelete utility, 387
  Unformat utility, 387
DOSHIGH, 72, 325, 353
DOSKEY, 325, 353
DOSShell program, DOS 4.0, 382-383
DOSVER, 139, 149
drive designations, 139, 149
  check disk (CHKDSK), 200, 267-268, 319-320, 351
  last-used drive (LASTDRIVE), 62-63, 72, 334, 357, 378
  make electronic drive (VDISK.SYS), 61, 73, 361, 383
  modify parameters (*see also* DRIVPARM), 325, 354
  move files (JOIN), 333, 357
  path settings (PATH), xviii, 66-68, 141, 150, 290, 291, 293-295, 297, 336-337, 358
  reassignment (ASSIGN), 317, 349
  subdirectory used as drive (SUBST), 67, 344-345, 360
DRIVEEXIST, 139, 149
DRIVER.SYS, 61, 73, 354
DRIVPARM, 325, 354
DR_BOX utility, 126
DUMMY.BAT, 264-265

E

E43V50, 139, 149

ECHO, 6, 13-20, 138, 148, 270, 272, 325-326, 354, 375
  % use prohibited, 17
  @ command to suppress, 316
  bell sounds (BELL.BAT), 19
  blank lines (LINE1.BAT), 19
  dot as replacement, 16
  ECHO1.BAT, 14
  environmental variables (%variable%), 16, 29-33, 314, 330-331
  limitations to use, 17
  line-drawing characters, boxing messages, 15
  LINE1.BAT, 19
  menu display batch file (MENU1.BAT), 89
  PATH use, 16
  prompt-removal, 16
  redirection commands prohibited, 17
  replaceable parameters (%0 through %9), 11, 22-25, 16, 313-314, 340
  SKIPLINE.COM, 20
  spacing on lines (SPACE1.BAT), 17-19
  status on/off, problems, 20
ECHOMESSAGE.BAT, 326
EDIT, 326, 354, 365-367
EDIT1.BAT, EDIT2.BAT, 224-227
editing files (*see* EDIT; EDLIN)
Editor utility, DOS 5.0, 386
EDITPATH.BAT, 224-227
EDLIN, 9, 326, 354, 365, 367-371
  Copy, Move, Transfer, Page commands, 371
EGA display mode, 139, 149
electronic drives (VDISK.SYS), 61, 73, 361, 383
EMM386, 73, 326-327, 354, 386
end-of-file marker (^Z), 314, 363-365
environment, 289-301
  COMMAND.COM, 290, 298-300
  COMSPEC, 29, 291, 293, 297, 321, 352
  CONFIG.SYS, 55, 57-66, 72-73, 297, 321-322, 379

enter or delete variable settings (SET), 68, 290, 291-295, 342, 359
  expand environment (COMMAND), 351
  GOHOME.BAT, 291-292
  increasing size, 297-301
  NEWPROMPT.BAT, 297
  PASSWORD.BAT, 296
  PATH, xviii, 66-68, 141, 150, 290, 291, 293-295, 297, 336-337, 358
  PROMPT, 16, 29, 68-69, 290, 291, 292-293, 297, 339-340, 358
  RAM usage, 289
  SET, 68, 290, 291-295, 342, 359
  SHELL, 63-64, 72, 297-298, 343, 360, 378
  SHOWENVI, 130
  surveying environment, 77-82, 199
  TESTENVI.BAT, 300
environmental variables, 16, 29-33, 239-240, 314, 330-331
  GET command and parameters, 127-128
  save disk space (SAVESPACE.BAT), 284-285
EOF.TXT, 364-365
ERASE, 2, 5, 354, 385
ERRORLEVEL, 33-34, 44-47, 327-328, 354
  BACKUP use, 45
  CHECKER.BAT, 248-253, 285-287
  CLOSE.BAT, 253-256
  DAILY.COM, 253
  DIGIT-1/3.BAT, 258-259
  KEEP.BAT, 253-256
  RESTORE use, 45
  SAVE-BIG.BAT, 257
  SAVE-ERR.BAT, 259-261, 285-286
  SetError program, 129-130
  WEEKLY.COM, 253
  XCOPY use, 45
EXAMPLE1.BAT, 8-9
EXE files, convert to binary (EXE2BIN), 2, 328, 354
EXIST, 43-44, 328, 354

EXIST (*cont.*)
  NOT command, 47
EXIT, 328, 355
expanded memory, 139, 149
  BUFFERS setting, 351
  DOS 4.0 support, 383
  EMM386, 73, 326-327, 354, 386
EXPMEN, 139, 149
Extended Batch Language Plus (EBL Plus), 155-164
extended key codes, InKey, 118-123, 393-399
extended memory, 139, 149
  expanded memory emulation (EMM386), 73, 326-327, 354, 386
EXTMEN, 139, 149

F

FASTFIND.BAT, 200-202
FASTOPEN, 328, 355, 383
  DOS 4.0 installation, 378
FastScreen, menus, 90
FC, 329, 355
FCBS, 62, 72, 329, 355, 378
FCLS1/FCLS2 utilities, 126
FDISK, 86, 329, 355, 384
file allocation table (FAT)
  directory matches FAT, 319
  large-capacity hard disks, 380
file control blocks (*see* FCBS)
FILEFOUND, CHECK, 112
filenames
  find available names (FINDFREE.BAT), 283
  listing names (HELP.BAT), 202-205
  redirection commands, 374
files, 62, 72, 329-330, 355, 378
  appending (+), 316
  archival files (*see* archival files)
  attributes, 305, 349
  backup creation (BACKUP), xviii, 4, 41, 317-319, 350, 385
  bad-disk errors, recovery data (RECOVER), 340, 359
  BAT files, 2
  check data after read/write (VERIFY), 69-70, 346, 361
  check subdirectories/files

(CHKDSK), 200, 267-268, 319-320, 351
COM files, 2
compare, (*see* also COMP), 352
compare, show difference (FC), 329, 355
convert EXE to binary (EXE2BIN), 2, 328, 354
copying (COPY; XCOPY), 2, 7-10, 45, 137, 148, 266, 321, 346-347, 352, 361, 385
copying, all files on disk (DISKCOPY), 324, 353
copying, to disk, subroutines, 181-185
copying, use replaceable parameters (*see also* SHIFT; TOA1.BAT), 25-29, 183, 313, 343, 360
delete (DEL), 266, 323, 352, 385
directory listings (DIR), 86, 267, 324, 353
distributing files on hard disk, 185
editing using ASCII editor (*see* EDIT; EDLIN)
erasing (*see also* KILL.BAT), 6, 354
examine and modify (DEBUG), 323, 352
EXE files, 2
existence testing (EXIST), 43-44, 328, 354
file control blocks (FCBS), 62, 72, 329, 355, 378
filenames available (FINDFREE.BAT), 283
find file on hard disk (FASTFIND.BAT), 200-202
hidden, 305
move drive designation/ subdirectory (JOIN), 333, 357
opening, FASTOPEN, 355
opening, maximum number allowable (FILES), 62, 72, 355
read-only, 305
recovery of deleted data (MIRROR), 334, 357
rename (RENAME), 340, 359

replace deleted files with back-ups (RESTORE), 45, 317-319, 341, 359
replace files (REPLACE), 340-341, 359
sharing (SHARE), 343, 360
system, 305, 360
testing for viruses (TESTCOMM.BAT), 108-109
transferring, File Transfer utility, DOS 5.0, 387
tree structure of directory (TREE), 8, 86, 345, 360, 385
type ASCII file to screen (TYPE), 90, 266, 345, 361
unerasing (UNDELETE), 361
write-protection, 105-106
FILESIZE, CHECK, 112
FILETEXT, CHECK, 112
filters, 355, 374
FIND, 330, 355, 374
FINDFREE.BAT, 283
floppy disks
  boot disks, 83
  cataloging batch file (CATALOG.BAT; REMOVE.BAT, 216-218
  compare (DISKCOMP), 324, 353
  copy (DISKCOPY), 324, 353
  copy files to disk, subroutines, 181-185
  formatting (FORMAT), xviii, 5, 86, 141, 151, 331, 356, 384
  volume labels (LABEL; VOL), 334, 346, 357, 361
flow control, batch files, 37-51
  ERRORLEVEL, 33-34, 44-47, 327-328, 354
  EXIST, 43-44, 328, 354
  FOR, 48-50, 330-331, 356
  GOTO, 38-39, 237-239, 314, 331, 356
  IF, 31, 39-43, 229, 331-333, 356
  NOT, 47
FOR, 48-50, 330-331, 356
  case tests (CASE.BAT), 261-263
  DO command, 324, 353
  DOS variables (%%j), 314

execute commands using
(3COMMANDS.BAT), 267-
268
IN command, 333, 356
nested FOR
(NESTFOR.BATs), 265-266
wildcard support using, 266
FOR-BAK.BAT, 49, 324
FOR2.BAT, 49
foreign characters
(DISPLAY.SYS), 61, 73, 353
FORMAT, xviii, 5, 86, 141, 151,
331, 356, 384
FORMAT.BAT, 6
formatting (*see also* FORMAT),
141, 151
format error (*see* MIRROR;
REBUILD; Unformat;
UNFORMAT)
FORMAT.BAT, 5-6
FROMA.BAT, 185

G

GET command and parameters,
127-128
GET.BAT, 185
GETKEY, 140, 150
GETVOL.BAT, 212-216
GOHOME.BAT, 291-292
GOLOTUS.BAT, 5
GOTO, 38-39, 237-239, 314,
331, 356
DUMMY.BAT, 264-265
GOTOEND.BAT, 263-265
SKIPEND.BAT, 264-265
GOTOEND.BAT, 263-265
GRAFTABL, 331, 356
GRAPHICS, 331, 356

H

hard disks, 85-88
check subdirectories/files
(CHKDSK), 200, 267-268,
319-320, 351
directories and subdirectories,
85-88
distributing files, 185
find files (FASTFIND.BAT),
200-202
formatting (FORMAT), xviii,
5, 86, 141, 151, 331, 356,
384

initialize and partition
(FDISK), 86, 329, 355, 384
large-capacity, DOS 4.0 use,
379-382
unformatting (*see* REBUILD;
Unformat; UNFORMAT)
volume labels, show (*see also*
LABEL; VOL), 334, 346,
357, 361
hardcoding, hardwiring, 22
hardware requirements, xviii-xix
help, DOS 5.0, 386
HELP.BAT, 202-205
hidden files, 305
high memory (*see* memory)
HOUR, 140, 150

I

IBMBIO.COM, 55, 306-308
IBMDOS.COM, 55
IF, 31, 39-43, 229, 331-333, 356
case tests (CASE.BAT), 261-
263
nesting, 248-253
NOT command, 47
IF3.BAT, 45
IN, 333, 356
INDEX.BAT, archival files, 103
indexing files, archival files, 95,
102-104
inflexible programs, running
(STARTDATA.BAT), 196-199
initializing hard disk (FDISK),
86, 329, 355, 384
InKey, 118-123, 389-399
$ characters prohibited, 118,
389
2-3.BAT, 123
entering scripts, keyboard-
manufacturers' variations, 390-
392
extended key codes, 118-123,
393-399
keystroke reporting function,
392-393
POPDROP program, 118
redirection command symbols
prohibited, 118, 389
upshift values, 118-123, 393-
399
INSTALL, 65, 72, 333, 357,
378, 384

installation, DOS 4.0, 377-379
invalid clusters (CHKDSK), 320
ISVOL, 140, 150
IS_TODAY utility, 126

J

JOIN, 333, 357

K

KEEP.BAT, 253-256
KEYB??, 333, 357
keyboards
alternate formats, foreign formats (SELECT), 342, 359
ASCII value of keystroke
returned, 140, 150
CHECK, 112
customizing (ANSI.SYS), 60-
61, 73, 137, 148, 316, 349,
384
InKey program, 118-123, 389-
399
key reassignment, foreign
characters (*see also* KEYB??),
333, 357
redirection commands, 374
typematic rates, 142
KEYPRESS, CHECK, 113
keystroke reporting function,
InKey, 392-393
KILL.BAT, 6, 112

L

LABEL, 334, 357
LABEL.BAT, 202
LASTDRIVE, 62-63, 72, 334,
357, 378
line-drawing characters, 15
LINE1.BAT, 19
LINK, 334, 357
LOADHIGH, 334, 357, 386
LOGBOOT.BAT, 271
logging computer usage (CTTY),
270-272
logic devices, rename
(DRIVER.SYS), 61, 73, 354
LOOPBOOT.BAT, 271
LOOP1/LOOP5.BAT, 38-41
loops, 37-51, 141, 151
breaking, 49
ERRORLEVEL, 33-34, 44-47,
327-328, 354
EXIST, 43-44, 328, 354

LOOP1/LOOP5.BAT *(cont.)*
  FOR, 48-50, 330-331, 356
  GOTO, 38-39, 237-239, 314,
    331, 356
  IF, 31, 39-43, 229, 331-333,
    356
  naming program lines for jumps
    to loop, 37
  NOT, 47
lost clusters (CHKDSK), 320
Lotus
  GOLOTUS.BAT, 5
  shelling to DOS
    (LOTUS.BAT), 191-193
LPT1, 334

M

mailing labels (LABEL.BAT),
  202
MAINMEM, 140, 150
MD *(see* MKDIR)
MEM, 334, 357, 384
memory, xviii, 140, 150
  amount available (MEM), 334,
    357, 384
  bank switching, 383
  CHECK, 113
  DOS 5.0 requirements, 386
  environment, 289
  environmental variables
    (SAVESPACE.BAT), 284-285
  examine and modify (DEBUG),
    323, 352
  expanded memory (EMM386),
    73, 139, 149, 326-327, 354,
    383, 386
  extended, 139, 149, 354
  graphic mode, load characters
    (GRAFTABL), 331, 356
  high memory, device driver
    load (DEVICEHIGH), 324,
    352, 386
  high memory, DOS 5.0 require-
    ments, 386
  high memory, load DOS
    (DOSHIGH), 72, 325, 353
  memory-resident programs, 71,
    357
  minimize DOS requirements,
    installation 4.0, 378
  pages, 383
  RAM configuration at boot-up,
    56

saving space
  (BIGMENU.BAT), 218-221
memory-resident programs, 71,
  77
  AUTOASK.BAT, 84
  background printing (PRINT),
    358
  conditional loading, 83
  file-sharing (SHARE), 343,
    360
  keyboard key reassignment
    (KEYB??), 333, 357
  load to high memory region
    (LOADHIGH), 334, 357, 386
  POPDROP, 118
  run (INSTALL), 65, 72, 333,
    357, 378, 384
MENU1.BAT, 89
MENU2.BAT, 90
menus, 88-93
  1.BAT through 6.BAT, 91-92
  color selection, 91
  display using ECHO
    (MENU1.BAT), 89
  display using TYPE
    (MENU2.BAT), 90
  FastScreen, 90
  Menuware Batch File Utilities,
    128-129
  message display, 91
  run menu applications
    (SHOWMENU.BAT), 91
  saving memory space
    (BIGMENU.BAT), 218-221
Menuware Batch File utilities,
  128-129
messages
  boxes and borders, line-drawing
    characters, 15
  display on screen (ECHO), 6,
    13-20, 138, 148, 270, 272,
    325-326, 354, 375
  improving display (CTTY),
    272-275
  suppress (>NUL), 315
MIDDLE.BATs, 276-278
MINUTE, 140, 150
MIRROR, 334, 357
MISSING.BATs, 281-283
MKDIR, 86, 334, 357
MODE, 70, 335, 358, 384
MODEL, CHECK, 113
MODE_ON utility, 126

MONTH, 113, 140, 150
MORE, 270, 335, 358, 374
MUL-COPY.BAT, 227-229

N

NEST.BAT, 248-253
nested FORs, 265-266
nested IF, 248-253
NESTFOR.BATs, 265-266
network control
  (NETWORK.BAT), 229-232
NEWPROMPT.BAT, 297
NLSFUNC, 335, 358
NO-EOF.TXT, 364-365
Norton Batch Enhancer utilities,
  130-137
Norton Text Search, 242
Norton Utilities, modifying DOS,
  305
NORTON.BAT, 130-137
NOT, 47, 335, 358
NOT-DEL.BATs, 269-270
NOTUSED.COM, 107
NUL, 8-9, 270, 272, 336
  CTTY and keyboard use, 275-
    276
  redirection commands, 374,
    375
NumLock key toggle, 140, 150

O

OBJ files, archival files, 99
OCCASIONAL.BAT, 210-212
operating systems, 54

P

parameter passing, complex
  parameters (TEXTFIND.BAT;
  TRANSFORM.BAT), 242
parent and child subdirectories,
  87
partitioning hard disk (FDISK),
  86, 329, 355, 384
passing complex parameters
  (TEXTFIND.BAT;
  TRANSFORM.BAT), 242-248
password protection
  (PASSWORD.BAT), 234-236
PASSWORD.BAT, 234-236, 296
PATH, xviii, 66-68, 141, 150,
  290, 291, 293-295, 297, 336-
  337, 358
  adding or deleting paths

(PATH.BAT), 221-227
APPEND, 317, 349
capitalization problems, 240-242
ECHO use, 16
editing paths
(EDITPATH.BAT), 224-227
SET, 68, 290, 291-295, 342, 359
PATH.BAT, 221-227
PAUSE, 20-22, 337, 358
PAUSEIT.BAT, 22
periodic backups and archival files, 95, 96-99
piping (*see also* redirection commands), 338, 373-375
FIND, 330, 355, 374
NUL routing of message (>NUL), 315
SORT command, 98, 344, 360, 374, 375
POPDROP memory-resident program, 118
POPPATH, 141, 150
ports
AUX, 317
LPT1, 334
PRN, 338
redirection commands, 374
POST testing, 53-54
PREPARE.BAT, 272-274
PRINT, 338, 358
PRINTER.SYS, 61, 73, 358
printing
background printing (*see also* PRINT), 358
foreign character sets (PRINTER.SYS), 61, 73, 358
mailing labels (LABEL.BAT), 202
mode setting (MODE), 70, 335, 358, 384
print screen, 140, 150
printer control, compressed print (COMPRESS.BAT), 199-200
redirection commands, 374
PRN, 8, 100, 338
programming, DOS as programming language, 7
programs, running inflexible programs
(STARTDATA.BAT), 196-199

PROMPT, 16, 29, 68-69, 290, 291, 292-293, 297, 339-340, 358
PROMPT1.BAT, 339
PRTAT utility, 126
PRTSC, 140, 150
PRT_ON utility, 126
pseudocode, 37
PUSHPATH, 141, 150

Q

QBASIC, 340, 358
QFORMAT, 141, 151
QuickBasic, load (QBASIC), 340, 358

R

random access memory, environment, 289
RD, 359
read-only files, 305
Reboot, 125
reboot, cold, 138, 148, 149
REBUILD, 340
RECOVER, 340, 359
recovery of deleted data
bad-disk errors (RECOVER), 340, 359
MIRROR, 334, 357
replace files with backups (RESTORE), 45, 317-319, 341, 359
Undelete utility, DOS 5.0, 387
unerase files (UNDELETE), 361
Unformat utility, DOS 5.0, 387
unformatting (REBUILD; UNFORMAT), 340, 361
redirection commands, 316, 373-375
devices, 374
ECHO use prohibited, 17
filters, 374
"hung" computer problems, 375
InKey prohibits use, 118, 389
problems with use, 375
REM, 11-13, 65, 72, 340, 359, 383
remarks and comments (*see* REM)
remote terminal use (CTTY), 352
REMOVE.BAT, 216-218

RENAME, 340, 359
RENDIR, 141, 151
repeating batch files (MUL-COPY.BAT), 227-229
REPLACE, 340-341, 359
REPLACE.BAT, 28-29
replaceable parameters, 22-25, 313-314, 340
moving between file formats (SHIFT), 25-29, 183, 313, 343, 360
reserved names, using, 168-169, 268
RESTORE, 45, 317-319, 341, 359
ERRORLEVEL use, 45
RETURN.BAT, 193-196, 278-281
RMDIR, 86, 342, 359
root directory, 87-88
ROWS, 141, 151

S

SAVE-BIG.BAT, 257
SAVE-ERR.BAT, 259-261, 285-296
SAVESPACE.BAT, 284-285
Schweiger, Frank, 124
screen display, 139
clear screen (CLS), 351
customized settings (ANSI.SYS), 60-61, 73, 137, 148, 316, 349, 384
message displayed (ECHO), 6, 13-20, 138, 148, 270, 272, 325-326, 354, 375
mode setting (MODE), 70, 335, 358, 384
redirection commands, 374
screen printing (GRAPHICS), 331, 356
scroll data (MORE), 270, 335, 358, 374
suppress all message display (*see also* @ command), 316
type ASCII file to screen (TYPE), 90, 266, 345, 361
scrolling, 141, 151, 358
SECOND, 141, 151
SELECT, 342, 359
SET, 68, 290, 291-295, 342, 359
%variable% use, 16, 29-33, 314, 330-331

SET (*cont.*)

  PATH, xviii, 66-68, 141, 150, 290, 291, 293-295, 297, 336-337, 358
SET1.BAT, 30
SETCURSOR, 141, 151
SetError, 129-130
SETLOOP, 141, 151
SETVER, 343, 360
SHARE, 343, 360
shareware programs, 152-153
SHELL, 63-64, 72, 297-298, 343, 360, 378
shelling to DOS, 191-193
SHIFT, 25-29, 183, 313, 343, 360
SHIFT ALT/CTRL, 142, 151
SHOWECHO.BAT, 326
SHOWENVI, 130
SHOWGOTO.BAT, 314
SHOWIF.BATSHOWIF2.BAT, 332
SHOWIF3.BAT, 333
SHOWMENU.BAT, 91
SHOWNOT.BAT, 335
SHOWNUL.BAT, 315
SHOWPAR1.BAT, 23-24
SHOWPARA.BAT, 313-314
SHOWPAUSE.BAT, 337
SHOWREPL.BAT, 24
SHOWSET.BAT, 342
SHOWSHIFT.BAT, 343
SKIPEND.BAT, 264-265
SKIPLINE.COM, 20
software requirements, xviii-xix
SORT, 98, 344, 360, 374, 375
SPACE1.BAT, 17-19
spaghetti code, 11
stack frames (*see* STACKS)
STACKS, 64-65, 72, 344, 360
START-UP.BAT, 305-306
START1.SYS, 305-306
STARTAPP.BAT, 82
STARTDATA.BAT, 196-199
STOREVOL.BAT, 212-216
strings, compare, 138, 149
subdirectories (*see* directories and subdirectories)
SUBROUTINE.BAT, 186-187

subroutines, 179-190
  all-in-one batch files, 187-190
  BIGSUB.BAT, 187-190
  copy files to disk, 181-185
  distributing files on hard disks, 185
  SUBROUTINE.BAT, 186-187
  "tricking" DOS into running subroutines, 179-181
SUBST, 67, 344-345, 360
SWITCHES, 65, 72, 384
SYS, 345, 360
system files, 305, 360
systematic copies of data files, 95, 99-102

T

TESTCOMM.BAT, 108-109
TESTENVI.BAT, 300
TEXTFIND.BAT, 242-248
times, 140, 141, 150, 151, 345, 360
  CHECK, 113
  current, 205-209
  foreign formats (SELECT), 342, 359
TINYAPP, configuration of computer, 79-82
TMP files, archival files, 100
TO.BAT, 181-185
TOA.BAT, 181-185
TOA1.BAT, 25
TOB.BAT, 181-185
TRANSFORM.BAT, 247-248
TREE, 8, 86, 345, 360, 385
TRUENAME, 345, 361
TSR programs (*see* memory-resident programs)
TYPE, 90, 266, 345, 361
  add wildcard support, 266
  menu display batch file (MENU2.BAT), 90
TYPEMATIC, 142, 151

U

UNDELETE, 361
Undelete utility, DOS 5.0, 387
UNFORMAT, 346, 361
upshift values, InKey, 118-123, 393-399

USER keyword, 346
utilities, 126, 152-153
  DOS 5.0, 386
  Menuware, 128-129
  Norton Batch Enhancers, 130-137

V

variables, environmental, 16, 29-33, 127-128, 239-240, 284-285, 314, 330-331
  GET command and parameters, 127-128
variables, FOR loops, 48-50
VDISK.SYS, 61, 73, 361, 383
VER, 346, 361
VERIFY, 69-70, 346, 361
version numbers, 113, 360-361
VGA display mode, 139, 149
VIDEOCARD, CHECK, 113
VIDEOMODE, 113, 142, 151
viruses (*see* anti-viral batch files)
VOL, 346, 361
volume labels, 140, 150, 212, 357, 361
VOLUME.BAT, 212-216

W

WAITFOR, 142, 151
WAITTIL, 142, 151
WARMBOOT, 142, 152
WEEKDAY, 142, 152
WEEKLY.COM, 253
wildcards, FOR to add wildcard support, 266
WINDOW, 142, 152
write-protection, 105-106, 105

X

XCOPY, 8, 45, 184, 346-347, 361

Y

YEAR, 142, 152
YES_NO utility, 126

Z

ZyIndex, 103
^Z command, 314, 363-365

The enclosed disk contains zipped files, which have been compressed with the program PKUNZIP and have a .ZIP extension, that contain the batch files discussed in *MS-DOS Batch File Programming, 3rd Edition,* by Ronny Richardson. It also contains ASCII text files with the same names as the zipped files, but with a .TXT extension. The text files list each batch file contained in the corresponding .ZIP files. The author has also included a README.COM file, which you can run by simply typing README at the DOS prompt.

Before you can access the batch files, you must create a directory on your hard drive, put the contents of this disk there, and unzip (decompress) the files. At the C>, type:

MD C: \ *directory name* < Enter >

You have just created a directory on your hard drive to hold all your batch files. Now copy all the files on the enclosed disk to your newly created directory by typing:

COPY A: *.* C: \ *directory name* < Enter >

Now you can safely decompress your files. Call up the README menu by typing README at your C: \ *directory name* prompt and follow the directions under the *How Do I Uncompress All These Files?* option on the menu.